# Framework for
# Industrialization in Africa

# Framework for
# Industrialization in Africa

Thomas A. Taku

PRAEGER

**Westport, Connecticut**
**London**

*For my parents*

**Library of Congress Cataloging-in-Publication Data**

Taku, Thomas A.
    Framework for industrialization in Africa / Thomas A. Taku.
        p.   cm.
    Includes bibliographical references and index.
    ISBN 0–275–96498–1 (alk. paper)
    1. Industrialization—Africa.   2. Africa—Economic policy.
    3. Industrial policy—Africa.   I. Title.
    HC800.T35   1999
    338.96—dc21         99–21592

British Library Cataloguing in Publication Data is available.

Library of Congress Catalog Card Number: 99–21592
ISBN: 0–275–96498–1

First published in 1999

Praeger Publishers, 88 Post Road West, Westport, CT 06881
An imprint of Greenwood Publishing Group, Inc.
www.praeger.com

Printed in the United States of America

The paper used in this book complies with the
Permanent Paper Standard issued by the National
Information Standards Organization (Z39.48–1984).

10 9 8 7 6 5 4 3 2 1

# Contents

1

# Background for Industrialization in Africa

There is no place in the world where well-educated people permanently form the neediest economic group.[1] Conversely, anyone who never went to school, or who possesses no useful skill, or whose health is broken, or as a youngster falls through the cracks of an urban environment, or if opportunity is denied . . . then that man or woman will be poor and the family will be poor, and that will be true no matter how opulent others become.[2]

In an industrializing environment, those who extricate by themselves from the clutches of paucities tend to have certain characteristics, which in some combinations allow them to adapt to the discipline of modern life. Unfortunately, only fractions of every generation have or know those combinations. This is because poverty is a vicious circle. Governments and other institutions typically come to the aid of the most needy. Unfortunately, however, governments and such institutions have limited economic resources. Choices, therefore, have to be made in the allocation of limited resources. Choices have to be made in the proportion of resources allotted to education, food, shelter, health, transportation, national security, and so on. Industrialization increases the resources available, thus making it easier to deal with the problems of poverty.

It will be necessary, at this early juncture, to recede into the past—to the cradle of industrialization—in order to command a profound understanding of the nature of poverty in Africa, during industrialization: Until the advent of the Industrial Revolution, wrestling with the plight of poverty was the order of the day: "From the earliest times of which we have record—back, say, to two thousand years before Christ—down to the beginning of the eighteenth century, there was no great change in the standard of living, of the average man living in the civilized centers of the earth. Ups and downs certainly. Visitations of plague, famine, and war. Golden Intervals. But no progressive violent change." Around the end of the Medieval times and the beginning of modern times, possibly between 1380 and 1510, workers and skilled artisans appeared to have lived in relative prosperity in Europe. However, this progress and prosperity were transient. The good times, as before, had to come to an end: the purchasing power of the artisans lost more than 50 percent of its value. This, coupled with the sheer nature and practice of agriculture and household industry, was inherently retrogressive. Population tended to increase, but agricultural production did not always increase in surplus proportions. This lack of a clear and enduring margin of production, beyond mere subsistence, was often jeopardized by the damage wrought by feudal plundering, crusading armies, or lack of a guarantee of internal order. In the Middle East, the effects of the destruction, pillage, and massacre by Genghis Khan were felt for several generations.

Thomas R. Malthus (1766–1834) tells us that his most famous work, "An Essay on the Principles of Population" was suggested by Goodwin's *Inquiry*, but it was really prompted by the rapid growth of pauperism that Malthus saw around him. Between 1795 and 1834, the problem of pauperism visited people in its most terrible form. In his famous work, Malthus stated that the number of people who can live is limited by the food supply. An increase in food supply would lead to an increase in population. However, any surplus over subsistence might be tempered by "moral restraint" and somewhat more ambiguously by "vice."

Both Malthus and David Ricardo (1772–1823) saw population as a dependent variable, with advancing wealth and productivity resulting in more people. Malthus presented his "law of population," stating that population when unchecked increased in geometric progression, while subsistence increased at best in arithmetic progression. That is, every twenty-five years, population tends to increase at the rate of one, two, four, eight, sixteen, thirty-two, and so forth, while the rate of increase for subsistence is, at best, only one, two, three, four, five, six. He alluded to the India and China of his day with respect to population growth.

Ricardo endorsed the population theory of Malthus, but without much dogma. Ricardo was a veritable apostle of economic growth. In his "Principles of Political Economy and Taxation," he stated the following:

It has been calculated, that under favourable circumstances population may be doubled in twenty-five years; but under the same favourable circumstances, the whole capital of a country might possibly be doubled in a shorter period. In that case, wages during the whole period would have a tendency to rise, because the demand for labour would increase still faster than the supply. (Ch.5)

In a lighter vein Ricardo penned in a letter:

Now that I am grandfather I should be puzzled, even with the assistance of Mr. Malthus, and Major Torrens, to calculate the accelerated ratio at which my progeny is increasing. I am sure that it is neither arithmetical nor geometrical. I have some notion of consulting Mr. Owen on the best plan of establishing one of his villages for me and my descendants, admitting only in addition a sufficient number of families to prevent the necessity of celibacy.

Ricardo, who married at the age of twenty-one, had eight children and twenty-five grandchildren. Malthus married at thirty-nine and had three children but no grandchildren. Some jokingly mention that had this progression continued, England would have been overrun with Ricardos. Malthus did not disagree with the general belief, then, that poverty and misery are the natural punishment for the "lower classes" that woefully failed to restrain procreation. His highly significant policy conclusion was that government should not give relief to the poor. The analogy for this alarming policy conclusion was that aid to the indigent would cause more people to survive, consequently worsening the problem of hunger. Some of Malthus's ideas were adopted in the Poor Law Amendment of 1834. The law abolished relief for able-bodied people outside workhouses. The implication was that a man applying for relief had to pawn all his earthly possessions and then enter the workhouse to have assistance granted. The rest of the family (usually the wife and children) also entered the workhouse. In some cases, they were sent to work in the cotton mills. The family, in either situation, was broken up. Treatment was generally harsh, to discourage families from becoming public responsibility.

The workhouse—not unexpectedly—was invested with social stigmas, and entering it was a psychological and moral torture. Public assistance became (for many) such an unbearable ordeal that, most people elected to starve quietly rather than submit to its indignities. Until the early twentieth century, this system was the basis for poor-law policy, in some places. Malthus also drew attention to the overwhelming propensity of prevailing adverse factors among indigents to check population growth. The catalogue included narrow streets, overcrowding in houses, filth and unsanitary conditions, villages near stagnant pools, settlements close to marshes, and other unwholesome conditions, and indigent neighborhoods, that courted the return of the plague.[3]

Malthusian pessimism was not divorced from the law of diminishing returns. As the population escalated, over the years, more workers would be required to grow more food, and the average and marginal yields per worker would decline. This law assumed that conditions were relatively static to the extent that technology did not change. Malthus and his theory on population may still be useful to those who tend to attribute poverty to excessive and indiscriminate fecundity among the world's indigents.

Whereas Malthusian pessimism was grounded in diminishing returns, Henry George (1839–1897) was overly optimistic in his views. George embraced and projected the economic significance of improved technology. He demonstrated that with technological improvements over a period, the average output per unit of labour and capital trends upward. Land cultivated under intensive agriculture, through the investment of more labor and capital per acre, eventually experiences diminishing returns. By optimally applying improved technology, diminishing returns will be negated, resulting in greater output that can sustain a growing population: "If the value of land increases in greater ratio than productive power, rent will swallow up even more than the increase; and while the produce of labor and capital will be much larger, wages and interest will fall."[4]

In the preindustrial world, land was historically deemed a very important resource, often the most valuable resource. Until 200 years ago, no perceptive person would have entertained any doubts that power was decisively and inextricably linked with land. Along with *landownership* came wealth, esteem, and sanguinary authority over the lives of the local populace. The landowner was self-assured of a position of eminence and power in the community. In the old world and the new, it was assumed that power belonged, as a right, to men who owned land. Democracy, in its modern meaning, began as a system that gave the suffrage to those who had proved their worth by acquiring real property, and to no others. It must be remarked, however, that the paramount nature of land in the preindustrial world with the incentive to acquire it was grounded in economics—the economics of agricultural production.

Malthus and Ricardo had extrapolated the imminent scarcity of land. It was projected that a demographic increase would be in accordance with a biological dynamic of its own. This surge in population would put pressure on the relatively limited food supply, thus elevating food prices. Increasingly, land would garner more value as it became ever more scarce. While this philosophical analysis was theoretically valid, the extrapolations never materialized. In fact, with improvements in technology and the advent of the industrial revolution land was dethroned as the most potent force of production.

This was because, until the Industrial Revolution, nonagricultural economic activity was relatively unimportant. Agricultural output had been limited by simple and stable technology, and by implication the demand for capital was minuscule. Nevertheless, with the advent of mechanical inventions and the growth of metallurgical and engineering knowledge, opportunities expanded for the employment of capital. More use of capital led to more advanced technology that in turn led to greater production and higher incomes and savings.

In the countries in the new world capital was usually scarce and the cost was high, unlike in some parts of Europe where the rates of return were lower. Coal, iron and steel, railways, locomotives, ships, textile machinery, buildings, and bridges increasingly commanded a bigger share of the national product. Conversely, land commanded a diminishing share. The person who commanded capital could now also control the needed labor and land: the command of land and labor did not allow one to own capital, but capital could easily obtain land and labor.[5] The historical staying power of land diminished, as power gravitated from land to capital.

In an industrializing environment, production was unequivocally dominated by those who controlled the supply of capital. Savings and capital were the decisive factors and *thrift* was the most applauded of social virtues. It did not matter very much that the majority of the population lived and died in abysmal illiteracy and ignorance. The owners of capital fixed prices and wages, determined investments, declared dividends, and decided production, within certain market limits.

By the second half of the twentieth century, this plenary power enjoyed by the stockholders again slowly gravitated away from its nexus. The power center shifted into the hands of top *management*. Majority of the stocks could, from then, be voted by proxy (in stockholders' meetings) for directors who were typically handpicked by management. This was tantamount to a usurpation of the legitimate power of capital.[6]

The power of the stockholder regressed, to all intents and purposes into a myth (in this context).

Management commands immense power in simple organizations. Although power is assumed to flow from top to bottom, this is not necessarily or always the case with much more complex organizations, in which decisions typically require information. In practice, some of this concentration of power is delegated (with some reservations) to the appropriate /immediate lower level.

In an *information age*, power increasingly has dispersed within organizations to those who have the information. Increasingly, *knowledge* has become the key resource in the work environment—and with knowledge comes responsibility.[7] Similarly, in an industrializing environment, knowledge ceases to be *private goods*, confined to the individual.[8] Instead, it becomes *public goods,* pertaining to society and is sought after by corporations. This is especially important in the competitive marketplace, where many corporations may switch from a labor-based manufacturing to knowledge-based manufacturing, in order to enhance productivity.[9]

When decisions require the combined information of a group, power tends to be irrevocable, and decisions cannot easily be reversed by an individual. Within the organization, people work in committees. Group decisions, unless acted upon by another group, tend to be absolute. By the same token, it may be expedient to arrive at decisions based on developing consensuses, from the bottom up, to gain the support of bureaucratic subordinates.[10] Group decisions and ratifications by chief executive officers (CEOs) should not be misconstrued because the latter—in this context and only in this context—remain the most responsible for the application and performance of knowledge. However, CEOs must cede some power to knowledge workers (who must use their initiative in frequent decision making) to enhance the overall organizational productivity.

The application of knowledge to technology was the spark that illuminated the early industrial economies. For centuries there had been no increase in the ability of workers to turn out or transport goods. Workers on the eve of the Industrial Revolution were no more productive than the workers who built the roads in Imperial Rome. Similarly, goods were typically transported at the speed of the horse.

These industrial nations applied Frederick Winslow Taylor's *Scientific Management* to industry. Taylor was horrified by what he understood to be systematic inefficiency and the inability of managers to do anything about it. He therefore went on to work on what is said to be the first writing about management in organization theory.[11] Taylor maintained that authority in the plant should be grounded in superior knowledge (professional management) and not based on ownership. His axiom was that every act of every worker could be reduced to a science, and skilled and unskilled work could be analyzed and organized by the application of knowledge. This was a difficult sell in a period when craft skill was still universally believed to be shrouded in mystiques. Despite resistance emanating from unions and intellectuals, Taylor's Scientific Management gained widespread acceptance in the developed world, by the 1930s. The standard of living of many poor people was greatly enhanced. Karl Marx's *proletarian* became the *bourgeois*. Management had created an escape hatch from the clutches of paucities, while enhancing productivity.

Management may choose to fortify its power center through affiliations. For example, the name of a renowned banker on a board of directors used to be an indirect announcement to the world that the corporation had access to the full capital resources of an economy. Similarly, the name and image of famous scientists or university presidents may be sought to invoke a sense of alignment of the corporation with the latest in technological innovation. An early example was the financing of the railroad construction boom in northern America, during the last two decades of the nineteenth century. Although the banker's relationship, as the financial adviser and the fiscal or the transfer agent of the railroads he sponsored, could be traced back to the 1840s and 1850s, the railroad/banking alliance was more evident in the 1860s. The use of syndicates to underwrite and distribute railroad bonds was introduced in the 1870s and institutionalized in the 1880s, during which investment bankers accepted directorships and positions in key committees. Until this time, bankers met with officials, informally, several times a year rather than serving as directors in formal meetings. The implication, therefore, was that investment houses would commit more time to the railroad business irrespective of other pressing and time-demanding business issues. The banker's presence on the board eased sales of a railroad's securities; boosted investors' confidence; and appeared to constitute an endorsement of the issue's "investment quality," or its "guarantee." On the part of the bankers, such representation safeguarded their reputations. The banker's role was, therefore, institutionalized as the "financial watchdog" of the railroad operations he endorsed. He was within proximity to encourage corporate policies that enhanced stability and profitability, as well as alert against corporate policies that planted the seeds of financial adversity. As the originator of an issue, the investment bank was appointed the registrar of the railroad's securities and the official bank of deposit. Besides, the investment houses increased their knowledge of the railroad operations. In case of additional capital requirements, the management of the railroad operation was, therefore, most likely to contact the investment house that was most conversant with its daily operations. These advantages of banking representation were so important that many railroads included the names of the investment bankers on their boards in newspaper advertisements and prospectuses announcing new offerings.[12]

In some advanced countries, like England and Holland, relative national wealth came in the eighteenth century, with the advent of industrialization. However, such wealth, in the early years of the industrial revolution, more than proportionately favored the new entrepreneurs.[13] Entrepreneurs were owners of factories, raw materials, railroads, and the banks that served them, and increasingly and accordingly lived in luxury and opulence. This contrasted significantly with the paucities in the conditions of many workers that is still reminiscent of parts of the developing world at the dawn of the twenty-first century. Such prevailing conditions may include noisome hovels, cramped and dirty streets perambulated by a working class that toils long hours for a pittance. With industrialization, real wages improved in the developed parts of the world, with expansion in production and relative output per worker. Until then, as in several places in Africa at the dawn of the twenty-first century, misfortune and failure among the poor were normal. What needed sage explanation was success! Enduring success!

If workers' wages were low, it was because of marginal products that had remained low.[14] Raising wages without a corresponding increase in marginal productivity was tantamount to putting labor beyond their contribution to production. Like labor, capital obeyed the principle of marginal productivity. When early gains in capital investments are not ploughed back into industrial expansion, this may retard the rate of expansion. Here, therefore, an effective mechanism for making the distribution of national income more equitable will tend to favor consumption, accumulated savings, and investments. When the converse is a truism, depression of popular living standards will be a looming possibility in a glutted labor market.

Unlike the laboring poor, owners of capital were known to accrue enormous returns. This problem was exacerbated by the relative immobility of labor.[15] For example, between 1892 and 1899, John D. Rockefeller's personal dividends from Standard Oil were valued at between $30,000,000 and $40,000,000. Andrew Carnegie's income from his steel companies was $23,000,000 in 1900.[16] These returns were quite astronomical then, when compared with that of each of the wage earners in their respective companies.

This disparity in incomes, between labor on the one hand and the owners of capital on the other hand, became a cause for concern among the advocates for *income redistribution*. The idea here was that the abject conditions of the poor will be improved by income redistribution. Nevertheless, this appeared to go against the grain of *natural law* and equity, which conveyed that what an individual has received, save for overt larceny, is rightfully his or hers. In addition, if income were widely distributed, it would be spent haphazardly, with little or nothing left for savings. Perhaps, also, it would create a persistent longing to buy those attractive and luxurious goods from distant lands. However, if income flowed in a concentrated stream to the rich, part of it would be saved and invested, thus enhancing capital formation and production and eventually greater rewards for all. Taxing the rich, according to conventional wisdom, destroyed the happiness and security blankets of the wealthy. The overall feeling was that of *penalizing success*, destroying the incentive to work hard and amass wealth, discouraging investments that generally created new jobs, and putting a damper on ambition and the spirit of free enterprise.

The privileged protected themselves from erratic economic changes because they were custodians of fortunes. By contrast, the indigents, who barely subsisted, were preoccupied with the agonies of paucities. They typically did not entertain thoughts of old age and pensions because they did not expect to see it. This was especially so, in the face of malnutrition, sickness, and a plethora of other unmet and dire obligations.

In many cases throughout history, the peasants made handsome contributions toward economic growth and general welfare. Unfortunately, these contributions have not always been appreciated. For example, in some places in preindustrial Europe, the peasants were subject to taxes on land and on profits from farming, while the nobility and the clergy were exempt from taxes. Taxes varied from year to year, depending on the whims and caprices of the collector and the wealth of the peasant. Peasants had to pay dues to the lord when a holding was inherited, or when a transfer through sale was made. In addition, business transactions, with lords' millers, bakers, and wine pressers, required the payment of heavy charges. Meanwhile, the nobles reserved the right to hunt games across the cultivated fields of the peasants. Game laws prohibited weeding and hoeing, should young partridges be disturbed.[17]

In some places, industrialization was very promising from the outset: the world of business and industry required a free, mobile, inexpensive, but hardworking labor force. In such places, government steps were no longer necessary to restrain wage increases, because of high birth rates and declining death rates that increased population and by implication the labor pool. *Enclosures* preempted disputes but drove tenant farmers and many small landowners off the land. Wage earners lost their right of access to village pastures and woodlands where they used to gather fuel and graze a cow or a pig. As adversity increased in the countryside, many farmers and farm laborers drifted to the cities, attracted by the carrot of better opportunities and driven by the club of rural poverty.

These developments exacerbated poverty among those directly afflicted. Landowners (in such places) were taxed to provide funds for poor relief, payable through local governments. The parishes were overburdened with indigents and efforts were made to repatriate them to their parishes of origin. Sick people with bleak prospects for recovery, including women in labor, were often rushed back to their places of birth by officials who wished financial burdens to be shifted elsewhere.

Prevented expulsion had been a bulwark to mobility until 1795, when it was abolished. The Spleenhamland Law, for example, was introduced in the same year and provided a minimum income. Family income was pegged to the price of bread. If, however, earnings depreciated below the prescribed level, allowances from taxes would be used to make up for deficiencies. Until 1834, when it was abolished, the Spleenhamland system prevailed in the rural areas and some manufacturing districts. This was the year when the laws were made so harsh that many people would rather starve than undergo the indignities of poor relief. By the same token, 1834 was the year when a competitive labour market was fully established. In retrospect, the workers initially bore the brunt of industrialization, through long hours and low wages. However, it is absolutely necessary to remark that, although their slice of the total pie was minuscule, the growth of the pie—through their sweat, blood, and tears—benefitted succeeding generations of workers along with other groups. Long after the onset of the Industrial Revolution, at the dawn of the twenty-first century, the standards of living of the workers in the industrialized nations are on the average still the highest in the world.

The success and market reach of industrialization was not without snags. In the 1800s, a small farmer's infected milk supply might have sickened a few neighbors, whereas a century later contaminated milk was almost tantamount to a massive epidemic.[18] The workers of the new urban industrial workforce, as a group, were the new mass of consumers. If the industries were not going to self-regulate, on their own initiative, somebody had to impose regulations to prevent the capitalists and workers from self-destruction. Because of the likely consequences of such developments, the role of the public sector strengthened with industrialization; government undertook the responsibility for regulating private industry.

Government regulations enhanced and directed private industry where and when the road map appeared hazy. Investment opportunities expanded and continued, since a sizable cross-section of the demographics still indicated want and paucity. Unlike the subsistence farmers that seemed self-sufficient and consumed much of their own output, while purchasing very little from the marketplace, the urban industrial workers of the late 1700s purchased a preponderance of market articles. Capitalists plowed back their profits accordingly, to take advantage of business opportunities. The result was increased capital formation and rapid expansion of the private sector.

In the preindustrial environment, the social and economic state of affairs had been volatile and inconsistent. Many people were used to living from hand to mouth. Unemployment was endemic, and individual incomes, for many, was extremely low. It was often easier to dream than to plan in the long term. Marriage rates declined, and fewer children survived. But with industrialization, economic well-being ameliorated, and misfortune became less episodic and avoidable. Life could be said to be more enjoyable, and people lived long. Long-term security became a major cause for concern. The prospect of old age without an adequate safety net was a discomforting thought for many workers. Economic security was guaranteed through strategies such as fire insurance (in case of a conflagration); flood insurance (in the event one's property or business was engulfed by water); and so on.

Industrialization had successfully transformed many displaced subsistence farmers into productive industrial workers. Industrial production had been determined to be the key to mitigating poverty—the indispensable elixir for anxieties, discomforts, and privations that were often the companions of economic insecurity and abject poverty.

## NOTES

1. This statement does exclude groups bound by vows to the rules and practices of a religious order.

2. John Kenneth Galbraith, "Wealth and Poverty," speech given before the National Policy Committee on Pockets of Poverty, Washington, DC, December 13, 1963 in Galbraith, *A Journey Through Economic Time* (Boston: Houghton Mifflin Company, 1994), p. 180.

3. Bernard J. Stern, "The Health of Towns and the Early Public Health Movement," in *Historical Sociology: Selected Papers of Bernard J. Stern* (New York: Citadel Press, 1959), pp. 386–394.

4. Henry George, *Progress and Poverty* (New York: 1942), pp. 171–72. (Originally published in 1879. Recent publication: New York: Robert Schalkenback Foundation, 1992).

5. When feudal land laws were abolished in Britain, land could serve as security for credit. Landowners were able to raise large sums for investments in agriculture or industry.

6. Adolf A. Berle, Jr., *Power without Property* (New York: Harcourt, 1959), p. 98.

7. Peter F. Drucker, *Post-Capitalist Society* (New York: Harper Business, 1993), pp. 106–109.

8. Before the Industrial Revolution, the possessor of craft skill was generally sworn to secrecy. This was because a craft by definition was inaccessible, except by those who had been

apprenticed by a master. The English used the word "mysteries" and did not speak of "crafts." The mystery of a craft skill or *"techné"* could only be demonstrated. It could not be explained in spoken or written words. The advent of patents and rewards to inventors, provided they published their inventions, brought an end to craft mystery and secretiveness. This marked the shift from skill to technology.

9. Ibid., pp. 70–73.

10. Paul Volcker and Toyoo Gyohten, *Changing Fortunes: The World's Money and the Threat to American Leadership* (New York: Times Books, 1992), p. 264.

11. Frederick Taylor, *The Principles of Scientific Management* (New York: Harper and Bros., 1917). See also Schuman David and Dick W. Olufs III, *Public Administration in the United States* (Lexington, Massachusetts: D.C. Heath and Company, 1993), pp. 103–125.

12. Vincent P. Carosso, *Investment Banking in America: A History* (Cambridge, MA: Harvard University Press, 1970), pp. 29–32.

13. E.J. Hobsbawm, *Laboring Men: Studies in the History of Labor* (New York: Basic Books, 1964), p. 65.

14. Historically, however, laborers commanded a higher purchasing power: "At no time since the passing of the 43d of Elizabeth, . . . could the labouring classes acquire such a portion of the necessaries and conveniences of life by a day's work, as they could before the late unparalleled advance in the price of the necessaries of life." Eden, I., in Arnold Toynbee, *The Industrial Revolution* (Boston: Beacon Press, 1956), p. 41.

15. In 1872, there were labourers in Devon who had never heard of Lancashire, where they might have been earning double their own wages. Human beings, in the words of Adam Smith are "of all baggage the most difficult to be transported." Ibid., p.43.

16. *New York Times*, March 4, 1957.

17. This is reminiscent of no-till planting, a form of conservation currently practiced in the industrialized world. It reduces soil erosion while providing cover for ground-nesting wildlife. In this case, hunting also keeps wildlife in check. Jim De Quattro, Emma Corcoran, Claire Emory (eds.), *1983 Yearbook of Agriculture, United States Department of Agriculture* (Washington, DC: GPO, 1983), p. 438.

18. The *Lancet* inquiry in the 1850s determined rapid growth of *adulteration*: All bread tested in separate samples were adulterated; more than 50 per cent of oatmeal tested as adulterated; all but the highest-quality teas were similarly adulterated; about half the milk was adulterated; all the butter was watered; and more than half the jam and preserves included deleterious matter possibly due to poor production. Sugar, although filthy, was the only commonly used commodity unadulterated.

# 2

# Specter

A specter haunts the economies of Africa at the dawn of the third millennium. After some thirty-five years or so of tinkering with economic progress, it is now transparent in many places that this was an exercise in a vicious circle. Efforts to enhance economic prosperity, based on an amalgam of policies forged on the anvil of the cold war, created or ignored other problems that increased the difficulty of industrialization.

Much of Africa is festering in a crucible of despair. Many Africans have felt a dire sense of entropy about the future of economic matters. The celebration of the warm and happy feeling derived from a sound education is increasingly halfhearted in the face of rising unemployment. The sense of economic security seems to be disappearing, and with ominous consequences. For the erstwhile communist-oriented nations of Africa, the virtually overnight switch to capitalism has been a baptism of fire.

The general state of poverty is deplorable. In urban settings the poor have been relegated to a precarious, insecure, hand-to-mouth existence. The very conveniences of modern living, may pose a threat to the urban poor: environmental pollution is rife, and hygiene standards are despicable. Without adequate economic relief for those who are down on their luck, the tendency is to perpetuate the scourge of corruption and street crime. Overcrowding in substandard housing, coupled with abysmal illiteracy and stark ignorance exist in enclaves where infections and diseases might be constant companions. All of this, coupled with the rising specter of unemployment, has made life untenable for many of the urban poor.

Some of the rural poor are still living in rugged isolation, clinging to the codes of living in places where the toothed wheel of the clock seems to have lurched to a halt.

Others may be trapped between the goodness and innocence of a simple past and the risky fringes of contemporary industrial prosperity.

In order to know the path into the future, knowing where the world has been is imperative. Nevertheless, the danger is in the glorification of the past and in the prison of uncorrected obsolescence. Engineering an escape from these phantom forces of captivity of a bygone era may require the fusion of the strands and remnants of the glorious past with the promising and confusing present.

While looking back into our collective past is appropriate, in the hope of finding meaning in the present, an economy that conducts its affairs in accordance with the rules of a bygone and poorer age foregoes opportunities for buoyant industrial growth. In this vein, anachronistic rules and procedures that tend to engender disorder and recalcitrance may be attuned to, or superseded by, coeval rules and regulations that fit into the fabric and texture of a contemporary industrial infrastructure. Into the bargain, opinions may not be quickly discounted because laws are the codification of opinions.

Like bread, humanity cannot live on laws alone. However, in an industrializing environment, laws tend to offer protection against the danger that the lives and livelihood of individuals will become pawns, in the game of human ambition, and fair prey, in the race for economic power and dominance.

The industrial revolution was as profound as the neolithic revolution. First, the nomads became farmers, and then the farmers became manufacturing labor. The efficiency of farming methods relieved previously useful labor from the farms. Methods such as crop rotation, mechanized ploughing, and seed drilling boosted crop production and increased animal feed. Selective breeding superseded the notion of merely increasing feed quantities. As a result, it was easier to obtain, healthily, more marketable farm animals. In parts of Europe and the New World, the Industrial Revolution transformed the urban landscape creating factories and industrial cities that absorbed millions of persons, who had been relieved of their farming chores. Industrialization was so successful that in the late 1800s it was even suggested in some places that the patent office be closed. Apparently the premise was that every possible invention had already been invented.

The industrial revolution could be a very good servant, but an unpredictable master. Left unchecked, it becomes a destructive engine of material progress. In an industrializing economy, it is imperative to install a governor in the system, such as statutes that canalize, regiment, and direct the nature of progress, correcting inconsistencies promptly, in order to foreclose unbecoming propensities. Statutes obviously are not an end by themselves. In which case, industrial policy remains a servant of national purpose instead of degenerating into the awkward role of master.

Technology and innovation are among the greatest strengths of industrialization—the power of creative destruction. The market does not reach its point of saturation because innovation relegates the old products into calculated obsolescence. In science museums in the industrialized nations, one may find a plethora of mechanical and electrical inventions (including valves, pumps, and gears) produced more than a century ago. Innovations such as these advanced the frontier of industrialization, enhanced the quality of living, and thus unleashed what might as well be eternal prosperity for all.

Technology depends on power and energy to be efficient. The lack of an ample source of power and energy was largely responsible for the relatively low technological environment that prevailed before the invention of the steam engine. Industrialization in Africa, from the outset, will inculcate manufacturing and capital investment, coupled with research and development. Once economies begin industrializing, research and development become an indispensable arm of the economy. Nations or corporations that neglect research and development will sooner or later experience a technological gap.

Communication is intrinsic to the financial and banking systems and the economy at large. Industrial growth, expansion, and efficiencies are enhanced by communications and information networks. These include libraries, telephone networks, on-line computer networks, information services, multicultural and multilingual programs, and the news media. These information infrastructure and communications networks tend to interlace regional trade while efficiently locking in the economies of Africa with the rest of what seems to be a global village. Sound communications systems, in conjunction with efficient transportation networks, are fundamental to industrialization.

Transportation is a platform for industrial development. In Africa, there has been considerable effort made in road construction during the last three decades or so. Unfortunately, these modern route systems are still dominated by the coastal-interior alignment of railways and road infrastructures, justifiably, for the speedy evacuation of natural resources (raw materials) and for the importation and distribution of some manufactured (finished) products. Throughout much of Africa, this enduring feature has given very few and relatively well served urban centers considerable advantages of accessibility. As a result, a few (mostly coastal) urban centers have inherently considerable head-start advantage in urban development, while small towns have been virtually stagnating under the weight of inadequate infrastructural facilities.

Very marginal effort has been made in much of Africa to link major internal routes, efficiently and effectively to take advantage of local and regional trade. Transportation systems from the national to the local levels are not always reliable and dependable. In an industrializing environment where the time factor may make the difference between profit and loss, the problem of transportation becomes a priority. In cities and small towns alike, many imported and locally manufactured goods are finally distributed by head-carriage over short distances. Many problems plague transportation over long distances. Long-distance transportation problems include poor roads and seasonally navigable waterways, unpredictable or no official departure and arrival schedules, slow vessels, and the general state of disrepair of many transport vessels. Inefficient transportation systems unnecessarily add cost to products, thus reducing their profitability in domestic markets.

Meanwhile, around the world, innovations such as standardized containers, computer power, and increased speed have revolutionized transportation in the second half of the twentieth century. Transported products are much more safe and secure, while scheduling integrity has been significantly enhanced with minimum margins for error. In many African countries, the relatively high costs of internal transportation also tend to reduce the profitability of some export products. All things being equal, otherwise profitable international markets have been mathematically foreclosed to many African export products.

Modern industry is based on organization. Money and credit activities are absolutely invaluable in an industrializing environment: they are instruments of social organization. They bring together humanity and resources. Banking becomes even more urgent because division of labor evolves to such levels that most people in a given community must work for nominal incomes. Capitalism by its very definition is based on some postponed gratification, whether by governments or by persons. This waiting period allows for capital to be originated, invested, and compounded.

As contradictory as latter chapters will *seem* to suggest, persons who, in the early phases of industrialization, resorted to the ubiquitous informal savings, credit, and "improvement" associations, such as *esusu* and "meeting" (in parts of West Africa) eventually will require professional services, in an urbanizing and industrializing environment. Among the sources of tragedy for Africa is the hand-to-mouth existence of a sizable cross-section of the population, and the propensity of many people to form self-help groups that reside without the official financial infrastructure. Worse still, these associations compete for funds with the local banking system.

The tax system conjoins two coexistent and equally significant spheres of influence: taxation is used simultaneously as a vehicle for collecting government revenue and as an instrument of social and economic policies. Tax deductions, tax credits, and tax exclusions are all designed to induce specific economic behavior. The power to tax is the power to encourage or discourage particular economic activities and trends. It is the power to distribute/redistribute income. It is the power to rearrange economic activities that may range from corporate finance to family relations. Tax measures are often means, employed by authority, to show that positive strides are being made to deal with what the public perceives as major problems.

Health care is one latent problem of industrialization. The quick and stressful paces of industrialization and mass production tend to overwhelm and debilitate workers—especially first generation industrial workers. Defective products rolling off the assembly line, undetected, could cause injury to many. The health of the workforce is very important to enhance productivity and ensure quality products.

Health is by definition a state of physical, mental, and emotional well-being, and not merely the absence of disease. Discoveries such as bacteria, anesthesia, steam sterilization, and the X-ray radically transformed the hospital, from a place where the sick and homeless found refuge and caring, into coeval institutions that more accurately diagnosed patients and administered treatment with the aid of technology.

Although in the last century, declines in morbidity and mortality could be attributed more to improvements in living conditions than to specific medical interventions, the availability of effective medical therapy mitigated against increases.

Just as a person who lacks good health is not happy and efficient, a nation whose citizens are not healthy cannot be efficient and happy. It is believed that the development of many great civilizations was either impeded or reversed because of the injured state of health of the people.

Wide ranges of phenomena have intermittently disturbed the tenor and rhythm of economic life, throughout the history of capitalism. Inflation is one of these lingering occurrences. Historically, inflation occurred in a myriad of communities with diverse institutional structures and monetary standards. The scourge of inflation was felt in ancient empires and modern kingdoms, as well as in modern preindustrial and industrial nations.

In Africa, in recent years, the effects of inflation have similarly ravaged many economies. As early as the period of the Roman Empire, wage and price controls were imposed to curb inflation. In those days, violators of the edict were punishable by death. This iron law proved abortive and was later repealed in favor of more efficient taxation. In Medieval Europe "the great debasements" were the personification of inflation in many European currencies. Debasement benefitted debtors, renters, peasants, among others, and attempts at coinage reforms were often met with revolt from the disaffected. In France the currency, the *tournois*, lost 80 percent of its value between 1338 and 1342. In 1343 monetary reforms reset the *tournois* to its initial precious metal content. However, the royal authority was forced to return to debasement because of wars.

The paper currency called the *assignat*, issued in postrevolutionary France, was also wracking with inflation. It must be noted that inflationary episodes that occurred in earlier epochs, such as 1790s France, took place in very dissimilar economic, political, technological, and social environments. This was so, when compared with twentieth-century examples such as Germany (1920s), Latin America (1980s), and the erstwhile Eastern-bloc nations (1990s).

It may be a truism that depression, if left alone, will eventually provide its own cure. However, it is not far-fetched to imagine that by that time the patient might have died because of social dislocation, exposure, and psychological shock. Industrial economies do not have to withstand, unperturbed, the social wreckage engendered by prolonged unemployment, and economic stagnation. Since the economic depression of 1929, it became obvious that society cannot afford to jettison its basic production units, which, in this case, were large corporations. To forestall disintegration through international deflation, corporations had to be shielded against the vicissitudes of international and domestic forces. This was the analogy for the policy of government subsidies that was independently consecrated in all industrial nations during the last great depression. This was also the intention for the radical revision of bankruptcy laws in the industrial economies.

Many start-up businesses in Africa have not been able successfully to ride the economic cycles. As a result the microeconomic front of industrialization has often fizzled.

Expansion of industry could be based on the endowment of natural resources and on manufactured capital. This was true of the rest of the industrialized world and particularly England, where natural resources were substantially appropriated from without rather than from the home front. It is no longer feasible and practicable to base industrialization mainly on appropriation and depletion of "natural capital."

The unsystematic destruction of the rain forest and the share exploitation of irreplaceable fuels and ores in many places in Africa have resulted in soil erosion, depletion of soil fertility, and even desertification immediately south of the Sahara. This has been jeopardized by overgrazing and inadequate farming practices, coupled with rains that tend to nourish the coastal areas and punish the inland.

The industrial machine that will generate economic wealth in Africa is simply too large to be supported by the fragile foundation of endowed "natural capital." Expansion based on risk premia is a master key to industrialization. Capital formation, therefore, will be based on a regulated environment of profit, the one resource that reproduces itself instead of being destroyed. In different words, what is significant is a business that is profitable, not simply a firm that produces.

Much capital is needed to foster industrialization, but much of that capital must be generated domestically. This will mean modeling financial institutions after those of industrialized nations. Capital, by its very nature, tends to be both nervous and greedy, and it will flow into regions where it can reap the rewards of its investments. In this case, the wealthy classes of Africa invested their savings in Europe during the cold war years. On the other hand, the capital of European institutions, simultaneously, streamed into Africa, not for simple investments opportunities but systematically and effectively to garner might for themselves and efficiently gain access to needed resources.

Industrial economic policy may inculcate full employment policy in order to mitigate against the nightmares of chronic unemployment. Extensive work programs, such as highways, waterways, irrigation, electric power generation, and reforestation, should not be overshadowed by political expedience. Instead, programs should be seen in terms of their economic contributions: for example, elimination of transportation bottlenecks, flood control, low cost of industrial energy supply, and land rehabilitation.

Consistent economic progress should be the goal and not just economic security. This may be accomplished by radically reducing risk factors such as revamping antiquated bankruptcy laws.

Money alone is not the answer to industrialization in Africa. Many African countries seem to have halted in the tracks of industrialization or are stagnating in development efforts because of lack of money. Money should not, by itself, restrain development efforts. Many voids have yet to be filled that do not require money. Africa has invested considerably in education. The knowledge and expertise of the workforce, overall, and the educated elite, in particular, can be mobilized with focus, organization, and determination for industrialization.

It is also noteworthy that the erratic nature of economic growth in some places in Africa in the previous three decades, may be paralleled by the fable of the random night-walk of the jovial, inebriate laborer who abruptly lost possession of his key in the dark alleys. A passerby observed him laboriously searching for something under the lamp post. When the passerby inquired what he was doing, he replied that he was looking for a lost key. The passerby persuaded to know the vicinity in which he lost the key. The laborer muffled, in response, that it was lost down in the alley. "Well then," he asked, "why are you spending much time looking here?" "Because the light casts a brighter glow."

The keys to African industrialization lurk perhaps undiscovered or overlooked in the nooks and crannies of the dark alleys and the untended bushes of the wayside. Opportunities for initiative may never again be as bountiful as they are on the eve of the third millennium. Although Africa may be engaged in an unholy encounter with its economic nadir, these are auspicious times all around the world that should not be squandered.

3

# Fresh Water: A Tonic for Industrialization in Africa

In an industrializing environment, the demand for fresh water increases to meet the needs of new factories, expanded agriculture, accelerated population densities in company towns/industrial districts, and expected higher living standards. The danger for some countries may be that in the face of drought and pollution this increased demand will be too costly and difficult to meet immediately. In other countries, the time frame for industrialization may be squandered because of the effects of war and mismanagement. When water demands are not anticipated, shortages tend to threaten previous investments in agriculture and industry and even national food security may be at stake.[1]

Although Africa is directly under the equator, where the rate of vaporization is very high, there is still an ample supply of untapped water resources on the continent. The main problems with water include accessibility, purification, variability, and distribution.

South of the Sahara, less than 5 percent of the land suitable for irrigation has been irrigated. Ten percent of Africa is underlain by high-yielding aquifers. The rivers and tropical rains of West Africa offer sufficient water.[2] Water has not yet, however, been adequately harnessed to meet the demands of an industrializing environment. For nations around the seacoast with inadequate rainfall, it seems a last resort will be desalination—the process of separating fresh water from dissolved inorganic salts in sea and brackish water. The ancient dream of converting saline water to fresh water is now technologically feasible. Saline water, though not chemically complex, is comparatively stable. This source of fresh water, therefore, tends to be cost-prohibitive, because of the huge amount of energy required to run the desalination plants, based on theoretical computations.

A cubic meter of fresh water produced by desalination may in a developed nation cost as much as a hundred times more than the same volume from some well-managed waterworks. However, bringing down the cost is not impossible. An option, it seems, will be a mutual investment between contiguous nations. Recycling urban waste water for agriculture is feasible, given current technology. Drip irrigation and greenhouses will also avert water waste in arid regions.

While significant resources have been expended, especially in urban settings, on the provision of basic facilities, such as water supplies, sewers, and paved streets, much work remains to be done in these areas. One study, not very long ago, determined that in the unplanned suburb of a large city in Africa, seven street fountains provided water for 25,000 people. While one would imagine that conditions might have improved since then, such allocations are still cause for concern, in an industrializing and urbanizing environment. In many African countries, communal water taps (standpipes) seem standard fixtures in towns and even cities. Archaic public water taps are not only affronts to environmental aesthetics, but outward symbols of the myriad of developmental opportunities yet to be seized. The failing patchwork of leaky pipes only adds insults to injury. Many people do not have indoor plumbing and must spend untold number of hours annually in queues around communal water taps just to obtain water for domestic use. This is valuable time that affects national productivity. In the rural areas, the situation is not very different. In many communities, the women and children instead of water pipes are typically responsible for providing the family with water. Often, this itinerant chore requires a great deal of time and effort. Water therefore tends to be used very sparingly, in households of the lower socioeconomic rungs.[3]

In urban settings, however, indoor plumbing is more common than in rural areas. Some of this plumbing is old, defective, and perhaps improperly designed for the high and constant water demands of an industrializing environment. Antiquated and faulty plumbing fixtures may be a source of contamination of drinking water, and water used for food processing. Such contaminations, in other parts of the world, have been known to result in amebic dysentery and even death. The possible sources of water contamination are many and various. For example, cross connections by plumbers may result in water flow in the reverse direction or even uphill, when valves fail or if flush-valve water closets lack vacuum breakers. In another example, the pressure in the water supply line was cut off, when the valve from the main line was turned off. Atmospheric pressure in the toilet bowls moved the water up to the drinking water-supply reservoir of the storey building. The water was contaminated on the first floor of the public building, causing an outbreak of gastroenteritis.[4] In another case, a hydro aspirator (a device employed in extracting body fluids during embalming) was improperly connected to the municipal drinking water supply. This error in connection contaminated the water delivered to other houses in the neighborhood. The water from the faucets appeared unusually rusty.[5] Although, in this case, the neighbors had ample water, it was not safe for drinking.

It is good practice to boil water before drinking when it may be contaminated by bacteria and other microorganisms. However, hot tap water in indoor plumbing is not a good substitute for cold water. One reason is that hot water tends to leach contaminants (such as *lead*) in pipelines. Hot water in indoor plumbing is not a substitute for drinking water when the municipal water supply is temporarily shut down for one reason or the other. Hot tap water, therefore, should not be used in preparing baby foods, tea, hot chocolate drinks, and the like.

The high temperatures prevalent in   much of Africa require much water consumption. Without adequate water, children run the risk of dehydration. A study of 800 urban families determined that where water consumption "was less than 22 lads, children had higher rates of diarrhea, scabies, conjunctivitis, febrile illness, and malnutrition, than comparable children in families consuming more water."[6] It was also presumed that the quantity of water consumed by adults could affect the health and labor productivity as well.

The quality of water for household, commercial, and industrial uses is enhanced, if sewer treatment plants are used in urban settings. Treating waste is vital, not only from industrial plants and households but also run-off from agricultural land. When run-off is not properly handled, the damage could be very costly. For example, overirrigation and poor drainage could sooner or later destroy the environment. In southern Iraq a field that once grew barleys was rendered barren, frosted by salt due to run-off from fields upstream from the river Euphrates. In this case, stagnant water collected in the field and as it evaporated it left behind a residue of salt.[7] The down-stream effects of river pollution tend to compound for settlements around the tail end of rivers, resulting in intermittent outbreaks of waterborne diseases.

Another danger with pollution is that it reduces available water. More polluted water means less useful water, available for industrial, municipal, and farm irrigation. For example, it may take as much as 110,000 gallons of water to make a ton of steel. When a body of water becomes polluted, life in the water begins to die.  This may even be difficult to detect casually, since many industrial age pollutants at low concentrations are colorless, odorless, and tasteless.[8] In largely diluted municipal water, ingesting them without knowing is easy.

Fish are good indicators of  the dangers of polluted waters. There are many streams and rivers in Africa that only thirty years ago teemed with a variety of fish. On the eve of the twenty-first century, the variety and quantity of fish have diminished in many rivers, streams, and lakes. Besides other forms of abuse and mismanagement, pesticides may be suspect. In one study, one part of DDT per billion parts of water was found to kill crab in eight days.[9] Some more sophisticated detergents have been known to kill fish eggs. Many Africans living close to rivers, streams, and lakes tend to use rivers and streams to do laundering, especially when the municipal water supply is shut down for extended periods. In northern Malawi, a business in Dwangua (around Lake Malawi) switched from growing fish to raising crocodiles for export.[10]

Africa is endowed with many lakes, both natural and manmade. These lakes are valuable resources. However, not properly managed, they lose some of their value and instead become  a threat to humans. For example, *bilharziasis* or *schistosomiasis* is a serious disease caused by a wormlike parasite called a schistosome or blood fluke. The eggs are deposited into ponds and streams and hatch to produce free-swimming larvae that penetrate and develop inside tiny freshwater snails. A subsequent larval stage matures in snails and can penetrate the skin of the human foot when the victim enters a contaminated body of water. In infected humans, the larvae mature into adult worms that mate and develop eggs. This cycle begins again when such human feces is released in streams, rivers, lakes, etc.[11] Like malaria, schistosomiasis causes general debility and lassitude. Obviously, it is not good practice for persons to defecate or wash clothes in streams and rivers. This is especially so if these water bodies are used downstream for drinking, swimming, irrigation, and so on. Schistosomiasis is almost as common as malaria in some communities. About 800,000 people die each year from this infection.[12] The damage inflicted by the worm is indirect. Female worms deposit eggs in human tissue and the body responds by walling off the eggs into cysts known as granulomas. These granulomas tend to block capillaries, impede blood flow, and cause scarring. Many scarring in internal organs may result in cirrhosis, bladder tumors, and kidney failure. Left untreated, this may result in loss of life.[13]

Many African countries tend to rely on tourism as a source of income, but it must be added that many tourists are not particularly excited by the quality of water in many African countries. The fact that purified bottled water is available does not in any way mean the problem has been resolved. Sanitary standards that are at parity with global standards are vital, not only in the tourist industry but also in the trade in cash crops and manufactured items. Fruits and vegetables, which tend to be eaten without cooking, require washing and processing with clean water. Unless these nuances are urgently addressed, expanding the volume of trade will be difficult. In the international trade arena, entrepreneurs cannot afford to be permissive. The intrinsic mechanisms of capitalism are not etched with sympathy.

It has been said that Africa's greatest strength was her weakness. In the post cold war environment, this is no longer the case—substantial strength derives from the ability to compete, successfully, in the global marketplace. Many African governments have relentlessly worked at water supply and waste disposal problems, and it appears that carefully coordinated, detail-oriented, modern, and well-integrated plans with staying power can resolve this issue. Until then, the increased and innocent misuse by the public of pesticides, chemicals, detergents, cleaning agents, machinery, and so on, will continue to exact a costly toll on aquatic life, humans, and the environment at large.

## LESSONS FROM THE PAST

Many ancient civilizations owed their greatness to the proper use of water. Ancient Egypt owed its greatness to the Nile river. Ancient Babylonia owed its greatness to the Tigris and the Euphrates rivers. Ancient China owed its greatness to the Yellow River, and India to the Indus. The Romans recognized the need for clean and pure water and secured their supply of fresh water from the streams in the distant mountains, rather than the more convenient but murky Tiber River.

Throughout history water has played a fundamental role in human settlement. Like air, water is a necessity of life. When primitive people stopped wandering and decided to settle in one place, they located their homes near water. Water was obtained from rivers, streams, and lakes. Great civilizations sometimes mushroomed from these settlements.

Later developments, however, superseded the physical location of water as the overwhelming determinant of the location of initial human settlement. Humanity learnt to balance such needs as security and food with the need for water, by digging wells. The Romans took this idea a step farther. They brought water to their cities from distant mountains by means of aqueducts.[14] This great idea is still used today.

Gravity is the fundamental technique for transporting water. The source of the water is usually higher than the destination/outlet, connected by an inclined aqueduct. Gravity is the cheapest and most reliable force in the world for carrying water. At junctures where gravity is insufficient, because of relative distance and transport terrain, the water must be propelled through by pumps. Sections of these huge pipes, called inverted siphons, curve downwards to pass, beneath stream beds and other low places.

Artifacts of ancient aqueducts have been found in the city of Jerusalem. The aqueduct in Jerusalem is constructed of limestone blocks, in which fifteen-inch holes had been hand-drilled. To supply the cities with water, the Greeks built masonry conduits. One of these conduits, that supply the city of Athens is 4,200 feet long and probably built 2,500 years ago. The city of Rome had arteries of aqueducts. Frontinus, the first superintendent of Roman Water Works, appointed in AD 97, had nine aqueducts built.[15] These aqueducts supplied approximately 85,000,000 gallons of water per day, from the mountain springs. Four masonry aqueducts were later added to meet increased demand. Almost 200 cities in the Roman colonies were supplied with aqueducts. Among these cities were Metz in France, Tarragona in Spain, Antioch in Syria, and Carthage in northern Africa. Remains of these aqueducts are extant over this region.

Modern Rome is supplied with eight aqueducts, two of them dating in part from the original ancient sources. Another two were constructed in the last three decades or so.[16] Although Rome has an adequate supply of water, the per capita water flow is about half of that of two millennia ago.[17] Early aqueducts ended in basins called *Castella Aquarum* (or *châteteaux d'eau* or display fountains), which conveyed water to small reservoirs—*fontes*—furnished with taps for the exclusive use of certain streets. A *castellum* typically carried a plaque announcing to the public the emperor or potentate who sponsored the project. The fountain may bear coats of arms. Water that was not drinkable ran out by means of large pipes into extensive enclosures, where it served to water cattle and as a ready resource in case of an urban conflagration. At these places, people could wash their linen. The Athenians named four officers to keep watch and ward over the water, an example followed by other Greek towns. Greek fountains were remarkable for their architectural beauty and the extreme delicacy of their execution. Greece virtually exhausted the treasures of its poetical imagination to embellish her fountains. Some fountains (e.g., Lerna) offered loungers an elegant portico, under which commodious seats allowed enjoyment, during summer, of the freshness water communicated to the atmosphere.

"The Romans take great care of three things above others, which the Greeks neglected," wrote Strabo, a Greek geographer, "That is in opening roads, building aqueducts, and sending residue underground into sewers." The Etruscans invented sewers but the Romans were quick learners.[18]

The greatest ancient aqueduct was the Aqueduct of Carthage (now Tunisia, in Africa). It ran 87.6 miles from the springs of Zaghouan to Djebel Djouqar. It was built by the Romans around 117–138 AD.

Sewerage systems may be traced back to ancient cities, including Athens and Rome. The great sewer of Rome, *Cloaca Maxima*, drained into the Tiber and had dimensions reaching 10 feet wide and 12 feet high. Rome also had public latrines. At least 150 could be counted at the time of Constantine. However, these achievements were not without a dark side. The masses were not always permitted to enjoy the available hygienic facilities.[19]

Dilapidated and open drainage ditches may be found in certain sections of some big African cities.[20] Here, gutters may flood during unusually heavy rains and perhaps elevate the risk of infection from microorganisms that may inhabit the drains. This not only poses added health problems but also tends to discourage some tourists and visitors from making repeat visits or recommending that other travelers visit. Waste matter in a community is often disposed of as sewage. In small communities such as farms and villages, sewage is often disposed of in the soil. This is obviously unsanitary in thickly populated human settlements such as cities and may indirectly burden budget allocations for health care. Savings in this area may be applied to industrialization efforts.

The sewer system is generally divided into *sanitation sewers* and *storm sewers*. Sanitation sewers are made up of an artery of drainage pipes that serve as receptacles for waste matter from households, factories, schools, office buildings, shopping malls, and other private and public buildings. A storm sewer empties all or part of the rainwater from the streets. The storm sewers are designed to avert flooding after rainfall or heavy storms. For this reason, they are called storm sewers. Although combination sewers are possible, they are not practicable. When cities try to cut costs by having combination sewers, the system is likely to be choked by unusually heavy storms. When this happens, sewage may back up and seep into basements and cellars or low-lying buildings. Even when this does not happen, waste matter is speeded through the *sewer treatment plants*. During a heavy storm, the volume of water may be very much for the treatment plant to handle immediately. The result is that a great amount of untreated sewage, including animal and human waste, is dumped untreated into nearby streams, rivers, or other bodies of water. A well-designed sewage disposal system is very important in large modern cities.

Because of the large concentration of urban population, sewage must be deposited at safe and sanitary distances. Decomposed sewage matter emits poisonous and explosive gases. To forestall calamities, sewers are ventilated at critical junctures by shafts with iron gratings. When these gratings are large enough for workers to lower themselves through and inspect/clean the sewers, they are called *manholes*. Manholes are at points in the sewer line where there is a change in direction or intersection. The sewer is expected to maintain a flow of at least one and one-half feet per second. Any deficiency in speed must be aided by a pump. It is important for building drains to be fitted with an elbow in the pipe, to prevent a possible backup of poisonous gases. This elbow, in building construction nomenclature, is a *trap*. Bad odors can be prevented if sewage is diluted with water that is about twenty to forty times its volume.

When sewage is not treated before being released into the river, lake, or ocean, it causes pollution. This is especially true if the water from the river is used downstream for agricultural and industrial applications. For example, polluted water may contaminate fresh vegetables. On a positive note, the action of bacteria is very important in sewage treatment.

Sewer construction must be able to factor-in contingencies. When sewers are built, they are generally constructed to last for ages. Because of this longevity, the planners are expected to anticipate future urban growth or the paths of urban development. Some sewers are built to sustain the weight of buildings and parking lots overhead, as well as vibrations from heavy traffic in the vicinity. Others are built to withstand only a few feet of overhead soil. If sewer lines are superposed by dump sites, landfills, and housing developments, there may be a propensity for underground sewers to collapse under the pressure of such unprecedented mass and vibrations, including earth movements speeded by unusual rainfalls. When sewers collapse in developed zones of the city, they may add collateral injury to the city infrastructure. Examples will include damaged roads, parking lots, and buildings.[21] Damage may also be caused by leaks in the sewer lines, which gradually erode the soil structure, engaging a cavity that eventually initiates a sinkhole. To avert this calamity, maintenance workers religiously inspect sewer lines and carry out anticipated repairs accordingly. Steel reinforced concrete is a prevention that is better than the cure.

## HEALTH CONSEQUENCES OF UNSAFE WATER

There are twin dangers in water pollution. The first in the danger to health, and the second is the danger of shortage. Polluted waters tend to cause illness around the stomach and intestines, nostrils, mouth, and eyes. Hepatitis is a waterborne disease that afflicts the liver. Typhoid fever, cholera, among many others, are water-related diseases that may not only impinge on national productivity but may even result in the loss of labor force.

*Typhoid fever* is an infectious disease that causes ulcers in the walls of the intestines. It is caused by the germ bacillus. During an attack, the germs multiply and infect other organs of the body, especially the spleen, which typically enlarges. Typhoid fever is contracted from unsanitary drinking water, milk, and infected food. The breath of a patient does not carry disease, but the discharges from his bowels and kidneys are infected with millions of germs. The bodily discharges of typhoid patients must be carefully disinfected or disposed of. When the bodily discharges of typhoid patients are not carefully handled or disinfected, they may infect the sewage and water supply. Houseflies that come in contact with the bodily discharges of typhoid patients may carry the germs into houses and food. Some people are immune to the disease but carry the germs in their system. Such people are a source of constant infection. When milk is infected, it is not because cattle are infected by the germs, for cattle cannot contract typhoid fever. Milk becomes infected when impure water is used to dilute the milk or when utensils were washed with impure water.

*Cholera* is often spread by infected water, infected milk, infected raw food, flies, and soiled hands. The victims of cholera often experience constant violent vomiting and severe, watery diarrhea. The victims do not expel urine, the body temperatures drop, and the victims lose weight rapidly. Untreated, the patient eventually collapses in shock and often expires.

Infectious hepatitis, a disease of the liver, can be traced to polluted water. It spreads under crowded conditions and when sanitation is poor. Infectious hepatitis may be fatal. The symptoms include yellow skin, yellow eyeballs, and enlarged and tender liver that may be coupled with fever.

Schistosomiasis, caused by the tiny flatworm known as blood fluke occurs when the worm reaches the bloodstream of people who wash themselves or their clothes in contaminated water, wade in it, or drink it. Recent research indicates that within a few days after the worm enters the blood stream, it changes its chemical nature to resemble that of a human cell, making it difficult for the body's immune system to respond to this foreign organism. Unlike the young schistosome, which enters the body by boring through the skin of swimmers and waders, other flukes enter via intermediate hosts such as freshwater crabs, snails, and insects. All flukes begin their development in snails.[22] In areas where these and other similar afflictions prevailed, work and school absenteeism tended to increase. This was the case in 1987, in Nigeria, when the waterborne guinea worm parasite became endemic in some rural areas. According to the World Health Organization (WHO) there were about 3 million cases, then an unusually high number relative to the estimated 140 million cases around the world. Since then, there were campaigns to eradicate this worm that causes recurring illness in humans and provide pure drinking water to the rural areas.[23] Another water-related affliction is river blindness. Not very long ago, rural populations were known to move entire villages away from the river to other areas because of simulium flies (blackflies), the main carriers of the cause of river blindness (onchocerciasis).

## ENHANCING FARM HARVEST

It is not difficult to fathom why, at the dawn of the third millennium, water, a necessity, still poses one of the most arrant problems facing much of Africa. Some 5,000 years ago Egyptians built dams to conserve water for irrigation. Since then, not much has changed in the basic idea. Of course irrigation is still used in Africa, but several countries in the very Africa became net food importers in the recent past. While the solution is not as easy, it is still imperative to increase the use of irrigation in arable lands (which already command high rates of crop output, but variable precipitation) and in nonproductive lands in the arid regions. The idea is to optimize the use of water at the proper times. This enhances the application of farm technology—including fertilizers, crop rotation, and more productive crop varieties.

In many countries in Africa, only a small proportion of the cultivable land is actually being farmed; yields have remained much lower than they need be.[24] Africa is a part of the world where many people still await for the rains to fall. Experience in recent years has determined that relying on annual rainfall (an act of nature) is a very unreliable and very risky way of doing agricultural business. In an industrializing environment, hundreds of millions of people and billions of dollars worth of investments in food crops and cash crops cannot depend entirely on natural precipitation. For agrobased economies like those of Africa, it is very risky indeed. To negate this predicament, it is only logical to tap auxiliary sources of water, such as mining underground lakes and rivers to make up for natural deficiencies. This may sometimes mean sourcing water from hundreds of miles away. This method, in conjunction with simple forms of irrigation, has been very beneficial and productive to farmers in other places, where as much as 33% of the irrigated land may be supplied by underground water. Water may be pumped by windmills, gasoline engines, electric motors, and so on.

Irrigation is by definition the watering of plants by artificial means. This is necessary if the plants do not receive water at the proper time and in the proper amounts and form. As a rule, land that receives an annual rainfall of less than 10 inches is deficient in producing crops of any kind. To avert this shortage, the advantages of irrigation must not be discounted. Irrigation not only makes up for natural deficiencies but also ensures water supply whenever it is most needed. This boosts productivity of land, reduces crop failures, and often leads to the attraction of new settlements, that eventually blossom into prosperous communities in a once barren region.

Irrigation water is chiefly sourced from the most dependable and most convenient locations. Although simple irrigation for a farmer's garden may be sourced from a hill top location, a country mile away, generally water for large scale irrigation may come from hundreds of miles away, by means of dams and canals.

Dams are very important because they hold back water in artificial lakes (or reservoirs). Where annual rainfall is ample but all the rain falls in one short season, the reservoir conserves the rainfall for the long dry season that follows. A greater variety of crops can be grown with irrigation. Irrigation increases the yield and grade of crops. Irrigated land must be graded or leveled so that water flows evenly over the land. A less undulating terrain also becomes handy in mechanized agriculture. A slope of ten to twenty feet per mile is acceptable, to optimize use of water. Although like everything else under the sun, irrigation has its own problems when *mismanaged*, essentially, irrigation can change wasteland into farmland and flat dry land into rich fertile land.[25] Minerals necessary for plant growth can be taken up from the soil in water or capillary action. Water consumed by a crop, from planting to harvesting, varies with the length of the planting season, the climate, and available soil water. Water consumed by a crop like corn for a whole season may range from 500 to 1,000 gallons of water, depending on the yield per acre.[26] More grain is produced per unit of water consumed, as yield per acre increases. A soil rich in plant nutrients such as calcium, iron, phosphorus, nitrogen, potassium, and magnesium may as well be useless without water. This explains why hydroponics is increasingly being used in the cultivation of vegetables in greenhouses. Yields are not only quadrupled but a stock of clean, fresh vegetables is also guaranteed.

Besides plants, animals also need a regular supply of water. Typically animals require water once a day, but water requirements may vary with the type of feed available. Range cattle may drink between four and eight gallons of water per day, while high producing milk cows may require as much as 25 gallons per day. Irrigation, piped-in well water, and technically approved water storage tanks, enhance constant supply of water requirements in isolated farmsteads and similar places and may become handy during the long dry seasons in Africa.

## BACK TO THE FUTURE

In a period of industrial growth, much water is needed. Factories use greater quantities of water than households. The problem usually is whether enough water will be available, to meet the demands of industrial growth. For example, as much as 325 gallons of water may be required to make one gallon of alcohol, and about 375 gallons to grow a one-pound sack of flour.[27] In an industrializing environment, therefore, surface water will be put where and when nature did not so do. Through a system of water storage dams and giant multipurpose dams, the scene of arid and semi arid places can be tempered and reclaimed into huge decorative artificial lakes and irrigation districts. Here, perhaps, millions of acres of rich irrigated farmlands will support huge urban populations and industrial demands for water, in places where nature had put only harsh and adverse climatic conditions.

## NOTES

1. Melvin Kranzberg and Carroll W. Pursell, Jr., *Technology in Western Civilization Vol. II* (New York: Oxford University Press, 1967), p. 419.

2. In an industrializing environment, a water source that was once considered safe may be contaminated even when the water looks like clear crystal and is free from odor and unpleasant taste.

3. It is difficult for persons living far from water sources to develop the minimum levels of acceptable hygiene habits in household and personal cleanliness, thus increasing the health risk of preventable diseases. It was observed during the Industrial Revolution, in Britain, that when supplies of water into the houses of persons of middle class were cut off, by the pipes being frozen, and when it was necessary to send for water from a distance, the house cleansing and washes were diminished by the inconvenience. Thus habits of household cleaning were presumed to deteriorate "if it were at all times requisite for them to send to a distance for water, and in all weathers." Report on the Sanitary Condition of the Labouring Population, 1842, pp. 69–70, in Pauline Gregg, *A Social and Economic History of Britain, 1760–1950* (London: George G. Harrap & Co., 1952), pp. 198–199.

4. Ruth Winter, *Poison in Your Food* (New York: Crown Publishers, 1969), pp. 151–163.

5. Ibid.

6. S.B. Thacker, S.I. Music, and R.A. Pollard, 1980. "Acute Water Shortage and Health Problems in Haiti." *Lancet* 1(8166): pp. 471–473, in Simon M. Fass *Political Economy in Haiti: The Drama of Survival* (Transaction Publishers, 1993), p. 175.

7. *National Geographic Magazine*, May 1993, pp. 48–49.

8. Leinwand G. P., *Air and Water Pollution* (New York: Simon and Schuster, 1969), p. 141.

9. Howard Earl, "Water Pollution, That Dirty Mess," *Today's Health*, March 1966, in Ruth Winter, *Poison in Your Food*, p. 152.

10. Winrock International, *African Development: Lessons From Asia* (Arlington, VA: Winrock International Institute for Agricultural Development, 1991), p. 163.

11. Richard Anthony, "Global Balance," *Harvard Public Health Review*, II, no. 2, Winter 1991, p. 27, in Robin Marantz Henig, *The People's Health: A Memoir of Public Health and Its Evolution at Harvard* (Washington, DC: Joseph Henry Press, 1997), p. 38.

12. Greg Folkers "A New Vaccine Strategy Promising against Schistosomiasis," *NIAID News*, April 27, 1994, p. 1. in Marantz Henig, *The People's Health*, p. 38.

13. Ibid.

14. An aqueduct is a man-made channel through which water is conducted to the place where it is used. In building aqueducts, the typical materials used would include (masonry) concrete, cast iron, steel plates, or even natural rock, through which a tunnel is dug, and then lined with reinforced concrete.

15. George Rosen, *A History of Public Health* (Baltimore, MD: Johns Hopkins University Press, 1993), pp. 15–16.

16. "The Grand Design of 23 Centuries Ago Is Still Watering Rome," *Smithsonian Magazine*, September 1992, pp. 88–101.

17. Ibid.

18. Ibid., p. 90.

19. Rosen, *A History of Public Health*, p. 18.

20. U.S. Department of Commerce, *Nigeria: A Survey of U.S. Export Opportunities* (Washington, D.C.: GPO, 1981), p. 45.

21. *Atlanta Journal/Constitution*, June 19, 1993, pp. A1 and A4.

22. "Man and His Environment," *Britannica Year Book of Science and the Future: 1970*, p. 396.

23. Helen Chapin Metz, ed., *Nigeria: A Country Study* (Washington DC: Library of Congress, 1991), p. 151.

24. William A. Hance, *African Economic Development* (New York: Frederick A. Praeger Publishers, 1967), p. 16.

25. Where soils are irrigated with low-quality water and inadequate drainage, salts slowly accumulate. High levels of salts drastically reduce crop production, and may flocculate the soil surface, rendering the soil susceptible to wind and soil erosion. Severe physical and chemical degradation can make the soil worthless, even if attempts are made to reclaim it. Good soil stewardship is, therefore, is a common responsibility: *1983 Yearbook of Agriculture: United States Department of Agriculture* (Washington, DC: GPO, 1983), pp. 18–27.

26. Ibid.

27. Winter, *Poison in Your Food*, p. 152.

# 4

# Productivity in Africa

Productivity is like money saved in the bank. It increases the purchasing power of nations and improves the general standard of living. It is a key that unlocks the shackles of the hobbled masses. Well-harnessed and organized corporations are more likely to succeed in the near and long term. It will be difficult to industrialize when productivity issues are not consistently addressed.[1]

Productivity in Africa has generally declined or stagnated through the years, while population has virtually exploded. In a continent where the majority of the population are farmers, productivity in agriculture still leaves much to be desired, jeopardized by skirmishes and inclement weather conditions in some countries.[2] When outputs in the manufacturing sectors of infant industries have increased, often such gains have not been accompanied by increases in quality. While the qualities of products have generally improved in much of the world, the converse has been true for much of Africa. When the costs of manufactured products have similarly increased, qualities were not given adequate consideration.

In North America, Europe, and Japan, the Industrial Revolution greatly improved productivity. Productivity in developed nations expanded forty-five fold compounded over a period of 125 years, at an average annual rate of 3 to 4 percent.[3] Before productivity explosions, it took at least fifty years for a country to become "developed." More recently, it took Korea only twenty years to become developed. This transformation began around 1955. This radical compression of the time span was largely the result of productivity revolution.[4] Industrialization in Africa will greatly improve worker productivity.

In the last two hundred years or so, corporations have been founded and built around the wisdom of Adam Smith's pin factory—the idea that industrial work is more productive when broken down into its simplest and most basic tasks. Adam Smith observed the technological changes around him during the Industrial Revolution and recognized atypical opportunities for manufacturers to increase worker productivity by orders of magnitude. Until then, productivity could be increased by nudging the artisan to work a little faster. In his famous work *The Wealth of Nations*, first published in 1776, he illustrated this principle of division of labor as follows, in the trade of the pin maker:

A workman not educated to his business (which the division of labour has rendered a distinct trade), nor acquainted with the use of machinery employed in it . . . could scarce, perhaps, with the utmost industry, make one pin a day, and certainly could not make twenty. One man draws out the wire, another straights it, a third cuts it, a fourth points it, a fifth grinds it at the top for receiving the head; to make the head requires two or three distinct operations; to put it on, is a peculiar business, to whiten the pins is another; it is even a trade by itself to put them into the paper; and the important business of making a pin is, in this manner, divided into eighteen distinct operations, which, in some manufactories, are all performed by distinct hands, though in others the same man will sometimes perform two or three of them.[5]

Adam Smith's analogy, thus, successfully determined that division or specialization of labor dramatically increased the productivity of pin makers: "Ten men, therefore, could make among them upwards of forty-eight thousand pins a day. Each person, therefore, . . . making four thousand eight hundred pins a day. But if they had all wrought separately and independently, . . . they certainly could not each of them have made twenty, perhaps not one in a day."[6] He later went on to explain that the advantage was due to "three different circumstances; first, to the increase of dexterity in every particular workman; secondly, to the saving of the time which is commonly lost in passing from one species of work to another; and lastly, to the invention of a great number of machines which facilitate and abridge labor, and enable one man to do the work of many."[7] This dimension of organization not only sometimes alleviated human suffering that was typically engendered in the workplace but ushered the age of automation and mass production. Automation not only sped up production but also ameliorated the mental numbness that sometimes accompanied machines.

Today this is still the central idea around which productivity is enhanced in manufacturing and service sectors. To take advantage of specialization of labor, work tends to be fragmented into basic tasks, for example car manufacturers, computer chip makers, food processors, and packaging companies. Similarly, in the service-oriented sectors such as distribution, finance, insurance, airlines, and accounting firms, the propensity to increase productivity is magnified, when labor is infused with planning, sweat is replaced by knowledge, and brain supersedes brawn.

Productivity is regarded as a litmus test for organizational performance. Management is charged with the foremost task of balancing a diversity of input variables, in order to increasingly improve productivity. This means, therefore, that the calculus to factor-in capital investments in production is only initiated when it increases productivity. Unfortunately, such changes have sometimes met with ample resistance, especially when labor feels threatened. For example, workers more often than not have demonstrated a poor receptivity to technology that threatens job opportunities in the short term. In the 1950s, an available option was to use computer-controlled machine-tool technology that could shape with precision intricate, structured components of major aircraft. This ingenious new technology attained dimensions and consistence that superseded human performance and capability. Unfortunately, this also meant the skilled machinist's job was in jeopardy.[8]

Labor, as a factor of production, has played a very significant role in economic policy formulation in Africa. The abundance of unskilled labor, as a resource relative to other factors of production, has translated into labor-intensive industries. This is especially true in agriculture, mining, manufacturing, and the transportation industries. When there is an abundant supply of unskilled labor and a limited supply of capital, using labor intensive methods to increase production is efficient. By the same token, using very costly capital when it could have sufficed to use cheap labor will be wasteful. Although labor intensive methods tend to increase total output, output per person does not increase as much as when capital intensive methods are employed. Capital-intensive methods of production are likely to increase output per person *faster* than labor-intensive methods. This explains the relatively low income levels in Africa and other developing countries.

Specifically, "in the manufacturing industries, productivity is directly controlled by the degree to which work is mechanized; that is by the amount of powered machinery placed under the command of industrial workers and technicians."[9] For example, when the options for combining machine and manpower were considered and arranged from most mechanized to least mechanized, in materials handling tasks, the most mechanized combinations prevailed. In one observation, output per worker hour was used as the yardstick, with a score of one being the least output while a score of ten was used as the most output. The most mechanized arrangement handled ten times as many materials per hour as the least-mechanized combination.[10]

In order to migrate from a low level of mechanization or production environment to a high level of mechanization or production environment, a supporting infrastructure is necessary. Therefore, requisites will include a guaranteed supply of power, transportation, communications, water supply and housing in an environment that demonstrates an affinity for the least cost combination of machines and other factors of production. Therefore, in a resource scarce and industrializing environment, optimal cost minimization to maximize outputs can be religiously practiced. Here, the benefits of optimal cost minimization reinforced by increasing wages are strategically commendable.

Unlike Africa where there has been an abundance of unskilled labor, in the preindustrial New World, there was a scarcity of labor and an abundance of land. This meant land was cheap and everybody could own land. Because labor was scarce, it was relatively expensive. In 1833, E.G. Wakefield wrote: it was a place where "Land is very cheap.... Where everyone who so pleases can easily obtain a piece of land for himself, not only is labor very dear...but the difficulty of obtaining combined labor at any price."[11] There was a great need for the fabrication of machine tools. This void was a catalyst for the Industrial Revolution in parts of the New World. A business that hires high wage labor to do tasks, with low productivity, may be paving its way to bankruptcy. When wages are high, and the productivity is not high enough to meet the competition or to exploit the potential or real opportunities, this will increase the likelihood to substitute labor-saving machinery for human labor.

The availability of cheap and accessible energy to power factory machinery was the spark of the Industrial Revolution. Up to this point, the alternative was natural energy, from the brawn of the muscle or by the beast of burden, and it was less efficient and less productive than artificial energy. Coal, water, and hydroelectricity became important factors in the location of industry. The cheap energy that spurred mechanization in turn increased productivity. For industrialization efforts in Africa to be effective, having lowcost, reliable, and affordable energy for industrial users will be necessary.

In Japan, the rapid introduction of electric motors between 1914 and 1930 spurred industrial dualism (i.e., traditional and modern sectors). Most manufacturing establishments with at least 1,000 workers were completely electrified by 1914 and those with less than 100 by 1930. The diffusion of cheap electric motors stepped up labor productivity in the small manufacturing industry, and reduced economies of scale in several industries.[12] In 1909, the cost of labor in the United States of America averaged 19.3 cents per hour while electricity was 2.2 cents per kilowatt-hour. In other words, manufacturers could purchase 8.8 kw/hr of energy or one hour of factory labor. By 1950, 157 kw/hr of energy could be exchanged for the same one hour of factory labor. This achievement, through external efficiencies, represented an improvement in favor of industry to the tune of more than 1,500 percent. The outcome of this transformation was a reduction of labor, while output per unit of capital assigned for production and distribution increased. Fuel consumption per kw/hr was made more efficient. There was efficiency in conversion (heat rate). The heat rate was improved from 25,000 British thermal units (Btu's) per kilowatt-hour, in 1925, to 10,400 Btu's per kilowatt-hour, in 1965. New efficient plants replaced old and less-efficient plants.

Amazingly, the majority of tools have not changed significantly through the millennia. Many hand tools that people used in their quest to increase productivity have remained simple in designs and applications, for example, hammers. Hard tools, such as dies and molds, have similarly remained basic in their orientation. What has changed, has been the source of energy. Tools that were once powered by human energy were also powered by animal muscle, the wind, water, and later fossil fuel and nuclear energy. So, although a recent word like *mechanization* is akin to modern technology, in reality, all tools by definition have always been mechanized from the days of the early man until today.

Optimal tool engineering requires that a tool performs with minimal effort, minimal complexity, and minimal power. Contrary to popular myth, most assembly line work is done with hand tools—fully mechanized, very simple small but often powered hand tools. *Automation* is not a higher order of mechanization. It is not a definite arrangement of machines and machine parts. It is simply a concept. It is a concept that is different from mechanization. Consequently, automation may be found in *mechanized* and *nonmechanized* environments. An example of automation is the *abacus,* used by Japanese and Chinese children. The abacus, noted for its relative high speed and accuracy, is automation and data processing without the requirements of machines or high technology.

Just as mechanization freed the human from physical labor, automation somehow freed the human mind from human fatigue, in guiding and controlling machines. Line productivity could be increased without increasing the numbness of the mind. The main distinguishing feature of automation vis-à-vis mechanization, is its *feedback* mechanism. In this case, the feedback control—hailed as the heart of automation—provides information concerning machine operation, continuously compared with desired performance. An example is the *thermostat*, in home heating and air-conditioning systems. Another example is the mechanical *cam*, found in many early machines is one of the most common control devices.[13] Electrical, hydraulic, and pneumatic control devices including computers have been also used since the cam. Specifically, computer programs are an evolution of this concept. Computer control applications can direct a single machine or a total production system. Today, computer-controlled programs are widely used in industry. Examples include electric power plants, chemical plants, steel rolling mills, and blast furnaces.

Automatic machines and automatic control do not, by themselves, result in automatic production systems. An automatic production system also requires automatic movement of materials through the production sequence. In this case, most of the productivity gains are derived from continuous movements.[14] Until the advent of the computer, the moving assembly line epitomized the vitality and efficiency of mass production. Some critics, however, revealed the other side of the coin. They saw continuous movement as a symbol of monotony and relentless pressure on workers. Continuous movement is used in a wide variety of production settings that may range from auto assembly, painting automobile bodies, manufacture of automobile parts, to beverage, newspaper, soap, and food production.[15]

Although corporations dramatically increased the productivity of the worker, using Adam Smith's organizing principles, there were also inherent snags and challenges—the more fragmented work became, the more workers were required. The urgent challenge was to coordinate workers and production, as output virtually exploded.[16] Management, therefore, had to establish procedures (manuals) and make rules for any imaginable contingency in order to ensure consistent and accurate performance. For organization to be effective, therefore, workers had to be virtually programmed to conform to established rules and procedures in the workplace. Essentially, an efficient worker performed a task; was expected only to do the job, not to think or make decisions about it. Such prerogatives were the provinces of management. A reason was that management did in fact command broader perspectives, based on more information, than did lower-level workers.[17] These changes, coupled with planning and control, were the essence of twentieth century business bureaucracy. Much of this organizational innovation in the American industrial infrastructure is attributable to railroads. Necessity was the mother of invention.

The railroads were faced with the daunting challenge of making *one-track systems* practicable, since they carried trains in both directions. Railroads not only enhanced the distribution of nationally advertised, mass-produced, branded goods; they were by their very nature large-scale employers of labor. In the meanwhile, industrialization had come to depend on railroads, because of quick and cheap bulk transportation of raw materials such as lumber, iron ore, limestone, coal, and clay. Essentially, mass production had an unbridled counterpart in mass consumption, and the railroad was at the very center of this relationship. The railroad meticulously and successfully established procedures, with very distinct lines of authority—a hierarchy. This new bureaucracy made one-track systems predictable, workable and safe, thus enhancing the integrity of the physical relationship among suppliers, manufacturers, consumers, and government. The railway is still crucial in industrialization efforts in Africa, especially when the fixed cost of capital is a significant factor.[18]

A very significant change in productivity was Henry Ford's improvement of Smith's concept of fragmenting work into repeatable tasks. In the Ford Motor assembly plant, each worker was typically charged with the responsibility of installing a specific part in a prescribed manner. Previously, workers walked from one assembly stand to the next stand to fit parts. With the installation of conveyor belts, work came to stationary workers, at their respective workstations. Although productivity increased, this new form of factory work organization also had collateral effects—a new bureaucracy of middle managers that needed structure. Huge volumes of output, timely procurement of raw materials, and marketing, all became important areas that needed professional attention.

The task of efficiently organizing this new sprawling huge bureaucracy was successfully accomplished by Alfred Sloan of General Motors. He created the prototype of the management system that Ford's immensely more successful factory system demanded.[19] This was another significant change to mass production that increased productivity. In other words, Alfred Sloan was applying Adam Smith's principle of division of labor to management; just as Ford had applied it to production.

Sloan created smaller, decentralized divisions that management could oversee by monitoring pertinent numbers such as sales, profit, loss, taxes, and inventory. The next significant phase in mass production and productivity engendered planning. Developed after 1945, planning accelerated organizational growth. Corporations had to think through the type of business they wanted to be in, determine capital investment allocations, expected returns, and so on. The large staff of corporate controllers, and planners acted as the eyes and ears of the executives. The disadvantage of this new structure was the increased distance between managers and customers.[20] With more innovative use of technology, a more recent trend in industrialized nations has been toward a flattened organizational structure.

Hierarchies flatten, not because democracy is suddenly bestowed on the workforce or because computers can cut out much of the middle management. They flatten to be more effective, often organized in small teams that may report to the CEO or to a board.[21] This organizational tendency, however, does not necessarily apply to bulk-processing industries such as steel and meatpacking. The reason is that, industries that are light on resources and heavy on information processing and application of ideas have become increasingly significant. High-technology products of these industries tend to be complicated in design and to deliver to the marketplace. Examples include pharmaceuticals, computer hardware and software, aircraft, telecommunications equipment and bioengineered drugs. They sustain themselves in an environment of increasing returns.[22] This is unlike Alfred Marshall's world of diminishing returns and the bulk processing of metal ores, aniline dyes, pig iron, coal, heavy chemicals, soybeans, coffee, and so on—commodities heavy on resources and light on know-how.[23]

Corporations should not fall into the trap of just buying expensive and big machines without initially and properly thinking through what the present and future applications will be, during the life cycle of the machine. When a corporation ignores this process, management may be entangled with a big and expensive machine and excess capacity that may never be used. This is waste. Alternatively, it may be necessary to keep running this very expensive machine, twenty-four hours a day, to justify the cost. Given this environment, the later tactic may lead to another trap ; that of producing expensive garbage that nobody wants. By determining the current level of productivity, and establishing time frames for the systematic improvement of productivity, the objectives become well organized and measurable.

Productivity increases must not be achieved at the expense of quality. When this is the case, output increases also precipitate unanticipated cost and speed. In the face of intense price competition, it may not be feasible to increase price to absorb higher cost. A tendency, therefore, will be to offset cost by exploiting productivity gains.[24]

Productivity may also increase by other methods such as shortening product life-cycle development (i.e., partnerships, etc.); truncating overall cost of product programs (i.e., engineering, research, and development); facilities and tooling (i.e., welding lines, presses, dies, molds, etc.); preproduction and marketing (i.e., reducing procurement costs by streamlining supplier base, bidding, negotiation, contract costs, etc.); and increasing market share and profitability (i.e., unit sales, return on assets, etc.).

Generally, productivity is positively influenced by production techniques. In industrialized or industrially oriented countries, the policy makers have had to constantly dispel the fear of *technological unemployment*. It is a false belief that machines displace human labor. Productivity is influenced by the type of equipment employed. In an industrializing environment, *steam shovels* and *conveyor belts* will be needed. This is unlike some places in Africa, where labor was plentiful and the initial tendency was to employ hand shovels with wheelbarrows. These implements are still very useful, as long as they are used efficiently and effectively toward industrialization. Production efficiencies, which enhance quality and productivity, are likely to achieve sustainable market penetration.[25] Increasingly, it will be necessary to combine labor with highly productive capital and resources.[26] This is because, when the marginal value of labor is low, incomes are low and output *per capita* is generally low. This disparity in organizing production, between the industrialized and industrializing environments and developing nations, is repeatedly prevalent in agriculture, mining, manufacturing, and the transportation industries. The outcome has protracted lower labor productivity in developing countries.[27]

Although machines do the jobs of human beings, human beings are not machines and don't work like machines. Machines are most effective when they perform simple repetitive tasks. This explains why complex tasks, for example car manufacturing, are best broken down into a series of simple tasks in an assembly line. Similarly, while technology may enhance productivity, the real power is not that it can make the old processes work better. The true power of technology is often in solving problems people, corporations, and entities do not know they have.[28] It enables organizations to break old rules and create new ways of working—that is organizational engineering.[29]

Unlike the machine, the human being, when confined to a single task, that demands repetition at a constant speed, becomes bored, fatigued. He or she may even become angry and irritable. This is because lactic acid tends to build up in the muscle. Visual acuity sags, and reaction time is prolonged. It is not unusual for employees in such work stations to daydream, and even become erratic and capricious. In this work environment, there is no one best speed or any one best rhythm. They frequently vary with the individual.

Although it is often not possible under every work environment and work process to adapt totally to every worker's needs, it is important to understand the human as a worker. It is important to understand the exogenous rhythms, speeds and other factors that may be a source of stress for the worker. It is a fundamental challenge, for management to align this mutual incompatibility between human engineering and industrial engineering, vis-à-vis organizational objectives.

From the factory floors to the office buildings, workers alike suffer productivity loss because of a multiplicity of reasons. The reasons for this loss in productivity may be exogenous to the workplace or endogenous to the individual. It is the responsible domain of management to (tactfully) help employees in dealing with personal problems that may jeopardize job performance, in particular, and productivity in general. Problems affecting employee productivity may range from job stress and family problems to medical problems, abuse of substances, and financial problems.

Employees may make individual efforts to improve their respective output on the job by focusing on issues like time management, work habits, and the reduction of procrastination. Labor is demanded because it is productive. The more productive it is, the higher the demand. High productivity of labor generally supports high wages.

*Office fatigue* is a syndrome that afflicts workers in the workplace. Left unaddressed, it impinges on productivity. The issue of office exhaustion in much of Africa, especially outside the big cities, has received almost superficial treatment for the most part. As a result, output has been negated. Office environments sometimes make it difficult for workers to think clearly. The humidity during the rainy seasons, coupled with the debilitating heat during the long dry seasons, results in exhaustion. Exhaustion increases the chances of making errors during work. Errors at work compound into lost time because of "rework" that may be measured in terms of lower productivity.

Air-conditioning tends to enhance worker efficiency. It is not a status symbol. It is beneficial to the health of the worker. It reduces fatigue during the hot dry season, and the office is generally cleaner and quieter due to closed windows.

While *fatigue* is largely due to impure and tepid air, there are other factors, such as the need of adequate supply of fluids, especially during the hot dry season. Fluid intakes in the office promote good health, alertness, and a better-sustained work environment.

Uncomfortable office desks and unscientifically designed chairs are also contributing factors to office fatigue and loss in efficiency and productivity. This is very important, since many office workers spend 90 percent of their time at work sitting down. The utilization of more comfortable chairs, for example, will enhance productivity. Maintaining the proper posture while sitting in a well-designed chair eliminates strain on nerves, muscles, or spine. It also reduces eye straining. It definitely enhances proper breathing and permits blood to ascend easily to the brain, through the great arteries of the neck. Uncomfortable chairs may result in self-choking postures that constrict the blood vessels. Often the effects are so mild that the worker is not immediately conscious of the contributing cause of his or her state of exhaustion.

Eye fatigue and nerve strain are especially common among typists, machine operators, and computer users. Some offices are laid out in such a manner that employees work under rather difficult conditions. The lighting is not optimal. Employees tend to sit facing windows, or they may work directly into a light source. This is further jeopardized by offices that may be painted brilliant white, which reflects glares. Eye fatigue and nerve strain contribute to worker exhaustion increasing the propensity for work errors and consequently lower productivity.

Noise is another significant factor that affects worker productivity. Noise that affects worker productivity may come either from within or from outside the office building. Generally noises originating from outside require insulation, while noises emanating within the office space require absorption. Acoustic bombardments from without may emanate from traffic, trains, construction equipment, pedestrians, and so on. Office noise may be caused by slamming doors, rattling windows, the clacking and clatter of hard heels on floors, loud talking, squeaking casters on chairs and machines, telephones, bells, typewriters, computer printers, and so forth.

Acoustical engineers measure sound as accurately as light is measured by light engineers. The unit of measurement is called a *decibel*. It was determined in an experiment that an acoustic intensity of just below 50 decibels reduced the output of a typist by 5 percent, while the efficiency of an executive was reduced by 30 percent.[30] Office noise may be magnified by *reverberations*. Hard plaster, metal, wood, and glass partitions and other similar materials reflect a high percentage of sound waves. Sound may result from *transmission* through partitions, ceilings and floors. Sound may be the result of *mechanical noises*, by mechanical equipment in buildings. In order to maximize office productivity, acoustical engineering is useful in computing the desired level of noise in an integrated office environment.

The rate of flow of information in the office also affects productivity. Timely receipt of information for effective decision making is crucial. Pertinent questions include the following: (1) Is too much time spent on information handling? (2) Can the time be parried, and if so do information flows need automation to enhance productivity? (3) Overall, what is the status of record keeping, pertaining to productivity? In a dynamic industrializing environment, it is expedient to continually evaluate and reevaluate the state of information in relation to the organizational objectives. While organizational memory is as important as human memory, the shelf-life of news is generally very short and much information (as opposed to knowledge content) tends to become stale very quickly. An organization at the leading edge of information avoids exhausting energy on yesterday's victories. In order to increase performance and productivity, an organization constantly moves onto new challenges and scouting for novel opportunities.

## NOTES

1. A loose definition of productivity is the output of a worker during a given period of time (e.g., one hour) above a minimum quality standard.

2. In the Western Sahel (Gambia, Guinea, Guinea Bissau, Mali, Mauritania, and Senegal), for example, between 1971 and 1991, food import averaged an increase of 5 percent per year, while populations increase averaged 2.5 percent per year. Increase of grain consumption, per capita, from 135 kilograms to 183 kg, was largely attributable to import. This was a research by National Institute of Agricultural Research, Montpelier, France, The Institute of Development Method Research and Application, Paris in France, and National University of Benin, Cotonou in Benin. *The Courier*, November-December 1991, p. 45.

3. Peter F. Drucker, *Managing the Future: The 1990s and Beyond* (New York: Truman Talley Books/Plume, 1993), p. 93. The explosions of productivity may be considered among the most important social events of the past hundred years or so.

4. Ibid., p. 94.

5. Adam Smith, *The Wealth of Nations* (New York: Modern Library, 1994), pp. 4–5.

6. Ibid.

7. Ibid.

8. Seymour Melman, *Profits without Production*, p. 5.

9. Ibid., p. 162.

10. Ibid.

11. Hrothgar J. Habakkuk, *American and British Technology in the Nineteenth Century* (New York: Cambridge University Press, 1962), p. 4.

12. Minami Ryōshin, "The introduction of Electric Power and its impact on the Manufacturing Industries: With Special Reference to Smaller Scale Plants," in Howard Stein, ed., *Asian Industrialization and Africa: Studies in Policy Alternatives to Structural Adjustment* (New York: St. Martin's Press, 1995), pp. 77–78. Japan had a dual economy: (1) a traditional, peasant, agricultural sector (including petty trade and cottage industry) producing primarily for family and village subsistence, with little reproducible capital, using old and intermediate technology, and a marginal productivity of labor lower than the wage; and (2) capital-intensive manufacturing and processing operations, mineral extraction, and commercial agriculture, producing for the market, and using reproducible capital and new technology, experiencing high and growing labor productivity, and hiring labor commercially. This dualism was exacerbated by Japan's rapid growth, especially in technology. Large firms with price-controlling power in product markets and credit rationing could therefore afford to pay higher wages.

13. The *cam* mechanically adjusts the position of a lever or a machine element as it rotates, thus causing the machinery to carry out a fixed set of events. It may be seen as a "program" control.

14. Melvin Kranzberg and Carroll W. Pursell, Jr., *Technology in Western Civilization* (New York: Oxford University Press, 1967), pp. 646–651.

15. By using overhead monorail trolleys and applying movement to powered chain drives, assemblers maintained stationary locations provided with parts and workstations. Productivity

increased because of timed work pace, job specialization, and minimization of unnecessary movement by workers and of materials. The Ford Motor Company, early in 1913 installed, experimentally, a moving assembly line for magnetos (small generators of alternating current). Each magneto, previously assembled entirely by a worker, had to be assembled in discreet stages by 29 workers, each doing a single operation. The use of this system of conveyor belts tripled production of flywheel magnetos. Convinced by the success, management replicated the idea in the assembly of the entire car. Here again, productivity gains were realized. The unit time per car assembly plummeted. It took an average of only one and one-half hours, compared with the old average of twelve and one-half hours, a significant disparity between the concept of conventional stationary assembly stations and the powered movement to chain drives. Kranzberg and Pursell, *Technology in Western Civilization*, pp. 42–48.

16. Expansion of output is not immune to Alfred Marhall's laws of diminishing returns.

17. Michael Hammer and James Champy, *Reengineering the Corporation: A Manifesto for Business Revolution* (New York: Harper Business, 1993), p. 96.

18. Peter Lane, *The Industrial Revolution: The Birthplace of the Modern Age* (New York: Barnes & Noble, 1978), p. 237. In Britain, during the Industrial Revolution, it was recognized that if the fixed cost of capital is high, and capital equipment is used only eight hours a day, the real cost of capital is much greater than if it can be used twenty-four hours a day. This was the case with tin and coal mining. Until the advent of the railway, there was little demand for large lumps of industrial capital, relative to the industrial capacity of British industry and agriculture. Most of the increase, in output and productivity, was achieved with low-cost capital. Capital did not absorb an inordinate share of productivity or output. When capital represents a great proportion of national output (say 50 percent), consumers may sustain a long period of deprivation. This was the case of Russia in the 1930s (p. 249).

19. Ibid., p. 14.

20. Ibid., pp. 15–16.

21. W. Brian Arthur, "Increasing Returns and the New World of Business," *Harvard Business Review*, July-August 1996, p. 104.

22. William S. Dietrich, *In the Shadow of the Rising Sun* (University Park: Pennsylvania State University Press), pp. 64–65. In Japan, for example, "The production of low-technology, labor-intensive products, is gradually moved to less-developed countries...Exits in the case of textiles and shipbuilding were nearly industry-wide. With automobiles and consumer electronics, labor-intensive assembly and routine manufacturing are pushed offshore, while sophisticated manufacturing, design, and engineering are jealously safeguarded, through restrictions." In addition, the knowledge-based industries, which tend to revolve around the extended electronics industries—including computers, computer peripherals, consumer electronics, lasers, liquid crystal displays (LCDs), office automation equipment, semiconductors, and telecommunications equipment—have been selected as the pivot of economic development. Information is now viewed as the singular productive resource that may even substitute for factor inputs of land and energy.

23. Ibid., pp.101–109.

24. Ibid., p. 69.

25. "The Japanese have recognized more clearly than their global competitors that, despite an appalling lack of natural resources, they are not deficient in one resource, people. And that is today's most critical resource. " Ibid., pp. 61–64.

26. Labor-intensive or capital-saving techniques in manufacturing can easily be adapted where there is a reservoir of engineering and technical skills, as was the case with Japan. Heavy demands may be made on machine operators to read blueprints, set up tools, and substitute human skill for machine accuracy. Presuming a high degree of industrial organization, subcontractors will systematically work as part of an industrial complex. In this case, small

machine shops and town factories must be able to coordinate their activities (production schedules, engineering standards, etc.) with the larger industrial complex.

27. Peter F. Drucker, *The Concept of the Corporation*. pp. 229–231.

28. Hammer and Champy, *Reengineering the Corporation*, p. 88.

29. Ibid., p. 90. By using a production schedule database and electronic data interchange (EDI), General Motors enabled its Saturn plant and its supplier to operate as one company. Its on-line manufacturing database was made accessible to its component parts' suppliers. Instead of using purchase orders and invoices, suppliers simply went on-line to consult the car manufacturer's car production schedule in a database. They in turn initiated physical delivery of the parts, with an electronic message detailing shipment. At GM's receiving dock, a clerk acknowledges receipt of delivery by scanning bar codes printed on shipped boxes with an electronic wand. Finally, scanning initiates payment to vendors. The computer data may also indicate exactly where next to forward shipment within the plant.

30. *Executive Handbook: Financial Management* (Dartnell Publications), p. 154.

5

# Quality of Products for Industrialization in Africa

As Africa expands its manufacturing base, infant industries that had once enjoyed protection will eventually have to face marketplace competition because of brand proliferation. This will be especially so when corporations decide to expand market reach across national frontiers. As assembly plants begin manufacturing component parts, quality will also become an important consideration. When a consumer buys a finished product or when a manufacturer orders an input product, both expect value and performance. Although quality is ultimately a customer-driven definition, a firm that produces relatively poor-quality products cannot expect to be in business for long in a free enterprise market system. Because of the ramifications of quality in the marketplace, government usually steps in to provide rules and regulations. Manufacturers are generally conscious of this role of government and may opt to self-regulate before the government steps in. As entrepreneurs take advantage of unfolding opportunities in an industrializing environment, it will be necessary to have a grasp of the dynamics of quality in the marketplace. Methods used to enhance quality in manufacturing tend to include product grading, product testing, open dating, seals of approval, and government research on products, in the interest of the government and the public at large.

The government not only makes sure that the qualities of products meet certain standards, but also prevents useless and harmful products from being traded in the marketplace. Government assures the qualities of products, which enter the marketplace, by stipulating the expected minima standards. For example, products may be inspected and assigned a *grading system*. Such a grading system (e.g., for meat) may include the following: Grade A (fancy), Grade B (choice), Grade C (standard), and Substandard. Grades are generally easy to read and understand. They are also simple enough that they can be easily recapitulated. One more illustration of quality standards is in the export/import trade. For example, dessert bananas are subjected to stringent quality evaluations before and after each shipment. Fruit quality standards may be grouped into five categories: (1) fruit blemishes and defects (2) minimum finger length (3) minimum and maximum diameter grade (4) cluster size and arrangement (5) net carton mass. In this case, fruit defects include blemishes that affect the peel and pulp, of which mechanical scarring and bruising are the most common and serious.[1]

Another method used to assure quality, is the *seal of approval.* Seals of approval or stamps of approval generally indicate that products bearing the seal have measured up to certain rigid standards. Examples of organizations that confer seals of approval are Underwriters Laboratories and Good Housekeeping. In *Good Housekeeping* (a magazine) the seal is more than just a rubber stamp of approval of a brand or product—it is a legal warranty.[2] Seals remain important, but they are not as important as they used to be. This is especially true for easily recognizable brands that are often household names, and have stood the test of time. The danger, however, is that workers may rest on their laurels and hide behind successful brand names or seals. In this case, costs may increase without corresponding increases in quality. These increased costs may be shifted to the final consumer in higher prices.[3]

*Product testing and product rating,* without a seal of approval, is another method used to assure quality. This may be done by either profit or nonprofit organizations, to give consumers information and advice on goods, services, health, and personal finance. Products are typically rated, after rigorous subjection to laboratory tests and controlled-use tests, tempered with expert judgment. Products are rated without regard to price. All products tested are sourced from the open market.

In another case, a government agency may carry out research in the interest of the government and the public. The agency's research is typically geared toward improving methods of standardizing measurements and collecting data. Such an agency helps to establish industrial standards for private business. Consumer groups also use the agency's testing methods and reports. The agency also produces and distributes standard reference materials and promotes dissemination and accessibility of scientific information. By establishing standards, the government, ensures the quality of purchases.

Another example is in the European food sector: *ISO 9000 Standards* have become normal business practice. In this case, the idea is to increase the efficiency of the whole food chain using ISO certification, which ultimately benefits the consumers and the food processors alike. ISO standards provide some guarantee of access to export markets.[4]

Product testing and product rating have not only been auxiliary in enhancing the quality of products but have also alarmed consumers when quality deficiencies threatened the safety of end users. For example, a young woman who buys lipstick does not expect her lips to become dry or cracked, nor does she expect it to cause her lips to burn and swell. A chemical analysis is made of the lipstick to determine what it is made of and whether any of the ingredients are harmful.

It pays to make products right the first time. It pays to inculcate the best possible quality into a product. Poor-quality products may not only injure the consumer, but may also be catastrophic to the manufacturer. This cataclysm may come as a *product recall* or a *lawsuit*. Recalls can be very devastating. They threaten market shares and revenues and may even put marginal firms out of business. Companies endeavor to avert this predicament by stepping up efforts in product engineering. Consumer satisfaction is foremost in product engineering: materials such as cables, wires, ropes, and belts are tested for *tensile strength;* pillars, posts, and foundations are tested for *compression strength;* propeller shafts undergo *flexural* and *torsional stress tests;* fuel-efficient automobiles endure *aerodynamic tests* in wind tunnels. Tests to determine the quality of television sets include image quality, color fidelity, black level, brightness, geometric distortion, interlace, color correction, color control, airplane flutter, adjacent channel, fringe VHF, fringe UHF, spark rejection, audio tone, stereo separation, ease of use, remote control, code entry, antenna, video, audio, price, warranty, and even repair history, among other nuances.

A government may reserve ultimate authority to investigate the quality of products and prescribe standards. Here, a minimum quality for consumer products is ensured by law. For example, a consumer product safety commission may be set up to conduct research on product safety and maintain a clearinghouse "to collect, investigate, analyze, and disseminate injury data, and information relating to the causes and prevention of death, injury, and illness associated with consumer products."[5] This commission may reserve the right to ban the manufacture and sale of any product deemed hazardous to end users. Its mandatory safety regulations are not only focused on specific products, but tend to affect whole industries. For example, bicycles sold may be required to incorporate prescribed safety features. This structural facelift may include reflectors on the front, back, sides, and pedals, to make bicycles visible at night; protective edges on metal fenders and coverings for protruding bolts; locking devices to secure wheel hubs to frame; chain guards for bicycles with pedals that cannot be reversed; locking devices to secure seat, handle bar, and stem clamps; brakes capable of stopping the bicycle within fifteen feet, when used by a person weighing more than 150 pounds, at a test speed based on the gear ratio; and instructions for the vehicle's maintenance.

Consumer protection laws and regulations greatly enhance the quality of products sold in the marketplace. For instance, the commission ensures that there is no asbestos in products such as children's modeling clay and artificial fireplace logs. It is responsible for issuing safety standards for products such as Christmas lights, contact adhesives, and baby rattles. A prices act may mandate the display of average and comparative prices of goods of the same quality. Similarly, open dating for perishable products ensure that consumers enjoy fresh groceries.[6]

A close-up view of kerosene regulations manifests this quality culture. Kerosene is used in space heaters and lamps. The authorities not only make sure that kerosene, at retail outlets, is clearly labeled, priced, and graded, but perhaps also test 500 samples of this fuel annually. Sample tests are made for color, flashpoint, sulfur content, and end point. Standards require that the color of kerosene should be close to the color of tap water, but it may have a slight pink or light blue tint. The sulfur content is monitored, in order to prevent the emission of high quantities of sulfur dioxide into the air. When ambient standards of sulfur dioxide are exceeded, they contribute to acid rain and breathing problems.[7]

In an industrializing environment, therefore, inordinate proclivities of businesses tend to be canalized and regimented through government intervention. Rules and regulations, product testing, product grading, open dating, consumer education, and product standards are among the methods used by government to check any parsimonious propensities in business transactions. Into the bargain, government strives to etch integrity onto the relationship between the manufacturer and the final consumer.

Although businesses generally need to be under the watchful eyes of government, corporations have come to realize that quality is paramount. Quality can either make or break a business. Companies that hope to command a staying power in the competitive realm of business must, therefore, demonstrate an absolute commitment to quality.

In Africa, the quality of goods produced by large domestic manufacturing outfits does not seem to have ameliorated significantly after a span of about twenty to thirty years. The qualities of products, it seems, have been frozen in time. Such status quo is the antithesis of industrial power.

In an industrializing and increasingly competitive business arena, the customer reigns. Quality is largely a customer driven definition.[8] It is the maxim of business. A dictum! The pulse of quality must be taken regularly from the customers and their needs and wants met accordingly. Quality is never the problem; it is the solution.

In order to improve quality, it is crucial to understand what contributes to customer satisfaction. In a competitive market environment, a customer who is satisfied with a product is very likely to be a repeat customer. The dimensions of product qualities, which satisfy a customer typically include the following: performance; reliability; durability, before, during, and after-sales service; needed or desired features; and aesthetics.

When consumers buy a product, they expect the product to accomplish certain tasks or satisfy a need or desire. When the product does not measure up to the expectations of an educated consumer, then the product has failed to perform. For example, kerosene stretched with water performs poorly as a fuel for kerosene lamps and stoves and space heaters.

In order to produce reliable or dependable goods, it is imperative to contract with quality-oriented suppliers or vendors. This means explicitly dictating the requirements for component parts or services. Stringent supplier requirements have sometimes meant increased costs. This appears to contradict the principle of awarding contracts to the lowest bidders. Awarding contracts to the lowest bidders (without adhering to strict quality guidelines) has sometimes led to the procurement of poor-quality materials and components in order to show profit or increased earnings. This does not, however, make guaranties that high bidders will not be tempted to become greedy and resort to poor-quality materials and components, as long as they can enhance their organizational goals and objectives. The ultimate solution is, therefore, to have checks and balances that preclude any costly embarrassments and setbacks.[9]

Durability is the expected useful life of a product, its longevity. Although extending the life of machines by religiously making repairs and maintenance is technically feasible, continuing further repairs beyond their useful lives may not be economically rational. Some companies, however, may vote to continue using an old machinery beyond its useful life, for whatever reasons. An important consideration here is that equipment and tools retain the capacity for holding design tolerances that enhance quality and provide sufficient outputs at competitive cost structures. When old machinery cannot accurately and reliably meet design tolerances, then high costs, scrap, and rework are likely outcomes.[10]

Before, during, and after-sales-services may enhance the competitive position of manufacturing equipment in the marketplace. This also protects the firm's image as a manufacturer of reliable equipment. In small, developing countries, the dearth of expert technicians in manufacturing equipment is often a major consideration in capital investment decisions. This is because of capital investment decision analysis, which considers equipment maintenance and equipment repair services in case of expected breakdowns.[11]

In the case of consumer products, the quality of a product is also a function of the ease, speed, and frequency of repairs. Increasingly, it has become difficult for consumers to personally repair certain consumer products. This is because of the increased sophistication of many products. For example, the television, the videocassette recorder (VCR), the personal computers (PC), and the photocopy machine all tend to require experts' repair.

Attractive features in products also add function, character, and quality. Consumers generally welcome improvements as long as they are not gimmicks to increase price. For example, a VCR may have on-screen programming from remote control, daily/weekly programming capabilities, ability to eject tape with power off, ability to search for unrecorded tape segment, and power backup. These are all attractive features that tend to tickle the desire of the consumer.

The aesthetics of a product is a determinant of quality. The consumer's perception of a product's beauty and smell influences quality. Similarly, the sound or taste of a product (where applicable) determines whether a consumer may like or dislike a product. Of course, individuals or groups of individuals have dissimilar preferences and unlike judgments. A grasp of the essence in product aesthetics is often necessary, however, in order to execute quality improvements in competitive target markets.

Organizational decisions made by management may also enhance the quality of products directly or indirectly. Organizational policy, for example, is a major contributor to quality. Such policies are often strategic when organizations must address the issue of quality. When quality is not adequately addressed, more often than not, inadequate quality results. Less-adequate quality is never a goal in manufacturing but may be strategically acceptable under certain circumstances. For example, management may follow a system by which quality is graded into *premium, standard,* and *ordinary* qualities. Therefore market segmentation, in this case, enhances quality-oriented policy formulation.

Although a minimum inferior quality in mass production may be strategically acceptable, this is not always true. In fact, there are many instances in manufacturing in which defect-free production is the goal, because of the adverse ramifications. In this case, there is a culture of continuous improvement.[12] The aim, therefore, is to do things right the first time. Again, this is because when things are not done right the first time, they may result in material waste, such as scrap and other wastes, lost time, rework, repairs, and rewriting reports.

The cost of ignoring quality could reach tremendous proportions. Quantity cannot be achieved at the expense of quality. There must be a balance, at least, in the eyes of the beholder—the customer.[13] "In most traditional factories, that cost is probably the biggest item on their list of expenses and it is always bigger than gross profit."[14] In such outfits, therefore, it is not unusual to employ 25 percent of the workforce in reworking things that were not done right the first time. Needless to conclude that 25 percent of the workforce, by implication, does not produce anything!

It is important to scan the quality spectrum, in order to understand the ramifications of premium quality and the pregnancy of microcosmic deficiencies. A 99.9997 percent perfect quality could mean 3.4 defective products per million output. This may come across as impressive, but only to the extent that the full range of the ramifications for the corporation, the customers, and the community at large have been analyzed and evaluated.

Let us put the case of a client who buys a brand new car. After driving the car around town for a week or so, the owner of the brand new car is involved in a minor wreck. Technical analysis determines that the gear slipped into reverse, thus causing the accident. Within a span of one month, two more similar cases are reported. All three cars are made by the same manufacturer. The news media pick up the story and disseminate this frightening news. Owners of such cars are afraid to drive their cars. The image of this foreign car manufacturer is seriously dented. Management surveys imminent litigation looming in the horizon; probable fall in market shares; a costly recall effort; a credibility gap; design engineering; a fall in the equity value of the firm; a fall in bond rating and possible trouble with government authorities for infractions of technical stipulations and standards. Although statistically the manufacturer was 99.9997 percent perfect in production, the .0003 percent defect may still be a very pregnant problem. Quality is very important. It can make or break a company.

A manufacturing director of a cellular phone equipment factory illustrated the consequences of quality by pointing out a device about the size of a refrigerator. He said that the device had 1,700 parts and 144,000 opportunities for someone to make a mistake. If the company ended up with a 99 percent quality that meant 1,440 mistakes were made per piece.[15] The cost of hiring technicians to repair such mistakes could be very costly for a business. It pays to do things right the first time, every time!

Well-designed products greatly enhance quality. Quality designs usually accommodate the consumer, the manufacturer, and the repairer. Poorly designed products may be difficult to produce or to service. They may be awkward or clumsy to the end user. For example, very compact machines may pose problems for manufacturers, consumers, and service personnel. Such inconveniences negate quality and may detract otherwise willing consumers. A well-designed product optimizes size, shape, color, materials, use, operation, and serviceability.

Not very long ago, it appeared that Ford Motor Company was taking its success for granted. It was, it seemed, losing touch with the marketplace. A consumer research of car buyers in California in 1980 revealed utter dismay on the part of the public. The shocker was the preponderance of persons then of college age, who conceded they did not own a Ford automobile.[16] This imminent danger propelled Ford executives into action. The whole concept of manufacturing was revisited, and the voice of the consumer was factored into the decision-making process. For example, design engineers invited consumers to input their opinions on the Taurus and Sable prototypes. When consumers complained of a lack of leg room, the design engineering promptly accommodated adjustments accordingly. The result of this new effort was magnificent! For at least the subsequent five years, Ford was the best-selling nameplate in California. Quality is rewarding![17] The Japanese rode into the American market on the back of quality!

Ideas to improve quality do not only come from research and development (R&D) groups, and clients. Ideas may come from other employees, management, and even competitors. A preponderance of substantial ideas to improve quality comes from the external environment. Ideas may emanate from competitors and non competitors alike. In the quest to improve quality, companies around the world are often sourcing ideas from within and without. The U.S. companies gave Japanese access to American companies in the 1950s and 1960s. Adding that such access is typically feasible among companies that are not competing is important. For example, when Motorola (U.S.A.) wanted outside ideas, it sourced "islands of excellence" around the world. It did not go to companies that manufacture pagers, like Motorola. Instead the company's management approached manufacturers of cars, watches, cameras, and other technology intensive products.[18] In another example, to encourage product/service quality in nations, awards are typically given to companies judged to be the best over a given period. One condition for accepting the award, it seems, may be that the winners are willing to share the secrets of their success with all comers.[19] Information may not simply be garnered from without; such information must also be accurate and timely. An Information Response System that tolerates a time lag is like an albatross around the neck of a corporation. Great services enhance consumers' product satisfaction. However, service is not a substitute for quality.

## NOTES

1. J.C. Robinson, *Bananas and Plantains* (Wallingford: CAB International, 1996), p. 207. A checklist of factors evaluated by banana quality inspectors at a Central American port of departure and after ripening at the export destination include the following: *Physical defects* (% of clusters)—Bruises, Latex stains, Neck injury, Scarring, Fingers too short, Fingers undergrade; *Physiological condition* (% of cartons)—Ripe fruit, Color changing, Underpeel discoloration; *Carton attributes* (% of cartons)—Average net mass, Cartons less than 18 kg., Cartons more than 18 kg., Jumbled pack, Slippage; *Carton condition*—Creased cartons, Crushed cartons, No carton code, Illegible carton code; *Fruit defects after ripening* (% of clusters)—Bruises, Crown

rot, Latexes stain, Neck injury, Neck rot, Off color, Scarring, Fingers too short, Mutilated fingers, Fingers undergrade, Withered pedicels. See also R.H. Stover and N.W. Simmonds, *Bananas*, 3rd ed. (London: Longman, 1987) in Robinson, p. 208.

2. *Fortune Magazine*, September 1997, p. 8.

3. Edward Cohen-Rosenthal, *Unions, Management, and Quality: Opportunities for Innovation and Excellence* (Chicago: Irwin, 1995), p. 27.

4. Lokman Zaibet and Maury Bredahl, "Gains From ISO Certification in the UK Meat Sector," *Agribusiness*, Vol. 13, No 4, pp. 375–384. ISO 9000 is a series of six standards ( 8402, 9000 to 9004) that detail internationally accepted procedures and guidelines to maintain quality in product design, production, installation, and services. ISO 9000 to 9004 are two standards to help firms design the system internally and choose a quality model. ISO 9001—3 are models for systems of different stringency for external representation in contractual or non-contractual relationships. ISO represents generic standards developed by the International Standards Organization with headquarters in Geneva, Switzerland. The standards are based on BSI 5750; the quality assurance standards developed by the British Standards Institute. They have been adopted at the European level as EN2900 and in the United States as Q90-4. These standards are voluntary principles of good practice and not intended to replace product safety or other regulatory requirements. HACCP (Hazard Analysis Critical Point) procedure was developed in the U.S. to enhance food safety in the 1970s. The object was to ensure food safety by negating hazards during processing and handling operations. This voluntary system became mandatory in 1977. The scope of the management plan of HACCP is not as wide as ISO 9000 and is therefore considered a subsidiary of the ISO 9000. Inherent benefits of such voluntary standards include reduced transactional costs associated with negotiating, monitoring, and enforcing contracts; reduced total cost of production (at least in the long run); and almost invariably increased efficiency of the firm/factory.

5. K.W. Clarkson, R.L. Miller, and G.A. Jentz, *West's Business Law*, p. 830.

6. Open dating means that the date by which a product should be sold to ensure freshness is clearly marked on its container: *Consumer Protection Gains and Setback*, (Washington, DC: Editorial Research Reports, 1978), p. 5.

7. Darrell Campbell, Lamar Graves, Robert Hatz, Iris Hill, Wes McDowell and Thomas Taku. *Acid Rain: Review and Recommendations*, group presentation, November 1989, Atlanta, GA: Mercer University.

8. Tom Peters, *Thriving on Chaos: Handbook for a Management Revolution* (New York: Harper & Row, 1987), p. 78.

9. Checks and balances must also preclude bribery and corruption.

10. David Bain, *The Productivity Prescription: The Manager's Guide to Improving Productivity and Profits* (New York: McGraw-Hill, 1982), p. 117.

11. U.S. Department of Commerce & International Trade, *Overseas Business Reports (OBR), Marketing in Cameroon* (Washington, DC: GPO, 1990), p. 23.

12. Edward Cohen-Rosenthal, *Unions, Management, and Quality: Opportunities for Innovation and Excellence* (Chicago: Irwin Professional Publishing, 1995), pp. 281–283.

13. Bain, *The Productivity Prescription*, p. 113.

14. "The Push for Quality," *Business Week*, June 8, 1987, p. 132.

15. "What Motorola Learns from Japan," *Fortune*, April 24, 1989, pp. 157–168.

16. "King Customer," *Business Week*, March 12, 1990, p. 90.

17. In what seems to be a global environment, it will be difficult to ignore the trends in quality among multinational corporations. A study revealed that "On the average, those firms whose products score in the top third on relative perceived product quality outearn those in the bottom third by a two-to-one margin." Just about the same conclusion was reached when further comparisons were made by sector (Manufacturing); by geography (North America vs. Europe);

or by market trajectory (Low growth vs. High growth, Low inflation vs. High inflation): Peters, *Thriving on Chaos,* p. 82.

18. "What Motorola Learns from Japan," pp. 157–168.

19. Ibid.

# 6

# Regional Integration of Business Activities in Africa

In order to complete effectively in the global marketplace, African businesses will also have to practise within the more familiar confines of their neighborhoods. This means looking for opportunities that reside in cross-border trade and taking efforts in regional industrial integration more seriously. Today's international economic conditions may not be as favorable to export expansion from the less developed countries, as they were during the Meiji period (1867–1912) in Japan; when Japan abandoned a 250-year period of cultural and economic isolation, and successfully embarked on modernization and industrialization using Western ideas. Without discounting the significance of these opportunities, in much of the last quarter century or so, the fastest expanding export items have been in textiles, clothing, footwear, and basic consumer goods, which require widely available labor-intensive technology. Nevertheless, parent companies of several nations, increasingly, offered other significant opportunities to efficient and effective indigenous businesses, in this domain. Here, good examples will include Japanese companies.

There are several advantages in regional industrial integration However, like everything else, there are also disadvantages. The challenge, therefore, will be in optimally balancing the benefits and detractors. Fortunately, there are many examples of international trading strategies around the world that suffice as guiding posts. An assessment of international trading activities in Africa will indicate that a preponderance of export activities was in primary products, which were essentially exchanged for manufactured products and capital equipment. While this system of trading was functional and rewarding in the past, it has become increasingly difficult to take on the challenge of full fledged and sustainable industrialization, based solely on this strategy. Within a context of mutually antagonistic and inconsistent objectives, a feasible approach will be in balancing in some optimal combination regional trade and trade with industrialized nations.

Integrating regional trade in an industrializing environment bristles with export possibilities for entrepreneurs, since most of the capital equipment in the nonindustrialized economies in Africa are not yet manufactured locally. It is possible for entrepreneurs to export manufactured products to industrialized nations. It will not be without some difficulties along the way, however, in spite of the cheap labor. African businesses engaging in the export of mass-produced goods to industrialized nations and without government intervention will find difficulties in sustaining profitability, indefinitely, using equipment from such origins. This is because domestic firms in industrialized nations engaging in mass production tend to be more competitive in domestic markets, using domestic capital resources.

Regional integration increases the variety and available quantity of foods. Increased and consistent supplies of agricultural output during industrialization will ensure at least a well-fed labor force and supplies of agricultural resources with industrial applications. However, the more significant effect will tend to be in relieving the pressure from excess farm labor, from the rural areas, seeking employment in urban settings. In an industrializing environment, where significant proportions of urban labor incomes are expended on food, surplus food tends to keep food price low, increase savings, investments, and the initial profitability and expansion of industrial operations.[1] In this regard, the ancient practice of *stockpiling* may be worth considering. Agricultural surpluses were used to precipitate initial industrial expansion in Japan. Here, the significance of irrigation may not be discounted. Irrigation has the potential for expanding output and labor use simultaneously. Japanese agriculture succeeded in generating a rapid increase in rural incomes while maintaining its structure of small farms, largely because of irrigation.[2] In fact, without the opportunities that irrigation provides, the prospects of many developing countries will be dimmed. As early as the *Meiji* period, Japan had resorted to inexpensive rice imports from Korea and Taiwan in order to maintain low food prices. Japan's agricultural technological progress was fast (between 1880 and 1920) and increased farm productivity per worker, thus facilitating substantial surplus transfer to industry. Large-scale enterprises created external economies in the supply of raw materials, working capital, and markets. These large-scale enterprises, however, could not manufacture every item needed and found it cost-effective to buy parts and components from independently run small workshops.[3]

Although export opportunities in agriculture will derive from regional integration, primary commodities (chief export earners) are increasingly less significant because of improvements in technology and substitutes, which are being synthesized frequently in laboratories. For example, iron ore is used to manufacture durable steel products, especially in the automotive and construction industries, which are generally recyclable when they become obsolete. The possibilities for substitutes are almost without limits. Substitutes may range from synthetic rubber, artificial vanilla, salt substitutes, and sugar substitutes to artificial flowers. Glass can be annealed to the strength of steel. The industrialized countries in the north do not necessarily have to depend on the southern neighbors for winter vegetables. They are readily grown in commercial quantities in greenhouses under more economical, very hygienic, and computer-controlled conditions. Cheap food in urban Africa will enhance the health and aptitude of workers, and release funds that may be expended or invested in other sectors. Therefore stepping up agricultural trade with other African countries will be crucial, especially those that consistently demonstrate net food import tendencies. Africa has yet to embrace optimally the benefits of regional trade in this domain. Early humans discovered that domestication of animals was more efficient and effective than running around in the forest to catch an animal every time meat was needed. By domesticating favorite meats, fruits, and vegetables, people did not only keep the animals, trees, and plants without the reach of predators but also increased production into the bargain. This ancient idea has been very productively applied in modern farming of chicken, fish, and pigs, and other food sources. To this extent, it is feasible to meet, with efficiency, the demands of local markets and even regional markets.

Regional trade has the potential of expanding the volume of international trade, especially intra industry trade. In the industrialized nations, the relative share of intra industry trade comprised roughly 60 to 80 percent of all trade. In the European Economic Community (EEC), between the 1950s and the 1970s, intra EEC trade, as a share of gross domestic product (GDP), rose from 5 percent to 10 percent with intra-industry trade being the most significant component.[4]

Regional cross-border trading allows firms, particularly small firms, to take advantage of economies of scale, which is possible with large markets. As firms expand capacity, this process usually means that longer production runs, for products lines, are practical; there are potential for larger transactions in buying, selling, and shipping and opportunities for geographic specialization that may mean less transportation of products. Business activities expand, possibly requiring more labor hours and, therefore, increases in income. However, many firms could not establish, profitably, in many places in Africa, because of the traditionally small markets. In this case, either the number of customers was limited, or the populations did not command the purchasing power. Regionalization also means opportunities for greater specialization, both among and within industries, firms, and establishments. As markets and outputs grow, knowledge of business organization and technology also develops and adapts to new and changing conditions.[5]

Regionalization pushes some firms to avoid nontariff barriers by redeploying manufacturing capabilities inside the region of target customers. This move may be accomplished through foreign direct investments (FDI). Although foreign direct investment tends to be attractive in industrialization, it was perceived as a threat to national sovereignty. This was a primary reason for the proliferation of state-owned enterprises in the 1960s and 1970s in developing countries.[6] Some industrializing countries, however, resorted to other methods of reduced or nonequity forms of foreign investments, such as subcontracts to local producers, licensing, and joint ventures. Here, Japan and Korea were examples of countries that were successful in relying heavily on licensing and similar arrangements. In any case, FDI may also be a natural outcome of the economic climate in industrialized nations. For example, in the 1960s, when Japan experienced labor shortage and wages started increasing, Japanese firms resorted to subcontracting labor-intensive production to firms in developing countries.

However, by the 1970s, the inroads of newly industrialized economies (NIEs) were perceived in some quarters as potential threats to unskilled jobs in advanced countries. Overall, the contributions of FDIs to industrialization may or may not be substantial. Industrialization, therefore, cannot overly rely on FDIs. Historically, FDIs have not been known to bring about mass production and mass consumption, in similar magnitudes over comparable periods in the industrialized nations. To promote industrialization, countries relied on strategies that were either outward-looking or inward-looking or some similar combination. Specifically, Korea (1964), like Taiwan (1962), and Singapore (1965) resorted to export-oriented industrialization. Most countries, however, pursued import substitution industrialization (ISI) as in Africa and Latin America. Such import substituting strategies resulted in market-creating schemes with neighboring countries.[7]

Although regional integration presented opportunities for economies of scale, domestic entrepreneurs often did not demonstrate the scanning capabilities that will allow for the development of markets beyond their respective national markets. On the other hand, multinationals flush with resources were more likely to establish national operations much faster than local firms, and when feasible were inclined to pursue rent-seeking operations within highly protected national borders. A survey of 225 European companies, many of whom ran operations in ten or more countries, determined that regional integration will be beneficial to their business environment. They did not consider lower tariff barriers very important. Instead, they maintained that the nontariff barriers were impediments (e.g., import licensing procedures, administrative procedures, quantitative restrictions, and the like). Understandably, it is naive to entertain the thought that every policy enforced will satisfy the needs, desires, and goals of every firm. Because it is not always feasible to satisfy everybody or every firm, every time, firms and groups of firms are forced to forego certain potential benefits for the good of society or to choose from a scale of preferences. By the same token, the "visible hands" of government are forced to make choices that strive to optimize domestic and external/regional needs and objectives of the community at large.[8] Another disadvantage is that export-oriented firms may find themselves overly dependent on other nations as suppliers of marketing channels, including brand name and technological requirements.

The benefits of regional integration may not be seen solely through the lenses of industrialization. Regional integration is a dynamic environment that may best be understood within the context of the overarching goals and objectives of nations in the region. For example, U.S. support for reconstruction in Europe after World War II led to the Marshall Plan and the Organization of European Economic Cooperation (OEEC), which evolved into EEC and EC.[9] The European Economic Communities were initially founded primarily as a response to security concerns. Besides the loose policy of coordination, undertaken within OEEC after 1948, then, the goal was to avoid any catalyst that might precipitate renewed Franco-German armed conflict. The formation of European Coal and Steel Community in 1952 was the result of economic considerations. In 1957, the Treaty of Rome created the EEC or the Common Market. This was more or less the foundation upon which the "golden era" was launched. This era spanning the 1950s and 1960s was characterized by sustained economic growth. The Common Market boosted the growth of intra-EEC trade, which during this period exceeded EEC trade with the rest of the world. Here a significant growth prevailed in intra industry trade. "EC 92" may be seen within the context of dynamic sea changes in the growing and competitive economic vigor of Japan, along with the "Four Tigers," or newly industrialized economies (NIEs), of Asia. In other words, the center of global economic gravity was visibly shifting, from the Atlantic to the Pacific. Obviously nations in the Atlantic could not just sit and gape as this phenomenon transpired. In order to fine-tune the efficiency of the markets, deregulation was effected in the United States. The response in Britain was deregulation and privatization. The European Community opted for a collective and different response: increased regional integration. Stagnation in the European Community (EC) single-market programme, launched earlier in 1985, was magnified by events in the Pacific. The idea behind EC 92, therefore, was not just to remove remaining barriers to intra regional trade; ensuring or priming the pumps of market efficiency was important.

The roots of regionalization may perhaps be retraced to Europe's centralizing monarchs, notably in England and France. Here, the mosaic of feudal fiefdoms, towns, and guilds, which acutely impeded trade and mobility of capital and labor were given centralized protection, under mercantilist policies. Both economies extended their respective powers of state and degree of economic integration, emasculating the powers and privileges of parochial baronies and manors, the virtually autonomous towns, and the self-governing merchant and artisan guilds under their jurisdiction. The outcome was the creation or consolidation of the nation-state. In England, the effect was a nationwide market, created through regional integration, which reduced internal trade restrictions, such as trade tolls and factor movements. In France, under Louis XIV and Jean-Baptiste Colbert, similar gains were also made toward unification. National markets set the stage for industrialization. In Germany, industrialization took off after the creation of the Customs Union (Zollverein), in 1834, coupled with political unification in 1871. The *Meiji* restoration in nineteenth century Japan also contained the seeds of economic regional integration.[10]

Nations began working in similar lines in Central and South America and in Africa, as an initial response to the trend toward economic cooperation in Europe.[11] The result was the emergence of regional organizations. Despite some successes, the essence of economic integration is yet to be realized in much of Africa. This is even more urgent if Africa has to keep abreast in a dynamic and competitive global environment. Intra industry trade is positively correlated with the level of economic development.[12] A nation cannot fully develop without industrialization. In a world where countries have been gravitating to form trading blocs, it is more urgent than ever to strengthen the economic ties for cooperation and integration.[13] It is imperative that countries define the objectives and benefits they expect to derive from regional trade and cooperation. It is also important that developments in regional integration be disseminated for optimal public consumption. Such a strategy will lay the foundation for the introduction of necessary but unfamiliar and possibly unpopular policy reforms. This will also guarantee that concerned parties take optimal advantage of such developments.

Incidentally, not all regional reforms or policies tend to interest all participating nations to the same extent. Expecting them to move always in lockstep with each other is, therefore, unrealistic. Regional integration, which focuses on the common problems in Africa, is a firm foundation for regional prosperity. In the process of integration, progress will be determined by the fastest, not the slowest members. Members prepared, willing, and able to take advantage of unfolding opportunities in the region will form core groups and proceed. Members that are dragging their feet, for one reason or the other, will be respectfully allowed to catch up at their own paces. Streamlining the activities of other regional entities in Africa is also equally important. Efficiency and effectiveness will be attained through executing value-added, coordinated, and synergistic functions, without duplicating and competing for scarce resources.[14]

In order to positively and irreversibly improve intra-African trade, the efficiency of communications and transportation infrastructures becomes a priority, since they enhance the cost-effectiveness of interregional trade. Relations in many areas and among most African states have remained healthy; however, economic relations still leave very much to be desired. Economic relations among African states, big and small, have always been and will remain indispensable keys to African industrialization.

Regional economic integration tends to call for harmonization of legal and administrative systems. It tends to require harmony or standardization of technical rules that address issues like noise pollution by plants, construction products, pharmaceuticals, food products, and so on. Increased trade and traffic across frontiers also means an increased propensity for a black market in contraband. Such contraband may include personal weapons, drugs, radioactive substances, explosives, and so forth. Increased trade also requires more efficient and proper management and coordination of external borders. This is especially the case when one factors in the ramifications of higher traffic volume and the coordinate potential for the spread of disease by rats, fleas, mites, pets, and other animals, plants, and microbes.

Paradoxically, a growing country may become worse off with growth. In an economic climate in which nations export primary products in exchange for manufactured goods, the tendency is to increase output of agricultural products in order to procure an increased stock of manufactured goods from industrially advanced countries. Naturally, developing countries have for ages found themselves in this conundrum in which increased amounts of primary products must be exchanged for manufactured products. This is one fundamental reason that a country remains underdeveloped.

This economic phenomenon afflicting some developing countries, is even more apparent when one considers the fact that manufactured products typically tend to improve in quality while primary products basically do not. For example, a car manufactured in the 1990s is of a much better quality than its counterpart manufactured in the 1920s or 1930s. While plant engineers may develop hardy wheat or a tomato with a longer shelf life, such marginal quality gains often accrue to production and distribution. Consumers often tend to be skeptical and sometimes outright resistant, to genetic engineering and other technologies like food irradiation that tinker with nature. This basically explains why the prices of manufactured goods increase with quality and sophistication, while the prices of primary products have generally stagnated and/or depreciated in real terms. Technical progress that orients toward raw-material savings/innovations is often detrimental to primary products. For example, synthetic rubber consequently led to a fall in price of natural rubber.[15]

The desire to precipitate the pace of economic development in Africa, through capital formation, industrialization, and a larger share of the gains from international trade, have not been undiluted with distortions. Endogenous distortions or distortions that affect market mechanisms may be caused by external economies that result in market imperfections. Economic distortions may also be policy induced. Economic policies such as tariffs, production subsidies, and consumption taxes may be used to promote noneconomic objectives, thus distorting the economic process. Examples of policy induced distortions in the economy may include the following: (1) infant industry protection; (2) a minimum level of production, perhaps for military reasons; (3) autarky or a minimum level of economic self-sufficiency; and (4) an acceptable level of employment of the factors of production, for example labor.

Optimal policies for correcting distortions must intervene with surgical precision, at exact points of distortion. In the case of noneconomic or policy-induced distortions, the point of intervention is typically a subsidy, and not a tariff. For example, production for national security reasons. If on the other hand, consumption must be restricted for policy reasons, then the optimal intervention is consumption tax. If the volume of imports must be truncated, then tariffs may appropriately suffice. By the same token, labor employment may be generated with subsidies. In protecting an infant industry, the optimal policy tends to be a production subsidy and not a tariff.

Incidentally, tariffs are the cash cows of economies at low levels of development. Tariffs are a major source of revenues for these growing economies. High tariffs or the fear of high tariffs may force multinationals or foreign-owned corporations to locate within tariff walls. Tariffs may cause resources to shift from export industries to import competing industries. As enticing as the positive repercussions for tariffs may be, they are optimally not the impetus to industrial development. In a fussy economic climate, tariffs foster a false sense of national well-being that eventually degenerates into low levels of welfare and a contraction of world trade.

Because trade imports represent a leakage in an economy, they play a significant role in capital formation. Sustainable industrialization requires a stock of capital goods. This arsenal of a "produced means of production" is feasible through savings and investment and reduces the marginal propensity to import.[16]

In North America, Japan, and Europe, the stock of capital goods increased faster than labor (population), thus ensuring higher per capita income and improved living standards. The infant-industry protection policy that was formulated, in 1791 appealed to many developing countries in the 1950s. By protecting infant industries, it was hoped, growing economies would accumulate ample capital. Unfortunately, many infant industries in Africa have sustained at this stage. Resources have been used to export primary products, and the industrial sector has either stagnated or declined, relative to global standards. Some countries have blamed this shortcoming on the export primary products, and the industrial sector has either stagnated or declined, relative to global standards. Some countries have blamed this shortcoming on the limited size of their respective national markets. It appears a more aggressive and strategic regional trade will be helpful in this domain. Trade among African nations is not only vital as a matter of principle but will also serve as an impetus for industrialization.[17]

Conducting business regionally is not a new phenomenon in Africa. For many centuries trading activities thrived between the different ecological zones. Typically, the principal markets/entrepôts were at the peripheries of these ecological zones. Some examples of these markets, at the borders, will include *Kano,* the center of the African "Caravan" trade; *Salaga,* a very important cola market in *Dagomba;* and *Kukuwa,* the capital of *Borno.* Important trading agents, in this dynamic and extensive ancient commerce included: the *Yoruba* of present-day Nigeria; the *Akan* of Ghana; and the *Dida* of Ivory Coast. These pre industrial trading networks were very helpful for many centuries, supplying the various settlements of Africans with an inventory of necessities for a happy, subsistent lifestyle.

Unfortunately, the myriad of dynamic changes in twentieth-century commerce and industry had, in principle, relegated these cherished African trading networks into an anachronism. Modern forms of transportation such as automobiles, trains, and airplanes have imposed themselves relentlessly on other modes of transport such as the camel used by African caravan traders. Radios, telephones, televisions, computers, and satellite technology have virtually diminished the world to what seems to be a global village. Electronic banking has significantly replaced paper currency and hard money. In a contemporary economic environment, the money supply comprises forms such as currency in circulation, checking account balances, NOW accounts, and share draft accounts at credit unions; savings accounts and time deposits such as CDs, money market deposit accounts, and repurchase agreements; money market fund balances held by institutions. Any attempts at modern regional economic integration that are based on centuries-old traditional African trading systems are likely to suffocate healthy prospects for industrialization and regional growth. Traditional African trade has evolved with resiliency through the ages into cash-based commerce from a system that employed cowries as local and regional currency, and retained gold as the international medium of exchange.

This cash-based commerce, which overwhelmingly conducts business transactions in paper currency and coins, neglects other more efficient forms of money, in a relatively competitive twentieth century global trading environment. However, it is significant that, like the traditional subsistent African farmer, the plight of the traditional regional trader is a major cause for concern on the eve of an industrial takeoff. At this juncture, it appears a more universal solution will be an extrapolation that factors the positive points of ramifications of traditional trading into the trajectory of regional economic integration.

Another impediment to regional integration is the rather anemic disposition of banking relations among countries of the same geographic region. This is especially true for banking between Anglophone and Francophone countries. This is further aggravated by the fact that "most of the African central banks do not allow their commercial banks to hold funds, in accounts with commercial banks in other countries."[18]

Left unaddressed, linguistic disparities may impose themselves as stumbling blocks in intra-African trade. However, making a trade document more user friendly will expedite commercial and industrial information exchange among trading countries. For example, if the national languages in an economic region are English, French, and Swahili, then each and every document should be printed in these three official languages, as a matter of principle.

Economic integration and cooperation are not an end by themselves. They are means to an end. Other means, which integrate national markets, speed economic growths, enhance living standards, are also important. The efficient maintenance of various institutions and the frequency and regularity of conferences or policy meetings, in which resolutions and declarations are adopted, is auxiliary. These auxiliaries only become potent if and only if they are canalized as direct extensions of the organizational vision.

In summary, regionalization is obviously not new to Africa. However, the opportunities still bristle for industrialization. Regional economic integration neither, means that international trade with traditional partners should be relegated nor that other unfolding opportunities in the international marketplace should be discounted. Regionalization enhances the opportunities for increased quantities and varieties of agricultural output, badly needed by countries that are net food importers; creates opportunity for economies of scale; creates employment opportunity; increases the possibility for enhanced standards of living; and expands trade. It is conducive to foreign investments. However, the benefits may not be seen solely through the lenses of industrialization: regionalization is a dynamic instrument of policy. Under the prevailing trading systems and without regionalization, some nations may be worse off with economic growth. When African businesses practice within the familiar confines of the neighborhoods, the effectiveness in competing, in a dynamic free market and global environment, will be enhanced. Regionalization ultimately reinforces globalization.

## NOTES

1. E. Wayne Nafziger, "Japanese Development Model," in Howard F. Didsbury, Jr., ed., *The Global Economy: Today, Tomorrow, and the Transition* (Bethesda, MD: World Future Society, 1985), pp. 111–134.

2. Here dams, irrigation canals, and large pumps serve rather large areas, while tube-holes (boreholes) with diesel pumps, which feature in Indian and Pakistani schemes, are best suited for areas of about ten acres or more. Irrigation schemes are more appropriate in larger farming units. Static power sources, like diesel pumps and electric motors are used to move water in a scale far beyond the capacities of human and animal power: G. Borgsstrom , "Too Many: A Study of the Earth's Biological Limitations," in David Colman, and Frederick Nixson,

*Economics of Change in Less Developed Countries* (New York: John Wiley, 1978), pp. 128–160.

3. Ibid. Here large firms provided the small, independently run firms with technical advice, scarce inputs, credit, and where needed, access to a large international trading company (*sago shosha*). Small-scale industry (establishments with less than fifty workers) increased its real output, though not output shares, between 1884 and 1930, contributing 65 percent to 75 percent of Japan's employment and about 45 percent to 50 percent of its gross manufacturing output in 1934. But many small firms were dependent, since they were being dominated by major banks, industrial companies, and trading corporations. The idea here was to promote small industry by upgrading, workshops, handicrafts, and cottage sectors. China called this approach "walking on two legs." Subsequently, in the 1930s, the Soviet Union accumulated industrial capital by squeezing it from agriculture. Low agricultural incomes and savings and perhaps no tax on agriculture result in a net inflow to agriculture.

4. Charles Oman, *Globalisation and Regionalization: The Challenge for Developing Countries* (Paris: Organisation for Economic Co-operation and Development, 1994), pp. 44–51.

5. Edward F. Denison and William K. Chung, *How Japan's Economy Grew So Fast: The Sources of Postwar Expansion* (Washington, DC: Brookings Institution, 1976), p. 91.

6. Oman, *Globalisation and Regionalisation*, p. 43.

7. Ibid., pp. 37–50.

8. Byung-Sun Choi, "Financial Policy and Big Business in Korea: The Perils of Financial Regulation," in Stephan Haggard, Chung H. Lee, and Sylvia Maxfield, eds., *The Politics of Financing Developing Countries* (Ithaca: Cornell University Press, 1993), pp. 23–54. In the early stages of industrialization in Korea (1946–1961) the government initiated subsidized credit to encourage big business. In the 1970s, heavy and chemical industries were targeted for industrialization. Industries selected as strategic included iron and steel; machinery; nonferrous metals such as aluminum, copper, zinc, and lead; electronics; shipbuilding; and petrochemicals. But there were looming adversities, for as long as the economy boomed, debt financing proceeded smoothly but when the economy slowed down, debt-ridden companies were compelled to fall back on government for relief.

9. The Marshall Plan also inculcated a massive program of technical assistance. The outcome was significant surges in productivity, which contributed to the development and infusion of mass production in Europe. After the Marshall Plan, the Common Market greatly spurred economic progress in Europe. Since then, trade transactions intensified among industrial countries, including the area of intra industry trade.

10. Oman, *Globalisation and Regionalisation*, pp. 37–41.

11. Orville L. Freeman, "The Farm Family: A Success Story with Global Implications," in Didsbury, *The Global Economy*, pp. 136–137. Of course, it is commonly known that millions of acres in Africa have the potential of becoming productive. It is also known that Sudan alone has as much unplowed land as the land currently being used for agricultural production in the United States of America. But, the problem with Sudan is that there are inadequate infrastructures and no storage facilities. This explains why, unlike Sudan, the average American farm family, which fed ten persons in 1940, could in the 1980s feed seventy-seven persons.

12. Hiroshi Kitamura, "Japan and Asian-Pacific Integration," in Didsbury, *The Global*, p. 199.

13. "Promoting Regional Cooperation and Integration in Subsaharan Africa." *The Courier*, Brussels, no. 134., July-August 1992, p. 77.

14. *The Courier*, Brussels, July-August 1992, p. 81.

15. Price stagnation and deterioration of the overall terms of trade may be strategically ameliorated through regional economic trade with other, growing nations. The terms of trade will tend to stagnate and/or will deteriorate if the exporting country is growing, while the importing country is not expanding. On the other hand, if both economies are growing at about

the same rate, then the volume of trade of both countries will grow *pari passu*. In this case, the terms of trade will not deteriorate, and technical progress that ensues from the import-competing sector tends to improve the terms of trade. But generally, as an economy grows and expands, the terms of trade tend to deteriorate. Per-unit price of export becomes cheaper. This is true when the volume of trade increases at constant prices and vice versa.

16. Kiichiro Satoh, "Japan," in Herbert V. Prochnow, ed., *World Economic Problems and Policies* (New York: Harper & Row, 1965), pp. 98–117. It is common knowledge that the Japanese economy expanded at an exceptionally fast rate, immediately after 1945, relative to the growth rates of other nations. This high rate of economic growth in Japan was attributed mainly to the sharp expansion of private plant and equipment investments. Japan was desperately intent on catching up with advancing countries, and resorted to technological innovation as a means to achieve this objective. As the cotton industry began to recede, the industrial structure was diversified and resources were shifted to the more value-added products of the heavy and chemical industries. Of the factors of production, Japan's only clear advantage was a labor force of 95 million skilled and semiskilled workers, who were also eager consumers. Unendowed with adequate natural resources, Japan had to import raw materials and turn them into products for domestic consumption and export markets. The export markets were segmented into (1) advanced countries, (2) developing countries, and (3) The (now-defunct) communist bloc.

17. Fortunately, regional economic integration remains an overriding objective for many African countries. This has been demonstrated by the plethora of regional organizations that have been formed during the last three decades or so. Such organizations range from UDEAC, (Central African Customs and Economic Union), established in 1966; and ECOWAS (Economic Community of West African States), established in 1975; to SADC (Southern African Development Community), established in 1980 as SADCC; and the PTA (Preferential Trade Area for Eastern and Southern African States), established in 1981. Unfortunately, efforts toward regional economic integration have not been without collateral difficulties.

18. *The Courier*, ACP-EC (Brussels, Belgium), November-December 1993.

# 7

# Taxation for Industrial Momentum

In an industrializing environment, society tends to undergo a metamorphosis that is characterized by an overwhelming affinity to amass private wealth. There is an emphasis on privately produced goods, sometimes at the detriment of public services. In Africa, since 1960, there has been what may be an irresistible tendency for a small minority of characters to destroy, abuse, and misuse property that they collectively own, while simultaneously respecting personal property. Such individuals do not take personal responsibility for highways, streams, rivers, lakes, public offices, public libraries, schools, universities, air, parks, and other public spaces.

Residents tend to be indifferent to the consequences of misuse of public spaces and property that are owned in common. Dirt is thrown onto streets; neighborhood streets are allowed to degrade into disrepair; garbage is dumped into ditches and storm drains. School premises are vandalized, and money earmarked for new school buildings and repair is misappropriated. Effectively, parents or future parents are squandering the future benefits allocated for their children and their children's children. In some communities, children are forced to attend classes in half-completed buildings, sometimes without doors and windows. Some poorly constructed classrooms and dormitories (violating initial blueprints) are easily accessible by mosquitoes, mites, and other parasitic insects. Increasingly the weaker and often inadequately nourished children fall sick. Many children suffer from malaria, filariasis, yellow fever, and the like. These children have paid their school fees, but they cannot attend classes; they instead spend school hours in hospitals, clinics, dispensaries, or recuperating at home. The government allocated funds to educate the young future community leaders, but the total benefits just never accrued to them. This is overwhelmingly tantamount to national self-destruction. There must be progressive synergies between public and private goods and their uses.

It is important to remark at the outset that this attitude is not universal. Perhaps it is the case of a few bad apples. However, Africans generally have very constructive attitudes toward development projects that originate in villages, tribal associations, and other social organizations that tend to revolve around the numerous informal savings, credit, and improvement associations. There are numerous examples in West and Central Africa, including the *Esusu* among the Yoruba and the "meeting" among the Ibo, both of Nigeria. Improvement associations tend to be elaborate, serving social, political, and community development functions. Here, taxation is through membership and takes the form of compulsory and morally obligatory payment of dues for all adults and special assessments for community projects. This voluntary contribution of funds is not confined to West Africa. The Kikuyu of Kenya for a long time imposed a form of self-taxation that was fairly heavy, through local native councils, typically for educational purposes. This self-taxation was (besides the government tax) contribution to local development.[1] As was stated earlier, synergies are enhanced through taxation. Taxation is the price of growth.[2] In a growth-oriented industrializing environment, an important consideration will be to use taxes, not only to meet necessary public expenditure, but to finance, indirectly, the expansion of private investment. When a community consumes more privately produced goods but is poor in public goods and services, an obvious tendency is to tax the former to provide the latter.

Private goods and services are, therefore, taxed so that public goods and services may be more adequate. More is paid for automobiles and petrol in order to have better roads on which to drive the cars. Cigarettes and liquor are taxed so as to provide adequate medical services, in time of sickness. Many entrepreneurs may oppose or openly grumble about tax obligations. By opposing taxes, one is perhaps opposing better schools, better roads, adequate health care, and general economic stability. In fact, in a free market system, the danger is not taxation. The real danger is in over-taxation. As early as 1790, Andrew Hamilton made the following observations in his monograph *The Principles of Taxation:*

Taxes on articles of immediate consumption appear to be the easiest and most productive sources of revenue. There is nothing to hinder the rate of such duties to be perfectly certain; they are always paid by the consumer at the time most convenient for himself; they are voluntary; and blended with the price of the goods, the generality of the contributors soon forget that they are taxed at all. . . . It is universally allowed, that a tax may be so high on an article that it would be impossible to levy it; the temptation to smuggling may be so great that no fiscal regulations however perfect, no laws however severe, and no police however strict, would be sufficient to prevent it. A commodity taxed to this degree is, with the greatest propriety, said to be over-taxed. But though a rate of duty should not be so high as it is here supposed, yet if it is high enough to be ample encouragement to smuggling, in opposition to strictest regulations sanctioned by the severest penalties. . . . Smuggling always prevails when the rate of duty is too high. . . . [T]he quantity of a taxed article always decreases on the revenue books after it is over-taxed.[3]

In an industrializing environment, in which a sizable cross-section of the population is still steeped in poverty and illiteracy, certain services may be best provided by the public sector. The underemployed or unemployed leave the countryside to look for better employment in the cities. While in gainful employment, their employers, as a rule, are required to deduct taxes, social security, and unemployment contributions. These deductions are used to build roads, schools, bridges, and provide services such as national defense and security. They also provide for the cost of hospitalization in case the worker falls sick, for unemployment compensation in case of an adverse economic downturn, and for pension benefits in case of retirement.

The pre-industrial precept that "He who does not work cannot eat" is antiquated. Well-managed industrializing environments sought to protect all workers during working life, during periods of unemployment and even in retirement. Through taxes, the government is able to allocate funds or social security for those whose working life may be cut short by blindness, deafness, and other disabilities that may derive from the hazards of exertion at work.

When a nobleman pays his taxes, he does not have to feel a sense of guilt every time he sits to enjoy his dinner, nor be accused of being nonchalant to the dire circumstances of the most needy around the corner. Instead, he should ponder what happened to tax revenues that base needs sustain in the community. In an industrializing environment, more economic opportunities are created that in turn create opportunities for incomes for individuals and businesses. The gap between the well-to-do and the lowest income groups is narrowed. Part of the burden of taxation is, therefore, shifted from the well-to-do and distributed more equitably.

Taxes are, first of all, determined by law.[4] As economies become industrialized, increasingly people support themselves not from property but from exertion. Property tax, once intended to be a tax on all wealth, ceases to be general in coverage. The test of ability to pay taxes is shifted from property to proceeds and earnings. Property tax is gradually supplanted by taxes on production facilities, wages, salaries, interest, profits, and so on. The medieval basis of taxation of mass property (in Europe) was abandoned as nations attained industrialization and because it no longer corresponded to the demands of justice.[5]

In fact, modern property tax is a metamorphosis of the medieval taxation. Through everything, in substance, though not in the name, it has undergone just about every phase of development. In its modern meaning, it is more adaptable to the needs of local government. The danger, however, is to apply local property tax to the extent that it discourages local development. For example, high taxes on housing may be expected to discourage demand for housing development.

"Circuit breakers" may be used to protect taxpayers against a property tax overload. Here, the circuit breaker is engineered to trigger when the income of a taxpayer drops below certain levels or when a refund is made when the income tax is not large enough to absorb the entire credit or when the payer is in fact not subject to income tax. Essentially, tax relief is made available to those who at one point in time or another demonstrated inability to pay. In some cases, homeowners and renters regardless of age are made eligible. The benefits may be financed by the state government, to avoid diminution of local government fiscal resources.[6]

Typically, government finances its activities to the community by either raising revenue through taxation or taking on debt obligations. The latter occur when revenues are less than planned public expenditure. Federal budget policy may be based on the rule that tax receipts must be approximately equal to annual expenditures. Therefore, when there are declining receipts, during periods of business contraction, the policy calls for reductions in expenditures or increases in taxes. During periods of prosperity surplus receipts develop, thus calling for lower tax rates or increased expenditures. Budget surpluses are used to restrain private spending during prosperity, while deficits are used to stimulate spending during recessions.[7] In a growth environment, surplus tends to be coupled with measures to stimulate investment, so that the aggregate savings lead to capital formation instead of being wasted in unemployment and loss of consumption. Fiscal policies and monetary policies are administered independently in promoting long-run economic growth as well as short-run stability.[8] It is, therefore, superficially paradoxical to combine anti-inflationary fiscal policy with an expansionary monetary policy.[9] The objective of industrial growth policy, therefore, is to provide full employment for labor force and industrial capacity in a relatively stable price environment.[10] When the tax system is rather antiquated and the monetary system is very rigid, it may not be suitable for a modern fiscal policy in an industrializing environment.[11] The powers of the government in this domain are, however, not without limits.

There may be a constitutional provision for a balanced budget or one limiting the degree/level/spectrum of deficit financing. The government's scope of tax extraction may also be canalized (i.e., preventing the tendency of government becoming the industrial sole proprietor) by taxpayer recalcitrance/obstinacy. These factors establish thresholds that limit the ratio of government taxes to national income (GNP) in an industrial environment, with a well-informed constituency. The danger, however, is to hamper national fiscal policy, where a significantly sizable proportion of taxes and expenditure reside in the hands of local governments.[12]

In local referendums, voters may ballot for or against proposed tax increases. Here, communities may be required by law to exercise this right, thus giving residents a say (rightly or wrongly) in the destiny of their neighborhoods, counties, districts, towns, and cities. They have a stake in local debt obligations. The local taxpayer (individual, family, office, or factory) has a voice in local tax expenditures that may range from schools and recreational facilities (swimming pools, playgrounds, parks) to traffic conditions, crime prevention, and capital improvements (sewers, water mains, sidewalks, a library branch, etc.). This is especially feasible where communities do command the critical mass of fiscal resources within their local borders. Generally, metropolitan areas tend to have a wider tax base. Unusually high local taxes, however, may prompt the flight of residents and businesses to more conducive tax jurisdictions, thus shrinking the tax base.[13] It is also easy to overstate this propensity.[14]

Ultimately, in an industrializing environment, taxes are meant to grease the wheels of the vehicle for positive economic change. Taxes ultimately benefit individuals, families, businesses, in the short and long term, either directly (e.g., as extra spending power, when it is most needed) or indirectly, for example in decent and well-maintained public infrastructures and services.

## NOTES

1. Margaret Katzin, "The Role of the Entrepreneur," in Melville J. Herskovits and Mitchell Harwitz, eds., *Economic Transition in Africa* (Evanston, IL: Northwestern University Press, 1964), pp. 179–198.

2. James Tobin, "Growth through Taxation," in B. Hughel Wilkens and Charles B. Friday, eds., *The Economists of the New Frontier* (New York: Random House, 1963), p. 270.

3. Andrew Hamilton, *An Inquiry into the Principles of Taxation* (Clifton:Augustus M. Kelly Publishers, 1975), pp. 1, 6–7 (first published in 1790). To prevent smuggling, certificates were required to accompany goods from port to port under penalties of forfeiture. Ports were established to prevent smuggling, and shipmasters were required to give regular notice of arrival and departure schedules. By law, ships could only be landed in daylight and ships could only load and unload during specific hours.

4. Acts of Parliament/Congress determine the spectra of economic activities that constitute the base for taxation. Typically, not all income is subject to taxation. The law allows for a variety of deductions, to be made from gross income, for minimal living expenses, interest payments on mortgages, children allowance, and so on. The law therefore taxes net income. Because of the ease of collection, organizations may be endowed with the legal duty of collecting taxes. In this regard, income taxes are deducted from employee wages, coupled with other tax obligations that may include VAT (value added taxes), sales taxes and industrial property taxes. It is easier to collect taxes from a cigarette manufacturer than from a cigarette smoker. Likewise, it is easier to collect taxes from a liquor manufacturer than from a liquor drinker. Poll taxes or herd taxes are less easy to collect because they tend to apply to more mobile populations with fewer guaranteed addresses.

5. Edwin R.A. Seligman, *Essays in Taxation* (New York: Augustus M. Kelley Publishers, 1969), pp. 56–61.

6. Joseph A. Pechman, *Federal Tax Policy* (New York: W. W. Norton & Company, 1971), pp. 258–265.

7. Ibid., p. 7. An expansionary budget runs a deficit while a restrictive budget runs a surplus. As an automatic stabilizer, taxes tend to affect savings, consumption, work, and investments.

8. The mysticism that cloaks monetary policy makes it a reliable weapon in performing some of the more intriguing jobs of policy.

9. Tobin, *The Economists of the New Frontier*, p. 272.

10. Pechman, *Federal Tax Policy*, pp. 23–31.

11. Angus Maddison, *Economic Growth in the West* (New York: Twentieth Century Fund, 1964), p. 116.

12. Maddison, *Economic Growth in the West*, p. 115.

13. Nine studies on tax rate changes indicate that change in tax rates *per se* is uninterpretable as an indicator of fiscal consequences of industrial development. Gene F. Summers, Sharon D. Evans, Frank Clemente, E.M. Beck, Jon Minkoff, *Industrial Invasion of Nonmetropolitan America* (New York: Praeger Publishers, 1976), p. 84.

14. The tax base may also vary based on the dynamics of annexations, consolidations, incorporations, and zoning restrictions coupled with valuations of the proportions of industrial, commercial, and residential units that may help carry the tax load. Older cities may be reluctant to forge rather one-sided relationships with small communities when the cities have already fully paid for their capital improvements. A study did not find any correlation between population density and per capita property values, thus revealing no correlation between a community's age and its per capita property value. Per capita property resources were not significantly correlated to the absolute size (i.e., a population and the area span) of a locality. Donald J. Curran,

*Metropolitan Financing: The Milwaukee Experience, 1920–1970* (Madison: University of Wisconsin Press, 1973), pp. 4–36, p. 50.

8

# Mosquitoes: War to End All Wars in Africa

Up to this point, many places in Africa seem to be desperately and fatally losing the war against a very lightweight adversary, the mosquito. But the tables can be turned around. Humans have won the war on mosquitoes in many other parts of the world, and it is also feasible in Africa. To win this war in Africa, no stone shall be left unturned. In other words, the onslaught will be three pronged: (1) A complete detailed understanding of mosquitoes is necessary; (2) Massive, relentless broad-spectrum onslaughts will be unleashed with surgical precision, until the last vector is exterminated; (3) Among other measures, benign creatures that also feed on disease-transmitting mosquitoes will be supplanted in appropriate locations, in the regained territories. These insectivorous creatures (patrol soldiers) will also include the giant species of African mosquitoes that tends to feed on these vectors and other insects such as dragonflies that also feast on mosquitoes.

Unfed and thirsty, a mosquito weighs up to a mere one-ten thousandth of an ounce, yet it is probably responsible for more deaths in Africa than all the shooting wars put together. According to the *Economist*, malaria affects about 200 million to 400 million people each year. Of this number, around one million die of the disease. Ninety percent of these deaths are in Africa.[1]

The nemesis is the female mosquito which prefers to feast on warm-blooded animals. This invasive, aggressive, and unrelenting mosquito will risk death to quench its thirst for blood. It invades with a humming dirge of death, plundering the blood supply by biting or piercing the victim and sucking the blood. Pathogens are deposited during its meal.[2] At the end of its meal, it will sluggishly lift off, swollen with a spoil of two to three times its body weight. In its wake, the victims are scourged with abominable afflictions ranging from malaria to filariasis, dog heartworm, encephalitis, yellow fever, dengue fever, temporal insanity, and about eighty viral diseases.

Human diseases caused by these metabolically dependent creatures (mosquito-borne pathogens) debilitate the workforce of a nation. They are responsible for the countless worker-hours lost annually to infirmity. Lost work hours are not only inconsistent with and inconvenient to employment, but also increase the cost of production and tend to make businesses less competitive. Scarce human resources are used either to cure or prevent a pandemic that had been eradicated in many parts of the world, including parts of Central and South America. It is not impossible to do the same for the many places in Africa that are still suffering from this scourge. These "flying hypodermics" have been catalogued among the causes of the downfall of ancient civilizations, particularly those around the Mediterranean.

Malaria is caused by a pathogen called *Plasmodium* (Plasmodium vivax, Plasmodium malariae, Plasmodium falciparum, Plasmodium ovale). *P. vivax* and *P. malariae* cause benign tertiary (tertian) and quartan malaria, respectively, in humans.[3] *P. falciparum*, also known as jungle fever, is much more serious and often fatal.[4] *P. ovale* is the fourth and rarest form of malaria. It is similar to the benign tertian malaria. In all forms, the disease tends to be less regularly spaced in some people.

Mosquitoes are territorial. Each specie occupies a specialized area where it can survive with minimum competition from other species. For example, a specie may prefer to establish a niche around fresh waters, while another may prefer polluted waters. Other habitats include standing water or where water tends to overflow, brackish water, and wild terrain. The cosmopolitan species tend to prefer water in cans, old tires, water barrels, trash, and uncovered sewage adjacent to human settlements. It is easy for this species to establish and propagate in urban settlements, where there is no centralized trash dump.

In order to resolve the menacing problems of mosquitoes, it is significant to analyze the gender disparity in their habits. Unlike the female, the mouth parts of the male mosquito cannot suck blood. Each kind of female prefers certain kinds of food. For example, some prefer birds while others prefer the cold blood of frogs. In order for most females to successfully reproduce, they must eat blood. By contrast, males are not attracted to human beings. Instead, they are usually found around grass and bushes, swamps, streams, lakes, ponds, and so on. Males typically get food from stems of plants or the surface of leaves and fruits. Swarms of mosquitoes are usually found near breeding grounds.

A striking feature of males, unlike female mosquitoes, is their swarming habit. They may be found flying within a limited vertical space and centered above, below, or beside a particular land marker. This marker is often a small bush or post. Swarms are usually almost entirely composed of males and occur mostly at dawn or dusk. Since mosquitoes are not conspicuous by virtue of their size and acoustics, but a swarm of males is much more obvious, it may be that in swarms these functions are magnified, so that females enter it in order to find a mate.[5] This may also suggest why some of the most brightly colored mosquitoes do not swarm.[6]

Mosquitoes remain free from malaria and are infectious when they bite persons having the disease.[7] The female *anopheles* mosquito (vector of a malaria parasite) typically bites at night. Malaria tends to prevail where there is a critical density ("reservoir") of susceptible hosts and a critical density of mosquitoes.[8] This is because, as a vector, a mosquito requires at least two bites to transmit disease. The first bite picks up the parasitic microorganism from an infected person. The subsequent bite infects the wounded victim with a salivary fluid, that first causes swelling and irritation.[9]

Initially eradicated in many places in the Northern Hemisphere in the 1950s, malaria stubbornly persists as a monumental problem in Africa and other developing regions of the world. Finding any person in Africa who has never been bitten by a mosquito is perhaps impossible. Malaria not only causes massive destruction of the blood cells but often leaves the patient with severe anemia. During severe attacks, the blood vessels of the patient may become clogged and may even result in death.[10] Malaria causes more deaths than any other disease. In the case of *filariasis*, caused by a small parasitic worm transmitted from mosquitoes to humans, the worm can block the victims' lymph passages, resulting in elephantiasis.

Generally, malaria patients may experience chills, fever, and sweats that leave them very weak. Malaria is responsible for the loss of countless number of working hours each year. Even when a patient recovers, the lingering effect of anemia may affect his physical efficiency at work, resulting in lower productivity. Malaria may also affect a person's mental growth disposition.[11]

*Yellow fever* is spread by Aedes aegypti. The Aedes aegypti mosquitoes are completely dependent on man and are often found within half a mile from human settlements. The eggs are laid just above the water line of containers. They bite around the clock and prefer to bite just above the ground. The Aedes aegypti mosquitoes are most attracted by dark colors and usually approach the shaded parts of the host. Ambient carbon dioxide levels, and perhaps warm moist convection currents also, guide the mosquito to warm-blooded hosts.[12] Yellow fever is an infectious virus disease that tends to attack the liver and the digestive tract. Like the Anopheles, the Aedes aegypti contracts the virus by feeding on blood of persons with the disease. Although yellow fever has been brought under control in the developed world, it is still a menace in Africa and parts of South America. Before modern medicine, yellow fever was infamous for spreading death through whole cities. A mosquito can pick up the yellow fever virus if it happens to bite a patient during the first three days of illness. The mosquito is capable of transmitting the germ after twelve days of becoming a carrier. Yellow fever typically attacks the patient within six days of being bitten. Patients usually experiences headache, rapid pulse, and high fever and then go through remission. Next, the state of health changes for the worse: the skin turns yellow and the patient may expectorate black blood or black vomiting. Yellow fever could be most *effectively* controlled by eliminating mosquitoes and by protecting the sick from mosquito bites.[13]

This anthropoid vector, the mosquito, by which malaria is carried from one human host to another, can be brought under control in space and time.[14] Important considerations here will be measures to truncate the "adequate life expectancy" and reproduction rate, which negates the maintenance of pathogens.[15] Another approach will be to sever the weakest link in the chain of transmission. In other words, this is possible through an integrated approach that eliminates environmental conditions conducive to mosquitoes, diligent application of chemicals, and natural biological controls. Mosquitoes can best be brought under control by destroying the breeding grounds. The adequate use of chemicals to eradicate mosquitoes can be beneficial. As strange as it may seem, sublethal quantities of certain insecticides will actually increase the rate of reproduction in the female mosquito.[16] However, indiscriminate chemical applications will not only kill pests but will also exterminate bugs that prey on insect pests and friendly *pollinators,* such as bees and butterflies.[17] During the last two decades *pheromones* have been successfully used commercially for insect control by applying a technique called mating disruption. Compared with the controversial aerial insecticides spraying programs, pheromones had an advantage because of low toxicity, low usage rates, and high target specificity.

Bed nets, were used since the days of ancient Rome to protect humans from mosquito bites. Until the 1960s, bed nets were very common in Africa, but somehow they disappeared from the scene, perhaps with the introduction of prophylactics. They are still useful today, especially for architectural designs that do not factor in the consequences of adverse environmental predators. For some reason or another screens have not been widely used. Insecticide-impregnated bed nets were reported to reduce childhood deaths from malaria by almost a third, according to studies in Kenya, the Gambia, Ghana, and Burkina Faso. Bed nets were said to be superior to many antimalarial drugs, since antimalarial drugs had side effects when taken over a period of several years. Bed nets have no side effects, it was reported, and could be arranged to be affordable.[18] In a series of trials carried out in areas where malaria was most difficult to control, but with different levels of endemicity, the number of clinical attacks of malaria in children protected by treated bed nets was said to reduce by thirty to sixty percent. The most dramatic results were in the Gambia, where overall child mortality rates dropped by more than sixty percent.[19]

Sterilization is another special weapon that may be enlisted in the war against mosquitoes, ensuring that the females do not go forth and multiply. In this case, mosquitoes are raised in the laboratory and sterilized. These male mosquitoes are then released in the millions above the affected areas.[20]

Strategic applications of chemicals that do not adversely affect the soil, plants, birds, and other benign and helpful insects tend to be acceptable in some locations. Spraying swamps and other stagnant water with oil can be an effective control method. *Toxorhynchites* (formerly called *Megarhinus*) are a subfamily, with about fifty species. The larvae are obligatory on those of other species. Various small aquatic animals serve as prey, but the principal delicacy consists of the larvae of other mosquitoes. A giant species is found in Africa, *Toxorhynchites brevipalpis*, and tends to destroy other mosquito populations. As larvae, they can devour hundreds of larvae of other species. As adults, the *Toxorhynchites brevipalpis* are benign: they neither feed on blood nor spread disease. The adults of both sexes are highly modified. The proboscis is long and recurved through an obtuse angle, rendering blood feeding impossible. Instead, they feed on nectar and plant juices. The breeding places are container habitats such as tree holes or rot holes that are constantly filled with water, in certain waterside trees (*phreatophites*). The size of the rot-hole or at least the aperture seems important often.[21] "The genus is found throughout the old and new world tropics with excursions into the eastern United States, the maritime provinces of the [former] USSR, and Japan. No species occur in Polynesia other than those introduced by man."[22]

Another effective method is to introduce fish that feed on mosquito eggs such as *Gambusia holbrooki*. This fish has been shipped to most parts of the world, to help control mosquitoes. Another tiny fish, the minnow, may be used in a tandem with other methods, to keep mosquito population down. It is about nine cm or three inches long. The minnow lives in streams rivers and lakes and may be found in Europe, North Asia, Britain, east to Siberia, south to Pyrenees and north, to Sweden. It is an abundant fish found in schools. They live on insect larvae and crustaceans. They also feed on plants. Minnows are eaten by larger fish and fish-eating birds. Breeding takes place in spring, when the males develop attractive red bellies. They spawn in gravel-bottomed water. The eggs find lodging among the stones until they hatch. Hatching usually occurs within five to ten days.

The guppy is another pest controller. It lives in streams and pools. Its natural range is northern South America to Brazil, Barbados, and Trinidad. It has been introduced in many tropical areas because of its beneficial characteristics. It feeds on the aquatic larvae of mosquitoes. It tends to reproduce in prolific numbers in brackish and fresh waters. The guppy may eat other insect larvae, small crustaceans and the eggs, and the young of other fish.[23]

Guppies are year-round breeders. Reproduction is by internal fertilization. Up to twenty-four offsprings may be born at anyone time. Sexual maturity is usually attained within four to six weeks. Sexual maturity may be affected by the temperature and the surroundings. The guppies are called millions fish in many areas, because of their ability to reach maturity rapidly and to breed many times a year. They are very small, brilliantly colored, and they make good aquarium fish.[24]

Some bats are known to have a voracious appetite for mosquitoes. They have been known to consume as many as 500 mosquitoes each per hour. Bat houses, almost similar to birdhouses, are a good method of harnessing the beneficence of the bats in residential settings. As in every other case, the ecological/environmental impact of the bats must be thoroughly analyzed. Ignoring the net environmental impact may be disastrous over time. For example, some bats may eat beneficial insects such as the *praying mantis*. However, bats are generally useful and harmless. These animals are among the most susceptible of all animals to the poisonous effects of pesticides.[25] In some places in the industrialized parts of the world, conservation organizations distributed, free of charge, bat boxes to home owners. The insectivorous nature of some bat species has made it popular to set up bat boxes in residential quarters to control insect pests. Bats catch insects by echolocation at night and have been known to eat as much as 100 percent of their body weight in just one night.

In Africa, there are many beneficial bat species. Bats indigenous to Africa include Yellow-winged bat (*Lavia frons*). It may be found between Senegal and Kenya, around swamps and lakes in forest and open country. Its roosts are trees and bushes.

The flickering of its long ears gives away its presence. They often fly in the daytime but seem to feed only by night. They wait until an insect flies by before swooping down from the perch to snap it up. They breed throughout the year. Males do not leave the communal roost for the birth season. *Hipposideridae* is distributed in tropical and subtropical Africa and southern Asia. This bat belongs to the Old World leaf-nosed bat family. There are 40 species of this bat. They are extremely numerous and are of incalculable benefits to humankind, since they feed entirely on insects. They destroy many insect pests. The Lesser horseshoe bat (*Rhinolophus hipposideros*) may be found in Europe, Asia and North Africa; Peters disk-winged bat belongs to the family *Thyropteridae*. There are two species in this family which may be found in Central America and in tropical South America. This insectivore can climb up smooth surfaces such as glass by means of its sucker disks. Some bats are fruit-eating bats. An example is Franquet. It ranges from Nigeria to Angola, and east to Zimbabwe and Tanzania. The Hammer-headed bat is another example. It feeds on the juices of mangoes and soursops and displays carnivorous propensities. The Painted Bat (*Kerivoula argentata*) is found around Southern Kenya, Namibia, and Natal. It is common in arid woodland. They roost in small groups. They may be found in the most unlikely roosts, such as in suspended nests of weaver finches or under the eaves of African huts. The Painted bat belongs to the family of evening bats known as *Vespertilionidae* and nearly all of the 275 species are insectivorous. The exceptions are one or two that feed on fish, which they scoop from the water. They massively consume blackflies, midges and mosquitoes, thus making life for human remarkably much more comfortable.[26]

Even with spectacular results such as those in the Gambia and in Kenya the war against malaria, to be effective, should be a national priority of all nations simultaneously. The goal should be massive, targeted, and relentless onslaughts, intended to quickly, eliminate these vectors. Such measures will tend to utilize every practical weapon in the arsenal, followed by permanent monitoring. It should not only be a national priority, but regional and continental, very closely following transportation and migration patterns. The war on mosquitoes is just the beginning. There are many other blood-sucking flies, fleas, and other parasitic insects and organisms that pose a threat to the physical and economic environment of Africa. These (i.e., houseflies, sand flies, tsetse flies, midges, lice, fleas, etc.) must be confronted with passion and commitment, in an urbanizing and industrializing environment. Here, the Jamaica quassia, *Picrasma excelsa* (Swartz) Planch., is a valuable tree in an industrializing environment and may not be discounted. No insect dares to attack this elegant tree. Its bitter compound called quassin is effective as a natural insecticide that eradicates many pests (including body lice) without exterminating beneficial insects such as bees. However, honey made from the bitter quassia nectar of the rose-colored flowers is inedible. Again, left unaddressed, the toll on the work force only gets worse with time. Again, more than eighty-five percent of the world's malaria-related morbidities and mortalities are in Africa, and children are the most vulnerable. Competing optimally in a competitive global environment will be difficult when a significant proportion of the workforces are unhealthy or when resources are expended on populations with shortened average life spans. There is much work available to do. Civilizations have been brought to their knees before, in history, by the mosquito.

## MISERY AND VECTORS

*Kala-azar* is a serious fever-causing disease that grasped the attention of the sanitary community around 1858. During this time kala-azar appeared as a quinine-resistant virulent form of a fever epidemic in the district of Burdwan, in lower Bengal India. This epidemic of fever was debilitating and decimated  populations. This "contagious fever," as it was then believed, greatly affected productivity and the ability of workers to pay their taxes and consequently reduced expected government revenues. Locally, the disease was called  kala-azar or *black fever*, which is the meaning in the Hindustani language.[27] A Special Commission of Inquiry was appointed, whose report was quoted as follows in the Annual Reports of the Sanitary Commissioners for Bengal:

Many large baries, in which there were formerly thirty or forty residents, have now been left with perhaps one solitary occupant; whole mohullas and streets have been deserted, and large villages which formerly told their residents by the thousands, can now almost number them by hundred. . . . Upon the whole, we believe that about 30 per cent of the whole population of the infected area have died.[28]

An inspection and report to halt the disease noted the following: "The disease is brought on by repeated attacks of intermittent or remittent fever; the spleen becomes enormously enlarged; appetite very great; the sufferer loses flesh, and becomes a perfect skeleton, and, in general dies within a year."[29]

A later expansion of this report noted the long duration of the disease and discoloration (blackening) of the skin, from which the name kala-azar was derived. This report also attributed the disease to "a malarious remittent fever with enlarged spleen" caused by dirty habits and the swamps around the villages. It added that it was well known that changing the sites of the villages would halt the disease and that the local population would not submit to removal to dispensaries for long courses of treatment.[30] This epidemic continued to spread. In 1885 mortalities was high in Assam and between 1891 and 1901 mortalities had reduced the population by 31.5 percent.[31] An editorial in the *Indian Medical Gazette* noted that "the Government of India . . . should appoint a commission, composed of two, or better three, members, to carry out a thorough investigation during the next cold weather" in order to decide whether kala-azar was, as generally assumed, a form of malaria or a separate entity.[32]

It was proven in 1942 that sand flies are the intermediate host of the protozoan (a single-cell parasite) causing the disease, kala-azar.[33] In Africa, numerous sand flies were reported in some areas around the Sudan and Ethiopia. Sand flies are very small nocturnal insects. They tend to rest during the day in shady places, including houses. They generally inflict a painful bite, often around the ankles and wrists, in humans. They also bite domestic animals, frogs, and even caterpillars. In hot and dry regions the larvae may survive on damp surfaces, mossy ground, beneath rocks, or in shady rocks and in crevices, among other places.[34]

Leishmaniasis comes in several forms. One form causes ulcers on the skin, from which victims eventually recover. Another form, known as mucocutaneous leishmaniasis can metastasize and become very destructive. It can completely deform the nose, the larynx and the palate. The third form is associated with some areas in the Mediterranean and North Africa, where it is known as kala-azar. The patient experiences fever, weakness, and weight loss. It attacks the internal organs and is frequently fatal. Insecticides may be used to control sand flies. [35]

*Cutaneous leishmaniasis* is transmitted by the bites of sand flies and household flies.[36]

*Elephantiasis* is a chronic, often extreme enlargement and hardening of the cutaneous and subcutaneous tissue, especially of the lower body, because of the blockage of lymph ducts by parasitic, very thin nematode worms (filariae). This disease is also transmitted with the bite of mosquitoes. The mosquito population has been increasing, unabated, in urbanizing environments across much of Africa. This is worst in the lowest income squatter places in big cities, characterized by tin shacks and cesspools, where sanitation efforts have virtually grounded to a halt.

In 1942, a mosquito survey conducted in Kaduna (northern Nigeria) did not reveal any *culex fatigans*. Another attempt in 1960 uncovered up to 760 of these mosquitoes per room. This massive increase seemed to have taken place quietly, without significant notice.[37] Perhaps this coexistence may be explained by dependence on prophylactics instead of conventional methods of urban mosquito control. This remark echoes an earlier observation by J.R. Brown, noted in H.J. O'D. Burke-Gaffney: "the present conditions that have changed," he wrote, "belong to the individual rather than the locality. *"[38]*

The consequences of such proliferation of this vector are hard to predict, but they can scarcely be other than dangerous. The insidious nature of *filariasis*, without dramatic symptoms at the outset, however, does not leave room for speculation. The hideous *elephantiasis* caused by a very thin worm (filaria) is carried by the mosquito. Filariasis is a multi-patterned, tropical parasitic infection caused by several forms of Filaria. Each form of filaria is caused by a specific parasite—*Wuchereria bancrofti, Onchocerca volvulus, and loa loa*. The worm is introduced by the bite of an infected mosquito, usually the *Culex, Aedes, or Anopheles* genera.[39] When the mosquito bites, the worm enters the body and lodges in the lymph vessels. The name *elephantiasis* is derived from the rough texture of the skin that may eventually form. The new skin resembles the hide of an elephant.

Elephantiasis is characterized by fever, swellings of body parts (often around the leg), and roughened skin. The attacks are serial, with each attack rendering the body incrementally enlarged, until a state of maximum enlargement is attained.

Typically, the mosquitoes are themselves infected when they bite individuals with the clinically active disease. They pick up the young worms in the bloodstream. The young worms develop in the mosquitoes while the adult male and female inhabit humans. The microfilaria, transmitted by the infected mosquito, penetrates deeply into the skin. The female worms and eggs lodge in the lymphatic vessels. Although they disperse throughout the body, they prefer to localize in the lymph vessels and nodes. Localized, the adult worms mature, and the females discharge microfilariae, which in the case of the mature female filariae may measure up to 100 mm long and 0.3 mm in width. This may reveal anatomic manifestations (e.g., swelling of the organs). After a period of latency, the micro filariae gain access to the bloodstream, where they may be picked up by an insect vector.[40] The larvae develop in the mosquito and egress the proboscis, upon biting. The most harmful of the filaria is *filaria bancrofti,* which may (besides elephantiasis) cause lymph abscesses, varicose groin glands, and other diseases of the lymph system. *Filaria bancrofti* is common in tropical or subtropical regions and may be prevented by controlling the mosquitoes, which harbor the young worms.

*River Blindness* is another problem deserving attention. About 25 million persons have become blind from preventable diseases in tropical countries. Some people become blind because of lack of Vitamin A in the diet, while others are because of diseases transmitted by intermediate hosts, in this case the mosquito and the *blackfly*.

Rivers are important natural resources in an industrializing environment. For example, they serve as cheap and valuable transportation arteries; through irrigation they are used to overcome water shortages in farming; the muddy bottoms may be mined to supply rich earth *(loess)* for agriculture[41]; fishing provides employment and income to riverine populations; and they may be harnessed for hydroelectric power.

When rivers are colonized by *blackflies*, some of these economic activities by local populations are jeopardized. Employment activities are abandoned, family incomes disappear, families are distressed and dislocated, and local economies are depressed. This was the case in the Volta river basin in the mid-1970s, where once-thriving riverine communities became uninhabitable. Robin M. Henig, captured this crisis as follows:

The land along the Volta had become uninhabitable. Once known for its thriving communities, this region of Africa was becoming known instead for its "macabre processions" the tragic sight of young children serving as seeing-eye guides for craggy old men and women who had become blind in midlife. What made these pairings especially brutal to witness was the knowledge that the children, too, would very possibly be struck blind themselves in a matter of a few years.[42]

Onchocerciasis (river blindness), caused by microfilariae, may lead to disturbances in vision or total blindness. It produces skin irritations and nodules and may affect the conjunctiva, eyeball, and optic nerve.

Unlike a typical mosquito that breeds and lives out its entire life within a radius of one or two kilometers, the blackflies can be long rangers. Blackflies *(simuliidae)* breed in turbulent, well-oxygenated water, such as waterfalls, river rapids, and other places where the river runs fastest. Where their breeding grounds are remote, blackflies have been known to command a flight range of up to 500 to 600 kilometers. They are prepared to travel this much distance just to meet their human hosts, because these flies must feed on warm blood to survive.[43] These species are generally daytime biters and attack both birds and mammals.[44] Onchocerciasis is associated with inflammatory lesions in kidneys, spleen, liver, and lungs.[45]

## NOTES

1. Jeffrey Sachs, "The Limits of Convergence," *The Economist*, June 14, 1997, p. 22.

2. R.R. Askew, *Parasitic Insects* (New York: American Elsevier Publishing Company 1971), pp. 99–100.

3. P.F. Mattingly, *The Biology of Mosquito-Borne Disease* (London: George Allen and Unwin, 1969), p. 58. West African Negro (as opposed to Bantu) peoples show remarkable immunity to *vivax* malaria. This holds true for the descendants in the New World. *P. vivax* is largely absent in West Africa. *P. ovale* is more common, especially in the humid and forested areas.

4. Ibid. Infection is passed as a sporozoite into the blood of humans with the saliva of a biting anopheline mosquito. It lodges in the liver cells and then into the bloodstream, where these pathogens infest and debilitate the host by multiplying (an asexual cycle). Toxic products are released into the blood stream as a result of the metabolism. These toxins cause fever. It is in the bloodstream that they are also sucked by mosquitoes. In mosquitoes (a sexual cycle) the pathogens eventually lodge in the salivary glands. *Plasmodium malariae* is quite similar to *P. vivax*, but its asexual cycle takes three days and causes quartan malaria. The third form causes malaria in humans is *P. falciparum*. It differs from the first two pathogens mentioned because of a larger erythrocytic cycle and affects deep-lying blood vessels instead of peripheral vessels. They may block these vessels with fatal consequences.

5. Ibid., p. 50. In the case of *Aedes*, male mosquitoes have the ability to seek out females for themseves, from a range of approximately ten inches.

6. Ibid., p. 50; R.C. Shannon, 1931. "On the classification of Brazilian Culicidae with special reference to those capable of harboring the yellow fever virus."

7. Stanley L. Robbins and Ramzi S. Cotran, *Pathologic Basis of Disease* (Philadelphia: W.B. Saunders Company, 1979), p. 460. Four species of plasmodia (malaria) commonly infect people. *P. falciparum* (most virulent) causes malignant tertian malaria or falciparum malaria, *P. vivax* and *P. ovale* cause benign tertian malaria and *P. malariae* produces quartan malaria. *P. knowlesi* is also implicated in some cases of malaria.

8. Ibid., p. 459.

9. Malaria may also be transmitted by transfusion or contaminated hypodermic needles.

10. Mattingly, *The Biology of Mosquito-borne Disease*, p. 42.

11. "Malaria," in J.R.M. Kunz and A.J. Finkel, eds., *The American Medical Association Family Medical Guide* (New York: Random House, 1987), p. 125.

12. Askew, *Parasitic Insects*, p. 51.

13. George Rosen, *A History of Public Health* (Baltimore, MD: Johns Hopkins University Press, 1993), p. 302. This was the conclusion of the Yellow Fever Commission accepted in 1901. Measures along this line were effected in Havana. Within one year yellow fever was wiped out, and it never reappeared.

14. Mattingly, *The Biology of Mosquito-borne Disease*, p. 57. The following statement sheds light on the many possibilities:

P. falciparum was . . . the cause of widespread and highly lethal malaria . . . in southern Europe. It was responsible for severe epidemics . . . P. vivax . . . about the middle of the nineteenth century it began to retreat . . . it is believed, because of improved methods of agriculture involving the reclamation of marshland and the stabling of cattle which provided concentrated alternative host populations for the vector. Improvements in domestic lighting and hygiene may also have helped by reducing the numbers of vectors hibernating in houses.

Endemic malaria had been wiped out from much of Great Britain and much of northwest Europe by the dawn of this century. Besides fortuitous introductions and accidental infections, the whole of Europe is said to have been free of malaria throughout 1967.

15. Ibid., pp. 137–139.

16. *News Views,* College of Agriculture and Environmental Sciences, Rutgers University, New Brunswick, NJ, January 1968, in Ruth Winter, *Poison in Your Food* (New York: Crown Publishers, 1969), p. 32.

17. "Mass-reared Insects Get Fast-food," *Agricultural Research,* June 1997, pp. 4–7. It is possible to commercially breed an army of hundreds of thousands to even millions of insects and release them in selected habitats where they can feed on other insects that are considered pests. Typically such insects will demonstrate good search qualities and high kill rates and will not attack other beneficial insects. Beneficial predators have been used for decades for insect control. Mass production and distribution depends on more cost-effective artificial diets.

18. *The Economist,* August 1, 1998, p. 69.

19. Geoffrey A.T. Targett and Brian M. Greenwood, "Impregnated Bednets," *World Health,* no. 3, May-June 1998, pp. 10–11.

20. "Florida Fights Medflies with . . . More Medflies," *Christian Science Monitor,* July 30, 1997. In the case of the Mediterranean fruit flies, agriculture officials (in Florida) used Air Force cargo planes. Flying at about 2,000 feet above affected areas, sterilized male medflies were released in the millions. This was an effective method in the battle to protect the $53 billion food industry. The medflies were believed to have originated from equatorial Africa.

21. The *Aedes* subgenus *Chaetocruiomya* breeds in very narrow tree holes with apertures an inch or less in diameter, sometimes forming long pipes and located in very slender branches. Larval habitats of mosquitoes with container habits include snail shells, large tanks or reservoirs with absolutely clean edges, bamboo habitats (vertical), cut bamboos (horizontal), decaying coconuts, split cocoa pods, and split or rodent-gnawed coconuts. Cut pawpaw stems may teem with *Culex* (*Culiciomya*) larvae. Alternative larval habitats for some tree-hole breeders include heavily shaded places containing dead leaves with typical tree-hole fauna. Underground habitats may include crab holes, wells and cisterns, cesspits, pit latrines, and septic tanks.

22. Mattingly, *The Biology of Mosquito-borne Disease,* p. 76.

23. *MacMillan Illustrated Animal Encyclopedia,* p. 514.

24. Ibid.

25. Winter, *Poison in Your Food,* p. 32.

26. *MacMillan Illustrated Animal Encyclopedia,* pp. 38–52.

27. Mary E. Gibson, "The Identification of Kala Azar and the Discovery of Leishmania Donovani," *Medical History Quarterly Journal,* 27, p. 203.

28. Bengal, Sanitary Commission, First Annual Report, 1864–1865, pp. 58–59.

29. Bengal, Proceedings of the Government of Bengal in the Medical Department, no. 34, May 1869, p. 19.

30. Ibid., no. 52, February 1870, pp. 32–33.

31. Sir Leonard Rogers, *Happy Toil: Fifty-five Years of Tropical Medicine* (London: Muller, 1950), p. 29.

32. "The 'Kala-azar' or Black Death of the Garo Hills," *Indian Medical Gazette* 20 (1885): 83–84, in Gibson, "The Identification of Kala Azar and the Discovery of Leishmania Donovani," pp. 203–215.

33. Ibid., p. 212.

34. Askew, *Parasitic Insects*, p. 48.

35. Robin Marantz Henig, *The People's Health: A Memoir of Public Health and Its Evolution at Harvard* (Washington, DC: Joseph Henry Press, 1997), pp. 40–41.

36. Robbins and Cotran, p. 463.

37. Mattingly, *The Biology of Mosquito-borne Disease*, p. 63.

38. J.R. Brown, in H.J. O'D. Burke-Gaffney, *The History of Medicine in the Commonwealth* (function organized by the Faculty of the History of Medicine and Pharmacy, and held at the Royal College of Physicians of London on 23 September 1966).

39. Robbins and Cotran, *Pathologic Basis of Disease*, p. 469.

40. Ibid.

41. Michael W. Fox, *Agricide: The Hidden Crisis that Affects Us All* (New York: Schocken Books, 1986), p. 63.

42. Henig, *The Peoples Health*, p. 45.

43. Ibid., p. 46

44. B.O.L. Duke, *Onchocerciasis*, in Robbins and Cotran, *Pathologic Basis of Disease*, p. 470.

45. Ibid.

# 9

# Manufacturing in Africa at the Outset of Industrialization

A 1961 United Nations report stated that "The reason for emphasizing industrialization is that industrial development would absorb rural underemployed persons into those fields of production where higher productivity is possible without reducing total agricultural output."[1] Manufacturing is at the very heart of industrialization. It becomes a priority in countries that have decided to embark on industrialization. The hallmarks of manufacturing are domestic demand, input substitution, and export. Assuming sizable domestic markets, countries, endowed with natural resources, tend initially to lay emphasis on domestic demand, while countries with scarce resources may rely on international trade by importing raw materials and exporting finished products. In much of Africa, firms manufacturing consumer goods have generally predominated, unlike intermediate and capital-oriented goods manufacturing enterprises. Most of manufacturing in sub-Saharan Africa, in the last quarter century or so, pertained to consumer goods, while a small proportion of manufacturing pertained to areas such as chemicals and transportation equipment.

Although the manufacturing industry still deserved much attention, 47 percent of manufacturing export in 1970 from the developing countries of Africa went to other countries in Africa. However, by 1984 this share had plummeted to 24 percent.[2] A decomposition of data pertaining to output growth in manufacturing in some key countries indicated that growth in manufacturing was due to domestic demand rather than import substitution or export growth. The output growth data were as follows: Botswana 54 percent; Cameroon 55 percent; Kenya 69 percent; Nigeria 76 percent; Zimbabwe 72 percent. Domestic demand was also significant in Ivory Coast (Côte d'Ivoire) and Zambia.[3] Overall, according to a report in 1991, manufactured export contribution to total world trade by the countries in sub-Saharan Africa comprised only 1 percent.[4] While this shows that the proportion of export from this region has yet to appreciate, global market competition may not be taken for granted. This is especially the case, pertaining to the competitive positions of countries, such as South Korea, Taiwan, Hong Kong, and Singapore, which have been dominant players in manufactured export to developing countries.

It is, however, feasible for latent domestic manufacturing firms to retain or expand market shares in a competitive environment. Of the several methods available, one that serves as an appropriate illustration goes back to the early days of metropolitan industrialization. Then, some small manufacturers resorted to the strict craft standards and practices required of custom-made goods. Instead of engaging in what was then considered the manufacture of coarse and standardized goods. City firms prospered by manufacturing small-batch custom items to the specifications of their many clients. This method of production also prevailed in some large firms. In this way, there was diversity in the marketplace and firms engaging in manufacturing specialty items avoided competition from mass-produced import goods. In the case of fancy items, such as in clothing, hats, caps, and jewelry, firms could easily adapt to the seasonal changes in fashion.[5]

Besides trade agreements and strategic government interventions, other methods to increase export may include the introduction of new or innovative products. In the case of Japan, such products were in synthetic fibers, yarns, fabrics, plastics, electrical machinery (generators, transformers, motors), electric lamps,[6] television receivers, and motor vehicles.[7] Another method is through export price competitiveness, which may be aided by falling prices for raw materials. Export may also be enhanced through structural changes in manufacturing—coupling foreign technology with domestic research and development (R&D), as well as heavy investments in business plant and equipment.

When domestic demand is the modus operandi for manufacturing, the income elasticities for the various outputs must not be discounted in sustaining growth. For example, the following products tend to be income elastic: fats and oil; sugar; footwear; clothing and household textiles; fuel; light; water; household goods; purchases of transportation equipment; books, newspapers, and magazines. Although expanding markets (economies of scale) is a source of industrial growth, in a given country, market expansion *per se* is not likely to *increase* the consumption of alcoholic beverages, housing service, and education.

Besides manufacturing for domestic consumption, manufacturing for export markets is also important to the economy. In this context, the export sector is important because of several reasons that include the following: It generates foreign exchange earnings that are vital in capital investments, in managing exchange rates, in debt servicing, and in purchasing intermediate goods, consumer goods, and substitute items. When a nation depends on imported raw materials and food items, it is usually an indication that its well-being, as an industrializing nation, is likely to be determined by her success in exporting finished products. By the same token, selling manufactured products profitably abroad when such products are high in labor content and low in raw material content is easier for an industrializing nation. Growths in markets tend to bring about opportunities for greater specialization— both among and within industries—and opportunities for establishments and firms to become larger without impairing the competitive pressure. Small firms find opportunities that transform them into larger units, and sustain longer runs and larger transactions.

The manufacturing industries in some countries in Africa still face problems that may sometimes be mind-boggling. These problems have systematic solutions in a dynamic and industrializing environment. The problems were resolved or are being resolved in other places in the world, including a handful of countries in Africa. In order to take advantage of the opportunities for industrialization, the post-1960 infant industries will be brought up to speed with contemporary business practice. The agricultural sector will have to grow beyond the idea of "food self-sufficiency" adopted during the era of the Green Revolution. Tractors, CAD/CAM,[8] machine tools, spectrophotometers, electron microscopes and similar devices will be ranked among *priorities*. There is room for manufacturing in both the traditional and the modern sectors in an industrializing environment. For workers to take advantage of these opportunities, some  considerations, here, will include overall attitude toward work. In so many words, this refers to discipline at work, punctuality and orderliness, alertness, adaptability, ambition, the readiness and willingness to experiment and to change, aptitude for cooperation,  hygiene and medical care, nutrition, and so on. Institutional considerations will include development of such institutions, effectiveness of pertinent agencies, credit, infrastructure of voluntary organizations, trade, employment, and so forth.

Well harnessed, import substitution becomes a fillip to manufacturing specifically and to industrialization overall. In much of Africa, however, the effects of import substitution were not substantial. Import substitution manufacturing still commanded a high import content with a fixed focus on consumer goods. In some places, manufacturing outfits often operated below capacity, and ultimately folded in the face of economic adversity. In *Nigeria,* for example, firms that had operated under the import substitution regime of the 1970s engaged in assembly or screwdriver activities. Although manufacturing increased rapidly, such activities contributed a smidgen of indigenously value-added aid to employment. The overall effect was to negate subsequent industrial expansion, in the early 1980s. Between 1986 and 1988, conditions ameliorated and manufacturing contributed a larger proportion of GDP, which grew at 8 percent. In Democratic Republic of Congo (Zaire), import substitution began in earnest between 1969 and 1972. Manufacturing, through the years, was focused on consumer goods such as food processing, textile manufacturing, beer, cigarettes, metal working, woodworking, and auto assembly. Problems encountered along the way included scarcity of foreign exchange, limited or unavailable spare parts, limited access to international markets, questionable management practices, and a domestic market with little expendable income. Although the Democratic Republic of Congo (also known informally as Congo Kinshasa) had demonstrated a penchant for massive industrial and energy projects, interlinkages were weak, and  the rural sector and transportation were marginalized. As a result, throughout the 1980s most manufacturing operations were underutilized, averaging around one-third of their capacity. Some outfits of multinational corporations (for example, General Motors assembly plant and Goodyear tire plant) had problems competing with cheap imports that were sometimes smuggled into the country or technically qualified as exempt from import duties. As in many other countries in Africa, the import contents of manufactured goods were high. To fill the void created, because of unaffordable or unavailable domestic goods, the traditionally numerous domestic entrepreneurs operating micro-outfits (often three or four employees), and medium-size businesses availed themselves to unfolding opportunities. Such operations produced a wide range of goods, including furniture, clothes, crafts, food, and even vehicle chassis. In 1981, manufactures comprised 9 percent of GDP. By 1987 and 1988, conditions were not very promising in Zaire, and the contributions were much lower, at 1 percent and 1.7 percent of GDP, respectively. [9]

In *Egypt,* efforts at expanding manufacturing were outward looking, intended to enhance self-reliance through import substitution. The industrial sector did, therefore, discount comparative advantage in capital investment decisions. An example was in the areas of steel and chemicals. The costs, by definition, were relatively high. However, comparative advantage changed during the period spanning 1965 and 1985, as domestic resource cost for steel fell. This fall in cost was attributable to a learning curve, increased skills of workers, discovery of better quality raw materials, and improved economies of scale. Import substitution in Egypt began during the interwar years. Industrial output rose by 40 percent between 1939 and 1946 and by 63 percent during the boom years of 1946 and 1951. The high growth rates occurred mainly because the manufacturing industry was generally still in its latent stage. In the 1970s and the 1980s, manufacturing output increased as well, almost doubling in value between 1980 and 1985. In the 1980s, in Egypt, the most profitable firms were those engaged in the production of beverages, light tools, electronic products, printing, and apparel. Firms with the highest productivity rates were in food-processing operations, such as sugar, oil, fodder, canned fruits, and vegetables. [10]

*Singapore* is an example of a country with hardly any other resources besides people. Yet, at the dawn of the third millennium, the country's industrialization effort was so successfully carried out that it can choose the companies that may invest in the city-state. Some companies already established there were politely entreated to move to other developing neighboring countries, where their economic contributions were more suited. This long-established trading post, lacking the hinterlands characteristic of most other developing countries, had become a capital-intensive and high-tech manufacturing economy, flush with capital.

In Singapore, industrialization began in earnest in 1961, with import substitution, and later shifted to export-oriented industrialization. Also in 1961 an economic development board was established as the government's executive agency. This board was to coordinate the functions of the different branches of government as they related to industry and provide services to investors, both foreign and domestic. Industrialization was coaxed and directed through industrial investment promotion, development of an industrial infrastructure and facilities, feasibility studies, project evaluations, and tax incentives' administration. The first phase of industrialization was by import substitution. However, this phase, which ran through most of the 1960s, did not sustain manufacturing growth as had been initially envisioned. This was because other sectors of the economy were stagnating at the time and this city-state's small domestic market turned out to be a limiting factor. The next phase was export-oriented industrialization. In retrospect, import substitution was perhaps not the necessary foundation for the takeoff of the subsequent export-oriented industrialization although it eased the transition. In any case, several specialized state agencies proliferated that handled different aspects of industrialization, spanning education and technical training, land development and export promotion.

In 1968, the economic development board's technical division became a development agency, which operated industry-specific training centers. Here, in plant training facilities, crash training programs were offered to technicians and school dropouts who wanted to upgrade their skills. Technical courses were also introduced in the curriculum for secondary schools. Technically related educational institutions were established, such as vocational institutes, technical colleges, and polytechnics. At the university level, the engineering faculty was expanded. Overseas training was eased, and immigration of persons with technical and professional skills was encouraged. With the oversight of the economic board, industrial infrastructure and facilities were developed. To reduce capital outlays and the time required to establish a new industrial venture, industrial estates were established, with already-built and fully serviced standard factories that were later sold or rented. Information was made available to the manufacturing community, coupled with technical and consultant services. Offices were established in foreign countries to promote and provide assistance to prospective investors. In the second phase of industrialization, that is after 1967, a unit of the economic development board, responsible for industrial research, was spun into a separate institute for standards and industrial research. Another unit, an export promotion center, became part of a new government international trading company.

Labor-intensive export-oriented industrialization yielded significant results by 1973. Export increased to 53.6 percent in 1970, from 30.5 percent in 1967, led by new export-oriented industries (petroleum refining, transport equipment, and oil rigs, and electronic products and components). Growth in manufacturing had sped up, and by 1972 contributed to the full employment of labor. With full employment in 1972, the government formed a tripartite council, which issued national wage guidelines, to ensure orderly wage increases. A compulsory national savings and pension fund system was established, through which the government could affect labor costs, by varying the proportion of contributions from wages by employees and employers alike. Through this scheme, the government ably held down real wages and labor cost during the period spanning 1973 and 1979. As a result real wages and labor costs were below real productivity growth, determined by the free market forces of demand and supply. Here, therefore, low real wages and labor costs enabled labor-intensive export manufacturers and labor-intensive industries overall to remain competitive longer than would be expected under dynamics of free market forces.

In addition, the withdrawal of liquidity from the system enabled an environment of low inflation and appreciating exchange rate, within a regime of a managed float, in an open economy. On the one hand, such currency appreciation benefitted manufacturers, because imported raw materials and other industrial supplies were cheap. On the other hand, it challenged the competitiveness of exporters. Singapore could offset chronic trade deficits with large services account surplus, and with substantial net positive inflows of foreign direct investments. Generally, export-oriented industrialization also meant increased national exposure to global economic forces. The test of resiliency to extraneous forces came with the 1973 OPEC oil crises, and global recession in 1974–1975, which affected export-manufacturing industries. Several businesses were compelled to downsize, to adjust to these adverse economic environments. This outcome occasioned introspection and reevaluation of the achievements thus far, under labor-intensive export industrialization. The plan, to embark on higher-value-added output manufacturing using less labor-intensive processes and service activities, was shelved until 1979, when the government embarked on capital-intensive high-tech manufacturing.[11]

*Taiwan,* had problems with the economic climate in the 1940s and 1950s, which mirrored those of Africa, in many respects, during the last quarter century or so. Such problems in Taiwan included a severely overvalued currency, an economy dominated by agricultural commodity production, and an inflationary rate that reached 3,500 percent. It has been maintained in some quarters that Taiwan may not be an appropriate example for Africa to emulate because efforts in export, which prolonged economic expansion in the 1960s and 1970s were the result of fortunate timing.[12]

In any case, such expansion provided a convenient pad for wealth accumulation, and after 1972 Taiwan became very competitive in manufacturing. What is significant about Taiwan's transformation is that the economic policy stressed stability over liberalization. Essentially, Taiwan was more concerned with the climate and not the weather. Also, Taiwan, until 1968, relied substantially on aid from abroad, which was applied in filling the gaps in domestic savings and foreign exchange. U.S. aid financed at least 40 percent of import between 1950 and 1957, thus enabling Taiwan to carry out postwar reconstruction and expansion of the human and physical infrastructure. Aid financed about 40 percent of annual capital formation, 37 percent of infrastructure development, and 26 percent of human capital development between 1950 and 1965. Most import, financed under aid, comprised capital equipment, and more than 73 percent of commodity aid came as raw materials ready for industrial processing.

Factories in Taiwan were decentralized. Here, public investments in roads and railways reduced distances from village to town. This meant farmers could keep pace with urban dwellers and supplement their incomes by working in urban factories. In agriculture, factors such as investment in research, protecting farmers from risk, and an available supply of fertilizers increased farm productivity and contributed to support industrial growth in the 1950s and 1960s. Agriculture, therefore, served as a market for industrial goods (such as powered tillers and pumps), supplied the labor force with cheap rice and manufacturers with inputs for processing. Taiwan initially focused on primary import substitution (agricultural diversification) and then shifted emphasis to industrial manufacturing.

Much of the growth in the industrial sector was linked to export. The share of industrial products in export rose, from 8 percent in 1952 to 83 percent in 1972. Here, nontariff barriers had the advantage of reducing information uncertainty, increasing predictability and enhancing market stability. Non tariff barriers lowered transactional costs associated with unclear information, while quotas and other quantitative restrictions enhanced predictability. Export promotion incentives included: duty drawbacks; export-merchandise insurance; low interest rates; short-term loans; export finance credit; export-quality inspection; and marketing assistance, by branch offices, to export companies. Taiwan also established one of the world's first export processing zones, in 1965, to encourage technological advance and expand export. Through bonded factories outside the zones and a variety of export incentives, export activity was promoted nationwide.

However, Taiwan did not cling to its static comparative advantage in cheap labor and agriculture. During the 1960s and 1970s, the technology policy encouraged diffusion and adaptation, rather than outright invention. By purchasing used equipment or secondhand technology from a leader, Japan, Taiwan could expand production by following the technology curve and product cycle. By the early 1970s, however, Taiwan was losing the competitive edge in low-cost labor. It became evident that highly skilled specialists in natural science and engineering were needed at that juncture in industrial transformation.[13] Then afterward, the new focus was growth led by technological innovation and increased automation. In 1973, to enhance research and development efforts, an industrial technology institute was established.

Throughout the 1950s, foreign investment in Taiwan was negligible, until the 1960s when policy changes encouraged such investments. Unlike the 1960s, the government was more selective in the types of foreign investments approved in the 1970s. Foreign investments were reoriented primarily toward export, especially in areas where Taiwan was deficient in critical technologies. Overall, the least proportion of foreign investments were in labor-intensive industries, such as agriculture and forestry, paper and paper products, food processing, and in construction, transportation and banking. The highest proportion of foreign investments was in electronics, metal products and machinery, and chemicals. Export requirements ensured that foreign-established manufacturing firms would maintain a sharp and competitive edge internationally, while a local content requirement coaxed foreign investors to help upgrade domestic suppliers to international standards.

Manufacturing thrives in an environment that encourages appropriate investments in infrastructure, in productive facilities in business, in knowledge and human resources. Here economic policy—metaphorically—makes the patient feel good. It makes and keeps the patient healthy. It creates an economic environment in which the economy can grow; acquire resistance to infection, injury, and disease, acquire the ability to adapt and to change rapidly; and to stay competitive. This explains the enigma in the triumphs of Germany and of Japan. Both were successful as long as they stuck to policies that focused on creating the economic climate and as long as they largely downplayed the dynamism of the economic weather.[14]

Computer Industry in *India:* The computer industry began in earnest in India when the government articulated its computer goals pertaining to corporate organization, market structure, and technology transfer. Although meager progress was made at the outset, significant leaps in computer technology were eventually made. Some early techniques employed were maybe questionable, by contemporary archetypes, however, overall, India's success in a multinational environment smacks of a realistic standard to which countries in Africa might aspire.

In the mid 1960s, the goals in India pertaining to the computer industry included the following: equity participation in foreign computer subsidiaries; using domestic companies to supply most of India's computing needs, with foreign units ephemerally supplying exotic technologies and large systems; having accesses to and manufacturing the most advanced systems available internationally. The dominant international computer operations, then in India, were IBM (International Business Machines) and ICT, the appellation for Britain's International Computers and Tabulators, Ltd.. (In fact both companies have common origins).[15] During this period, in the United Kingdom, two other important computer companies were emerging: English Electric, and Elliott-Automation. In 1967, English Electric bought Elliott-Automation, and the following year English Electric merged with ICT, to form International Computers Ltd.(ICL). International Computers and Tabulators, Ltd., therefore, became ICL, the largest computer manufacturer outside United States, with an unofficial preferred-supplier status in the public sector. In India, besides private wholly Indian systems-engineering firms, in the 1970s, the only wholly Indian computer enterprise was the central government's Electronic Corporation of India Limited (ECIL).

India's policy hegemony in computers ran aground at IBM, when India advised IBM in 1966 and 1968 to share ownership of its local activities. According to IBM, such arrangements were not feasible because of the highly internationalized and interdependent nature of its operations, which required a centralized control. When India pressed again in 1973 and 1974, IBM opted to pull out of India, rather than submit to equity participation and other controls of its local operations. As a result, IBM, instead of sharing equity with Indian nationals, settled the issue by offering new and high levels of manufacturing activities that would be useful in fetching foreign exchange earnings, in technology transfer, and in direct technical assistance to India's data-processing programs. In 1977, when India, again, brought up the issue of shared equity, IBM announced pulling out of India. In 1978, therefore, India lost the world's premiere computer enterprise. This departure posed a potential problem of withdrawal of service, since many systems in India were sourced singularly from IBM. This void was eventually filled when ECIL's products became available, and with the establishment of a computer maintenance corporation. In ICL's case, then the other dominant international computer operation, India gained ground: although the company initially did not relinquish control of the sales unit, India nevertheless succeeded in gaining 40 per cent ownership in the manufacturing unit. In the 1970s, the Indian government resisted Burroughs' efforts to establish a wholly-owed subsidiary. The result was a joint venture in 1977, with Tata Enterprises, each owning 50 percent of the new company. By the end of the 1970s a few Indian firms had emerged, designing and assembling systems. The government's ECIL employed 1,000 workers, or so; New Indian entrants employed about 1,900 workers, while Burroughs and ICL employed 600 employees.

Overall, therefore, the government by the late the 1960s had ensured effective Indian participation in ownership and direction of local units of foreign computer firms. However, India was not as successful initially in attaining the second goal, that is in fostering indigenous sources of supply. In fact, virtually no progress was made in this domain during the first six years. Between 1967 and 1972, India's ECIL was responsible for only 8.5 percent of all the systems installed or a market share that was perhaps 3.4 percent. On the other hand, during the same period IBM was responsible for roughly 75 per cent of all the systems installed, consistent with its market share in the pre computer policy period (i.e., 1960 to 1966). During the period spanning 1973 and 1977, ECIL's market share bolstered, and the company was the single largest systems supplier in India. But remarkably, other indigenous enterprises increasingly took on extremely important roles in the computer industry, and by 1980 had the giant market share. It is also noteworthy that the non-ECIL domestic industry had cost advantages. For example, in 1978, the *per-bit cost* of the main memory (used by the *central processor*) of an *ECIL TDC-316* was the rupee equivalent of US$0.14, while the per-bit cost of main memory of the *DCM Galaxy 11* was the rupee equivalent of US$0.06.[16] ECIL's systems, on the other hand, suffered a cost disadvantage and long delays, tallied at between 18 and 24 months. As a result, its market shares rapidly shrunk to about 10 percent, or close to the peak in the period up till 1972. Although market shares plummeted with the number of systems installed, the number of installations was still high by a factor of about 7.5 relative to the period spanning 1967 and 1972.[17]

Overall, India's temporal (technological) lag increased from 1967–1972, relative to the pre policy period of 1960–1967. This lag was attributable to manufacturing efforts that oriented toward importing previously used systems for refurbishment at local facilities of foreign units and then renting these systems to Indian customers. Between 1973–1977, this technological regression was reversed, and was narrowing at the end of the decade. Here, the positive change was attributable to import as the major form of access to foreign-origin systems: These systems were technologically more sophisticated than the refurbished systems. In addition, the proliferation of the number of foreign computer firms in the developing world, was also characteristic in India by this time, coupled with overall falling costs of computer systems. In addition, the systems manufactured in India continued to improve technologically: In an environment of rapid technological change, computers were increasingly more powerful, and their component parts were less and less expensive in the market, coupled with new types of fabrication procedures.[18] By 1980, therefore, India was making inroads in achieving the goal of acquiring and producing technologically sophisticated data processing equipment. However, these gains derived mainly from activities in the private sector. India's range of opportunities was also affected by the emergence in the international computer industry, of small systems architectures (that is, minicomputers and microcomputers). At this time, inexpensive minicomputers could execute functions previously done by mainframes, while microcomputers coupled with the floppy disk that provided auxiliary storage at low cost could replace minicomputers. In other words, inexpensive microcomputers were competing with highly-priced minicomputers and similarly minicomputers in some cases competed with the expensive mainframes.

This new paradigm in the marketplace was a smack of reality check for India's strategy, in the 1970s, to fabricate (with increase levels of value-added) mini systems. Earlier, in 1971–1972, the government had revamped its computer strategy and supporting policies. The idea was to encourage the use of small systems, instead of focusing on large systems, after the government found out it was feasible to design and assemble these systems in India using imported components and peripherals. Accordingly, India's ECIL was to be the "crown national champion" of mini systems: ECIL and ICL were expected to satisfy the bulk of India's minicomputer requirements. New wholly indigenous entrants were, therefore, implicitly refrained from competition with ECIL, as the government actions restricted new enterprises in microcomputers. Wholly indigenous enterprises that wanted to enter the systems-engineering industry did not find India's policy hegemony in computers especially conducive. Many Indian users, however, were inclined to rational decision making in the marketplace, judging mainly on price and quality. Users, therefore, believing the microcomputers could substitute for minicomputers, provided by ECIL, purchased the former instead of the latter.

The result was a rapid denudation of ECIL's market share, in an environment of increasing import. However, the net effect was not as devastating, due to the earlier creation of an export processing zone. Here, firms could retain most of their foreign exchange earnings from export of non computer products, and components needed for their manufacturing programs. Burroughs, for example could finance import through its export of software and dot-matrix printers. Other foreign exchange costs (that is, ECIL's and to some extent ICL) could be defrayed by other methods that included earnings of foreign electronic firms at the export zone.

The 1980s in India saw more liberal economic policies, away from the strong central government controls in development, dominant in the 1970s. The new policies would negate the inability of India's scientific and technical apparatus to transfer technology to marketable goods, a factor that kept many Indian firms from being competitive in international markets. Relaxation of the import-substitution policies, designed therefore to encourage Indian firms, benefitted the electronic companies.[19] Most of the expansion took place in the production of computers and consumer electronics. By the mid-1990s India's engineering sector was large and varied, comprising about 12 percent of export. Computer production rose from 7,500 units in 1985 to 60,000 units in1988, reaching 200,000 units in 1992. Electronics and motor vehicles were the most dynamic areas and consumer electronics made up 30 per cent of total electronics production. Production in FY (financial year) 1990 included 5 million television sets, 6 million radios, 5 million tape recorders, 5 million electronic watches, and 140,000 video cassette recorders.[20] Banglalore, the capital of Karnataka, is a center for high-technology, and a site for major research and development. Here, much of the activity is carried out through collaborative arrangements with multinational corporations in the fields of aeronautics, communications, and machine tools. Around 1990, at least 100,000 people were employed by 3,000 companies in the electronics industry alone.

It seems incomplete to discuss computers manufacturing in an industrializing environment without mentioning *semiconductors*. This is because this is the age of semiconductors. They are practically everywhere, these days. It is therefore difficult to discuss manufacturing and simultaneously ignore these ubiquitous objects. The mystery of the computer industry and manufacturing, in particular, is embedded in chips. These chips, increasingly, have infiltrated manufacturing, uplifting humans to new pinnacles of vision and might. They may not be immediately discernible, but they are more scattered around us these days than previously. Semiconductors are not only used in computers, in airplane cockpits, in photocopying machines, and to run industrial robots, they have also been increasingly built into diverse devices, including household thermostats, digital cameras, programmable VCRs, and in controlling the operations and providing the displays of modern cars. A significant area in semiconductor applications, in recent years has been in communications; network infrastructures have been enhanced by the proliferation of Internet and wireless communication. Here, two primary technologies may be identified as central to this process: the semiconductor chip and the *satellite*.[21] This has led to the emergence of an amorphous, new, and vigorous industry (coupling computers and telecommunications) in an increasingly globally interlaced economy. This global economy values a rapid information exchange and, therefore, a greater bandwidth (for example, in coaxial cable, and fiber-optics), presaging opportunities in semiconductor applications in both industrial and industrializing environments. Here, semiconductors can convert analog signals into digital signals, in real time. Analog chips (*Amplifiers, Voltage regulators, Interface circuits, Data converters*) process signals from real world phenomena such as light, heat, and pressure, useful in industrial and other applications. Digital semiconductors (*Microchips, Memory chips, Logic devices*) process information in binary form (series of 0s and 1s). So far, about half the value of semiconductor businesses have derived from the computing end of the market. Overall, semiconductors have contributed enormously, in increasing productivity in manufacturing. They have opened new production opportunities and are altering existing cost relationships, including efficiencies in information gathering, transmission, analysis, and storage. Their momentum to increase productivity rapidly in Africa during industrialization may not be discounted. Here, the experiences of some countries in the Asia and Pacific region are testaments of lurking possibilities in industrializing environments.

The computer industry may be segmented into Systems Manufacturers, Peripheral Equipment Suppliers, Software Companies, Service Companies, Supplies Manufacturers, and Data Communications Companies.[22] It may also be subdivided into computer makers, semiconductor manufacturers, and semiconductor-equipment companies.[23] Computer makers rely on semiconductor makers for raw materials (chips), to manufacture advanced products. Semiconductor makers, sell their products to computer makers, and a wide range of industries, including telecommunications, data communications, industrial, automotive, consumer entertainment, and electronics.

However, most of the chips are sold to original equipment manufacturers (that is, companies manufacturing computers and other electronic products). Semiconductor-equipment companies are virtually invisible to the public and are known within the industry and by investors. Most companies in this industry can be small, efficient, and specialized in making, say, the best possible chips, disk drives, or video display devices. However, some companies may also be big, efficient, and integrated.

In Japan, as factories became bigger and more efficient, producers learnt how to eliminate defects which translated into fewer flawed chips being discarded, and therefore lower cost per finished chip. In the 1970s, 85 percent of all the machines necessary in making semiconductors around the world came from North America. At this time, 80 percent of those used in Japan were also from the North America. However by 1985, the semiconductor industry had evolved in such a way in Japan as to promote linkages with other Japanese companies (for example, in supplying chip-making equipment). In recent years, growth in semiconductor consumption was faster in the Asia and Pacific region than in other locales. This growth was attributable to rapid economic expansion in countries such as Singapore, Taiwan, Malaysia, and Korea. Here, Taiwan emerged as the largest source of silicon for "fabless" semiconductor companies. A fabless company is an appellation for an outfit, which does not construct, own, or operate semiconductor fabrication facilities. Instead, such companies focus on designing innovative chips, while relying on contract manufacturers, or foundry partners, to manufacture their product. This method, when differentiated from traditional manufacturing companies, meant higher profit margins and impressive free cashflows. However, there are inherent detractors, in this industry, which may be seen as notoriously cyclical and volatile. For example, in times of rapid industry growth fabless firms run the risk of becoming chipless, since foundry space may be limited.

Unlike several other industries, semiconductors have nothing to do with strategic industries instead they depend on ideas. This may sound mysterious. This phenomenon is reminiscent of the nineteenth century, when no country could be a serious economic contender if it could not make engines, steel, and machine tools. Similarly, no country can expect fully to assert itself economically, today, without engaging in the business of manufacturing and using semiconductors. The Chinese and Mexicans recognized much earlier this dynamic of industrialization in the nineteenth century. Without a determination of the extent to which this dynamic has been widely recognized in Africa, it is only proper to ponder: What are the chances that *some* computers and telecommunications equipment that have been pouring into Africa, in recent years, will degenerate into tomorrow's equivalent of yesterday's (erstwhile) Soviet tractors and similar equipment, abandoned and rusting all over West Africa?[24]

Again, countries such as India, Singapore, and Taiwan (mentioned earlier), may cast more light on this environment. High-technology in semiconductors is a contemporary dynamic, which may not be discounted in an industrializing environment in Africa. Here, therefore, the role of the government in nurturing high-technology is crucial. The government does not have to own and run semiconductor factories, but the government can provide a conducive environment (for example a reliable market) that otherwise will not exist. Heavy involvement of government may be a determinant, in a high-technology manufacturing and industrializing environment.[25]

## NOTES

1. United Nations, ECAFE, *Economic Bulletin for Asia and the Far East*, 12, no. 3 (December, 1961), p. 11., in Gunnar Myrdal, *Asian Drama*, Vol. 2 (New York: Twentieth Century Fund, 1968), p. 1153.

2. Roger Riddell, "The Future of the Manufacturing Sector," in Thomas M. Callaghy and John Ravenhill, ed., *Hemmed In: Responses to Africa's Economic Decline*(New York: Columbia University Press, 1994), pp. 225–226.

3. Ibid. In Côte d'Ivoire and Zambia, much of the growth in the 1960s *originated* from import substitution. In Zambia, import substitution surpassed domestic demand in the respective ratios of 55 percent and 44 percent.

4. E. Wayne Nafziger, "Japan's Industrial Development, 1868–1939: Lessons For Sub-Saharan Africa," in Howard Stein, ed., *Asian Industrialization and Africa: Studies in Policy Alternatives to Structural Adjustment* (New York: St. Martin's, 1995), pp. 80–81.

5. Walter Licht, *Industrializing America* (Baltimore: John Hopkins University Press, 1995), pp. 30–35.

6. The manufacturing of electrical machinery and apparatus was fairly well entrenched in Japan before 1914 and grew rapidly in the subsequent two decades. The electric lamp industry comprised three types of producers: (1) High-grade lamps manufactured by Tokyo Electric Company in a few large and well-equipped factories; (2) Standard lamps manufactured by about a dozen odd midsized firms, utilizing parts and materials sourced from specialist suppliers; (3) Cheap lamps, made to the orders of merchants, miniature bulbs, and automobile bulbs, usually manufactured by numerous small factories and workshops. Production outputs of the first two were mainly destined for the local markets, and most of the outputs of the small manufacturers were earmarked for export. The expansion of the industry was coupled with the rise in output of electrical power: G.C. Allen, *Japan's Economic Recovery* (London: Oxford University Press, 1958), pp. 100–101; see also *Survey of Japanese Finance and Industry*, July-August 1954, p. 3.

7. In the more recent past, to enhance manufacturing productivity, robots have been increasingly introduced in environments that can be extremely hazardous to human beings, for example, the robots do tasks within toxic gas atmospheres. Increasingly, industrial robots have been populating factories around the world, often doing narrowly specialized functions, such as spray painting, sanding, welding, drilling, and cutting operations on the assembly line. In vehicle manufacturing plants, they move parts from supply to assembly areas and even attach modules to the vehicle structure. In factories, robot vehicles may self-load and transport materials for considerable distances, stopping or navigating around an obstacle in their path, and unloading at the right points of delivery. Japanese manufacturers are prolific users of robots, unlike the American counterparts. Important considerations, in introducing these humanoids include cost-effectiveness and high quality. However, the danger may be in automating inefficiency, in a dynamic and rapidly changing environment. Robert J. Cone, *The New Technology Works* (Phoenix, AZ: Oryx Press, 1998), pp. 76–79.

8. CAD/CAM is the acronym for Computer Aided Design and Computer Aided Manufacturing. The CAD programs contain whole libraries of component designs and can generate detailed instructions for automated manufacturing equipment, including parts and lists, blueprints, and specifications. These CAD programs tend to shorten the time it takes to bring

a new product from concept to production, reduce human error, and help workers explore the envelope of design possibilities. They also enhance the creativity in product designs, pertaining to the practical realities of production, such as dimensions, material characteristics, and time constraints. An example is in designing braking systems for automobiles. The CAM programs guide automated equipment through the manufacturing process. The computer may use sensors to monitor the process, dispensing changes of direction and corrections, based on its analysis of the reported data. A CAD program can also verify whether designs meet regulatory standards. "Jaguar 'Puts the Brakes' to CAD," *Investor's Business Daily,* September 22, 1998, p. A10.

9. *Zaire: A Country Study* (Washington DC: GPO, 1994), p. 184.

10. Helen Chapin Metz, ed., *Egypt: A Country Study* (Washington DC: GPO, 1991), p. 204.

11. Linda Lim, "Foreign Investment, the State and Industrial Policy in Singapore," in Stein, ed., *Asian Industrialization and Africa,* pp. 205–238.

12. Deborah Brautigan, "The State as Agent: Industrial Development in Taiwan, 1952–1972," in Stein, ed., *Asian Industrialization and Africa*, pp. 145–181.

13. Li K.T., *The Evolution of Policy Behind Taiwan's Development Success* (New Haven, CT: Yale University Press, 1988).

14. Peter F. Drucker, *Post-Capitalist Society* (New York: Harper Business, 1993), pp. 165–167.

15. Both companies owe their origins to Herman Hollerith, inventor of the punched-card tabulating machine. Hollerith devised his tabulator while working for the United States Bureau of Census, and the machine was first used to process the 1890 census in the United States, and again in the 1911 United Kingdom census.

16. The *central processor* is the unit that performs computations and controls the computer system as a whole.

17. Based on data in: Om Vikas and L. Ravichandran, "Computerization in India: A Statistical Review," *Electronics: Information and Planning,* December 1978, pp. 318–51; India (Republic), Lok Sabha, Estimates Committee, *Sixty-sixth Report: Department of Electronics* (New Delhi: Lok Sabha, 1974), p. 101., in P. Gopalakrishnan and N.S. Narayanan, *Computers in India: An Overview* (Bombay: Popular Prakashan, 1975), pp. 133–42; *Annual Report of the Department of Electronics,* New Delhi, 1978, 1979, 1980, in Theodore H. Moran *Multinational Corporations: The Political Economy of Foreign Direct Investment* (Lexington: Lexington Books, 1989), pp. 60–61.

18. In integrated circuits, the tendency of improvements has been toward miniaturization (that is, increasing the density embedded within a chip) and learning to decrease the number of circuit destroying impurities in production facilities. Such advances have contributed to increase the rate at which integrated-circuits are produced. Consequently, performance has been increasing, while per-component costs for an integrated circuit have been dropping. The introduction of the integrated circuit in the 1960s, was a far cry from the years of germanium point-contact transistors (manufactured in the 1950s), and silicon planar transistors (in the late 1950s through the 1970s).

19. During this period, restrictions were lifted on technology and component import . Strict and time-consuming procedures for obtaining licenses were relaxed, and excise duties were reduced.

20. James Heitzman and Robert L. Worden, eds., *India: A Country Study* (Washington, DC: GPO, 1996), pp. 32–335.

21. Technological improvements pertaining to transponders (the relay components for transmissions within satellites) have significantly reduced the cost of information transmission over great and sometimes small, distances.

22. Computer system manufacturers make and ship complete systems, which include processors, memory, peripherals, software, and company standard products. Here, applications may include process control, communications systems, data collection, laboratory instrumentation, and factory test equipment. Independent peripheral equipment manufacturers make and ship peripheral, data entry, or terminal equipment but no central processing units. Independent software companies supply software to systems manufacturers and users who may need expertise or enhanced productivity in a particular area or who do not want to hire a permanent programming staff to handle a short-term heavy programming workload. Here, users get generalized standard software (utilities, compilers, operating systems, and so on). Service companies may be involved in data communication services, including timeshareing. They may offer on-line services such as interactive access to common files (for example, credit, ticket reservation, and stock market quotation services). Anthony Ralston and Edwin D. Reilly, Jr., eds., *Encyclopedia of Computer Science and Engineering* (New York :Van Nostrand Company, 1983), pp. 336–345.

23. James Fallows, *Looking at the Sun* (New York : Pantheon Books,1994), p. 30.

24. Irvin Kaplan, Margarita Dobert, James L. McLaughlin, Barbara J. Marvin, Donald P. Whitaker, *Area Handbook for Sierra Leone* (GPO: Washington, DC, 1976), p. 214. Also see Kenneth B. Taylor, "The Economic Impact of the Emerging Global Information Economy on Lesser Developed Nations," in Howard F. Didsbury, Jr., *The Global Economy: Today, Tomorrow, and the Transition* (Bethesda, MD: World Future Society, 1985), p. 150.

25. Anthony Ralston and Edwin D. Reilly, Jr., eds., *Encyclopedia of Computer Science and Engineering* (New York : Van Nostrand Company, 1983), pp. 353–355. See also Fallows, *Looking at the Sun*, p. 58.

10

# Manufacturing and Some Key Natural Resources: Insights for Industrialization in Africa

It is important at the outset to take stock of the available or feasible resource base in order to ease the course of industrialization. However, resources by themselves do not determine the pace and directions of positive changes.[1] In order to sustain surpluses for investment, the pace and directions tend to be functions of demand.[2] During the early stages of development, the new patterns of resource utilization generally tend to be shaped by the requirements of industrialization itself—by the need to amass capital goods such as plant, machinery, materials, and various forms of "social overhead," such as transport services, urban housing, and utilities.[3]

In the face of these increases and changes in demand, the danger will be inadequate supply of skilled labor. In industrial nations, this deficiency was generally overcome by refining and increasing or introducing capital-intensive methods, such as improved tooling, better explosives, perfection of mechanized pumping, drilling, hoisting, and handling equipment. Another danger is to allow the efficiencies inherent in technologies to mask the deficiencies in other areas. For example, masking deficiencies in farming technique and the limitations of the soil is possible, with improvements in farm implements. In this case, increased competition may be accompanied by declining yields, for example, of fruit trees, thus questioning the whole exercise of mechanization.[4]

During industrialization, technique and organization are not confined to manufacturing and distribution. Instead, they are extended to other areas such as energy, mining, agriculture, and forestry, thus adding economic significance to these resources. There is no reason to doubt that countries, poorly endowed with germane preconditions on the eve of industrialization, could actually meet with greater success than those inheriting superior starting points.

In the 1960s, many latent industries in Africa were protected from foreign competition. While a handful of individual factories and firms might have prospered, the rate of development, of whole industries have gyrated on their launching pads.[5] The aluminum, textile, and the iron and steel industries have yet to avail themselves to the extensive opportunities that lurk in the wings. For example, the aluminum industry in Ghana—the country's most conspicuous effort to promote an integrated capital-intensive aluminum industry, was based on the exploitation of her sizable bauxite reserves and hydroelectric potential. This plan was intercepted by global economic conditions and coupled with severe drought in Ghana, which impinged on local aluminum production. The discovery of reserves of bauxite in Australia and Brazil generated a world glut of the mineral, inducing a protracted recession in the aluminum trade. The arithmetic of the conflicting factors, of the prevailing circumstances considered, suggested that it would be cheaper to import semiprocessed alumina from Jamaica and South Korea than to rely on local supplies. Drought ultimately truncated the electricity-generating capacity of the Akosombo Dam, to the extent that the aluminum smelter it supplied was shut down, between 1983 and 1985. Aluminum production slowly recuperated in the wake of the shutdown. By the early 1990s, aluminum production and export were still considered less than optimal.[6]

## ELECTRICAL ENERGY

The production of minerals, like manufacturing in general, may require substantial supplies of *energy*. In fact, supplies of electrical energy should be organized so that manufacturing operates without significant interruption. In Ivory Coast, Nigeria, and other countries in Africa, droughts were impediments to the supply of hydroelectricity. In Ivory Coast, the lakes behind all five dams were nearly dried up. Electrical output fell by 18.3 percent causing blackouts in Abidjan, and productivity losses that were estimated at 35 percent in the industrial sector. Four turbines had to be shut down and the country relied on thermal energy. Four large gas-powered turbines were purchased in the drought of 1983–1984. In Nigeria electrical failures also wreaked havoc on the industrial sector, through a national grid linking many urban centers. This was as a result of the drought spanning 1977 and 1978. The water level of the Kainji Reservoir was significantly lowered during the drought, causing frequent blackouts. In manufacturing, work in process was disrupted, and machine operations were interrupted, reducing productivity. Some of these townships were previously served by diesel power stations. In Tunisia, the sources of energy were diversified: there were four steam-power plants, four hydroelectric plants, seven combustion turbine plants, and a few diesel plants. About 90 percent of the electricity was thermally generated, 2 percent was hydraulic, and 8 percent was produced by other means. In the 1970s and 1980s, demand for electricity increased at substantial rates. Plans to increase future supply included solar energy and a nuclear energy. The government at that time was contemplating also the use of coal instead of fuel oil and natural gas, even if it had to be imported, since oil and natural gas fetched more revenues as export products. In Egypt, it was expected that gas could be used mostly as an oil substitute. The total electrical power capacity was 21,000 megawatts and 35,200 in fiscal year (FY) 1981 and FY 1986, respectively. Twenty thousand megawatts of this total derived from the Aswan High Dam. The rest was supplied by thermal power. There was much anxiety in the air in 1988, when the profound negative ramifications of a drought in Ethiopia became apparent to the Egyptians. Most of the Nile waters originate in Ethiopia, and the drought there had significantly lowered the water levels in the Aswan High Dam's Lake Nasser, to the extent that it was beginning to threaten a complete shutdown of the turbines. This moment denoted the significance of diversifying sources of power supply. A constant source of power supply is *sine qua non* for industrial-scale manufacturing.

## CHEMICALS

Outside South Africa, and with perhaps the exception of a few countries, industrialization in Africa will require the dramatic expansion of the generally small chemical sectors. Such expansion will meet future domestic needs and will also cater to an export market. The *chemical industry* in Japan grew rapidly, especially chemical fertilizers and chemical products needed by the textile industries.[7] By 1937, Japan was competitive in most classes of chemicals, including nitrogenous fertilizers (especially ammonium sulphate), essential in the maintenance of agricultural output; sulphuric acid, used for manufacturing various chemicals and for processing in the textile and metal industries; caustic soda and soda ash, used for manufacturing rayon, glass, soap, dyestuffs, pharmaceuticals, plastics, and insecticides. After 1945, a greater proportion of fertilizers were manufactured using the gas process. Around this period, Japan not only satisfied its own needs in chemicals, but was soon able to establish an export trade amounting to half a million tons of chemicals per year.[8] Generally, government and business leaders agreed that the composition of Japan's output had to shift continually if living standards were to rise. In this regard, the Government played an active role in making these shifts, often anticipating industrial changes rather than reacting to them. After World War II, the initial industries that policy makers and the public felt were appropriate for the nation included, iron, steel, shipbuilding, the merchant marine, machine industries, heavy electrical equipment, and chemicals. Automobiles, petrochemicals, and nuclear energy were later added to this list and in the 1980s such industries as computers and semiconductors were also added. Government support for research and development surged in the 1980s, and government–industry collaboration in projects were also started. During the 1980s, government also promoted the managed decline of competitively troubled industries through measures such as tax breaks for corporations that retrained workers to work at other tasks. Such industries included textiles, shipbuilding, and chemical fertilizers. By the late 1980s, knowledge-intensive and high-technology industries had become prominent. Although other sectors were booming (such as fashion design, advertising, and management consulting), the government seemed indifferent in promoting such developments.

In Indonesia, much of the value of positive change in her initial industrial effort was based on increased processing of oil and gas. Indonesia's oil industry is one of the oldest in the world. Most mineral production exported to industrial nations was carried out after some degree of domestic processing. In the case of Indonesia, Japan was the primary importer. In some cases, Indonesia's mineral-intensive industries, such as steel and aluminum, relied on imported raw materials. A pertinent example was in 1989, when Krakatau Steel imported roughly 2 million tons of high-grade iron ore from Australia, and PT Indonesia Asahan Aluminum imported alumina from Australia. In 1989, the total value of her mineral export was US$10 billion, with almost 90 percent of the value deriving from oil and natural gas; mineral export comprised US$1.4 billion. Overall, Indonesia was a net exporter of minerals. In 1990, domestic consumption of petroleum increased to 50 percent of total production that year. In the same year, Indonesia was the world's largest producer of liquefied natural gas, with an export value of US$3.7 billion, or 20.6 million tons. Roughly 20 percent of the natural gas was used domestically, primarily in fertilizer plants, where it was processed into urea and ammonia. Overall, investment for industrial takeoff was characterized by government and private ventures with foreign partners, which in 1986 accounted for 40 percent of industrial output. Here, foreign investment was often crucial in the development of capital-intensive industries, and Japan, Hong Kong, and South Korea were the predominant investors. In several industries foreign corporations generally supplied technical assistance and arranged for domestic production under licensing agreements. They did not have direct equity participation in the domestic operation.[9]

Of course, the idea of establishing processing industries associated with mining is not new. Zambia long ago ceased exporting unprocessed copper and instead substituted a finished product—electrolytic refined copper. Liberia began producing iron ore pellets of high purity and uniformity that were much in demand for iron and steel manufacturing. Gold was refined in Ghana and petroleum in the Congo and several other countries. In this regard, Tunisia seems to be an example of the few African countries (outside South Africa) that have optimized the chemical value of an available raw material. Here, phosphate was the predominant mineral, and the phosphate industry was vital to the Tunisian economy. The yearly output was around 5 million tons in the mid-1980s, of which less than 50 percent went to domestic uses. Using several processing plants, Tunisia stepped up its production of phosphate derivatives because the demand for derivatives was less variable than the demand for phosphate rock. Phosphate derivatives included ammonium nitrate, and phosphoric acid. Typically phosphoric acid is used for the production of soft drinks, dental cements, in rust-proofing metals, and in making phosphates used in water softeners, fertilizers, and detergents. The growing chemical industry in Tunisia was dominated by the production of fertilizers, which had received substantial government investment. Tunisia was the world's third-largest producer of phosphoric acid, and in the mid-1980s production averaged 600,000 tons per year. Average annual production of ammonium nitrate to 250, 000 tons. When there was a fall in demand because of cuts in farm subsidies in importing countries, Tunisia went into barter agreements. In

Britain, phosphates were exchanged for small-scale capital equipment, and in Romania phosphates were traded for timber.

Like Tunisia, Morocco was proactive in establishing markets for manufactured products. In Morocco, phosphate production accounted for 75 percent of mineral contribution to GDP and a substantial portion of export earnings. The phosphate mining sector was the single largest customer of the Moroccan Rail network. As did Tunisia, Morocco opted to focus on producing phosphate derivatives, since their demand tended to be less elastic and processed phosphates allowed for enhanced market control and increased revenues with increasing prices. Phosphate rock was therefore processed in several plants into products such as phosphoric acid, monoammonium phosphates, and sulfuric acid. A 1985 plan to build a fertilizer complex in Saudi Arabia was based on an initial understanding among India, Saudi Arabia, and Morocco. In this accord, Saudi Arabia was to buy 1.4 million tons of phosphates every year from Morocco, process it, and sell the output to India. Earlier, in 1975, Morocco signed a trade agreement with Moscow, in which Morocco was to supply phosphates and phosphate derivatives to the Soviet Union for thirty years. The quantity supplied was expected to reach 10 million tons per year. In return, the Soviet Union agreed to develop the Meskala Mine. An agreement was also signed for citrus fruits; the agreement was to run until 1990. In the mid-1980s, Morocco was offering trade financing for its export to developing nations. Such a loan, valued at US$20 million, was granted to Iraq. Morocco at the same time turned around and secured credit agreements to import from the United States, Japan, and France. By nurturing a conducive trade environment, Morocco was able to plan with less doubt of the outcomes.

## MANUFACTURING

Minerals are important indicators of a nation's wealth and economic potential, because minerals are essentials in industry. However, resource endowments by themselves do not constitute wealth and economic power. Modern wealth and economic power are not gifts of nature or chance, like coal and iron. Wealth and economic power exude from the human mind. It is the ability to transform an idea into a reality through the industrial process: the talent of coordinating skills and making rigid organization susceptible to positive change.[10] In this regard, Brazil may be a convenient example.

Manufacturing was well established in *Brazil* by 1920. Based on census records, there were 13,000 plants and shops, engaging about 275,000 workers. Sixty-four per cent of manufactured goods were supplied from domestic sources; import provided the other 36 percent. Most of the domestic manufacturing outputs, around this period, concentrated on textiles and food processing industries, bringing imported items to less than 10 percent of total supply in these areas. Important additions in the 1920s included an integrated steel plant and a cement plant. In the 1930s and 1940s, the industrial base was broadened through direct investments, by international companies, in facilities to produce rubber products, chemicals, and aluminum, and to assemble automobiles. Manufacturing *capabilities* (apart from recession-induced problems) included automobiles, airplanes, large ships, heavy construction equipment, computers, modern communication systems, plastics, machine tools, and several other product categories. The war interfered with industrialization efforts, however, and output increased mainly through more efficient utilization of existing capacity. Excepting the steel mill, industrial and infrastructure development were very marginal. By the end of the war, Brazil's industrial and infrastructure capacity was obsolete, and the transportation infrastructure was inadequate and seriously deteriorated. By 1950, the broad range of manufactured products added significant value from industrial activities. Food, beverages, and tobacco were responsible for 25 percent of the value added, while textile products and shoes added another 24 percent. These two manufacturing industries comprised and remained the largest sectors in the economy.[11] This progress, on the industrial front after 1920, was coupled with the establishment of institutions to train engineers and scientists in several areas and conduct research and development.[12]

By 1950, Brazil employed 1.3 million workers in some 83,000 industrial establishments. As a response to government efforts to adapt advanced technology and enhance industrial capabilities, multinationals established large manufacturing and assembly plants. This industrialization effort had really begun much earlier, perhaps around the last decade of the nineteenth century. Government policies during the Great Depression curtailed supply of import, stimulating rapid industrial expansion.[13] Industry was the engine of growth, averaging an annual rate of 9 percent per annum, between 1950 and 1961, compared with only 4.5 percent for agriculture. The result was a nearly fourfold increase in industrial output. Until 1960, industrial expansion was mainly based on import substitution manufacturing. Although import substitution inherently created balance of payments pressures and other distortions, it remained the basic objective, even after the possibilities in food and textile industries were apparently largely exhausted.[14] The outcome of import-substitution industrialization instead increased import, notably in inputs and machinery, and did not alleviate the problems with balance of payments. Because of inadequate export growth during this period, the large influx of foreign capital in the 1950s resulted in a large foreign debt burden. In the second half of the 1950s, the government enacted a series of programs intended to refine the focus of the process of industrialization.

Bottlenecks were removed, and vertical integration was encouraged. Specifically, the government gave special attention to industries considered basic for growth, notably the automotive, cement, steel, aluminum, cellulose, heavy machinery, and chemicals industries. After 1960, growths in import substitution possibilities were largely confined to machinery, chemicals, fuel, and miscellaneous manufacturing, while traditional sectors, such as textiles, food products, and clothing declined as a proportion.

The period between 1962 and 1980 was mixed with stagnation and spectacular growth. From 1962 through 1967, the Brazilian economy lost much of its dynamism and stagnated in relative terms. The average rate of growth in GDP and industry declined to 4 percent and 3.9 percent respectively, compared with the preceding period between 1950 and 1961, when GDP exceeded 7 percent and the average annual growth of industry was 9 percent. A political impasse hindered the introduction of tough measures to combat inflation and obstacles to growth. However, conditions improved after reforms were made in 1964, and the period between 1968 and 1973 was outward looking and saw spectacular growth. An outcome of the post-1964 policies was an expansion in external trade, which grew faster than the economy as a whole. Nevertheless, amid this growth, import grew even faster. Massive inflow of capital counterbalanced the pressure, resulting in balance of payments' surpluses. The industrial sector experienced not only rapid growth but also considerable modernization. A rapid growth in income, for the upper-income strata and from credit plans for consumers and home buyers (by capital market reforms) increased demand for automobiles, durable and luxury goods, and housing. Within industry, the leading sectors were consumer durables, transportation equipment, cement, steel, and electricity. Because of the period's outward looking industrialization efforts, Brazil's industrial export increased from US$1.4 billion in 1963 to US$6.2 billion in 1973. Whereas in 1963 processed and semiprocessed manufactured export items accounted for 5 percent of total export, their share was 29 percent in 1974. The period of 1974 to 1980, in Brazil, saw relative growth with debt. By 1980, the goal was self-sufficiency; however, it turned out to be what may be seen (as in many other places) as a lost decade. By 1990, the nation was facing imminent hyperinflation. Between 1990 and 1994, economic measures taken were geared to drastically reduce inflationary pressure and lower inflationary expectations.

Coming back to Africa, what is troubling is the abandonment of strategic industrial incubators or their parochiality after several years in their implementation phases. Such abandoned projects ranged from paper mills to shoe factories that were unable to compete for one reason or another. On the other hand, Kenya, although lacking in significant mineral resources, was able with unusual soil fertility to sustain one of the best growth rates in Africa. There is still much promise for manufacturing in Africa. In fact, the only danger discernible on the horizon is the challenge in handling the noneconomical by-products of manufacturing, to the extent that they are rendered harmless to humans and the environment at large. In this case, government regulations are therefore indispensable.

For some countries in Africa to emerge as successfully modernizing and industrializing economies, the following conditions may not be overlooked: (1) An environment that presents opportunities for the exercise of leadership to persons (private and bureaucrats) whose interest is engendered in promoting economic change; (2) An inheritance of organizational capacity and skills; (3) Institutional arrangements that are conducive to rapid *deployment* and efficient accumulation of capital.

## TOOLING AND MACHINE TOOLS

As Africa expands the manufacturing base, expanding tool manufacturing will also be necessary. Machine tools are the foundation of modern industry and are utilized directly or indirectly to manufacture machines and tool parts. Specialized machine tools make it possible to manufacture standardized products very economically, using unskilled labor. Highly versatile and accurate tools are adapted to computer control.

With industrialization, there will be an expected increase in demand for tools such as screwdrivers, wrenches, saws, drills, pliers, staplers, spirit levels, calipers, lathes, dies, and presses. It will be also necessary to engage in the manufacture of conventional and unconventional machine tools to manufacture interchangeable parts. In this case conventional tools will include presses, cutting tools and fluids, saws, grinders, drilling and boring machines, milling machines, and lathes. Unconventional tools will include the areas of laser-beam machining (LBM); electrochemical machining (ECM); electrodischarge machining (EDM); electron-beam machining (EBM); ultrasonic machining (USM); and plasma-arc machining (PAM).[15]

## IRON AND STEEL

These are the most useful and among the cheapest metals known to man. They are used to make thousands of products that are useful in everyday life. These products range from paper clips, pins, nails, and razor blades to cans, furniture, and farm machinery. Machines made from iron and steel in turn help produce the many things we use such as paper, lamps, clothes, food, trains, automobiles, and ships. Industrialization is inextricably fused with iron and steel. Mauritania and South Africa are examples that illustrate economic growth and industrialization using heavy industry in Africa.

In *Mauritania* economic growth in the second half of this century was based on the contributions made by the  iron industry. For twenty years, iron ore was the nation's most important source of foreign exchange. In 1966, iron mining contributed 28 percent of GDP and as much as 92 percent of export earnings. At Kedia (in Mauritania) the surface mines were determined to be rich, with as much as 65 percent of iron content. Here, iron ore was mined from the sides of huge rock formations. The ore was then loaded on 100-ton trucks and transported to the railhead, where crushing and sorting took place. After this process, the ore was then loaded on the world's heaviest trains and transported to Nouadhibou for export. A typical train had twenty cars, averaging a length of two kilometers, with a total carrying capacity of 20,000 tons. The train made one trip daily in each direction along the 650-km line. By the mid-1970s, iron operations consumed about 40 percent of the nation's imported fuel oil and contributed 25 percent of GDP because of its high consumption of public utilities (water, power); commerce; transportation; and services. The construction of mines, rails, and port facilities were sources of income for thousands of laborers. By the 1970s and 1980s, this industry employed around 6,000 workers, 10 percent of the workers in the modern sector. Overall, it made a significant contribution in the various public-sector investments and current expenditures. Mining growth magnified national accounts, in the 1970s, mainly because of rising demand and favorable world commodity prices. This had a ripple effect on the nation's ability to meet her debt obligations. Here, mining speeded the development of urban centers. For example, in Nouadhibou and Zouîrât, the populations in both places grew from about 5,000 each to about 20,000 and 30,000, respectively, by the mid-1970s. It also spurred the growth of the capital, Nouakchott, to 125,000 in the mid-1970s from 5,000 in 1960. This initial iron-based growth was reversed in the recession of 1974–1975, because of the sharp rise in oil prices during this period, Mauritania's costly involvement in the Western Sahara Conflict (1975–1978), and a prolonged drought that had begun in the 1960s.

In 1979, Mauritania, it seemed, was determined to turn the tables around, still using the iron industry as a change agent for industrial growth. A new project, the Guelbs project, initiated in 1979, began in earnest in 1984. New surface mines were opened at El Rheins, in the Zouîrât district, twenty-odd kilometers from the Kedia district. However, the ore from the new deposits (38 percent) was not as rich in iron content as the Kedia ore (65 percent). In order to raise the ore content to competitive export market levels, this project therefore required the construction of concentration and beneficiation facilities. In addition, transportation, water, power, housing, and port facilities had to be upgraded to hold what was expected to be a surge in export volume. By 1987, it was evident that global market demand could not rise to expected levels. Instead there was a worldwide glut, mainly attributable to increased production by Brazilian mines. Meanwhile, in 1983, the value of Mauritania's iron ore, relative to its other export, had fallen below 50 percent for the first time. In that year, fish surpassed iron ore as Mauritania's most important source of foreign exchange. Although iron remained a key factor in the overall economy, in 1985, iron ore fetched 40 percent of export earnings, a decline from an average of 80 percent between 1963 and 1980.

In the 1970s, 30 percent of total government revenues had derived from iron ore, a proportion that probably declined in the 1980s. Mining royalties comprised 5 percent of government tax revenues, between 1981 and 1986. However, the proportion of the industry's actual contributions were much bigger when taxes paid on business profits, employers' payroll taxes, export taxes, turnover taxes, and public enterprise revenues are accounted for.

Although small by world standards, steel manufacturing in *South Africa* is the largest on the continent. The iron and steel industry is relatively well developed and satisfies much of the local demand, leaving enough for export. In the early 1990s, South Africa produced on the average about 9 million tons of steel annually. A substantial proportion of the output was used in manufacturing structural goods, transport equipment, and machinery for the engineering industry.

To encourage the fledging manufacturing industries, during the 1920s, the government established state corporations to provide inexpensive electricity and steel for industrial use while imposing import tariffs to protect local manufacturers. Large-scale production of iron and steel dates from 1934. South Africa Corporation (Iscor), is a parent company with several subsidiaries that own many iron ore, coal, and other mines throughout the country. Iscor is a dominant player in the iron and steel industry and the automobile industry uses a sizable proportion of the steel produced. Vehicle parts are manufactured locally by at least 150 plants. In 1994, South African automakers assembled more than 225,000 passenger cars and about 97,000 commercial vehicles. This was a significant progress in Africa since 1960, when Ford

Motors established the first assembly plant in Port Elizabeth. This progress may be attributable to the government's policy to encourage local content in manufacturing. Initially, the government encouraged local content based on weight rather than value. As a result, South Africa's vehicles were rather heavy and expensive. In order to reduce cost, manufacturers resorted to low-cost imported parts, with the objective of increasing the proportion of the value represented by local products. The lower cost of assembly was apparent in June 1991, when South Africa Motor Corporation (Samcor) announced that it had started exporting locally assembled Mazdas to Britain. In 1994, there were 6 million vehicles, including 3.5 million passenger cars licensed in South Africa.[16]

The heavy-engineering industry also consumes a sizable proportion of steel for construction, as well as for machinery and mining equipment. Many heavy-engineering firms are connected in one form or another with Iscor.

Most of South Africa's metals are exported, unprocessed, excepting iron ore, which is used in local industry. Although the largest known deposits of manganese in the world are in South Africa's, 90% of the manganese produced is used locally, in the production of iron and steel. On the other hand, chromium, used to manufacture stainless steel, was one of South Africa's export successes in the 1980s. About one-third of this alloy was exported in 1993, mostly to the United States. South Africa is also a leading producer and exporter of vanadium, used in steel manufacturing, to provide tensile and torsional strength, and resistance to abrasion. In the early 1990s, South Africa produced 45% of the world's supply.[17]

## GOLD

The muffled whisper of the word gold had a tendency to act upon prospectors like a fever—*gold fever*. Once this fever reached epidemic proportions, it often mutated into a gold rush among people who had learnt to cherish and adore the sparkle and glitter of gold. During the 1500s, the Spanish amassed lots of gold from the Aztecs in Mexico and the Incas in Peru. Many communities around the world owe their existence to gold rushes and the development of gold mining.

Gold is among the earliest known metals to humankind. From the ancient Egyptians to the Africans of the Gold Coast, the possession of this bright yellow metal symbolized wealth and prosperity. The radiant and seductive beauty of its lovely yellow color and soft metallic glow is almost irresistible and perhaps intoxicating. Many explorers in history set out in search the legendary land of gold called *El Dorado*.[18] They often thought they had found it. The rich gold discoveries of California, Australia, Alaska, and South Africa were perhaps inspired by the legend of *El Dorado*. Each discovery triggered a gold rush. The great gold rush to California in 1849 is probably the most renowned. For centuries Ghana produced and exported gold that eventually reached Europe through the trans-Saharan trade routes. In the fifteenth century, the Portuguese attempted to find and control the source but were not successful. In Zimbabwe, gold captivated the attention of Arab traders, Portuguese navigators, and British prospectors and entrepreneurs. Anxious British prospectors inferred that an abundance of existing gold mines promised equally substantial profits. It was not long before it was uncovered that the mines had already been worked dry, and in total value the sites that were mine worthy often did not even cover the cost of investments in capital equipment. Artifacts indicated that mining in Zimbabwe dated back thousands of years to the iron age. Excavations revealed a sophistication in the use of gold, such as delicate necklaces of twisted gold and seashells set in gold.

All the gold that has ever been mined is still around in one form or another. This is simply because gold cannot be destroyed. It is, one might say, eternal. This aspect explains how a pharaoh envisioned to convey treasures into the next life. Pieces of gold ornaments have been recovered intact from beneath the soil after thousands of years. This is because gold does not "age" even when buried.[19] Gold is extremely inactive.[20] It tends to be unaffected by air, heat, moisture, and most solvents. Its melting point is 1,063 degrees centigrade or 1,945 degrees Fahrenheit.[21] It does not tarnish.[22] It is a nonrusting metal that tends to be resistant to chemical changes. However, it may dissolve in aqueous mixtures, such as chlorides, bromides, and some iodides. Gold tends to maintain its value through the ages because of its relative scarcity.

Its softness makes it ductile, malleable, and easy to work with. This ductile nature means one ounce of gold can be drawn into a fine wire fifty miles long. The amount could plate a thousand-mile strand of copper wire. Similarly, an ounce of gold (just about the size of an American half-dollar) could be hammered into a thin sheet that will cover 100 square feet.[23] A little gold goes a long way. When gold is fashioned into a piece of jewelry, it must be combined with another metal (alloy). Gold alloys are measured in carats. A carat is equal to one twenty-fourth part. Twenty-four carats is pure gold (24K). Eighteen carats is eighteen parts of pure gold and six parts of alloy (18K). It is found in its native state as nuggets, spangles, grains, and streaks. Nuggets of gold may be found in streambeds. Typically such nuggets have been washed away by erosion from veins and cracks in the earth's crust, transported, and deposited in river and streambeds.

Gold mining has evolved into huge industrial enterprises that require substantial initial investments for operations to take off. Unlike the yesteryears of the lone miner who quickly turned a fortune, equipped with only a pick, a shovel, a pan, and an ore rocker, today's competitors in the global marketplace are large corporations. These large corporations may employ tens of thousands of workers garbed in boots, oilskins, and helmets with flashlights and armed to the teeth with air jackhammers, hand drills, explosives, mechanical loaders, and revolving mills. In one year, workers in a single productive mine may hoist about 6,145,000 tons of ore to the surface, in order to produce 66 tons of gold, or 2,122,285 ounces.[24]

Although gold may be mined from the surface of the earth, where it is contained in *open cuts,* it is also found in *veins* and *faults* deep in the earth. A mine yielding an average of one ounce of gold per ton of ore will be ranked among the richest mines in the world.[25] Gold-bearing rock with as little as one part of gold to three hundred thousand parts of other worthless material may still be mined at a profit. Industrially, gold mining could be very costly, requiring considerable capital equipment. It is not unusual, therefore, for a mine to extend about one and one-half miles down into the earth, for example, in South Africa. At 6,500 feet in the Vaal Reefs Mine in the Transvaal province of South Africa, the gold-bearing reef looks like gray asphalt in a streak eighteen inches wide. Here, white stones are scattered through the vein.[26] A visitor to one of the South African mines recounted being transported by an elevator down into the mine, where she found herself among whitewashed walls with ceilings of surprising height. Here are her vivid remarks :

Electric lights . . . miniature streetcar . . . whitewashed walls, . . . less orderly part of the mine . . . there was a smell of explosive . . . their excellent ventilation . . . Cars . . . carrying lumps of dynamited ore toward the lifts or rumbling back . . . . Outside . . . loads would be dumped into . . . machine that ground them up, sorted out the gold, carried everything by belt to its appointed destination . . . overpowering noise . . . the grinding of ore . . . fall of water, . . . down the rock wall.[27]

Gold is seldom found in an unalloyed or pure state. It is usually combined with silver, in a natural alloy called *electrum*. It may also be found with quartz, calcite, lead, tellurium, zinc, and copper. Gold is usually a by-product of these minerals.

Gold may still be mined by gravity separation (i.e., sifting/panning or hand mining). Mining by means of hydraulic pressure, dredging, and power shovels, tends to be effective however, but many countries, do not condone dredging and hydraulic mining because of their destructive ramifications on land, streams, and the ecosystem of coastal waters.

Gold is a very useful metal in an industrial environment. The hundreds of products manufactured for industry include the following: gold reflectors for spacecraft; gold-tipped contacts for electrical circuits; and frost-proof gold-impregnated glass for cabin windshields of jet aircraft.

Goldsmithing in ancient times used to be analogous to priestly rites, with the goldsmith regarded as possessing special god-given talent for working this noble metal. Like an alchemist, he brewed his batches of metal, according to his secret recipes, adding a touch of this and a pinch of that. Skills were sometimes handed down from father to son like precious possessions or perhaps the secret ritual of a mystical society.

The advent of industrialization and the introduction of controlled processing in the nineteenth century tipped the scales. With industrialization, machines have assumed many simpler tasks of the goldsmith and even some very complex processes. The cottage industry of the goldsmith has been dominated by machines for a mass-production, profit-oriented environment. In the jewelry industry, this means less expensive but still fashionable varieties of jewelry for those who might have otherwise done without a true work of art.

In an industrializing environment, the shops are replaced by factories, each with long lines of machines that do operations ranging from cutting, grinding, stamping, and squeezing to milling and drilling. These plants literally devour gold and churn the yellow metal into attractive jewelry. Gold chains (that may range from eight to eighteen carats) are manufactured for jewelers and watchmakers, who then cut them into appropriate sizes and shapes for necklaces or chain bracelets. In one plant, workers tend automated machines, with about five hundred such machines that stand row on row, each capable of ingesting from two to fifteen pounds of fine gold daily, depending of the weight and size of the chain. Artisans finish some pieces by hand, using tweezers, small gas torches, and so on. Commemorative pieces in the medallion department range from that of the pope to those of various heads of states, the Olympic Games, civic anniversaries of various cities, and independence days of numerous African countries.[28]

Gold is generally considered a good store of value. Sometimes people advocate jewelry purchases, as a form of investment against troubled times. Such investments may not always provide the cushion expected in trouble times. This is because jewelry markups are usually high—about a hundred to 200 percent or more. This may be an even unfruitful decision for mass-produced jewelry.[29] Economic cycles, as we know, are inherent of industrialization. During inflationary periods, investors have generally resorted to gold as a store of value. Gold is also a very good portfolio diversifier, especially for long-term bonds.

Transactions in world trade were facilitated by gold as a medium for settling international trade accounts. Although the use of gold coins dates from antiquity, the International Gold Standard, also known as the Golden Age of the Gold Standard, spanned from the 1870s to the eve of World War I (1914–1918). During this period, Britain, which had been on the gold standard since 1821, was the financial center of the world. By the 1870s, world trade flourished. International investments increased, promoting international specialization and global welfare. There was vigorous trade among nations. Accounts between nations were settled in theory and in practice by the exchange of gold. Gold coins could not only be exported, but they could be melted, hoarded, and so forth. Gold was equivalent to money at the mint price.

Some nations are endowed with substantial gold reserves. When a nation expends quantum resources in exploration and gold mining, to the extent that other sectors are disaffected, one would naturally expect the development of value added industries. A logical extension may be the production of luxury items. Such production will include areas such as gilded ornaments, jewelry, gold lace, gold leaf, ruby glass, and even tooth filling braces.

Despite the radical transformations of the international financial system in the twentieth century, gold has stood the test of change. It qualifies as an official reserve asset under the International Monetary Fund (IMF). Coupled with the creation of paper gold (or special drawing rights) it resulted in isolating the private gold markets from the International Monetary System.[30]

As is the case of diamond mining and mining of other minerals, the prosperity of gold mining communities cannot be guaranteed after the mines shut down. The will of the community must be etched into long term industrial planning in order to forestall an imminent economic cataclysm. Gold is a blessing only to the extent that it is used for integrated industrial development. In this case, much can be learned from South Africa.

## DIAMONDS

Diamonds are not the most valuable of precious stones, but they are unquestionably the most fascinating, the most interesting, the most important, and the most noteworthy of gemstones in the world.[31] Their extremely rare qualities rank them among the most valuable in the world. The crown jewels of nations have been known to be studded with some of the most valuable cuts of diamonds in the world. These shimmering gems exude luxury, glamour, warmth, and seemingly magical powers and eternal beauty. Diamond studded rings are the traditional jewels for engagements and weddings in Western-oriented cultures. Diamonds of a lesser grade are typically used for industrial application.

Diamonds are made of a pure crystallized carbon. Diamonds are one of the most perfectly crystallized of minerals. Almost every single stone is bounded by more or less regularly developed crystal faces. The faces of diamond crystals differ from those of most other minerals in that, as a rule, they tend to be much curved and rounded instead of being perfectly plain, as is usually the case. This curvature is due to the growth of the crystal.[32] Diamonds can be easily confused with other rock forms. In fact, some of the most renowned finds around the world turned out to be nothing more valuable than pieces of rock crystal or fine pieces of colorless topaz.

The specific gravity of diamonds varies from 3.3 to 3.7.[33] Within this range, the differences in specific gravity are probably due to the presence of various impurities that include color and bubble. Since colored diamonds always contain a small amount of impurity, the specific gravity will vary with the color.[34]

In their natural state most diamonds look rough and dull. Many are covered with a graying, greasy-looking film. In their pure form diamonds are supposed to be most beautifully clear and transparent, with visual renderings of a peculiar steel blue.[35] However, this natural transparency is not always achieved because of enclosures of foreign matter. Although a great number of diamonds are indeed perfectly colorless (about 25 percent), cloudy and opaque diamonds are actually more common than those that are clear and transparent. Diamonds, which combine great depth and beauty of color with perfect transparency, are objects of unsurpassable beauty. Black diamonds are often completely opaque. The transparency of crystals depends on the condition of the surface. Diamonds are, therefore, polished to unleash their *adamantine lustre*; their radiant power; their glimpses of metallic lustre; their high index of refraction, and their great power to disperse or break up white light into its constituent colors—their "fire." Hence and behold their most beautiful play of brilliant, prismatic colors, upon which the beauties of diamonds rest.

Originally, diamond cutters just polished the dull surface by rubbing one diamond against another. Around the 1400s, iron wheels coated with diamond dust were introduced as a polishing surface. By the 1600s, diamond cutting had evolved into a delicate art of fashioning diamonds in shapes that would render the greatest brilliance.

Diamonds are the *hardest known natural substance*. The Greeks named them *adamas* (invisible), in this context signifying unconquerable. They are easily recognizable because they will scratch all other substances without exception, while they remain unscratched by none. However, diamonds from one locality may scratch diamonds from other localities because of the varying degrees of crystalline hardness by geography. As hard as diamonds are, they are not impervious to damage. They are combustible at 1600° F (870° C) and tend to be brittle.[36] The hardness of diamonds has been historically confused with their *frangibility* or *brittleness*. Diamonds will possibly cleave, crack, or chip, under the severe shock of a sudden sharp blow. This characteristic allows diamond cutters to fashion certain pieces of these rough gemstones to appropriate sizes and shapes.[37] Faceting by *cleavage* is not only laborsaving, as opposed to the tedious process of grinding away portions that need to be removed, but also means that fragments carefully removed by cleavage can be utilized in fashioning smaller gems. By cleaving away the faulty exterior portions of large diamonds the per unit profit margins are greatly increased. Diamond cutting is traditionally a time-consuming and delicate art.[38] This labor intensive nature of cutting and polishing diamonds substantially increases the average cost of diamonds.

In some countries such as Israel, automated computerized machines have been installed to replace the manual labor of cutting diamonds. In other countries like India, the low cost of labor still makes the use of manual labor a cost-efficient option.

Gem diamonds are graded by their weight, purity, cut, and color. The weight of a diamond is measured by the *carat*. One carat is equal to two hundred milligrams. The purity of a diamond may be affected by fissures, cloudy texture, cut, scratch, uncrystallized carbons, and so on. The *colors* of diamonds are varied and may range from red, pink, blue, and yellow, to brown, green, and black. Some have a blue tinge, while others are colorless. Most commercial gem diamonds are colorless or very pale, steely blue. Strongly colored stones tend to fetch much higher prices. Red, pink, or blue diamonds are considered the rarest.[39]

*Industrial Diamonds.* At prices that have ranged from about $9,000 to $147,000 *per pound*, industrial diamonds are reputed among the most valuable of all minerals used in industry.[40] Their usefulness in industry derives from their hardness. About 75 percent (by weight) of diamond production are of an industrial grade.[41] The hardness of diamonds renders them invaluable in industrial toolmaking. Diamonds are fused to the ends of drills used in mining, tunneling, and the sinking of artesian wells; abrasive wheels and files; disc saws; finer mechanical tools; in the pivots of precision instruments; in wire-drawing dies; in cutting glass (glaziers' diamond); in boring holes in glass, porcelain, and such precious stones as ruby and sapphire; and other industrial applications. The benefits of diamond tools derived mainly from the savings in time and labor and from the demonstrated superiority of the results engendered in their use. At least in the past, the benefits tended to counterbalance the high initial expenses incurred.

General Electric (GE) is an American company that is a leader in the arena of synthesized diamonds. Synthesized diamonds are useful mostly in industrial applications. An average of half the weight of diamonds is lost during cutting. This diamond dust is carefully recovered and applied in the tool making industry. Stones with unpleasant physiognomical dispositions, such as those chipped, cracked, or disfigured by "clouds" are typically applied as *bort* for technical purposes. On the other hand, some stones may be bought because of their scientific interest.

Early finds of diamonds in South Africa were purely accidental. For example, diamonds were discovered in the walls of a dwelling house built of mud from a neighboring pond. In a more familiar story, a traveler in 1867 found a child playing with a bright and shiny stone that turned out to be a diamond crystal weighing about 21⅛ carats.[42] These finds were the catalysts of searches that eventually led to rich discoveries.[43] Although the first diamonds were found by chance, diamonds had very high per-unit weight. In much of Africa around this time transportation was not suited for many forms of trade. Most of the developments of railways had not yet reached Africa, and the automobile was just about to emerge on the scene. Under these conditions, the promising nascent diamonds business proved to be a blessing from the earth.[44]

Since then, some of the most important and richest diamond mines in the world have been known to be in South Africa. Many of the diamonds have come from diamond fields near Kimberley.[45] When initial surface workings were exhausted, diamonds were traced to their source rock and mined by large-scale methods. Historically, these mines have supplied about 90 percent of given market demand for diamonds. The diamond markets of the world effectively fell under the complete control of the owners of the South African mines. The market effects of Brazilian and Indian mines proved to be comparatively insignificant.[46]

De Beers Company, a London-based cartel originally founded in South Africa, has for much of the twentieth century maintained an iron grip on the world diamond trade. On the average more than 80 percent of the world's freely traded diamond supply passes through De Beers's fortresslike office building in London. This is the legendary Central Selling Organization, otherwise known by the acronym C.S.O. Typically De Beers's London office stockpiles diamonds. Potential competitors may sell to De Beers. The sources of diamond in Africa include Namibia, Angola, Zaire, South Africa, Botswana, Tanzania, and Sierra Leone. Outside Africa, the Soviet Union and Australia are the dominant players. The United States is a major market. Japan was a sizable market in the 1980s. It appears the next markets will probably be the Eastern European nations.

According to a 1979 report, only 230 tons of diamonds had been mined in the last three thousand years. To obtain a single rough diamond, an average of 40 to 250 tons of earth have to be excavated and meticulously sifted.[47] Between 1947 and 1970, diamond production increased from an average of ten million carats annually to fifty million carats annually. Production stabilized at fifty million and then contracted to forty million in 1977. In 1985, world production stood at 41,674,000 metric tons.[48]

The Jwaneng mine in Botswana was ranked as the best in the world. The capacity was determined at 7.6 million carats, evenly split between gem and industrial-quality stones. De Beers Botswana Diamond Mines (Debswana) is a joint venture of the Botswana government and De Beers Consolidated Mines Ltd. The diamonds are eventually sold to C.S.O. London. Botswana is one of the world's three largest diamond producers (along with Australia and the former Soviet Union). Botswana's three mines have a combined capacity of 13.1 million carats. Mineral production in Botswana has become the key to development. Mineral production accounted for more than 50 percent of real GDP, and 70 percent of export in the mid-1980s. In Botswana, the two most important commodities are diamonds and copper/nickel matte. Democratic Republic of Congo is among the leading producers of industrial diamonds. About 10 percent of its diamonds are of gem quality. Diamond ore in Congo Kinshasa yields roughly six carats per cubic meter; in 1984 and 1985 it accounted for 30% of the world production.

Although Africa supplies most of the diamonds in the global market, diamonds have been known longer in India than in any other country. Until the discovery of diamonds in Brazil, in 1728, the world supply of diamonds derived almost entirely from Indian sources. The supply of Brazilian diamonds in the world market was a chief blow to the diamond mining industry of India. There was no competition between these rich and untapped sources and the Indian mines, whose age could be counted in centuries and perhaps tens of centuries. This was jeopardized by the opening of diamond fields in Africa. New and rich deposits have generally not replaced the old mines. The proportion of diamonds that reach the European markets has been relatively insignificant. One reason was that a significant proportion of the stones remained in India to satisfy the demand for these gems with very highly desirable qualities by the privileged classes and magnates. Merchants were similarly induced to sell in the domestic market because the native diamonds fetched more attractive prices than in the European markets, where these gems had to be valued on the basis of comparative global market forces for treasures from around the world and the inexorable laws of demand and supply. In fact, India began importing diamonds from the Cape of Good Hope because of the brisk demand in the domestic market.[49]

When Brazilian diamonds first reached the market, perhaps because the only references then were Indian diamonds, they were not favorably received by the diamond-buying public. Some buyers had difficulties believing they were diamonds, while others asserted the differences between Brazilian and Indian diamonds.[50] On this account, many Brazilian stones were routed to Gao, then a Portuguese possession in India, where they eventually found their way into the market as Indian stones. When Dutch merchants got wind of these tribulations, they promptly contracted and secured the monopoly of the trade in Brazilian diamonds. Subsequent outputs of Brazilian diamonds were sent direct to Rio de Janeiro and Bahia to Amsterdam.[51] Consequent upon a treaty signed at a later date with the British government, the entire output of Brazilian diamonds was sent to London. In more recent times, the stones have been purchased by French houses and placed on the Paris market.[52]

If diamonds are said to belong to the "robber industry," then by definition, they are expected to be scarcer in the long term. The world market was flooded with diamonds in the early 1990s. Imminent market glut emanating from Angola and Russia had distressing tendencies for the De Beers cartel.

The commercial mining of diamonds can bring jobs and prosperity to an otherwise depressed area. However, when the proceeds from mining are not invested in capital formation, the inhabitants are rendered potentially vulnerable to economic adversities. Such adversities usually occur after the mining has stopped. The area may revert to its original state of economic depression, prompting net emigration that may threaten to create a ghost town in its wake. Like other minerals, when diamond resources are properly managed, they form a launching pad and trajectory for industrialization.

## SILVER

A mineral of excellent nature, silver is said to be as good as gold. Silver is cherished not only as a symbol of wealth but also because of its versatility and practicability in industrial and industrializing environments. Its usefulness ranges from applications in photography and medicine to even the production of solar energy. Besides its more apparent traditional utility in coinage, it is also used in silver-plating, catalysts, soldering and brazing, jewelry, tableware, ornaments, and other household ware as a portable store of value. Like gold and diamonds, silver endures as wealth in the hand. Through purchases of anklets, bracelets, and other jewelry, homemakers, historically in some places, used it as a savings account and as an avenue to some financial freedom in matrimony. Nations have maintained hoards of silver from centuries of trade.

To brighten festive meals, silver beaters transform this highly malleable, ductile metal into a featherweight foil. It is used as decoration and food, since it is benign and tasteless. In India, it is not unusual for an ambitious mother to go the extra mile and provide the guests with silvered roast chickens at her daughters wedding. Silver activates oxygen to kill bacteria. European airlines have been known to use silver in purifying their drinking water.

Silver is also used extensively by dentists, although it will not prevent tooth decay. In swimming pools, charcoal filters impregnated with silver eradicate germs. In hospitals burns are disinfected with silver creams, and broken bones are mended with cements containing antibacterial silver salts. Large amounts of silver are contained in X-ray films to reduce the exposure of the patient to radiation. Perhaps nothing else reflects light as well and uniformly as silver. It is therefore useful in concentrating the sun's rays on solar collectors, in backing the best mirrors, and in protecting the heat-reflecting gold films on office windows.

No other metal, including copper, is known to have a higher thermal and electrical conductivity than silver. Silver wires are used to lace solar cells, and silver oxide batteries may be used to power little gadgets such as hearing aids and pocket calculators and even large contraptions. Miniature disks of silver, hardened with tungsten or molybdenum, may be posited to tap together and switch current from wire to wire in lighting and in automobiles. In the case of machines such as a dishwasher, the timer may have a few dozens of electrical contacts that open and close without excessive heat or friction, since silver is a natural dry lubricant. In computers and electronics, silver is used in wiring panels and in printed circuits. A little silver can go a long way : an ounce of silver may be used to manufacture 5,000 color photographs. Silver is used in film since crystalline silver salts are sensitive to light sources, promptly detecting light falling on them and making a permanent record. When the film is processed, the salts become silver grains that amplify the image a billion times, thus producing a picture.

## OIL

Modern industrial civilization is more dependent on petroleum and its by-products than in any other single commodity. This is because of its extensive applications and its versatility, very familiar to people living in urban and suburban settings. Oil means money.[53] A country entirely cut off from oil cannot survive. Oil has a benign Midas touch on industrialization.

The word *petroleum* means rock oil. Its etymologies are the Latin words, *petra,* meaning rock, and *oleum,* meaning oil.[54] Humankind has used petroleum or rock oil since ancient times. Typically, when hard rock that contained oil underground fractured, the oil sometimes seeped to the surface of the earth. This was how humans found oil in ancient times. The builders of the city of Babylon used pitch or asphalt as mortar to strengthen the walls. The mother of Moses used pitch to coat the cradle, so that it might stay buoyant on the river Nile. The Indians in North America used oil for medicine, fuel, and war paint. In the more recent past, oil was used for lubricating axles, for medicinal concoctions, and as a household lighting fuel, presenting a significant competition with whale oil, which was still being used for lighting and lubrication. At this time, however, whale oil was getting increasingly scarce. The veritable search for a new source of fuel was no secret. A new source of oil was urgently needed.

In 1845, French scientists had discovered how to produce oil by heating a kind of rock called oil shale. By 1850, the British had discovered how to produce oil from coal and oil shale. It wasn't long before Great Britain could boast of 130 plants making shale oil. Increasingly in Europe and North America, coal oil, although costly, gained popularity as a lighting fuel. In fact, when kerosene was introduced in the market, it was sometimes called coal oil.

In North America, scientific investigations into the value of bottled medicine oil instigated George H. Bissel, a lawyer from New York, to delve into the possibilities of oil during his visit to his old college at Dartmouth in the winter of 1854. The professors there had been experimenting with crude oil in their laboratories, and they showed Bissel a sample of crude oil. The professors told him that if crude oil is suitably refined, it could produce a better lamp light than coal oil. Bissel was so impressed that he immediately formed a company to buy the farm near Titusville, where the sample had been found. A second opinion from Benjamin Silliman, Jr., a professor of chemistry at Yale, was in the affirmative: Silliman said the Dartmouth scientists were right. Enterprising coal oil dealers offered $20 a barrel for all the crude oil. The only obstacle between Bissel and his looming fortunes was his inability to produce his oil on a substantial scale, for the company was losing money. It was at this point that a young man appeared on the scene asking for a job and offering to put up some of the capital. He was hardly a man to inspire confidence. He had spent much of his life hopping from job to job and had virtually no formal education. Although he liked to call himself colonel, he had in fact never been to the army. The only uniform he had ever won was that of the railroad conductor. The company was, however, prepared to hire him since he had some money and seemed to command some knowledge pertaining to efficient and inefficient methods of drilling water wells. In

1858, this young retired railroad conductor, named Edwin Laurentine Drake, was hired and sent to Titusville to take charge of production.[55] In the summer of 1859, Drake set up his derrick, and the locals christened it "Drake's folly."

Drake's drilling equipment was made of wood and the drill was steam powered. His was very rustic drilling equipment or rig, compared with modern rotary drills and bit technology (such as directional drilling systems, MWD or measurement while drilling, and PDC or polycrystalline diamond compact bits) that tend to reduce the overall cost of finding new reserves.[56]

Because of the frequent cave-ins, Drake had his crew drive in an iron rod or casing thirty-nine feet into the ground to solid rock. Drilling was then done in the casing (coiled tubing). This method has since then developed as a standard in preventing cave-ins, in oil drilling.[57] After three months of pioneer drilling, Drake's folly paid off. His crew struck oil on August 27, 1859, at an exact depth of 69.5 feet.

This discovery marked the beginning of the rapid growth in the modern petroleum industry. Oil was pumped at the rate of thirty barrels per day, at $20 per barrel or a daily income of $600.[58] Within twenty-four hours, there was a rush to join this promising source of wealth. Ex-whalers and gold rushers joined the vanguard. Thousands of oil wells were drilled in the vicinity, and boom towns mushroomed virtually overnight. An oil boom took off in Pennsylvania. In sprouting settlements like Pithole, as many as fifty hotels were built in a space of a few months. Pithole was not very different from most mushrooming towns elsewhere around the world then. The streets were generally thronged with a curious admixture of opportunists. In an oil town like Pithole, such opportunists and treasure hunters included prospectors, drillers, lease grabbers, speculators, prostitutes, ex-soldiers, desperadoes, and hellions. Indeed, a bar was an invariable appendage to every building, and every other shop was a liquor saloon. The initial demand for the new product was insatiable. The oil boom created parvenus, dazed with sudden wealth and joyous with an inordinate propensity to squander it as rapidly as possible.

The transportation infrastructure then was not built to support this booming industry. Railroads, therefore, had to build spur lines to the oil fields. Speculators paid astronomical sums for land, hoping to garner quick returns on their investments. So much oil was being produced that it could not be hauled off immediately. Three years after Drake struck oil, there was an oil glut: oil prices plummeted from an initial $20 to 10 cents per barrel—a potential outcome overlooked in the heat of speculation.[59] Many original companies, including Bissel's, were forced out of business.[60]

Meanwhile, the oil industry proceeded with the pangs of birth. To overcome bottlenecks in the field, the first oil pipeline was built by 1865. It was five miles long. In need of a new source of foreign exchange, barrels of this valuable but inflammable liquid had to be exported abroad. Initial shipment, from Philadelphia to London, was not easy. Workers deserted the loading dock, for fear of being burnt, once they found out what they were handling. This problem was subsequently settled. In 1865, Britain, France, and Germany became substantial importers. For most of the rest of the century, out of every three barrels of kerosene produced, at least one fetched export earnings. Commercial oil production quickly spread around the world, and for a while, the main commercial product was kerosene. Kerosene was used for lighting lamps.

The now very important gasoline (petrol) was then practically useless. Gasoline exploded when put in lamps. Gasoline at this time was a waste product refiners dumped into creeks and rivers.

The invention of the automobile cut waste tremendously in the petroleum industry; automobiles burned gasoline. The main snag was that at the turn of the twentieth century, there were very few automobiles. Many people still considered automobiles very strange, noisy contraptions and preferred the safety and elegance of their horse-drawn carriages. A meteoric increase in demand for automobiles by 1910 irreversibly increased business for the petroleum industry. In 1910, half a million cars were on the road, compared with only eight thousand in 1900. In an industry where 100 gallons of petroleum fetched only 13 gallons of petrol, demand for fuel quickly outstripped supply. Improved methods of refining, between 1911 and 1913, subsequently ameliorated supply–demand conditions. Cracking (a process of decomposing complex hydrocarbons into simpler compounds) began in 1913 to increase the quantity of gasoline. Coincidentally this process also improved quality. The new and improved gasoline was a better anti-knock fuel, to all intents and purposes.

Throughout the twentieth century, the demand for oil as a source of energy has generally increased. By 1983, the world was producing approximately 53,000,000 barrels of crude oil per day. In Africa, in the same year, total production was approximately 4,425,000 barrels per day, with much of the production coming from Algeria, Angola, Egypt, Gabon, Libya, and Nigeria. By 1991 the world as a whole consumed approximately 23,000 million barrels each year. There are about 400 million cars in the planet, and the oil industry has been blessed with much business.[61] Oil once used for greasing axles is today used for lubricating the wheels of industry and commerce all over the world. Gasoline is used by cars, trucks, aircraft, and buses. Fuel oils are used in homes, office buildings, factories, railroads, power plants, and smelters, to name just a few.

The efficiency of the oil industry has been tremendously improved since the drilling days of the young retired railroad conductor Edwin L. Drake. By using equipment such as geophones, magnetometers, gravimeters, seismographs, and possibly satellite generated maps, geologists and geophysicists increase their efficiency at exploring and mining oil deposits.[62] Prospectors pay attention to nuances in the earth's structure, such as anticlines, stratigraphic traps, faults, salt domes and seepage. Geologists exploit underwater oil fields by drilling from piers, artificial steel islands, and anchored barges. Drillers may even "throw curves" to tap deposits located farther away. Efficiency has not been limited to work tools. Advances have been made in processes such as *catalytic polymerization* developed to meet the demands for high octane gasoline, *alkylation, hydrogenation, reforming* and *solvent refining*.

The petroleum industry is typically classed into: prospecting and production, refining, petrochemical, transportation, and marketing operations. This industry comprises myriads of companies, many of them relatively small in stature. By the same token, some giant corporations are petroleum-based companies. Typically, a preponderance of these companies specializes in one or the other aforementioned activities. Increasingly the larger corporations become fully integrated, fusing drilling, refining, transportation, and marketing. They possess oil fields around the world, control fleets of tankers, operate pipelines, build and operate refineries and various distribution facilities.

Again the modern industrial civilization is highly dependent on petroleum. As other nations industrialize, they inevitably increase consumption of oil.[63] The industrialized nations are, therefore, the greatest consumers of petroleum. Energy consumption by the United States, Europe, the erstwhile USSR, and Japan, comprised 75 percent of the world total, in 1990. The cheap and convenient nature of petroleum displaced coal, in the twentieth century, as an important source of energy.[64]

In spite of the overall low prices, developing nations blessed with petroleum have overwhelmingly depended on foreign exchange earnings deriving from petroleum. For example, the shah of Iran claimed that his country was being unfairly treated by oil companies in comparison with Arab nations. He indicated that because of the relatively larger population of Iran, among other reasons, he deserved the fastest rate of growth in oil production. He therefore requested a consortium to accelerate expansion, from about 12 percent to 17.5 percent and double output by 1970. In the recent past, efforts to monetize reserves by the organization of petroleum expoting countries, OPEC, in an environment of weak crude oil prices resulted in massive debt obligations. In other cases negating increasing cash flow pressure meant unbridled marginal propensities beyond stipulated production quotas, as was demonstrated in 1992 by Venezuela's defection. Cartel stabilization efforts may be jeopardized by oil-hungry non-OPEC countries, where supplies have been trending upward in recent years. Not long ago, OPEC appealed to the rest of the world to restrain future production [65]

Because of these production dynamics, petroleum and raw materials overall, while important, are not as coupled to industrial economies as previously: important manufactured products contain far fewer raw materials than before.[66] What seems to have been a collapse of the raw-materials economy has had almost no impact on industrial economies. Traditional development theories and traditional development policies need to be reevaluated.[67] The oil industry, however, remains a significant part of industrial economies. For example, in the United States, the Standard and Poors (S&P) 500 market value index, which comprises 500 companies from 90 industry groups, ranks the oil industry as the largest in terms of market capitalization.[68] For oil-consuming nations in general, trade balance improves with lower oil prices.[69] For oil-consuming nations that use boiler oil fuels in manufacturing, lower oil prices also mean lower energy costs that tend to boost profit margins. Lower oil prices also tend to damper inflation, assuming all other things remain unchanged, and interest rates are trending downward.

In the petroleum industry, gasoline or petrol is very price inelastic. In other words, a drastic swing in price, one way or another, is not compensated by an equally significant increase or decrease in the industry's total sales. Given the nature of the industry and product and the pricing behavior, it is therefore cheaper to confine competition as much as possible to the acquisition of outlets.[70]

In this case, successful sales promotion not only boosts the garage men's enthusiasm but may also increase the company's market share at the expense of competitors. By owning filling stations, companies can take advantage of economies of scale in distribution. For example, it costs less to deliver 4,000 gallons of gasoline or petrol than 200 gallons to a filling station. Companies can, therefore, choose to enhance their corporate image at the points of purchase by motorists and perhaps establish brand loyalty.

This is not, however, the case with fuel oil. Fuel oil has to compete for customers against coal and natural gas. A price cut, therefore, can lead to very significant increases in sales. But, in meeting a rapidly rising demand for fuel and heating oils, companies may find themselves with costly and surplus inventories of gasoline, since the demand for gasoline tends to be inelastic.[71] Because companies generally cannot afford to let their competitors use pricing to gain market advantage, they tend to follow the leader. Companies that cannot consistently manage wide bands of price cuts or fluctuations tend to leave the market entirely. Price wars are usually not to the long term interest of all the companies involved. Under most circumstances, it is more effective to employ cost cutting measures and sales networks. Cost cutting implies minimizing waste or finding a use for everything produced. Companies with many sales outlets tend to have larger sales volume than companies with a few outlets.

Although companies compete with each other, they also form joint ventures in production, pipelines, or refining and may find themselves interlocked with their competitors through various agreements for the sale and exchange of products. In other words they belong to a club, suggesting dimensions of a cartel, in these interrelationships, alongside areas of unrestrained competition. Historically most of these interlocking relationships took place in the Middle East. Although in newer concession areas companies preferred to operate alone instead of submitting to the burden of consultations necessary in important decisions, the inherent costs and risks tended to pull them together. This meant reducing costs or risking losses where feasible. For example, building crude oil pipelines cost a fortune. In Europe, the main crude oil pipelines—Trans-Alpine (TAL), Southern European (SEPL), and Rhine-Donau—had interlocking ownerships. Since all companies wanted to use them, the obvious tendency was to share in the costs.

Unlike pipelines, the tendency with refineries, at least from a historical perspective, was for companies to have complete ownership, unless where they were obliged by governments (in this case in many developing countries) to build plants before their local sales could justify such investments. Here, the refinery's ownership was based on each company's stake in the local market. Although it is not common practice, companies have been known to cooperate at the marketing level. For example, Shell and British Petroleum (BP) in Africa decided to sell through the same distribution company, sometimes under the Shell brand name. Administratively, at least in theory, joint venture companies were purely administrative concerns and policy decisions came from the parent companies. Although the rules governing joint-venture concerns were typically spelled out in great detail, thus leaving executives with little scope for initiatives, directors met in order to issue necessary instructions and to ensure that they were implemented.

Besides engaging in selling oil and its by products, the petroleum industry is also one of the world's biggest customers for iron and steel, vehicles, electric power, meters, pumps, pipes, measuring devices, lumber, tanks, ropes, cables, paints, hoses, cement, rubber, metal products, chemicals, containers, and so on.

There are at least 4,000 different occupations in the oil industry alone. These thousands of occupations may be grouped into seven chief classes:

*Science Oriented/University.* This includes petroleum engineers, geologists, chemists, chemical engineers, researchers, statisticians, administrative office workers, lawyers and personnel recruiters.

*Observational Group.* Jobs in this area typically involve reading gauges and meters. Such workers generally must demonstrate good judgment, keen perception/reaction, and precision in recording. A background in physics is helpful. Occupations in the refinery include treaters and stillmen.

*Mechanical Group.* Workers in this area typically employ tools and mechanical equipments. Good mechanical judgment, keen perception, and good bodily coordination are required. Occupations include machinists and instrument repairmen.

*Manual/Mechanical Group.* This group uses large tools and heavy mechanical equipment. Jobs generally require strong physique, mechanical judgment, and good bodily coordination with emphasis on the arms and hands. Occupations in this area include rig builders and cable drillers.

*Truck Driver/Observational Group.* Workers are typically required to know how to operate vehicles such as trucks, tractors, Jeeps, and possibly swamp buggies. Workers are expected to demonstrate quick reaction, keen perception, good bodily coordination with emphasis on appendages—the arms, legs, and hands. Occupations include truck drivers and tank truck checkers.

*Marketing Groups.* Sell petroleum products and services. This group requires business judgment, and personal qualities to attract and retain customers. Mechanical aptitude and knowledge are very helpful, especially with computers.

*Administrative/Clerical/Personnel Groups.* These groups require training in business administration, office management, and management. Frequently, people advance from clerical jobs to administrative jobs.

## Africa and the Oil Economy

The increase in oil prices in the 1970s meant windfall incomes for African oil producing countries, big and small. For many countries badly in need of hard currency, it was indeed a dream come true. Many nation-building projects, both short-term and long-term, were undertaken. For some countries, the relative profitability of certain industries was overweighted in investment decisions. Consequently, some relatively less profitable sectors of the economy were neglected in the 1970s. This is one of the major reasons for the economic stagnation of the 1980s, in Africa. In fact, the bright investment prospects of the 1970s dimmed as soon as oil prices began to plummet. Export of oil, gas, and minerals constitute the means of creation of a modern economy; they are not an end. They are only vital ingredients in industrialization efforts. Extreme reliance on a few commodities and a few markets tends to overexpose an economy to the uncontrollable external environment of world trade.[72] In this case, a developing economy may deploy substantial outlays in capital projects, then experience bouts of economic growth, but no spectacular industrial transformation, not a novel phenomenon in Africa.[73]

In the 1990s such projects, which were devoid of intrinsic sustainable growth mechanisms, littered the economic scape of Africa, half-completed or abandoned. Explanations have ranged from lack of investment capital to dilapidation consequent upon permissive accounting and managerial practices.[74] For the nondiversified African economies that overly relied on a few chief commodities, such as oil, coffee, and cocoa, the 1980s was indeed the lost decade.

Perhaps reassessing the role of foreign concessions may incorporate marginal discipline into their value in an industrializing environment.[75] The benefits of foreign concessions include technically skilled and reliable workers, effective managers and administrators, widespread knowledge of the use of efficient production techniques, agricultural research and extension, capital, government revenue, and as subsequent generators of employment and income. Given these benefits, reassessing the level of control of foreign concessions is therefore significant. Detailed procedures governing the conduct of business, reporting requirements, negotiations, renegotiations, and terms of agreements must mirror a climate of industrialization. As a basis for strategic planning, obligations to report information, therefore, must be scheduled, consistent, and adequate. Some examples will include statistics on employment, wages and salaries, income supplements (meals, medical services, schooling, and so on), costs of production, import, export, prices, markups, freight charges, warehousing, transport costs, investments, training facilities and results, and other quantitative indicators of economic activities.[76] In an industrializing environment, government equity participation, where analytically feasible, may not be encouraged, especially where equity participation has real opportunity costs.[77] For example, if government invests in a joint venture as an equal partner, this means sharing 50 percent of the profits. However, the same stream of revenues can still be derived from taxes instead of dividends.

The promise inherent in some resource-rich countries of Africa can be fascinating. Yet political turmoil has impeded significant opportunities for positive economic transformation. It has been said that economic development tends to follow political stability. In the last twenty-five years or so, in Angola and in Mozambique, it seems radical industrial change had to wait, in the wings, for political stability. The danger is that significant proportions of many generations of Africans, from cradle to grave, may come and depart in quick succession, disillusioned with only ragged memories of turmoil, hunger, and abject poverty in the homeland, a stark contrast to the impressions of tantalizing images and stories in newspapers, magazines, books, television, movies, of what must be (or at least seems to be) living in relative peace in a golden age in distant lands. History evidences that it is not impossible for political turmoil to continue for a hundred years. While relative peace and stability are not the only reasons that attract foreign investors and multinationals, they remain very significant pull factors in determining the fruition of business ventures in an industrializing environment. It is extremely rare for adequately nourished, clad, housed, educated, and busy, gainfully employed masses to be unreasonably disgruntled. It will, therefore, be necessary for pockets of political instability in Africa to wait for the heavenly magic of industrialization to come to fruition.

## NATURAL GAS

The potential impact of gas on the industrial revolution may be traced back to its application to lengthening the working day. Gas was first used to illuminate factories in 1805, in Britain, although there were earlier experiments in gas lighting.[78]

In the early 1600s, Jan B. Van Helmont, an alchemist in Belgium, was trying to make gold when he discovered manufactured gas. He called it "ghost" or "wild spirit." Some say gas was derived from the Dutch word *geest*, which means spirit. Antoine Laurent Lavoisier conducted experiments on how to light large cities. Circa 1780 he invented the gas holder. In 1792, a British engineer, William Murdock, applied coal gas for domestic household lighting.[79] He discovered that by letting gas flow in minute orifices, he could ameliorate the mixture of air and the quality of the flame enhanced significantly. Advances continued in improving the quality of lighting. By the 1850s, hundreds of cities and towns were using gas flame for street lighting. The gas mantle and the Bunsen burner were developed around this period. The Bunsen burner premixed air and gas and had an adjustable flame, ranging from a yellow, containing carbon, to a hot blue that was smokeless and soot free. Breakthroughs in light and lighting reached incandescent proportions after 1879, when Thomas Edison invented the electric light. The bright prospects of the gas lighting industry suddenly dimmed. Slowly, but surely, electricity began replacing gas in street lamps, and in industrial and domestic settings.

In some places, as early as 1824, residents were known to use wooden pipes to carry gas from small nearby deposits into their homes, where they employed it in cooking and heating.[80] When the wooden pipes proved unsatisfactory, they were replaced with lead and cast iron. Even then, natural gas was available only over short distances because pushing the gas through the lines at high pressure was then impossible.[81] For many years natural gas was considered a scientific curiosity and oil drillers saw it as a waste material that impinged upon oil exploration. Natural gas was inevitably produced with crude oil, and much of the energy languished in oil fields on a profligate scale, until distribution networks could be constructed. Casing heads were flared off like giant torches, and rich oil fields around the world glowed like furnaces in the night. The blessings of natural gas, as we know them in the twentieth century, were slow to come to fruition.

The turning point for natural gas was in the early 1920s, with the development of *acetylene* welding. A former waste product suddenly became a valuable economic resource. It became possible to construct high-strength thin-walled pipes that will transport natural gas under high pressure through long distances. In 1931 the first 1,000 miles of pipeline were completed, and by the 1940s natural gas was widely distributed throughout the United States from the gas fields in the Southwestern part of the country. [82]

In a competitive marketplace, with alternative sources of energy, natural gas was marketed as a clean and more manageable fuel that could be easily switched on and off like electricity. Natural gas lent itself to the use of an automatic burner and the thermostat. This sales pitch did not sell well for the coal industry, which had dominated the residential energy market for ages. The sales pitch of the natural gas industry silently magnified the ritualized ordeal of coal as a fuel for household heating. Would-be converts could envision a basement, then permeated by coal dust and choking thick fumes, gainfully transformed into playrooms or dens for casual entertainment. Coal for household heating was fast becoming a spine-numbing ordeal for some people. Although oil might have been a better choice than coal, it was economically less tenable; old furnaces, which had been retrofitted to use oil, notoriously leaked at the seams, thus releasing a smell that permeated the household. In some places, federal regulations choked off price increases, thus making natural gas a bargain fuel for home heating.

Before natural gas is used as a fuel, it is typically processed to extract important organic chemicals with useful applications in solvents, anesthetics, and alcohol.[83] Through processing, natural gas may be converted into automobile gasoline, oils, and waxes. After natural gas chemicals, also known as hydrocarbons, have been extracted in *cycling plants* the residual *dry gas* is the common gas fuel used in homes and factories. Besides industrial and agricultural applications, natural gas may be demanded domestically for cooking, water heating, refrigeration, house heating, air-conditioning, laundry, drying, and burning of waste in incinerators. This demand for natural gas, however, may not be consistent.

In the industrialized world, variations in demand were overcome logistically, by using underground storage facilities in proximity to communities where the gas is employed in relatively quantum proportions. Sometimes, these underground storage facilities were in fact abandoned or disused caverns, which once produced oil and gas. These geographically strategic loci negated any variabilities in the demand. The demand for natural gas is not only higher in winter months than in summer months, but may vary diurnally; the demand for heating is higher on a cold day than on a mild day.

Natural gas is typically distributed in pipelines in industrialized countries including South Africa. Because of the fugacious quality of natural gas, it lends itself to fluidized commercial operations. The practical applications of twentieth century science and technology have made it possible for both oil and natural gas to flow unseen and untouched by human hands, from the time they emanate from their subterranean caverns until when they are delivered to the end users' facilities. The petroleum industry uses sizable quantities of natural gas.[84] Because oil refining requires a lot of energy, strategic management may require use of in-house gas to the extent allowable by fuel efficiencies. For example, as early as the mid-1920s, Exxon and Mobil built giant refineries that required natural gas for fuel.

*Liquefied natural gas* (LNG) largely improved the distribution efficiency of the natural gas industry. A major technical problem pertaining to the supply and demand for natural gas was resolved by the efforts of a man who had no connection with the oil and gas industries. William Wood Prince, the president of Union Stockyard and Transit Company of Chicago, a subsidiary of Armour Meat Company, determined that his natural gas suppliers were demanding prices he considered exorbitant for company operations. In an attempt to find another source of supply, he conceived the radical idea of freezing natural gas to sub-zero temperatures, so that it becomes a liquid, and then shipping it up the Mississippi by barge from Louisiana.

By cooling natural gas to extremely low temperatures, it was possible to effect *liquefaction*. Compressed to one six-hundredth of its former state, it was likely to lend its bulk more readily to the fluidized operations of twentieth-century commercial science. In 1917, experts in this area determined that the idea was feasible in practice. What required more attention was basic research into the low-temperature properties of metals and insulating materials used for transportation. This effort attracted unusual attention. The World Bank published a report on this development. Continental Oil and the British Gas Council became interested and joined in the venture. In 1959, three years later, a converted dry cargo vessel called *Methane Pioneer* made its first of a series of trial voyages across the Atlantic, with LNG from Louisiana for delivery in Britain. The trials were successful, and in 1964, three LNG tankers began regular ferry service, transporting liquefied natural gas from Algeria to France and Britain.[85] The LNG, for the first time, bridged forbidding market distances that had relegated natural gas in Africa, the Middle East, and elsewhere as recrement. Liquefied natural gas, then, meant hundreds of millions of dollars in contracts for the construction of LNG ships.[86] Countries that were uncertain of developing a full fledged natural gas industry, because of minimal or no reserves, could at least entertain the thought of an import-based natural gas industry.

It is noteworthy, however, that a natural gas pipeline delivery network could be a relatively low-cost and efficient overland transit system. This was the case in north America, pertaining to the Alaska Natural Gas Transportation System, approved under the Natural Gas Transportation Act of 1976.[87] In this project, pipeline transportation was determined to have a relatively long and reliable record of safety, coupled with being a low service-cost system with minimal adverse environmental impacts. This was especially so because the overland pipeline system traversed existing utility and transportation corridors. Well-developed techniques for constructing pipelines in potential earthquake fault areas provided a degree of assurance, then unequaled by the proposed LNG system, in case of a seismic event. Pipelines proved to be a more viable, feasible transportation option than that of the LNG system, which integrated pipelines, liquefaction and gasification, and LNG tankers. In addition, LNG delivered gas at the peripheries instead of directly to markets, where gas was needed. In 1975 dollars it was also determined that, over a twenty-year period, pipelines commanded a lower service cost ranging from $1.03 to $1.05, compared with LNG service-cost option, which averaged between $1.19 and $1.21 per million Btu's over the same period.[88] Pipelines also commanded improved fuel efficiency, since pipelines were determined to require less energy for transportation than an LNG system.

Effectively, in this case, the pipeline delivered more gas at less cost than any other transportation system.[89] This benefit, may not easily accrue in geographical regions visited by political uncertainty.

In 1944, LNG suffered a setback, when LNG storage tanks blew up. By 1970, researchers announced they had surmounted the problem, when they built two double-hulled tankers to transport LNG at -250°F. Liquefied natural gas was successfully transported from Algerian oil fields to industrial markets in Europe and North America, where it was reheated and sold for distribution. Today, like the oil industry, the natural gas industry is a potent force in industrialization.

## WATER POWER

It is sometimes said that truth is stranger than fiction. This is exactly the case with the energy potential of Africa. The continent of Africa possesses the greatest water power potential in the world. Tropical Africa has about 37.5 percent of the total world potential at ordinary minimum flow. This tremendous potential is as much as the combined total hydroelectric potential of Europe, the Americas, and Australia. However, much of this potential is yet untapped. Around 1970, hydroelectricity comprised only 8 percent of the total energy consumption of Africa.[90] Enormous and constant, and cost-efficient energy supply is needed in industrialization.

In the past, water power was tapped as a natural resource to ease the daily burdens of work previously done with hand tools and muscular energy. [91] Such work was often laborious, quickly tiring, far slower, and of sometimes of inferior quality. Mills were therefore placed in motion to do simple and repetitive operations in tasks that required the application of considerable force. Examples of such tasks included crushing, hammering, pounding, pressing, sawing, pumping, and blowing. The rotary motion of the waterwheel was conveyed by cranks, shaft-mounted cams or lifters, or gearing to provide the required back-and-forth, or up-and-down, or round-and-round movements of the simple machinery. A small capacity of about three to five horsepower was usually required to operate a gristmill or sawmill. Even less capacity was required for water-driven bellows of blast furnaces making a few tons of pig iron a week. The water mill demonstrated the needed laborsaving benefits of machinery and mechanical power. The replacement of manual skills with water-powered machine operations was a significant turning point in modern transformation.

Because of the increasingly significant role of, and dependence on, water in many communities, keeping a pertinent database was crucial. Except where water was not a cause for concern, it was necessary to accumulate a record of local rainfall, average stream flow, and lake-stage—all invaluable factors in the computations of future water supply. Besides an analysis of the drainage basin, upstream reservoirs were also important. This upstream catchment for floodwater during wet seasons mitigated water shortages during dry seasons. Millponds were necessary for the overnight accumulation and storage of stream flow that otherwise would be wasted over the dam.

However, it was not long before a substitute was commercially available for this age-old yoke of water, to turn the wheels of industry. This substitute was steam power, in places where the supply of coal was plentiful and cheap. Steam power had an advantage because, it was more swift and powerful, and yet docile. It also allowed the factory to locate in the manufacturing district or closer to ports, domestic markets, bankers (who discounted bills), engineers (in case of repairs), and other businesspeople. Water was no longer a prime determinant of location of industry. Instead, coal transportation and delivery to the steam-powered plants became an important concern. In some places, industry came down from the hills to the more populated plains. The widespread use of steam engines practically changed the face of industry. Industrialists could now increase the size of factories, ironworks, coal-mines, shipyards, and so on.[92]

Before 1850, steam power in rural mill industries was not very widespread. This development of *stationary* power, often in obscure and damp sites in basements and outbuildings or even under urban sidewalks, led to remarkable advances in industrial efficiency and reductions in the cost of production. Transmission of power was secondary in importance to the generation of power. The mill was contained in an elegant and commodious building. Millwork or elaborate and extensive systems of shafting, pulleys, and belting through which power was distributed from engine or waterwheel in factories were more apt to confuse than to inform the visitor. Occasionally in the nineteenth-century factory, steam engines, with their polished brightwork, embellished framing, and rapidly rotating flywheels, were more of a showpiece, included in plant tours for important persons and gingerly placed within the purview of passersby.

The rebirth of waterpower had to await improvements in the waterwheel and the electrical generator. To stress superior efficiency and operating characteristics, the new and greatly improved waterwheels were given the name turbines, from the Latin stem denoting the motion of spinning or whirling.[93] Waterwheels had thus evolved into the complex development of the turbine that cleared the way for the development of hydroelectricity.

Today, hydroelectric stations convert the energy of water falling, from a higher to a lower level into electrical energy that is then distributed to consumers. The attractiveness of water as a source of power was largely because of its relative convenience and lower cost than other sources of fuel.[94] Besides power production, water also offered multiple uses, such as navigation, flood control, and irrigation. [95]

The problems pertaining to the relatively underdeveloped hydroelectric potential in Africa seem multifaceted and varied. For example, wood or timber is still widely used as a source of fuel. Wood is not only expensive to collect and distribute but potentially has better alternative uses. However, these problems are not insurmountable. Some reasons given for the relative underdevelopment of hydroelectricity in Africa include high costs, inaccessibility of sites, and long distances from markets. Because of some of these and other reasons, some countries with energy needs opted to import power. For example, Ghana exported electricity to Benin and Togo, with plans to extend the market to Burkina Faso (formerly Upper Volta) and Ivory Coast. However, in the mid-1990s, Ghana had to cease exporting electricity to these neighboring countries because of low water levels of the Volta River. In Ghana, major domestic industrial consumers agreed to adjust production accordingly. Governments, it seems, could advocate the production and sale of power to finance projects.

Not resolving the problems pertaining to energy supply will be an impediment to industrialization in a competitive marketplace. Broad-based solutions will include economies of scale, pumped storage, interconnections, synergy, and functional management information systems.

Economies of scale tend to reduce unit cost. The economies of scale in power transmission depend on both the quantity of energy and the distance over which it is transmitted. The capacity of the line varies roughly with the square of the voltage and decreases with the distance. By doubling the voltage, the capacity will increase roughly four times through a fixed distance. However, this function is not without limits.[96]

Pumped storage can be used to overcome the increased demand for electricity during peak periods. *Pumped storage* is a recent technique that utilizes two reservoirs at different elevations. During periods of low demand, surplus thermal power capacity is used to pump water to the higher reservoir; during peak demand the water is released to generate power. Although 3 kWh may be used for every 2 kWh produced, here it is still cost effective. This technique uses reversible blades on the waterwheel. The generator acts as a motor, and the unit becomes a pump. What is attractive about pumped storage is that it can operate without a stream. Both reservoirs, in this case, are entirely artificial.

Another recent progress in electrical system planning and operation is in the emergency use and surplus "economy" power. *Interconnections* between small independent systems can be introduced to enhance maximum reliability of power generation between two or more systems. The economies of scale and synergy realized in pooled systems have meant such interconnections could even span whole regions. As with everything else, however, such sophistication is not 100 percent foolproof. There is always the residual danger of a blackout. The challenge, therefore, is how to forestall such a calamity. It seems the best synergies have been computer-integrated supersystems that permit power generation at any given time from lowest cost facilities.

Since electricity was first harnessed more than 100 years ago, technological improvements have altered the panorama of the industry. However, the physics of generating this form of energy has not changed. Electricity is produced when a magnet is rotated inside a coil of wire. The spinning of the magnet may be caused by steam, as in coal, oil, and nuclear power plants; by falling water, as in hydroelectric plants; and by hot expanding gases, as in gas turbines and diesel generators. Because electric energy cannot be economically stored, it must be instantaneously generated and delivered based on customer demand (residential, commercial, and industrial). In an industrializing environment, there is usually a growth in demand for electricity, driven by economic expansion, increasing customer base, new applications for electricity such as electrical appliances. Industrial customers use electricity for more consistent and predictable manufacturing processes. Housing starts and purchases of new electronics and appliances may be used as predictors of growth in residential electricity demand. In a free market and industrializing environment, urban electric rates tend to be higher than rural rates because of the costs associated with decaying infrastructures, laying most transmission and distribution lines underground, and higher taxes. Although electric energy cannot be economically stored and it must be instantaneously generated and distributed, each utility must have a reserve margin of extra production capability to allow for maintenance, equipment outages, and unexpected variations in usage.

With abundant and steady supply of energy, the propensity to lower total cost increases without sacrificing long-term profitability. Although industrial plants may consider having in-house electric production facilities, one reason some industrial plants hesitated to locate in some places in Africa was the relatively high cost of energy. Obviously, not every place in African is adorned with abundant water resources. Cost-effective alternative sources of energy, it seems, have yet to be adequately explored. Other sources of energy that may be significant include natural gas, oil, wind power, solar energy, geothermal energy, and nuclear energy. Where oil is no object, fuel or steam-powered generating plants may be worth considering. Efficiently harnessed in some optimal combination, these alternative sources of energy will greatly enhance industrialization efforts. A very big problem, it seems, resides in the safety of nuclear technology. Although nuclear energy (enriched uranium fuel) could be a very attractive alternative source of energy, inherent problems have been associated with safety, safety regulations, and radioactive-waste disposal. Because of increasing environmental concerns, there has been more focusing on renewable energy sources. However, Ghana has a national Nuclear Research Institute and trains university students in the techniques of nuclear science application for peaceful purposes, such as agriculture, medicine, and research. In 1994, the construction of a nuclear reactor was almost completed. The Ghana Atomic Commission also recommended the addition of a second nuclear physics center.

## NOTES

1. When old forms of control and coordination are undermined and new technologies, cities, and organizational forms are grafted onto preexisting conditions, the tendency will be to create a new path to industrialization. This may set back the clock of industrialization, compelling leaders to take a respite and once again grope for alternative suitable and practicable strategies to accelerate the pace of positive change.

2. Cyril E. Black, Marius B. Jansen, Herbert S. Levine, Marion J. Levy, Jr., Henry Rosovsky, Gilbert Rozman, Henry D. Smith II, and S. Frederick Starr, *The Modernization of Russia and Japan: A Comparative Study* (New York: Free Press, 1975), pp. 342–354. In this case Japan and the Soviet Union stood out, among societies prior to initial industrialization, for the exceptional scale of mobilizing, coordinating, and controlling natural resources. Promodern Japan had relatively high literacy and urbanization rates, and this was reflected in the highly organized character of society. Russia was richly endowed with natural resources (including sparsely settled arable land) and the tendency was to employ them on a large scale and, in retrospect, perhaps lavishly. Inherent deficiencies were later transmuted in *reforms*, after the

1860s. Unlike the *extensive* nature of social organization of Russia, Japan resorted to *intensive* social organization and developed a great capacity for organizing a meager resource base. Japan radically utilized technology-intensive methods and, in the relay to industrialize, availed itself of a new generation of leaders. In the Soviet Union, the highly centralized administrative machine that was efficient in an earlier period proved to be rather rigid and slow to change to new patterns of control and coordination that were requisites in the subsequent phases of transformation. At the risk of digressing, since 1949, China moved from a basis of coordination and control highly decentralized and family-oriented to one capable of much greater degree of coordination and one oriented to some conception of the Chinese entity as a whole. The antecedent extensive-intensive distinction in the "seeds of industrialization" would appear more basic in nature than the ideological distinctions, canalized in highly convincing abstract principles, that have loomed large in this domain. Despite the undeniable need for strict coordination and control, a highly authoritarian approach is not the solution: Stalinist methods, in this regard, are more likely than not to produce similar complications.

3. Harvey S. Perloff, Edgar S. Dunn, Jr., Eric E. Lampard, and Richard F. Muth, *Regions, Resources, and Economic Growth* (Baltimore, MD: Johns Hopkins University Press, 1960), p. 194–309.

4. Ibid., p. 199.

5. *The Courier* (Brussels-Belgium), May/June 1993, pp. 58–59.

6. LaVerle Berry, ed., *Ghana: A Country Study* (Washington, DC: Library of Congress, 1995), pp. 175–176.

7. After 1945, the Japanese developed an intricate system of policies to enhance industrial development, which included close cooperation with private firms. Resources were deployed to specific industries to gain competitive advantage for Japan. The idea was to increase productivity of inputs and to influence industrial investment. Administrative guidance (*gyōsei shidō*) was the principal instrument of enforcement. Influence, prestige, advice, and persuasion were employed to cajole individuals and corporations, alike, to work in directions deemed to be desirable. Persuasion was exerted and advice was dispensed by public officials, who often reserved the right to provide or withhold loans, grants, subsidies, licenses, tax concessions, government contracts, import permits, foreign exchange, and approval of cartel arrangements. Administrative guidance was also used to buffer market swings, to anticipate market developments, and to enhance market competition. Rather than produce a broad range of goods, the Japanese selected a handful of areas and developed high-quality goods for mass production. An example of this effort was the camera industry. Here the Japanese could target market niches and gain economies of scale, albeit on a worldwide basis. The Kodak box camera was an alternative to the very expensive, largely German-made cameras of professional quality, produced in low volume as cheap standardized cameras for mass consumption. The Japanese dramatically lowered per unit costs on the single-lens camera by mass production. Historically, manufacturing sectors in Japan were characterized by competitiveness and were deliberately structured toward high value-added products and high productivity. Ronald E. Dolan, and Robert L. Worden, *Japan: A Country Study* (Washington, DC: GPO, 1992), p. 206.

8. G.C. Gallen, *Japan's Economic Recovery* (London: Oxford University Press, 1958), pp. 120–122.

9. William H. Frederick and Robert L. Worden, *Indonesia: A Country Study* (Washington, DC: Library of Congress, 1993), pp. 182–186. In the case of the automobile, the industry grew under heavily protected domestic markets: assembly plants in Indonesia produced roughly twenty international brand-name vehicles, ranging from Fiat to Toyota. By 1991, domestic firms were producing 250,000 units per year, comprising about eighty different types and makes of vehicles. Such production was usually under license agreements. This production strategy,

however, did not take advantage of the low-cost structures that tend to derive from economies of large-scale production for export.

10. Servan-Shreiber, J.J. *The American Challenge*, p.65.

11. Richard F. Nyrob, ed., *Brazil a Country Study* (Washington, DC: Library of Congress, 1982), pp. 181–197. In the 1920s, both sectors constituted nearly 70 percent of the value added from industrial activities. Chemicals, nonmetallic minerals, metals, and machinery—the basic heavy industries—were added between 1920 and 1950, and grew substantially. By 1950, basic heavy industry comprised one-third of the value added from industrial activities.

12. Ibid., p. 195. One-fifth of the expansion in industry between 1959 and 1970 was the result of technological advancement.

13. Ibid., pp. 181, 192. The two world wars and the Great Depression of the 1930s were stimuli to domestic manufacturing in Brazil. Import substitution, which began with manufacturing consumer goods (food processing and textiles) eventually inculcated finished clothing.

14. Here, even the substantial inflow of foreign capital was inadequate to compensate for the rather anemic growth in export. Consequently, by the early 1960s, needed import prroducts were constrained by controls. The stabilization program(1964–1967) resulted in slow annual growth in the economy and in manufacturing (3.6 percent) but corrected many problems of the rapid growth that followed between 1968 and 1973. Manufacturing growth averaged 13.9 percent per year, while manufactured export registered 38 percent per year. During this period, idle capacity was brought to use. Tariff levels were lowered and import restrictions were liberalized in what may be characterized as a stop-and-go pattern. Export was encouraged by fiscal and credit incentives, and foreign firms were encouraged to locate in Brazil. As a response to the surges in oil prices in 1973 and 1973, however, import restrictions were reimposed. The outcome was an emphasis on import substitution and an expansion of foreign debt (Ibid., pp. 181–197).

15. Among other tooling applications, *laser beam machining* (LBM) manipulates a beam of coherent light to vaporize unwanted material. It is also used for cutting stainless steel or materials that may be difficult to cut by any other means; EDM employs spark erosion; EBM uses electrons that are accelerated to a velocity that is approximately 75% of that of light. Electron beam machining is used mostly in the electronics industry to aid in etching of circuits in microprocessors. The process is performed in a vacuum chamber. *Ultrasonic machining* (USM) utilizes high-frequency, low-amplitude vibrations to create holes and other cavities. Plasma-arc machining uses high velocity jet of high temperature gas.

16. Rita M. Byrnes, ed., South Africa: A country Study (Washington DC: GPO, 1997), pp. 225–226.

17. Ibid., pp. 210–211.

18. Emily Hahn, *Love of Gold* (New York: Lippincott & Crowell, 1980), pp. 51–60. The Royal Academy exhibition was built around the Colombian legend of *el dorado*, the golden one. As the story goes, the coronation ceremonies of the Muiscan took place around Lake Guatavita. Rituals of the coronation called for purification, after which the first task of El Dorado was to pay homage to the spirit of the holy Lake Guatavita. In this part of the festivities the new king was covered (with the aid of resins) in gold dust, giving the appearance of a living gilded sculpture. He was then mounted onto a raft to the middle of the lake, where he made offerings of treasures (by submersion) to the lake-spirit. The subjects did the same amid music, dancing, and so on. Offerings ranged from golden figures, gold plates, coins, and nuggets to emeralds, bracelets, to other glittering adornments. After this custom was abandoned, several expeditions were launched to retrieve the treasures from the bottom of the lake. Muisca country is a tableland of Colombia. Also see Ray Vicker, *The Realms of Gold* (New York: Charles Scribner's Sons, 1975), p. 33.

19. However, gold is susceptible to forgery. Carbon dating of gold is useless, since there isn't any carbon involved.

20. Bruce A. Rogers, *Nature of Metals* (Cleveland, Ohio: American Society of Metals, 1966), p. 95. A British mint, clamped together two well-cleaned blocks, one of gold and the other of lead, and allowed them to remain in contact for four years. "Analysis made at the end of the period showed that gold could be detected in the lead blocks as far as five-sixteenth inch from the interface." This demonstrated the movement of atoms in solid metals.

21. It is also one of the heaviest metals, weighing as much as 19.32 times its own volume of water. The quality of gold is rated in parts per thousand. Thus, a rating of 995 is therefore being 99.5 percent pure.

22. When the number of carats is low, that is much base metal content, then it may tarnish. An example is a nine-carat gold or 37.5 percent purely.

23. Ray Vicker, *The Realms of Gold* (New York: Charles Scribner's Sons, 1975), p. 16.

24. Ibid., p. 128. This was the case of Vaal reefs (South Africa) in 1972. The richest mine in the world was determined to be Crown Mine, a Rand Mines, Ltd., property. It had a life span of seventy-seven years and produced more than forty-four million fine ounces of gold. At a price of $1.80 per ounce, it was worth nearly $8 billion.

25. Hahn, *Love of Gold*, p. 129.

26. Vicker, *The Realms of Gold*, pp.18, 126, 127. After gold-bearing rocks are transported above ground, with the aid of mechanical loaders and cars, the pieces of rock are pulverized in revolving mills. The ore may then be mixed with cyanide, which separates gold from the rock. Zinc dust is added to attract the cyanide from the gold. The resulting slurry is melted and refined in electric furnaces, then poured into 1,000-ounce bars and transported to the refinery.

27. Ibid., pp. 131–132.

28. Ibid., pp. 82–105.

29. Vicker, *The Realms of Gold*, p. 96. The French citizens like to hoard gold in the shape of coins, medallions, and small bars. They do not purchase gold jewelry for its store of value. It is, therefore, easy to shift from a solid-gold article to one that is gold plated, if the design of the latter tends to be appealing.

30. Edward M. Bernstein, *The Gold Crisis and the New Gold Standard*,Quarterly Review and Investment Survey. New York: Model, Roland & Co., 1968, pp. 1–12.

31. Max Bauer,*Precious Stones,* Vol. 1 (New York: Dover Publications, 1968), pp. 113, 119.

32. This is not without exceptions and/or irregularities. However, in substance they are identical chemically with graphite and charcoal. The remarkable disparity in the appearance of diamands relative to that of other for ns of carbon depends strictly on the crystallization of the material and the physical characters consequent upon this. An early experiment to prove this chemical identity of diamonds and carbon was based on the fact that soft-bar iron, when heated with charcoal, takes up a certain amount of carbon and becomes converted into steel. When charcoal was replaced with diamond in the experiment, the conversion of soft iron into steel recurred (*ibid.*, p. 113–115).

33. Another source indicates a range of 3.1 to 3.7.

34. Bauer, *Precious Stones,* Vol. 1, pp. 127, 128. The following are the specific gravities of the different colors of diamond: *Colorless diamond*—3.521; *Green diamond*—3.524; *Blue diamond*—3.525; *Rose diamond*—3.531; *Orange diamond*—3.550. Other values that have been given are: *Colorless diamond*—3.519; *Light yellow and green diamonds*—3.521; *Colorless Cape diamonds*—3.520; *Yellow Cape diamonds*—3.524. Determinations that give results which disperse widely from the mean value of the specific gravity of diamond, namely, 3.52, and those which approximate to extreme values, 3.3 and 3.7, must be regarded as inaccurate or having been made on impure material.

35. *Blue-white* diamonds are the most highly prized of all. The colorings of diamonds are so faint that to the unpracticed eye, it may be difficult to recognize that the stone is colored. This deficiency may be overcome by comparing such a stone to an absolutely pure diamond or to place it against a pure white background. Faintly yellow is not observable as such in any artificial illumination except with electric light and then appears to be colorless.

36. The temperature of ignition is between 690° C to 840° C. Another source stipulates that transparent diamond crystals, heated in oxygen, will burn at about 800°C (1,470° F), forming carbon dioxide. This compares to graphite, which is unaffected by temperatures as high as 5400° F (3000° C). This explains why graphite tends to be used wherever molten metal must be handled. It is the main constituent of containers, otherwise known as crucibles, in which steel, aluminum, brass, and precious metals are melted. Mixed with sand or clay, it lines the molds into which the molten metal is poured, thus giving the surface a smooth finish that allows easy removal of castings after cooling. Graphite is also used in bricks for lining furnaces in which steel is produced. Graphite also has applications as carbon brushes in electrical motors, in dry-cell batteries, in "lead" pencils, in paint, and so on. Synthetic graphite is manufactured from a by-product of petroleum refining and is used chiefly for electrodes in electric-arc furnaces.

37. Paul E. Desautels, *The Gem Kingdom* (New York: Random House), p.97.

38. Typically, the stone to be cleaved is fixed to the end of a rod with some kind of cement (e.g., a mixture of shellac, turpentine, and the finest brick dust or an alloy perhaps of lead and tin). At the end of the rod, the direction of cleavage is parallel to the length of the rod. A second diamond with a projecting edge is fixed to a similar rod with the edge uppermost. A nick is then initiated (by grinding the sharp edge of the second diamond against the first) in the direction in which the cleft is to be made. The rod supporting the diamond is set on a firm elastic base. A tool, usually a sharp, strong chisel is affixed in the proper direction in the nick. The chisel is then dealt a single sharp blow with This is not without exceptions and/or irregularities. However, in substance they are identical chemically a hammer, thus effecting a cleavage. The cement may be loosened by heating. The process is repeated to effect other cleavages. The powder abraded when the nick is initiated collects in a small box provided with a sieve and becomes handy in the process of grinding.Grinding and polishing can be easily accomplished if it is in the direction of least resistance, that is with the grain.

39. Ibid., p. 98.

40. Unit prices of industrial diamonds may range from about $4 per carat for small sizes to about $65 per carat for stones large enough to be used in wire-drawing dies.

41. Robert L. Bates, *Industrial Minerals* (Hillside: Enslow Publishers,1988), p. 37.

42. Versions of the details of these stories tend to vary, but the basic facts remain the same.

43. Of course, an initial find of a few gemstones is not a perfect guarantee of future discoveries. In a rare and unusual case, 80,000 carats of rubies and a single diamond weighing 108 carats were exhibited as initial finds. Later, a smaller lot of stones were included to the exhibition, as additional finds from a second search. Convinced by the exhibition, in 1872, government and capitalists subscribed funding of this promising mining venture. When mining started, 1,000 carats of diamonds and 6,000 to 7,000 carats of rubies were reported as output from mining. Well, to make a long story short, this scheme was an unusual case of a swindle. An official geological survey determined that the (supposed) mining-district had been "salted." The rubies were in reality ordinary garnets, and although the smaller diamonds were genuine, they were in fact imported rough Cape diamonds. The swindler had imported the diamonds and scattered them about in the neighborhood, so plentifully that stray stones could still be found several years later. The initial outlay of the swindler paid off (valued in 1872 at three quarters of a million American dollars).

44. Melville J. Herskovits and Mitchell Harwitz, eds., *Economic Transition in Africa* (Evanston, IL: Northwestern University Press, 1961), pp. 15–19.

45. Like many other early mining fields or districts around the world, the development of mining operations at Kimberly (after the discovery in July 1871) was not without inherent problems. Although many of the original miners made their fortunes in less than a month, the living and working conditions were not the best; nor was the climate the most conducive. The initial dwellings left much to be desired, and the sudden population increase had inflationary propensities. This was the case with Kimberley, then scantily populated. Transportation was slow, typically by wagons drawn by horses, mules, or oxen. Goods going from Capetown (port city) to Kimberley, a distance of about 650 miles, required about one month and two weeks. Eggs, cabbage, potatoes, beer, and wine fetched high prices. Deer meat was the cheapest food around and quickly became the staple article of food. Rainfall was concentrated in a few weeks of the year, and water had to be bought. Wages paid to overseers and miners were similarly high, to match the high prices. When Kimberley was connected, by 647¼ miles of railway line, to Cape Town in 1885 the cost of transport was considerably diminished. The cost of necessities similarly fell and it became feasible to extensively use coal, then from England and South African mines: Bauer, *Precious Stones, vol. 1.*, pp. 179–216.

46. Ibid., p. 180.

47. Jerome Smith, *Understanding Runaway Inflation: An Investor's Guide to Inflation Hedges* (1979), p. 52.

48. *Reader's Digest Almanac 1986* , p. 252.

49. Bauer, *Precious Stones, vol.1.*, pp. 140–155.

50. Among others, the following characteristics tend to be useful in identifying diamonds or in differentiating diamonds from imitations: (1)They are resistant to acids and bases; (2) They are cold to the touch and are excellent conductors of heat; (3) Diamonds are not good conductors of electricity and become charged with positive electricity when robbed.

51. Diamonds had been discovered in the state of Bahia (Brazil) as early as 1755. The immidiate reaction of the government, however, was to prohibit further search, afraid that the agricultural prosperity of the fertile state might suffer. Considerable finds continued until the beginning of the nineteenth century. Amsterdam evolved into the polishing and cutting center in the diamond industry, with many large and small establishments. However, there are other skilful cutters in many other locations, such as in Antwerp, Ghent, Paris, St. Claude in French Jura, London, Hanau, Berlin, Boston, and so on.

52. Bauer, *Precious Stones, vol.1.* pp.155–179.

53. The Rockefellers, the Gulbenkians, the Gettys and even the Rothschilds owe some or all of the fortunes to oil.

54. Betsy Harvey Craft, *Oil and Natural Gas* (New York: Franklin Watts, 1982), p. 4.

55. Christopher Tugendhat, *Oil: The Biggest Business* (New York: G.P. Putnam's, 1968), pp. 9–12.

56. "Oil & Gas including Drilling & Services: Basic Analysis," *Standard & Poor's Industry Surveys, vol. II* (New York: McGrawHill, 1996), pp. 32–35. Because of vibrations and pressure on the drill bit, MWD equipment may provide only a superficial analysis of downhole geology. In case of such deficiencies, *wireline testing* the old-fashioned way may be the best way. Wireline testing tends to be more comprehensive except that it is more expensive. In this process, a wireline—a cable woven from a series of steel strands— is positioned over a vertical well. Calibration tools are attached to the wireline. When a well is ready for evaluation, the drill bit and tools are removed and the wireline lowered into the borehole. Sensing equipment evaluates the geology for hints of potential hydrocarbons. The information is picked up by down hole sensors and transmitted to the surface where it is *logged* at the site or at offsite locations. High speed-computers facilitate the evaluation of geological data. *Platform Express* introduced

(1995) by Schlumberger is an example of a comprehensive wireline-logging tool. Different rigs are typically used for different projects: *Drillships, Semisubmersible rigs, Jackup rigs,* and *submersible rigs.*

57. More recently, to prevent boreholes from collapsing, latex-based cement has been used. This is because, latex-based cement helps maintain the borehole's integrity in a variety of geological conditions. Such downhole conditions may range from heat to extreme pressure. During drilling, special fluids or drilling muds are used to flush away excavations in the borehole, while simultaneously cooling and lubricating the drilling equipment. This is because cuttings and heat may damage the bit, motor, and sensors, rendering the equipment less efficient. Coiled tubing is a metal or steel tubing that is flexible enough to bend but rigid enough to navigate equipment through horizontal and directional boreholes. Coiled tubing, in the drilling world, is important in *remedial* or *reworking* projects, and in facilitating *downhole analysis* in directional drilling. With the aid of steerable motors, the coiled tubing is snaked through a broken borehole, piercing the damaged pipe and creating a new hole.

58. 1 barrels = 42 American gals. (gallons), or 35 imperial gals., or 159 litres; 1 imperial gallon = 1.2 American gals., or 4.6 litres.

59. Tugendhat, *Oil: The Biggest Business,* pp. 9–12.

60. Ibid.

61. *Reader's Digest 1986 Almanac And Yearbook,* pp. 245–253; *The Courier* (Africa-Caribbean-Pacific-European Community), Brussels, Nov/Dec. 1991, pp. 83–84.

62. Seismic analysis is the process used to evaluate subsurface geology before drilling. Seismographs measure the time it takes for an artificially induced vibration or acoustic signal to travel from its source and rebound to a receiver. The strength of the return signal is also evaluated. Because different geological formations reflect sound waves in predictable ways, the data are used to build a "picture" of a site's geological composition. Advances in 3D of three-dimensional diagrams let scientists process information, either at the site or at computer centers located throughout the world. Such data is transmitted at very high speed over long distances using satellites or fiber-optic cables. Computer imaging systems have significantly ameliorated the herculean task of processing seismic and drilling information. Perhaps the most important computer application has been the integration of various oil service functions. Oil service companies are developing total service project applications, which allow oil drilling and production companies use seismic databases coupled with downhole evaluation tools. For example, Schlumberger's *Geoquest* system is useful in data processing, interpretation, and archiving services in order to improve exploration and development success ratios. Using on-site workstations, information is sent to data service centers throughout the world.

63. This is because of oil's advantage as a chemical feedstock. It is principally composed of compounds of carbon and hydrogen, two of the most basic and versatile chemical elements. In the refineries, these are broken down and thrown together into new syntheses. Previously, they were evaporated into the atmosphere or they formed liquids that were often discarded when no use could be found for them. The petrochemical industry was born when the versatility of the applications of these waste products was determined independent of the fuel oil, gasoline, and lubricants with which they were being produced. *Ethylene,* as an example, is the source of ethanol, used for producing acetic acid and eventually cellulose acetate for rayon and plastics; ethylene glycol, used for antifreeze liquids and terylene fiber; polyethylene, used for films, extruded and molded plastics; ethyl benzene, used to produce styrene, polystyrene, emulsions for paints and coatings, and extruded and molded plastics; ethyl chloride, used for producing ethyl cellulose for films, lacquers, and so on; ethylene dichloride, used for producing vinyl chloride, polyvinyl chloride, and PVC plastics.

64. Oil companies did not take full advantage of the chemical potentialities of petroleum until 1939. Oil companies had been busy with meeting the ever-increasing demand for gasoline,

fuel, and lubricants. The chemical industry had similarly been contented with traditional feedstocks—coal, salt, wood, and animal and vegetable matter. Only small quantities of petroleum were bought for further treatment. Wartime shortages sparked the birth of the petrochemicals. For example, the shortages of rubber led scientists produce butane (an oil and gas derivative) and then use it to further manufacture butadiene, which was then combined with styrene to form a synthetic substitute. Fertilizers were manufactured to increase food production; detergents took the place of soap; and so on.

65. "Oil & Gas," *Standard & Poor's Industry Surveys: 1996*, pp. 19–22. The OPEC cartel at this time controled two-thirds of the world's oil reserves and contended that its market share (then at 40 percent) should be more in line with total reserves. In a diversification effort, Saudi Arabia's Star Enterprise went into a joint venture with Texaco; Kuwait resorted to distributing petroleum products in Europe under the *Q-8* brand and held 9.8 percent of the shares of British Petroleum. Venezuela distributed oil in the United States under *Citgo* and *Unocal* brands.

66. Pete F. Drucker, *Managing the Future: The 1990s and Beyond* (New York: Plume, 1993), p. 6. In the 1920s, for example, raw materials and energy comprised 60 percent of the cost of the key product at the time, the automobile. In the 1990s, the key product, the microchip, has a raw material and energy content of less than 2 per cent. Between 1965 and 1995, Japan increased its industrial production 250 percent, without significant changes in its raw material and energy consumption levels. Additionally, investors locate manufacturing plants almost at random in the global market, instead of the earlier practice of producing at home and exporting.

67. Peter F. Drucker, *The Frontiers of Management: Where Tomorrow's Decisions Are Being Made Today* (New York: Truman Talley/E.P Dutton, 1986), pp. 21–49. Among the rapidly industrializing nations of the nineteenth century, Japan approached development by exporting raw materials, silk and tea, in an environment of steadily rising prices. Germany, on the other hand developed by using an infrastructure of knowledge and education to leapfrog into the high-tech industries of that era—electricity, chemicals, and optics. United States used both corridors. Again, world commodity prices have been very low. One of the reasons is increased production efficiency , which tends to scale down raw-material needs. As an example, 50 to 100 pounds of fiberglass cable transmits as many telephone messages as does at least one ton of copper wire. Similarly, the energy requirements (especially petroleum) for one hundred pounds of fiberglass are about 5 percent that required to mine, smelt, and manufacture one ton of copper wire.

68. "Oil & Gas," *Standard & Poor's Industry Surveys: 1996* (New York: McGraw-Hill, 1996), p. 17.

69. Tugendhat, *Oil: The Biggest Business*, p. 219.This advantage can be easily captured in cases where annual oil requirements are put out for tender. This is because bid tenders require more than just prices. They also call for credit terms and currencies. The following example is merely illustrative, since these transactions are typically confidential. In 1966, United ArabRepublic's General Petroleum Corporation asked for bids totaling 2.5 million tons of crude oil, 300,000 tons of fuel oil, 100,000 tons of gas oil, and 100,000 tons of kerosene. Details of the companies' bids, later published in *Petroleum Intelligence Weekly*, indicated the following offers: Shell offered 120 days credit, and was prepared to take payment, 50 percent in pound sterling and 50 per cent in Egyptian pounds. Jersey Standard would accept only 90 days' credit and was willing to accept 90 percent Egyptian pounds and 10 percent dollars. Caltex offered no credit and 30 percent dollars. Mobil offered 60 days' credit and would only accept dollars.

70. Ibid., p. 224. Perhaps the greatest area of competition is in crude oil contracts or prospects for new concessions. But even here, the competition is tempered by the rate of return on investments.

71. Ibid., p. 222.

72. Drucker, *Managing for the Future*, p. 74. In economic history, the point at which a nation's dependence on one market becomes economically dangerous is somewhere in the neighborhood of 25 percent. Again this serves as a marker and does not mean that lucrative opportunities should be abandoned because of a datum. This merely means proceed beyond this point with caution and begin earnestly to explore opportunities in other markets.

73. Robert W. Clower et al., *Growth Without Development* (Evanston, IL: Northwestern University Press, 1966), pp. 90–91.

74. *The Courier* (ACP-EC, Brussels), Nov/Dec. 1991, p. 63.

75. Tugendhat, *Oil: The Biggest* Business, p. 268. A much earlier observation described oil companies' operations in developing countries as enclaves of twentieth century technology surrounded by economies that are to say the least underdeveloped. There is nothing to fall back on if anything goes wrong with oil, and the demand for oil is entirely dependent on the level of economic activity in the consumer countries.

76. Government without statistics is as unthinkable as business without accounts; no amount of intelligence or goodwill can offset statistical deficiencies. To collect information that is not used is wasteful, and so too is the misuse of valuable information and the uncritical application of nonessential or poor information. The collection and organization of data are a ritual. Without organized information, statistical series, and analysis, coupled with pertinent and timely data, administrative decisions are likely to be less effective or reliable.

77. Clower, et al., *Growth Without Development*, pp. 80–84.

78. E.J. Hobsbawn, *Industry and Empire: The Making of Modern English Society* (New York: Pantheon, 1968), p. 43.

79. Then, gas could be made by roasting coal in a tightly closed oven.

80. Tugendhat, *Oil: The Biggest Business*), p.192.

81. Kraft, *Oil and Natural Gas*, p. 3. In China, 2,000 years earlier, hollowed-out bamboo poles were used to transport gas needed to vaporize seawater. The salt residue was then used as meat preservative.

82. Tugendhat, *Oil: The Biggest Business*, 1968), p.193.

83. Ibid., 194. The main constituent of natural gas is methane and may range from less than 60 percent to more than 90 percent. The other constituents are ethane, butane, propane, other light hydrocarbon fractions, nitrogen, and sometimes hydrogen sulphide.

84. *Wet gas* contains heavy hydrocarbons such as propane, butane, pentane, hexane, and heptane. These heavy hydrocarbons can be easily liquefied and form the basis of the natural gasoline industry. They also provide important raw materials for the chemical industry. Dry gas, used as fuel by millions of customers, is natural gas from which heavier hydrocarbons have been extricated. *Sour gas* may contain impurities such as hydrogen sulfide. It may be sold in its original state for industrial and household applications. It is also possible to isolate sulfur from natural gas using modern techniques. *Sweet gas* is natural gas without hydrogen sulfide. It may also be used for industrial, commercial, and residential applications.

*Manufactured gas,* by contrast, is produced from raw materials. There are several types of manufactured gas and they are all used as fuel. When natural gas is combined with manufactured gas, it is called *mixed gas.* Examples of principal manufactured gases include *coke oven gas, carbureted gas,* and *oil gas.* Manufactured gas may be produced by using heat to effect decomposition or by chemical reaction that forms gases composed largely of carbon monoxide and hydrogen.

85. Tugendhat, *Oil: The Biggest Business*, p. 198–199.

86. Norman Melvin, *The Energy Cartel: Who Runs the American Oil Industry*, p. 36.

87. After months of hearings which developed more than 50,000 pages of testimony and exhibits, the Federal Power Commission (FPC) issued a one-volume report of recommendations to the president, urging the designation of overland pipeline system through Canada. After the

FPC report, pursuant of the statute, task forces were organized to report on various issues underlying the selection of a transportation system. Under the Trans-Alaska Oil Pipeline Act of 1973, Congress had authorized the president to explore the possibility of a gas pipeline across Canada with the Canadian government. The outcome was a Transit Pipeline Treaty with Canada, of general applicability to all energy transportation systems, shared by both countries. It was developed and signed in 1977.

88. This was a testimony of John G. McMillan, chairman and CEO of Alcan Pipeline Company, before the Subcommittee on Public Lands and Indian Affairs of the House Committee on Interior and Insular Affairs *and* the Subcommittee on Energy and Power of the House Committee on Interstate and Foreign Commerce (September 22, 1977, Washington, DC). The cost of service (or cost of transporting gas) pertained to Alcan Pipeline company.

89. A statement by James R. Schlesinger, Secretary of Energy, on the *Alaskan Natural Gas Transportation System* to House of Representatives, Subcommittee on Energy and Power, Committee on Interstate and Foreign Commerce, and the Subcommittee on Indian Affairs and Public Lands, Committee on Interior and Insular Affairs, on Friday, 23 September 1977, Washington, DC.

90. William A. Hance, *African Economic Development* (New York: Frederick A. Praeger Publishers, 1967), p. 14.

91. Peter Lane, *The Industrial Revolution: The Birth of the Modern Age* (New York: Barnes & Noble Books, 1978), pp. 67–68.

92. Ibid, p. 236.

93. Louis C. Hunter, *Water Power: A History of Industrial Power in the United States, 1780–1930* (Charlottesville: University Press of Virginia, 1979), p. 318.

94. Ibid, pp. 399–400.

95. Despite the obvious gains, multipurpose use of man-made lakes has not been without problems. For example, without proper micromanagement of projects the lake and shorelines may also pose a threat to human population because of waterborne diseases like schistosomiasis). Water impoundment for hydroelectric-power generation, irrigation, and conservation are frequently implicated. Snail and snail eggs are carried from place to place naturally by water, floating vegetation, and aquatic birds and by people who transport water, plants, dirt, and even tools. Human contact with water is an important component in disease transmission. Feces or urine of contaminated persons can be deposited directly or washed into fresh water. Small amounts of fecal material on clothing being washed may sufficiently contaminate water with eggs. Incidence, morbidity, prevalence and ultimate arrest of transmission is effected by preventing the completion of schistosoma life cycles. Integrated control strategies include chemotherapy, molluscicides (severing weakest links in disease cycle), checking water contamination and exposure, sanitary waste disposal, safe water supplies, health education, monitoring labor migration patterns, landscape alterations, and introducing predators in local ecosystems (e.g., mollusk-eating fish, larvae of sciomyzid flies, the snail specie *Marisa cornuarietis* is a predator snail) or engineering measures to remove snail food supply or to alter water characteristics like temperature and velocity. China used a method called bury the snail, filling in infested irrigation canals and constructing new ones. In St. Lucia and around Lake Barombi in Africa an effective and integrated onslaught against S. haematobium transmission was reported. See B.O.L. Duke and Peter J. Moore, "The Use of Mulluscicide in Conjunction with Chemotherapy to Control Schistosoma haematobium at Lake Barombi Foci . . . III. Conclusions and Cost," *Tropenmedizin und Parasitologie*, vol. 27 (1976), pp. 506–508.

96. Bruce C. Netschert, "Developing the Energy Inheritance," in Melvin Kranzberg and Carroll Pursell, Jr., *Technology in Western Civilization vol.2* (New York: Oxford University Press, 1967), pp. 237–256.

## 11

# African Forest: Treasure House for Industrialization

The idea of the jungle also conjures, at least in the mind's eye, an abundance of trees. In fact, Africa has fewer trees than any other continent. The Food and Agricultural Organization (F.A.0.) reports on the forest indicated an annual deforestation of 0.7 percent or 4.1 million hectares annually. The rate of deforestation was determined to be thirty times faster than reforestation in many African countries.[1]

The equatorial forest was apologetically known as the jungle. The jungle by implication was a connotation of backwardness, underdevelopment, and darkness. Such disaffection for the equatorial forest betrayed the jungle as a bulwark to civilization. In nervous haste, nations around the equatorial belt, it seems, have been cutting down the jungle, perhaps with a sense of apology and as a symbol of progress.

In Africa and other similar places, people have gladly cut down trees for firewood, furniture, lumber, and so on. The seemingly sheer abundance of trees relegated any thoughts of losing this vast treasure house of raw materials. To sensitize the inhabitants of the value of the equatorial regions, the jungle is recently, benignly, and popularly called the rain forest.

The rain forest people may find it difficult to understand the urgency of forest conservation when they are practically being choked by trees. The dim view from below, at least, validates this dilemma. But the simple truth is that the rain forest is disappearing at an alarming rate. Seventy percent of the earth is covered with water. Most of the earth is either too cold, too dry, too wet, or too mountainous for at least cost-effective crop farming. This precarious balance could be easily jeopardized by any further reckless decimation of the rainforest. Here, the dinosaurs are remote and quaint reminders of a worst-case scenario.

More apparent is the destruction of the natural vegetation through the centuries that can be seen on the entire continent. The traditional practice of using wood as a source of fuel is still widely practiced in Africa, out of necessity. Wood fuel remains the primary energy source for more than two billion people around the world. Such *bioenergy* consumption of wood-fuel resources may only continue to the extent that they are sustainable.[2] Centuries of forest fires and overgrazing have reduced parts of the continent to grassland and desert shrubs. As in the Sahel, in Africa, grazing animals have exacted their toll on the vegetation of Algeria, Tunisia and Morocco alike.

Besides man, the chief destroyers of the forest are fires, insects, disease, and wind. Unplanned forest fires can be very costly. When deliberately set, forest fires can be a source of regeneration and revitalization of the ecosystem. Some insects eat a ring around the trunk of a tree (girding), acutely draining the tree of sap, thus contributing to tree decimation. The larva of a moth could be very destructive to trees. Fungi cause tree diseases. This includes mildews, molds, mushrooms, and other related plants. Relatively, wind is not an enemy to trees. Lightning can be a terrible destroyer of trees if it strikes and causes fire, though the humidity in the equatorial regions negates some effects of lightning on trees. Livestock may also cause damage to the forest by injuring young seedlings and tree shoots and by trampling on the forest floor until the soil is too dense for sound root growth. Some animals gnaw the bark around the trunks of young trees and kill them.

## PROTECTING THE RAIN FOREST

In an industrializing environment, the tropical forest becomes a valuable resource that must be protected. Without protection, it may as well become an engine of destruction. Many valuable pharmaceuticals derive from the rain forest. Its abundant tropical plants are important in sustaining nutritional diversity of food crops. Protecting the rain forest during industrialization enhances the ability to prevent floods, soil erosion, and perhaps the spread of disease through changes in disease vectors.

At the dawn of the third millennium, there has been a resurgence of interest in exploring tropical rain forests for their medicinal value. About 65 to 75 percent of higher plant species are indigenous to rain forests, of which perhaps only 2 percent have been explored for their medicinal potential. Approximately 25 percent of prescription drugs contain a plant-derived active ingredient obtained directly from forest plants. For example, the rosy periwinkle plant is used in manufacturing drugs such as *vincristine* and *vinblastine*, which are antimitotic alkaloids; vincristine is useful in pharmacopoeias for treating a certain type of leukemia. A more familiar example is *quinine*, derived from the bark of the cinchona tree. When chloroquine and other synthetic derivatives became less effective prophylactics, quinine was the treatment of choice, almost indispensable for the acute stage of *P. falciparum* malaria. In addition, forest creatures such as leeches, snakes, ticks, and vampire bats are used in the development of new anticoagulants. Without discounting the importance of biomolecular engineering, natural products and particularly tropical rain forest plants remain an essential source of bioactive compounds. Clues to current efforts in the development of antiviral agents have come from the rain forest.

Industrialization, which is coupled with deforestation, may threaten the wild relatives of major crops and the supply of alternative foods. For example, one species of wild rice from India became useful in protecting the crops in Asia from four major rice diseases. The introduction of wild Brazilian cassava genes, to provide disease resistance, also introduced the potential to increase the yield of cassava by eighteenfold in Africa and India. When tomato seed no. 832, collected in 1962 from the Peruvian Andes, was backcrossed ten generations with a commercial tomato variety, the resulting tomatoes were larger, with an increased sugar content. In an industrializing environment input efficiencies such as these in preserving gene diversity enhance productivity, increase production, and reduce the potential for commercial crop failure. The future of nutritional diversity in Africa may well depend on the tropical forests. In Nigeria, for example, approximately 150 species of woody plants are used locally for nutritional purposes, and some 1,500 leafy plants from the forest are useful in the tropics as leafy vegetables.[3]

When forest margins are preserved (as opposed to their deforestation for agriculture), they enhance the maintenance of aquatic diversities  and thus, the preservation of a cache of significant animal protein. When forest aquatic margins are not sheltered, perhaps because of deforestation that may include catchment area, this encourages soil erosion and runoff. Deforestation reduces the water-absorbing capacity of the soil, which may be jeopardized when coupled with overgrazing, overcultivation, and salinization. In West Africa, a study determined that runoff rates were twentyfold higher from some cultivated and bare soil than forested areas. Without trees, erosion rids the soil nutrients, since mineral nutrients are not recycled from deep soil layers and the top soil is washed off. The ability for plant roots to take hold is reduced, and overall farmland productivity is negated. The consequences may be extensive: rivers, lakes, and even reservoirs become silted, reducing the storage size of reservoirs and increasing floods in the immediate and outlying areas.

Logging, clearings, and firewood are culprits in deforestation. Logging, however, does not have to be a problem where tree harvesting is systematic and regulated. With industrialization, people, especially educated specialists in respective fields, migrate to urban areas to work, since opportunities for gainful employment usually do not exist in their rural settings. This tendency generally puts a check to future forest clearings for agriculture, by future generations. Electrification is usually a standard fixture of industrialization, which therefore means less tree cutting for firewood and charcoal. Forest management that encourages continuous growth of hardwood trees can both protect the rainforest and generate  employment and income for timber-producing areas. Here, much can be learned from South Africa. Deforestation, overgrazing, soil erosion, and desertification are problems that cannot be overlooked in an industrializing environment.

Although Africa has not been neglectful of the plight of its ecosystem, there still remains much to be done. The forest provides products such as firewood, charcoal, fruits, fibers, medicinal herbs, leaves, fodder, grasses used for weaving, timber, and so on. It is very easy to deplete these resources without making allowance for natural regrowth or tree-replanting projects.

A good forester usually cuts trees only where other trees will grow to replace them. The wise farmer adds to the soil plant foods extracted from it by crops. Harvesting mature trees that will eventually die of old age, if left standing, gives young trees more room to grow faster. Selective cutting is a method of conservation. Selective cutting in this case may mean cutting in blocks, or thinning out. The idea is to ensure that there are seed trees or young trees in the nurseries that are constantly replacing the aged or grown trees. In this way, conservation not only sustains the forest but becomes a treasure house for industrial raw materials.

When conservation laws are ignored, the effects may be catastrophic. When forest is cut without replacement, it renders the soil bare, exposed to the elements of rain and wind erosion. Erosion increases the propensity for drought, because less moisture is retained in the vicinity. At this stage, the worst that can occur may occur—famine, which, caused by war, floods, harmful insects, or drought, is very destructive.

Typically forest activities go beyond managing timber extraction. Efforts are made to rejuvenate degraded streams and spawning grounds. When cutting forest may negatively impact stream sedimentation, it is discouraged. Forest clear-cuts are limited to a few acres, and trees have to regenerate naturally or be planted within a space of five years, whichever comes first. The impact of logging and mining on streams and rivers is carefully examined, and their effects on fish and aquaculture are considered. Investments are made to improve streams and fish habitats that are crucial for spawning. Wildlife habitats are not discounted. Paint is used to mark trees. For example, blue marks may indicate trees saved for seeds, shelter, stream improvement, animal denning, and so on.[4] Depending on other considerations, an average of, say forty trees, may be harvested per acre, while an average of fifteen trees is retained per acre, assuming these trees had been previously planted. The headwaters of tiny streams are designated protection zones, within, say, a fifty-foot band. Trees inclined to streams or rivers are generally not harvested, since they provide stability to stream banks.[5] When streams are not shaded, their rate of vaporization is increased, thus enhancing their marginal affinity to degrade into seasonal streams.[6]

By the same token, effective forest management is generally executed in conjunction with wildlife management and conservation. The populations of wildlife must be closely monitored. This is especially true for Africa, where many people rely on game as a source of protein. Hunting without regard to season, gender, or age, is not efficient. Relentless and continuous hunting of a very small population of wildlife species for food may endanger the species and ultimately result in extinction in some areas. With a rapidly growing African population, it is a good investment to ensure self-sustaining wildlife populations that may serve future generations as invaluable food and other resources.

It the case where wildlife habitats have been destroyed due to deforestation, fires, floods, and so on, providing artificial habitats may be necessary. For example, birds may be provided with nesting boxes. Like humans, wildlife is also exposed to the vicissitudes of the environment. It pays to use radio collars to monitor sample populations. It also pays to take blood samples for laboratory tests and even to administer antibiotics when and if necessary. Although conserving wildlife populations is necessary, it is equally important to remember that occasionally, some wildlife populations may be in conflict with ranchers and foresters. For example, some animals, because of overpopulation, may eat or destroy newly planted seedlings, endanger highway traffic, or even encroach on human settlements.

Efficient and effective forest management is not only the responsibility of the forestry officers. It is usually the integrated effort of engineers, soils scientists, hydrologists, biologists, geologists, entomologists, other experts in the community at large.

Forests in South Africa cover only 1 percent of the total land area. Although the land was naturally never forested, there was some denudation of its natural wood resources in the early twentieth century. Plantations to grow trees for commercial use began after 1918. Most timber plantations produce pine and eucalyptus trees. The forest produces at least 14.5 million cubic meters of unseasoned timber annually. Several hundred thousand people are employed in timber farms, and more than 240 wood-processing factories. Although most wood is used for fuel, industrial applications include construction and mine props, paper products, and diverse agricultural applications. The pulp and paper industry expanded operations for export in the 1980s. The industry was promoting the use of timber frame in housing to increase its share of the domestic market.

In *Ethiopia,* certain tree species such as *boswellia* and species of *commiphora* are grown in arid lowlands and produce gums that are the bases for frankincense and myrrh. A species of acacia, found in several parts of the country is a source of gum arabic, used in the manufacture of adhesives, pharmaceutical products, and confectionery. The eucalyptus, introduced in the nineteenth century and grown mainly near urban areas is a valuable source of telephone poles, tool handles, furniture, and firewood. It is also a major source of the material from which fiberboard and particleboard are made. The vast network of roots of the eucalyptus (in this case *Eucalyptus globulus Labill*) literally drains marshy areas in hot and humid environments, converting "fever districts" into healthful, dry areas.

In *Nigeria,* in the early 1960s, the government focused on fast-growing species such as teak and gmelina (an Australian hardwood). During the 1970s and 1980s, State plantations became an important source of timber, paper pulp, poles, and fuel wood. Despite these developments, forestry's share of GDP declined from 6 percent in the 1950s to 2 percent in the late 1970s and 1980s. The oil boom in the 1970s increased demand for wood in the domestic construction industry, which in turn slowed timber export. In the 1980s, demand (outside paper pulp and paper) for commercial wood products overwhelmed resources. An afforestation effort was announced in 1989.

In *Sierra Leone,* in the mid-1970s the government forestry policy focused on increasing the rate of exploitation of domestic forests in the hope of replacing import. In 1973, imported sawn and manufactured wood were equivalent to 15 percent of domestic consumption. Over a five-year period, from 1974 to 1979, the plan was to concentrate on sawmill development, and research into plantation silviculture was slated for intensification. The forest plantation was extended at a much slower rate than planned and comprised only thirty-three square miles, or 3 percent of forest area in 1974. Reserved forest comprised about 4.3 percent of total land area. These forest reserves and protected areas consisted of remnants of the original high forest cover that had not been cleared for cultivation and consequently often occurred on widely scattered small patches of steep hillsides or infertile soils.

*Bamboos,* and *Eucalyptuses* are examples of the many kinds of industrially valuable nonwoods and trees that may be used in afforestation. It must be noted, however, that such efforts are not without inherent problems. The nuances of the problems and solutions to adaptability or introduction of tree species pertain, in this case, to the specialists. Bamboo is the common name for forty-five genera of about 480 species of treelike plants of the grass family. Some bamboo species are very fast growing and may grow as much as twenty-four inches per day, eventually reaching a height that may be as much as 164 feet or 30 meters. Besides other common uses, bamboos are also used in paper manufacturing. Thomas Edison found carbonized filaments from a single fibrovascular bundle from an internode of the treelike plant. This was the ideal material for his early incandescent light bulbs. It was not until 1910 when this cellulose material, which forms conduction tubes for moving liquid in trees, was replaced in the globe by fine metallic wire.[7] Ranges of bamboo species vary with moisture. One kind may be on the wet southern slope of a mountain at a certain elevation, but not on the dry northern slope. Some bamboos may be well spaced out like a well-seeded field of corn. This is the case with *Arundinaria alpina,* the Kenya bamboo.[8]

Eucalyptuses are very useful in industry and have been planted in many parts of the world. They may be found on the continent of Africa in countries such as Egypt and Cameroon. These trees grow very rapidly, and some species may reach gigantic heights of 300 feet in four to six years. These trees are very useful for their oil, gum, and timber. After twenty to thirty years they can be harvested as timber. The *jarrah* is an Australian eucalyptus with a red wood much like mahogany. Eucalyptuses are very good as wind breaks around orange and lemon groves. They make good shade trees along roads and streets and are a good source of firewood.[9] There is no better wood than eucalyptus to make lumber for ships, railroad ties, paving blocks, telegraph poles, fences, and piers. At low moisture content, wood is classified as an electrical insulator. This explains why wood has been used as a common material for high-voltage power-line poles and for tool handles. These woods are a source of large amounts of resins called *Botany Bay Kino.* Kino protects woods against borers and shipworms. This makes it especially suitable under water. Some species contain tannin, which is useful for treating fevers. The bark of the *stringy bark* is used for making paper and rope. The leaves contain oil that smells like camphor. The oil is an antiseptic deodorant and stimulant. It has been used for lung and throat disease and for dressing wounds. These trees are used in building construction and make fine cabinet timber. Eucalyptus oil is an essential oil, derived from eucalyptus leaves and used as an antiseptic and disinfectant.[10]

## FORESTRY AS INDUSTRIAL SPRINGBOARD

Africa has been doing exactly what it did during the European Industrial Revolution—exporting raw materials and semi raw materials in exchange for imported finished products. In the forest domain, timber and other valuable goods have been exported.

Although many countries have paper mills, the pulp, paper, and board industry is largely not yet developed. In 1988, total paper production was 2,588,000 tonnes. By 1993, production had fallen to 2,353,000 tonnes. This was a contrast to the increased production registered in the regions of Asia and the Pacific and Latin America over the same period. Taking advantage of the unexploited opportunities in the paper industry will be competitively very difficult for Africa, if trees and nonwoody plants are not urgently cultivated in sufficient quantities. Non wood fibers with applications in paper and paperboard manufacturing may include straws, bagasse, bamboo, cotton, reeds, sisal, jute, abaca, kenaf, and flax. Paper is needed for commercial and industrial uses: newsprint; groundwood paper; uncoated converting paper; uncoated free sheet; bleached bristols; cotton fiber paper and thin paper; packaging and industrial converting paper; special industrial paper; tissue paper; and other machine-creped paper. Wood will also be needed for *Paper Boards*: unbleached packaging and industrial converting paperboard; bleached packaging and industrial converting paperboard; semichemical paperboard; recycled paperboard; wet machine board; and other nonspecified paperboard mill products. The forest resources are also needed for *construction paper and board*: these include insulating board, construction paper, other nonspecified building paper and board, and hardboard products.[11]

Extrapolating historical rates, some countries in Africa that are traditional timber exporters may run out of timber for profitable export in a decade or two.[12] However, this may be reversed by effective and aggressive programs that replace harvested trees and even go the extra and needed mile of establishing forestry as the basis for developing the paper industry. Industrialization does not in any way call for the reckless decimation of forest resources. This is why industrialized nations have been able to export wood products to other parts of the world, including from Africa. In fact, industrialized nations have some of the best-managed forests. When the management of forest is treated superficially, the ripple effects can be disastrous to the economy, the climate, and the environment at large.

## DESERTIFICATION

The largest desert in the world is the Sahara Desert in North Africa[13] In recent years, the tree line in northern equatorial Africa has been slowly pushed southwards. Left unchecked, it seems permanent desert conditions will increasingly impose on the sahelian region, amid lingering drought conditions.

The Sahelian region is a large ribbon of marginal land spanning the southern limits of the Sahara Desert and the fertile lands and the forests that stretch down to the West African coast. It stretches from the Atlantic ocean on the west through Mauritania, Mali, Burkina Faso, Niger, and Chad. Most of the northerly segments, Senegal, Ghana, Cameroon, Nigeria, and the Central African Republic, constitute the southern limits of the sahelian ecology. Nomadic people such as the Tuareg and the Fulani inhabit this area. Camels and cattle are typically important in the lives of these nomads. Southwards the populations are more settled in thousands of villages. Outside the towns and cities, the people are mainly subsistent farmers that depend on such crops as millet, maize, and sorghum. The *sahel* in Arabic means the shore.

The people of the *Sahel* for the most part thrived in the 1960s. There was relatively frequent rainfall. The cattle population rapidly increased, and the human population virtually exploded. The growing economies of Nigeria and Ivory Coast served as ready market for increased supply of beef. But the delicate balance of this desert shore could not stand the test of time. The increased populations of goats and cattle devoured much of the vegetation, further marginalizing an already marginal ecosystem. The Sahel, it appeared, had reached that fragile threshold where it could not take any more strain from overgrazing, let alone just one spell of drought.

In 1969–1970, a drought reared its ugly head in this region—a drought that arrested the seemingly eternal prosperity of the 1960s. Between half and two-thirds of the cattle population was devastated by 1973. Since then, the droughts in the *Sahel* have been intermittent, degenerating into desertification. It appears life for the nomads will never be the same again. Journeys of the nomads to the more settled south, to escape the adversities of drought in the north, were not without inhospitable gestures from the sedentary farming southern residents. The camel-borne trade that had survived centuries in the Sahel and the Sahara is gradually being replaced by airplanes, railways, roads, and lorries. Consequently, this has severely reduced the incomes that derived from caravan trade, transport, and camel breeding.[14] It appears, all across the Sahel, radical economic policies may be necessary to cater to the plight of the nomad on the eve of the twenty-first century.

Desertification in Africa presents an opportunity to revamp the traditional practices in agriculture and animal husbandry. There is room for land rehabilitation in Africa. The favorable land–man ratio on the continent means ample opportunities and potential for a vibrant agricultural base for industrialization *without* destroying the valuable resources of the fragile ecosystem.

While the tsetse fly and other disease carriers remain imminent dangers, they can be strategically exterminated, using current technology and scientific knowledge. There are at least seven million square kilometers of land that can be brought under cultivation.[15] For example, in 1986 it was reported that the people of Burkina Faso had been suffering from drought since 1970, and annual average rainfall had dropped to less than ten inches. The people here were resigned to dependence on international relief organizations for food. Although the Black, the White, and the Red rivers are by definition natural resources, much of the fertile land in the valleys remained fallow. Since the inhabitants were afraid of the river blindness disease carried by blackflies along the rivers, this fear arrested the will to cultivate the fertile river valley.[16]

The nomads who inhabit the semi-arid regions of West Africa typically demonstrate a movement governed by the seasons. For centuries, this lifestyle of pastoral nomadism was feasible, because of very low population density. Increasingly, the big picture is changing: aridification of the Sahel, relatively high population growth, increased pressure on land use by a statistically bigger population of subsistent farmers, and the persistent use of firewood as a main source of household fuel. It appears, for many West African countries, the urgent moment has come to rescue this precarious and fragile ecosystem from the weight of a much bigger population trapped in what seems to have become an ancient but simple and a convenient lifestyle.

Understandably, pastoral nomadism flourished for centuries in Africa, Europe, the Americas, and other parts of the world because of valid climatic reasons. Regions that were not suited for agriculture were employed as grazing territory. Since fodder and water had to be obtained throughout the year, the herders moved from one grazing ground to another. For ages, nomads in the Sahel have been driving their herds from place to place along the grassy areas in much the same way as the Hebrews of biblical times tended their flocks. Some nomads have attained high levels of learning, but overall nomadic life is much simpler than those of settled people. For example, nomadic habitats are often tents, which render added flexibility of moving around. This is unlike the permanent houses or homes of semi-nomadism and transhumance.

Persistent drought conditions in the Sahel have prompted nomadic tribes to drift much farther south. For example, in 1984 and 1985 when drought conditions were more dramatic, many nomads flocked from Niger, Nigeria, Burkina Faso, Togo, and even Ghana and Mali. In desperation, the traditional migration over the Sudanese zone unusually overlapped into southern and central Benin, where the more tropical vegetation is inimical to grazing. This brought herdsmen into proximity with peasant farmers, who were not used to nomadic herdsmen and their flock. The encounter was not without ensuing problems.[17]

The relationship with more settled peasant populations farther North is much more friendly. The farmers are used to the nomads and through the years, developed a symbiotic relationship. For example, in northern Benin, the Bariba and the Dendi people are agricultural and fishing communities, respectively. More than a hundred years ago, Peul herdsmen, searching for good grazing pasture, were accommodated in northern Borgou. Through a series of arrangements and understandings, both the farmers and the herdsmen thrived. After the grain harvest, the farmer allowed the herdsmen to graze their cattle on the plant stubs.[18] Considering the fact that cattle may deposit droppings on land as much as twelve times a day, the dung increased soil fertility. Before the herdsmen left the stubble fields for greener pasture, farmers consigned the few cattle they owned to the herdsmen, for grazing. In return for taking care of the farmers' cattle, herdsmen were typically allowed to keep the milk and some calves.[19] Nevertheless, in the face of desertification, what is acceptable and functional for the traditional lifestyles of pastoralists may no longer be good for the land. For example, pastoralists tend to need ever more land, because the more cattle a man has, whatever the quality, the higher his status in his community. Pastoralists also attach great and mystical value to livestock. They are like a bank account, a means for acquiring wives, who in turn will bear girls, who, when married, will fetch more cattle by custom.[20]

With lingering drought conditions since the 1970s, herdsmen have been bombarded with numerous problems. Some problems include restricted land use, limited or debarred accessibility to grazing lands, shortage of water holes, less interdependence between the farmers and herdsmen, and poor quality of cattle. Because of increased populations, more farmers have expanded agricultural lands. This agricultural land use has sometimes hemmed in grazing land, precluding herdsmen from an ingress. Sometimes, herdsmen had to traverse officially prohibited territory just to reach grazing land. An example is the National Park of "W"in Benin. Herdsmen overburdened limited pastures during protracted drought spells. Their grazing cattle on already grazed pastures, destroyed grass, shrubs, and young trees. Tree branches were cut off so that cattle might feed on the leaves. Under increased population pressure roaming cattle, coupled with unscientific brush fires, levied a cataclysmic toll on the Sahelian ecosystem. In some places, such as water holes, what remained was an expanse of cracked, sunbaked mud flat.

The strength of a nation resides in human resources. Pastoral nomads have fed an exploding urban population with untold quantities of beef. Although modern methods of agriculture and livestock husbandry in an industrializing environment measure against pastoral nomadism as more efficient, the plight of the nomad may be ignored. Strategic solutions such as intensive agriculture, artificial lakes, silos, crop rotation, water tanks, reforestation, and irrigation should not relegate the change implications for the nomad.

It appears the time has come for African economies to advocate, consistently, contemporary methods of raising farm animals. This is especially significant when one considers the ramifications of industrialization with a veterinary infrastructure in Africa. Many animal diseases are transmissible to humans. Many animal diseases are spread by insect vectors, meat, and milk. A frontal attack on the problems of raising farm animals will be beneficial in Africa south of the Sahara, where the patient–doctor ratio is still very low. Veterinary is at the very foundation of human and industrial development.

In some places, in the industrialized north, a day was set aside for the planting of trees. In this case, it became a day of observance especially by schoolchildren. This is usually crucial in an environment where many trees had been used for homebuilding and for firewood or to make room for farmland, or where traversing for miles without seeing a single tree is not unusual for a traveler. This is reminiscent of some parts of Africa today. The tree most distant from any other tree in the world was sited at Ténéré

Desert, Niger Republic. There were no other trees for thirty-one miles. After an incident in February 1960, the tree was transplanted and is now in the Museum of Niamey, Niger.[21]

Conservation in Africa still has much work ahead. Many Africans, with very tight household budgets, are quick to explain that the trees have to be cut down because people have to eat. The justification tends to be that, considering the income bracket and financial obligations, firewood is the only fossil fuel that is affordable. Such valid but simplistic arguments have been heard around the world for hundreds of years. Europeans may not be very vocal about the African situation, but many do know, very well, the tribulations that emanate from man's overly parasitic relationship with the environment.

Europe imported large quantities of food for more than a hundred years because populations exploded while the soil degraded. For 500 years or so sheep and goats destroyed trees and shrubs. The result was a ruined soil, from overgrazing, in Italy, in Spain, and in Greece.[22] Northern Africa had been devastated earlier to feed and sustain ancient Rome. This was aggravated by exorbitant mining practices and soil erosion, caused by relatively heavy rainfall in southern Europe. The effects of erosion were milder in central and northern Europe because of much lighter liquid precipitation, with a correspondingly less-erosive momentum. Central and northern Europe suffered loss of mineral and forest cover.

European nations embarked on conservation programs as early as the 1860s. Norway and Sweden adopted forest conservation programs. Denmark and Belgium demonstrated that poor sandy soil could be transformed into rich farmland with the application of fertilizers. By dyking and draining portions of the sea, Belgium and the Netherlands created some of the richest farmlands on earth. French farmers diligently saved and used available bits of animal manure. French foresters kept forest growing on mountain slopes and sand dunes. The northern plain of Germany that was wetland and poor soil was drained and fertilized. In Switzerland, the propensity for flooding from the mountain slopes was checked by effective forest management. The northern part of Italy around the Po Valley was drained and enriched. Land reclamation programs in Greece and Italy were considerably successful. When the northern forest of the former Soviet Union was damaged as a result of fire and logging, conservation efforts in Russia included planting trees in dry areas and controlling rivers to prevent flood damage.

In the Orient, Japanese learned very early and understood very well the value of the environment. Besides population pressure, three-quarters of the land is too mountainous for permanent cultivation. Land in Japan is very carefully conserved. Waste from homes and commercial fertilizers were used to keep the soil adequately fertilized. Today, the hills and mountains are covered with natural and *cultivated* forest. Although much of the soil in China had been damaged, careful methods of farming have preserved much of the soil fertility. To prevent soil erosion, the hillsides were carved out into terraces, where the farmers raise crops.

As populations have increased, there has also been a strain on the forest resources. Although measures have been taken to reverse forest loss, it appears much more work still has to be done, considering overwhelming demographic factors. In India, as in some parts of Africa, the least privileged in some places tend to use animal dung as fuel, rather than as manure. This has rendered some soils poor in nutrients. India, like Pakistan and Burma, has well-developed forest services to protect and sustain timberland. In Israel, irrigation projects have transformed desert wasteland into rich farmland. Swamps and lakes were also drained to provide soil for crops.

Whereas conservation has become an intrinsic part of industrialized and industrializing societies, to many individuals in Africa it remains an alien concept that attempts to impinge on traditional lifestyles. To put it mildly, many individuals in Africa have been more concerned with more fundamental and urgent problems like poverty, hunger, literacy, and health. Envisioning allocating food for wildlife during a drought spell is difficult for the Africans unsure of their next meal.

## SOLUTIONS NEARBY AND FARAWAY

Sometimes, urgent solutions to the drought problems may have to be sourced from without. Often, the answers to some problems are a stone's throw away.

There are projects in Africa that may serve as localized examples of a people dealing with the problem of aridification. One example is the Keita Project in Niger. This project transformed barren landscape into a flourishing environment of crops and livestock. In this project that is stark in the middle of the Sahara Desert, fifty-three village wells were drilled, coupled with 500 smaller wells for crop irrigation. Anti-erosion trees were planted. Life in some 205 villages has been ameliorated. This example just illustrates that hopes can be realized even in the middle of the desert.

Ten percent of Africa is underlain by high yielding aquifers.[23] Water good enough for human consumption and irrigation occurs naturally beneath vast tracts of the deserts of the world. In Africa, much of the desert water is "fossil" water that accumulated over the past 100,000 years. It must be remarked, however, that such subterranean water is irreplaceable.[24] The problem of water in these parts of Africa could be counterbalanced, not only by reforestation and damming but also by regulation and irrigation. Only five million hectares of the 150 million hectares suitable for irrigation have been irrigated. Irrigation will not only increase animal and crop yields but will also booster international and domestic trade and create buying power and jobs.

Zoologists researching in Africa remarked that the native antelopes, such as Grant's gazelle and oryx, can survive a severe drought, while domestic cattle typically die of thirst unless led to a good water hole every day or every other day. The reason for such stamina was that the antelopes fed between midnight and early morning, when night air cooled to almost 60 degrees Fahrenheit, and relative humidity rose to almost 85 percent. During the cool hours of the early morning, the vegetation absorbed moisture until the leaves were 40 percent water. By eating them, the antelopes obtained all their moisture requirement. In the daytime, the hot sun and the moisture starved (dry) air quickly reduced the moisture content of the leaves to about 1 percent. When the herdsmen led their cattle to feed on the same plants, only negligible moisture requirements were met. The only resort was to take the cattle to a good water hole daily or every two days. The scientists disclosed these findings to the herdsmen, but the herdsmen were afraid to feed their cattle at night because of the dangers of beasts of prey and rustlers.[25]

In North America, the problem of overgrazing at the turn of the century was surmounted by charging token fees from cattle ranchers that grazed on public land. In this case, about 9 percent of cattle graze on public land. The token fee is used to maintain the ecosystem and to prevent overgrazing that may result in soil erosion. Soil erosion not only destroys spawning grounds for aquatic life but also precipitate loss of vegetation. This loss of vegetation similarly increases the rate of vaporization, in the streams. As a result, the streams are exposed to degrade into seasonal streams that are likely to dry up during the hot summer months. In the vicinity, there may also be loss of desirable grass caused by suboptimal moisture conditions.

Regulation for cattle grazing, began in the United States in 1906. Fees for grazing on public land were not charged until 1934. The idea was not to burden cattle ranchers with added cost when they were barely breaking even in the cattle business. The fees only kicked in when the business in cattle started booming. The fees for grazing on public land have averaged about one-eighth the fees of grazing on private land, or about $1.86 per cattle per month. While this fee is used to conserve the public lands from overgrazing, it is only a little more than one-third the cost of conserving publicly grazed land. The government effectively subsidizes these revenue deficits with other sources of revenue.[26] At least, the cattle ranchers are sure they can afford to come back on public lands year after year to graze their cattle. Overgrazing is not the problem!

Several shrubs and trees have outstanding positive ramifications for conservation. The *clover* for example, is a very valuable plant used for improving soil fertility and livestock feed. The leaves have nodules rich in nitrogen. There are several kinds of clover. Many of them thrive in temperate regions. Clovers grow in mountain regions and in lowlands. They thrive in southern Africa and in South America. When the red clover was introduced in Australia, they did not produce seeds until the bumblebee was introduced to pollinate them. Other clovers include white clover, crimson clover, Japan clover, alsike clover, hop clover, ladino clover and so on.

The perennial *alfalfa* is preferred fodder. It enriches the soil greatly. Alfalfa grows best in warm temperatures and where the air is dry. A moist soil is conducive. Lime soil is best. Nitrogen-fixing bacteria are also necessary. If the soil is lacking the bacteria, then they must be artificially introduced by sprinkling the alfalfa field with small quantities of soil from other fields where alfalfa or sweet clover has been grown successfully. Bacteria culture that are prepared and sold commercially ensure positive results. Alfalfa roots may grow as deep as seventeen feet. They may give seven to eight crops per year. They have a high food value and high protein content. Bees make large quantities of honey from alfalfa. They may grow in mountain regions, arid regions, and at sea level. To obtain seeds hot, dry conditions are necessary. Crops of alfalfa are grown in dry, irrigated regions.

Human beings have probably cultivated alfalfa more than any other plant used primarily for animal feed. Cultivated in Persia during the Christian Era, it was introduced in Greece during the Persian invasion. Alfalfa got to Italy about 100 A.D., and much later into other parts of Europe. Spanish explorers took the alfalfa to South America and Mexico. Alfalfa was introduced into the United States of America from Chile, during the Gold Rush of 1854. Alfalfa is in Africa, but the value has not been adequately exploited. *Timothy Hay,* introduced in the Carolinas in 1720, is the most valuable cultivated hay in North America. Used in crop rotation with grains, it makes good hay, but not good pasture grass.

The *Mpingo* tree of Tanzania is a hard African blackwood used for making clarinets in the West. The native carvers use it to make sculptures. This tree is very resistant to drought and serves as a bulwark against desertification. Planting trees with the characteristics of the *Mpingo* along the southern front of the Sahara Desert will be a help in checking desertification

The value of the *African Lungfish* has not yet been properly harnessed. The lungfish holds an important place among fish. The lungfish has gills like other fish and a pair of lungs. These dual breathing organs allow it to breathe both air and water. Lungfish are naturally found in Australia, South America, and Africa. The lungfish can live in oxygen-poor swampy areas and even polluted waters because of its capacity to supplement oxygen obtained from the water with air at the surface. The lungfish is peculiar because of its ability to estivate. The lungfish lives through drought periods by building a mud shell (cocoon) around itself. The lungfish stays inside this shell until the rains return. It lines the inner shell with mucus secreted from its body. During this period of dormancy, it lives on its own body fat. The cocoon can be easily collected and shipped to other locations. When they are placed in tepid water, the mud softens and the fish is released. The African lungfish is also known as *protopterus aethiopicus.* It is common in eastern and central Africa, and lives in lakes and rivers. It is about 2 meters or 6 feet long. Three other African species live in swamps and estivate during the dry season.

Through *cloud seeding,* scientists have been able to precipitate rainfall in drought areas. As of 1949, scientists were able to make rain and snow fall, breaking the long dry spell that adversely reduced the water supply. This was effected by disturbing the state of thermal equilibrium or maximum entropy. There are several ways to create the condition for rainfall. One of these methods is drop chain reaction. This is feasible in the presence of deep heavy clouds called cumulus. There must be an upward blowing wind of at least 5 miles per hour and saturated water droplets. Using an airplane to fly over the clouds, large water droplets can be sprayed over the upward air currents. This repeated process precipitates condensation at higher, colder levels. Cumulus clouds are a common occurrence in Africa and other tropical regions of the world.

For more than two decades several places in Africa have been stricken be a lingering drought. The total cost of livestock and foregone crop harvests has been immense. One would imagine that cloud seeding is a blessing to farmers throughout the world. It is uncanny that some farmers in other parts of the world did not like artificial rain accidentally falling on their crops.

# NOTES

1. *The Courier* (ACP-EC), Brussels May/June 1993, p.74.

2. "Recent international fora and agreements have highlighted the environmental advantages of bioenergy utilization, mainly with regard to $CO_2$ cycle and greenhouse gas emission mitigation, creating an additional thrust for wood energy expansion." (UN, 1997): *UNASYLVA: International Journal of Forestry and Forest Industries*, FAO 49, no. 193 (1998).

3. Roger L. Shapiro, "Tropical Deforestation Is a Health Threat," in Charles P. Cozic, ed., *Rainforests* (San Diego: Greenhaven Press, 1998), pp. 46–63.

4. "When Folks Say Cutting Edge at Nez, They Don't Mean Saws," *Smithsonian Magazine*, September 1992, pp. 32–45.

5. Ibid.

6. John Mitchell Watt and Maria Gerdina Breyer-Branddwijk, *The Medicinal and Poisonous Plants of Southern and Eastern Africa* (Edinburgh: E.& S. Livingstone, 1962), p. 925. In South Africa, *Salix babylonica L. (Salicaceae)* is often grown on the banks of rivers and dams. The young foliage is said to have the odor of roses. The timber is used extensively in making brake-blocks, gate fixtures, farm buildings, and fencing poles. The young shoot is valuable as a stock feed in spring.

7. Laurence C. Walker, *Forests: A Naturalist's Guide to Trees & Forest Ecology* (New York: John Wiley, 1976), p. 256.

8. Ibid.

9. The eucalyptus belongs to the myrtle family. Other members of the myrtle family include clove and guava. The myrtle family belongs to an order that contains 9,000 species, placed in twelve families.

10. *Webster's New Universal Unabridged Dictionary.*

11. *Current Business Reports*, U.S. Department of Commerce, Nov. 1988.

12. "Tropical Timber Boycott," *West Africa Magazine*, May 2, 1988, p. 77.

13. At its greatest length, it spans 3,200 miles from east to west. From north to south, it ranges from 800 to 1,400 miles, bringing it to a total area of approximately 3,250,000 square miles. The land level is at its lowest at 436 feet below sea level in the Quattara Depression in Egypt. The highest point of the desert is Chad, on top of the Emi Koussi mountain.

14. Jan O.M. Broek and John W. Webb, *A Geography of Mankind* (New York: McGraw-Hill, 1989), pp. 236–237.

15. Indira Gandhi, *A World without Want*, Special Report, World Population Year.

16. *Reader's Digest: 1986 Almanac/Year Book*, p. 515.

17. *The Courier*, May/June 1992, p. 88.

18. Watt and Breyer-Brandwijk, *The Medicinal and Poisonous Plants of Southern and Eastern Africa*, p. 1128. This arrangement that suffices in desperate times may not be to the best interest of bovine populations—in this case because of *Fungi imperfecti*. For example, *Diplodia zeae* is a fungal infection of maize that may poison cattle and sheep, which graze on old maize land. Field poisoning may occur when cattle feed on infected cobs as well as infected maize stalks. *Fusarium moniliforme sheld. var. subglutinans Wollenw* was reported to cause abortion in cattle, under similar conditions.

19. R.R. Askew, *Parasitic Insects* (New York: American Elsevier Publishing, 1971), pp. 58–60. The implication of this relationship should not be overlooked. For example, tsetse flies which cause sleeping sickness in humans and *nagana* disease that wastes cattle. However, owing to modern drugs, sleeping sickness has ceased to be a main cause of death. The tsetse, such as *G. morsitans*, may travel distances of up to eight miles. The tsetses are only locally

common and tend to flourish in a shady but warm environment of tree and scrub cover, forming discontinuous "fly belts" south of the Sahara. *G. mortisans* feeds mainly on *suids* and *bovids*. Species of the *G.palpalis* are found, typically in dense rain forests, usually around rivers and lakes. Their diet consists mainly of the blood of large reptiles, such as crocodiles and monitor lizards, but tend to be more opportunistic feeders. Their diet, therefore, may include primates (mostly man), bovines, various mammals, porcupines, and birds. Most species of tsetse flies are day biters, and vision seems to play a large part in finding hosts. Species of the *G. mortisans* feed on temperatures between 18 degrees C and 32 degrees C. Below 18 degrees they are inactive, and above 32 degrees they are photonegative. Feeding stops in darkness, despite temperature.

20. Broek and Webb, *A Geography of Mankind*, p. 219.

21. *1987 Guiness Book of World Records*, p. 111.

22. *The Courier*, Jan./Feb., 1992, p. 58.

23. *The Courier*, May/June, 1993, p. 74.

24. Tony Allan and Andrew Warren, *Deserts: The Encroaching Wilderness* (New York: Oxford University Press, 1993), p. 86.

25. *1970 Britannica Yearbook of Science and the Future*, p. 397.

26. *MacNeil/Lehrer NewsHour, (PBS, WPBA ATL)*, July 1, 1993.

# 12

# Nature's Chest of Medicines

A healthy workforce tends to be productive in an industrializing environment. Here, nature's chest of medicines may become handy to some persons in times of tight budgets. Trees, shrubs, plants, have been and remain very valuable natural resources. Besides other uses, for example, as a source of food, they comprise a *living pharmacy*. Well harnessed, this effort will be of tremendous benefits to many persons in Africa who currently can barely afford the cost of modern medicine. The high cost of health care means many families may have to forgo many necessities, including food rations or even skip meals, just to meet the expenses that must be incurred in times of sickness. Nationally, this will in turn release funds that may be applied toward badly needed capital investments in industrialization efforts, including in health and sanitary services. The burden of this chapter is merely an infinitely small illustration of the tremendous bounties that lurk in nature and remain mostly untapped by many very needy families in Africa. Rare plants and trees may be very useful and should be conserved during industrialization.

*Ensete ventricosum Cheeseman* (banana) known under an early classification as *M. Sapientium* has also been affectionately called the "tree of paradise."[1] Bananas are chiefly eaten raw as a dessert fruit because in the ripe state they are sweet and easily digestible. The unripe fruit of this plant is an astringent, apparently from the presence of *tannin*. The amount of tannin diminishes as the plant ripens.[2] The main change in fruit ripening is the conversion from starch to sugars and peel color is correlated with the starch/sugar ratio. The starch content virtually disappears, from an average of about 20 to 23 percent at harvest to only 1 to 2 percent in ripe fruit. Sugars (sucrose, glucose, fructose) increase in about the same proportions.[3] Bananas are an important and immediate source of energy. They are also a source of vitamins.

Bananas are particularly high in *potassium*, having more than twice the concentration in ripe pulp than most other tropical fruits.[4]

This plant yields good fiber that is soft and fairly strong and is used by many Africans. The possibilities of using this plant in making paper have been investigated. The fully ripened banana is more *laxative* than the partly ripe one. This is because it contains free *pectin* and the *tannin* is bound. The pectin changes to acids when the banana is overripe. Banana *vinegar* compares favorably to apple vinegar. Ripe bananas are said to have a therapeutic value. The ripe yellow banana yields potent, physiologically active substances that are of great clinical significance—*serotonin*, *norepinephrine* (*arterenol*) and *dopamine*. There is neither *adrenaline* nor *histamine*. Extracts of the skin and pulp of the ripe banana effectively inhibit the growth of certain fungi and bacteria.[5]

The therapeutic values of bananas include the following: *Baby foods*—The easy digestibility and the mineral and vitamin contents make ripe and mashed bananas excellent food for babies from the age of three months. *Food for the elderly*—Bananas may be eaten in large quantities without adverse effects such as fattening and digestive disturbance. *Managing high blood pressure and heart disease*—Bananas are low in sodium and contain little fat and no cholesterol. *Managing gout and arthritis*—Bananas are free from substances that give rise to uric acid. *Peptic ulcer therapy*—Bananas have the capacity to neutralize hydrochloric acid. Ripe bananas mixed with milk have been recommended for ulcer patients. *As a special diet for kidney disease sufferers*—This is because of the low sodium and protein content. *Gastritis and gastro-enteritis*— It is usually introduced after nausea and vomiting are brought to bear. *Obesity*—The combination of low lipid with high palatability makes banana ideal for the diet of obese persons.[6]

The fruit of *Ananas comosus Merr* (pineapple) is rich in *vitamin C*. It also yields a potent protein digestant, *bromelin* (bromlain), found in the ripe fruit and in the leaf and stalk. This proteolytic enzyme is similar to, but not identical with *papain*. It can also dissolve blood clots. Bromelin is just as effective as papain in tenderizing meat. It is anthelmintic like papain.[7] The pineapple juice and bromelin affect living helminths in vitro, which gives some scientific support for the fruit as an anthelmintic. The digestive outcome is still effective in a dilution of 15 percent.[8] The leaf juice is regarded as an anthelmintic and purgative, while the fruit is an old Cape remedy for scarlet fever. The leaf yields 3 percent of a soft bright or yellowish white *fibre*, which is strong but very short. This fibre has been much used in China and Philippines.[9]

The fruit of *Carica papaya L,* popularly known as papaya or pawpaw, is obviously a table food among Africans. It is eaten green as a vegetable or ripe as a fruit. However, other uses may or may not be immediately discernible to many. Therefore, reviewing the various uses of this fruit by other Africans and in various parts of the world may be necessary. The ultimate ramifications of the *pawpaw* may be of considerable significance to families and to industry.

In eastern Africa and South Africa, the leaf is used to tenderize meat and as a vegetable. In West Africa, the young shoot has been used as an asparagus substitute.

It is also used as an anthelmintic.[10] In Ghana, the root is a remedy for *yaws* and *piles*. The leaf has been used as a soap substitute in many parts of Africa, while the young fruit may be applied to scarification over an *enlarged spleen* to reduce it. The milky juice has been used to draw *boils*. Some African tribes feed the fruit to domestic animals.[11] In Hawaii, parts of the tree have been used as an application to skin diseases and deep cuts. In Java, the fresh leaf has been used as a remedy for *beriberi*. Some American Indians wrap the leaf around the meat to make it tender. In Mauritius, the leaf is smoked for the relief of *asthma*.

Pawpaws are exploited for the latex, which contains *papain*, used in meat tenderizing; in pharmaceuticals; in shrinking textiles; in the leather industry; in the manufacture of chewing gum; and in the preparation of precooked foods. It has been prescribed to assist protein digestion in *gastritis, chronic dyspepsia*, and *gastric fermentation*. Viscous pus is lysed by 1.2 percent of papain in a water solution, in five hours, under controlled conditions. The leaf of the *papaya* contains *carpaine*, which has been suggested in the treatment of hypertension. When rabbits and horses fed on pawpaw leaves, there was no discernible adverse reaction.[12]

Pawpaws also kill and help expel threadworms and roundworms. They have the capacity to dissolve the protein in dead skin. Fresh leaves can be wrapped around wounds. It is especially effective for deep slow-healing wounds.[13]

*Adansonia digitata L* (the baobab tree) flourishes in extremely dry surroundings and stores as much as 1,000 gallons of water. Its diameter is about thirty feet and it is one of the most massive trees in the world. When an opening is drilled in the side of the bole and a bung inserted, the tree is used as a source of water in the Kalahari Desert.

In Sierra Leone, the leaf of this tree is used as a *prophylactic* against malaria, to check excessive perspiration, and as an astringent. The seed, embedded in whitish or yellowish acidulous pulp, when dried, has been regarded as a "cream of tartar." The pulp of the fruit (monkey bread) was also used as a leaven in bread during the East African campaign in World War I and in Transvaal. In Senegal the bark of the tree is eaten. In West Africa, the dried leaf is used as a condiment of seasoning, and the fresh leaf is used in soup. Nutritionists in Zimbabwe have also indicated that the edible and pleasant tasting fruit pulp, also used to make refreshing cool drinks, is high in *ascorbic acid*. The bark is fibrous and is used by Africans for making rope, string, snares, sacking, and mats. The wood has been used in making paper. Ash from burning the baobab wood has been used as a *salt substitute* in the Luanga Valley of Tanzania. The baobab tree is now cultivated in other parts of the world.

This plant, *chrysanthemum cinerariaefolium Vis* (pyrethrum), has been cultivated in commercial proportions in some African countries including Kenya. It is the source of *pyrethrum,* an *insecticide*. Dried flowers, or the extracts, are used as sprays suspended or dissolved in suitable solvents. As insecticides and fumigants, they are used to decontaminate aircraft of insect borne diseases and for verminous applications in household, horticulture, and on livestock.[14] It is used to kill mosquitoes, domestic flies, cockroaches, bedbugs, and so on. It may also be used in a dust form or insect powder. Pyrethrum loses its potency when exposed to sunlight. It is particularly useful because it does not leave behind a poisonous residue. The powder has been successfully added to a thin *cement* and sprayed on walls to control insects.[15]

A decoction of this plant *Beta vulgaris L* (*beet*) is taken in large quantities as a *purgative* by sufferers of hemorrhoids. It is cultivated chiefly for the large succulent roots, which are used as food and fodder. *Beet* roots are also a source of *sugar* and lend color to *fabric dyes*.

This hill-grown grapefruit, also known as *Citrus paradisi Macf*, has been stated to cause a rapid disappearance of sugar from the urine of *diabetics*. An extract of the leaf inhibits *Mycobacterium tuberculosis* while those from the roots inhibit *Micrococcus pyogenes var. aureus*.[16]

The extracts of the leaf and fruit of *Citrus reticulata blanko* (Naartjie, mandarin, tangerine) are strongly antibiotic to *Mycobacterium tuberculosis*. The leaf is rich in volatile oil, extracted from the branch and particularly from the fruit. The residue left after distilling the oil is a mixture of citral and citronellal.[17] Naartjie is also useful for digestion, *flatulence, vomiting* and *wet coughs, bladder disorders, bronchial congestion, mastitis,* and *lumbago*.[18]

Toothbrushes ("chew sticks") made from twigs have been made from *Clausena anisata Hook. f.* in West and East Africa. It is also used in West Africa as a remedy for *toothache, migraine, rheumatism, laxative,* as *eye medicine,* to prevent illness in children, and to treat women after *childbirth*.[19] The Hayas use the plant as a remedy for *gastroenteritis,* and the Shambalas use an infusion of the root and an inhalation of the leaf in the treatment of *dulazi* (a peculiar internal disease), *shafula* (infestation by hookworms with swellings and emaciation), *Mpempo* (a sudden infectious disease that causes pains in the chest, headache, cough, mental disturbance, impotence, and sterility). In the Moshi district of Tanzania, the bruised leaf (under the name *Clausena inaequalis Benth*) when mixed with butter, has been administered to *pregnant women* at the beginning of labor and postpartum. The steam from the leaf decoction has been used to steam a febrile patient. The roots have been used as a remedy for *influenza*.[20]

This tree is also known as moringaceae, drum stick plant, and ben tree. This tree (*M.Pterygosperma Gaertn*) grows in East African countries and in Angola. It yields an exudate known as *moringa gum*. The seed yields an oil. In East Africa, the exudate is used as a *diuretic, antifebrile,* and remedy for *asthma*. The oil is used as a remedy for *hysteria* and *scurvy*. In India, the root, bark, leaf, flower, seed, and gum have been used in the treatment of enlargement of the spleen and liver, in acute chronic rheumatism, fever, epilepsy, sores in the mouth, leprosy, and other conditions. The living tree is used for fencing in Tanzania. The oil, known as *Ben oil,* has been used by watchmakers and was known to the Greeks in classical times. The fruit is said to be helpful in diseases of the liver and pancreas. *M. Oleifera* is the commonly used species, and *M. Pterygosperma* is important in India; The young leaves, and young fruits are eaten as vegetables and the flowers are added to curry. The fruits are great favorites of India. The seed is eaten in Malaysia as a peanut. *Antibiotics* can be made from the plant.[21] In Africa, the roots of *M. Peregrina* are edible and the oil extracted is used for the treatment of infantile convulsions.

The bark of *Eucalyptus alba Reinw* has tanning capacity and its leaf and root have an antibacterial effect on *Mycobacterium tuberculosis* in a dilution of 1:80.[22] The leaves of *Eucalyptus globulus Labill* (blue gum, Tasmanian blue eucalyptus, Tasmanian blue gum) may be used in sprays against vermin-infested places. The vapor from water, in which the leaves are boiled, may be inhaled as a respiratory antiseptic, and for croup and diphtheria. A lightly boiled decoction or an infusion has been recommended for coughs, colds, and inhalation treatments. Among the very poor in South Africa, the finely powdered bark is used as a dusting powder. In Central Africa, the leaf is used as a leprosy remedy and as a febrifuge. The leaf juice is reported as a tonic, as an antiperiodic, and as an antiseptic. The leaf has given positive test results for antibacterial activity against Mycobacterium tuberculosis and partial inhibition with *Staphylococcus aureus*.[23] *Eucalyptus globulus* (blue gum) has been used in South Africa as a prophylactic against malaria.

The fruit of the guava tree (*Psdium guajava L*) has a high vitamin C content, which is not destroyed by canning or dehydration. The skin and outer flesh is richest in vitamin C. The vitamin C content is lower early in the season than late in the season and rises parallel to the fructose content. Extracts of the flower have shown considerable antibacterial activity. In Hawaii, the leaf has been used as a medicinal tea and as a remedy for deep cuts, sprains, diarrhea and intestinal hemorrhages. In Egypt and Hong Kong a decoction of the leaf is commonly taken to relief cough and pulmonary disorders.[24]

Onion (*Allium cepa L*) like garlic and leek, may be used internally and externally.[25] The odor of the breath after eating onion is thought to act as a mosquito repellent. The Arabs of East Africa have been known to use the skin of the onion as a sticking plaster on sores. In South Africa, a household remedy for whooping coughs is the syrup formed by sprinkling sliced onion and sugar. In India the onion is used medicinally and applied around window and door frames, as a snake repellent.[26]

It also has antimicrobial effects. Improvements have also been reported in sciatica, gastritis, chronic colitis, and whooping cough from taking onion extract. Onion tends to be more effective when crushed than when segmented. The intact undamaged onion bulb contains no pyruvic acid, but this is very rapidly formed from a precursor or precursors, when the onion tissue is wounded during processes such as mincing. The volatile substances emitted from fresh onion paste are highly effective in treating infected wounds in humans and dogs.[27] This is because onion is antibacterial.[28] Onions stored up to six days are as effective as freshly cut onions. Highly colored varieties are less effective (in this case) than slightly colored varieties. The anemia factor in onion can be extracted by alcohol but not by water or ether.[29]

An old Cape remedy for dropsy (edema) is *Allium porrum L* (leeks). In Europe, the leek has been used as a diuretic and anthelmintic. *Leeks* are bactericidal. The plant was determined to be a strong antibiotic against *Staphylococcus aureus*, which is responsible for skin infections such as whitlow, abscesses, and infections of wounds and burns.[30]

Besides its use as a condiment in food, garlic (*Allium sativum L*) has been used as a stimulant, carminative, antiseptic, anthelmintic, diaphoretic, expectorant, diuretic, hypotensive, antiscorbutic, aphrodisiac, and anti-asthmatic.[31]

The bulb has been used in the treatment of typhoid fever, cholera, dysenteries, gastrointestinal catarrh, and other gastrointestinal conditions. The juice has been used for lupus, laryngeal tuberculosis, duodenal ulcers, earache, in the form of ear drops and diluted as a lotion for wounds and foul ulcers. It was determined that, *sativum* tends to accelerate the healing of noninfected wounds in rabbits.[32] In World War I, before the discovery of penicillin and other antibiotics, garlic powder was used on wounds.[33]

The oral administration of garlic to children is said to be dangerous and may be fatal. Poultices of garlic have been recommended for the treatment of lupus and tubercular ulcers and inhalations of garlic for bronchiectasis and other pulmonary disorders. Observers have recorded that a concentration of 1:5000 of garlic juice completely inhibits the growth of *Mycobacterium tuberculosis*, and boiling and prolonged storage in the air does not destroy the effect. In guinea pigs, daily doses of two grams in food did not delay or prevent the onset of the disease. When fed to the milch cow, garlic produced disagreeable flavor in the milk. It was toxic to rats and mice. Mashed garlic, at one to three grams per kilogram, in the food of geese is 80 percent effective in removing cestodes.

The active antimicrobial effects of garlic are realized in crushed garlic in the presence of water or an enzyme. Garlic is more effective when crushed than when segmented and is also active at a distance through an envelope of air.[34] In a nutshell, garlic (like astragalus and echinacea, used extensively in Europe) builds the immune system, is useful as a natural antiseptic agent, an antibacterial, and an expectorant. It is antiviral and induces sweating, kills and helps expel worms, and tends to lower blood pressure, cholesterol, and blood clotting. It is a also useful in coughs, colds, bronchitis, and catarrh. [35]

This tree, *Canarium schweinfurthii Engl* (pink mahogany timber), exudes a pleasantly scented resin used as substitute for incense. It is used as a remedy for *round worms, colic, dysentery,* and *gonorrhea*. It is also used in fumigating dwellings. In Angola, the resin is also used as anticorrosive paint, insecticidal powders, and wood preservative. The fruit is used as a condiment, and the pulp when boiled with meat tends to soften it and give it a pleasant aroma.[36]

The gum resin is used in West Africa as an *insecticide*, especially as a termite repellent. The tree is also known as *Commiphora africana Engl*.

Cocoyam (*Colocasia antiquorum Schott*) is widely eaten. The tuber of this plant is rich in *starch, protein*, and *Thiamine* (*vitamin B1*). The Swati and numerous other Africans eat the leaves. The plant is grown behind the huts to keep termites away. A poultice for rheumatism is made from the rhizome. In Brazil the plant is used as an anthelmintic. The plant is styptic (astringent), stimulant, and rubefacient and is used as an application to scorpion stings. Other more common names for *Colocasia antiquorum Schott*, include *malombo* and *taro* in East Africa, and *eddoes* in West Africa.

Camellia sinensis (*Thea sinensis or tea*) is not just a medicine to banish drowsiness, an antidote to sleep with which one could solace the midnight hours, it is also remarkable for its wholesomeness. Writings as early as 1610 attributed Chinese longevity and freedom from serious illness to fondness for tea. A body of lore, tradition, and mystique has surrounded the tea culture for ages. In line with the somewhat mythical beginnings of tea, the Taoists asserted the importance of tea in the elixir of immortality and saw waste of tea through incompetent manipulation as one of the three most deplorable acts in the world. The others were false education of youth and uninformed admiration of fine paintings. The following note was captured from early writing (translated in 1598): "[W]hen they will entertain any of their friends, they give him some warm water to drinke; for the pots wherein they sieth it, and wherein the herbe is kept, with the earthen cups which they drinke it in, they esteeme as much of them as we doe of Diamants, Rubies and other precious stones, and they are not esteemed for their newness, but for their oldness."[37] Another writing, "Sinarum regio," mentioned, "It protects them from pituitary troubles, heaviness in the head and ailments of the eyes; it conduces to a long life almost free of languor."[38]

Green tea (*Thea viridis*) may prevent or control a host of ailments, according to many epidemiological studies. Green tea may prevent several health problems, ranging from heart disease, to sun burns. Tea catechins tend to protect the tissues or negate the adverse effects associated with sun damage, cigarette smoke, air pollutants, and radiation. Some bacteria are susceptible to catechins. Mice on a green tea regimen, when exposed to chemical carcinogens or ultraviolet light, developed a remarkably small number of tumors. This result was unlike that of another set of mice that were deprived of tea. This was mainly because tea is a potent antioxidant. Although EGCG, one of the catechins that is only found in tea, is found in black tea (*Thea bohea*), the proportion is high in green tea. The EGCG blocks an enzyme that tumors use to grow new capillaries. Tea catechins have an anti-clotting effect in the blood, and lower blood lipids without reducing HDL (the other cholesterol, known as the good cholesterol). Green tea has also been associated with inhibiting bad breath, gum disease, and tooth decay in laboratory rats. In the case of humans, a minimum of four cups of tea a day may be necessary to obtain associated benefits.[39] This seems to run against the attitude of those who celebrate and observe the rituals of tea, "Never take more than three cups unless you are quite thirsty, for tea is the very essence of moderation and helps to still the six passions."[40]

Turmeric (*Curcuma longa L*) is a plant well known as an aromatic in curry powders. The rhizome contains *curcumin*, a yellow crystalline pigment. In India turmeric has been used to relieve catarrh and purulent ophthalmia, as well as serving as an ant repellent. The volatile oil is carminative, inhibits the secretion of acid in the stomach, and in large doses inhibits excessive peristaltic movements of the intestines. The rhizome is also a *carminative* and a *diuretic*.[41] The cholagogue action is ascribed to stimulation of the bile secretion by both the volatile oil and the pigment while the pigment produces in addition a contractile effect on the gallbladder. Curcumin is also an *antibiotic*. Sodium curcuminate has a powerful action on *Staphylococcus aureus*. The substance is low in toxicity. In West Africa as in India, the plant is cultivated for use as yellow dye. The rhizome is well known as a coloring for basketware, mats, and even for dyeing leather. The pigment is prepared by grinding the root in water and soaking the article in the fluid.

*Catharanthus roseus* (Madagascar Periwinkle, Vinca rosea), although native to Madagascar, is a plant cultivated in many places in Africa. Periwinkle tea is drunk in Jamaica for its antidiabetic properties. In Cuba, Puerto Rico, Jamaica, and other islands, an extract of the flowers was commonly used as eyewash. In Central America and parts of South America, it was used as a gargle to ease throat and chest pains. In India the juice of the leaves was used in treating wasp stings. In Hawaii, an extract of the boiled plant was used to arrest bleeding. Scientific interest in *Vinca* (true periwinkle) began in the mid-1950s, prompted by word of periwinkle tea in Jamaica. Since then much has been learnt of its valuable and varied properties. The Madagascar periwinkle contains more than 70 known alkaloids agents, some of which decrease blood pressure while others decrease blood sugar levels. The plant contains two anticancer alkaloids—vincristine and vinblastine—that inhibit the growth of tumors. Vincristine is an effective treatment for childhood leukemia and vinblastine in treating testicular cancer and Hodgkin's disease (cancer of the lymphatic system). However, like many other drugs used in chemotherapy both alkaloids produce such side effects as nausea and hair loss.[42]

The seeds of the friut of *Balanites aegyptiaca Del* (desert date) are edible and are commonly sold in the food markets of West Africa. There are nine other species of Balanites in East Africa and may be easily confused with the *Balanites aegyptiaca* that produces a resin with pleasant but a faint aroma. The seed is bitter when unripe and becomes bittersweet when ripe. In West Africa and Chad, the seed is used in soup, the leaf as a vegetable, and the pericarp is crushed and eaten cooked. Although the fruit is edible, it is regarded as an *emetic*, a *purgative*, and as an *anthelmintic*. The bark is used as an anthelmintic and in the treatment of syphilis. In Tanzania the fruit and in West Africa the whole plant is used as a fish poison. The fish kennel, bark, root, and branch have proved lethal to molluscs (including bilharzias), miracidia, cercaria (schistosomiasis), fish, and tadpoles. A concentrated emulsion of the berry has been recommended for treating ponds and canal dead ends. It has been recommended to plant the fruit trees along infested waters, so that the fruit could drop in the water spontaneously. A high concentration may kill the larva of the *Culex* mosquito. Extracts of the root have been slightly effective in experimental malaria treatment. The flower is sucked by children and eaten by the West African in soup. The flower is also boiled and added to *daudawa,* a Hausa dish.[43]

## NOTES

1. J.C. Robinson, *Bananas and Plantains* (Wallington, U.K: CAB International, 1996), p. 8.

2. Ibid., p. 213–14.

3. Ibid.

4. J.F. Morton (1987), *Fruits of Warm Climates,* in Robinson, *Bananas and Plantains,* p. 216.

5. John Mitchell Watt and Maria Gerdina Breyer-Brandwijk, *The Medical and Poisonous Plants of Southern and Eastern Africa* (Edinburgh: E. & S. Livingstone Ltd. ), pp. 783–784.

6. Robinson, *Bananas and Plantains*, p. 8.

7. An anthelmintic is used to rid humans and other host animals of infestations by parasitic worms, such as tapeworms, roundworms, pinworms, schistosomes, and filariae. An anthelmintic is known as a vermifuge. They act by attacking the worms' neuromuscular or respiratory systems, interfering with the metabolism or making them susceptible to attack by the host's microphage. They are generally more effective against gastrointestinal infestations than muscular infestations.

8. Stanley L. Robbins and Ramzi S. Cotran, *Pathologic Basis of Disease* (Philadelphia: W.B. Saunders Company, 1979), p. 474. Among the many tapeworms, four in particular may cause intestinal disease in man: *Taenia saginata* (beef tapeworm), *T. Solium* (pork tapeworm), *Hymenolepis nana* (dwarf tapeworm), and *Diphyllobothrium latum* (fish tapeworm).

9. Watt and Breyer-Brandwijk, *The Medical and Poisonous Plants of Southern and Eastern Africa*, p. 150.

10. Before antibiotics became the generally accepted treatment, this tree, as an infusion, was administered as a remedy for the once notorious *syphilis*. In Tanzania, the tree supplies an indigenous *gonorrhea* remedy.

11. Watt and Breyer–Brandwijk, *The Medical and Poisonous Plants of Southern and Eastern Africa*, p. 173.

12. Ibid., p. 173.

13. Miriam Polunin and Christopher Robbins, *The Natural Pharmacy* (New York: Macmillan, 1992), p. 92.

14. Deni Brown, *Encyclopedia of Herbes* (London: Dorling Kindersley, 1995), p. 359.

15. Watt and Breyer-Brandwijk, *The Medical and Poisonous Plants of Southern and Eastern Africa*, p. 213.

16. Ibid., p. 916.

17. Ibid.

18. Brown, *Encyclopedia of Herbes*, pp. 263, 262, 390.

19. The Xhosa place leaves on hot ashes to fumigate the newborn by waving the infant to and fro in the acrid smoke. It is said this is supposed to clear and strengthen the lungs. The Xhosa also hold babies who are in delicate health in the steam from a pot of water containing some material from the tree. The Zulu use the leaf as a parasiticide and purgative and the leaves as an anthelmintic. The Europeans have used the leaves in febrile conditions and as a diaphoretic. The Masai chew the leaves as an emetic.

20. Watt and Breyer-Brandwijk, *The Medical and Poisonous Plants of Southern and Eastern Africa*, p. 917.

21. Ibid., pp. 781–782.

22. Ibid., p. 790.

23. Arnold and Connie Krochmal, *A Guide to Medicinal Plants in the U.S.* (New York: Quadrangle, 1973), p. 104.

24. Ibid., p. 799.

25. In East Africa, the onion is the indigenous remedy for fever and is used as an amulet against the evil eye and to drive out evil spirits.

26. Watt and Breyer-Brandwijk, *The Medical and Poisonous Plants of Southern and Eastern Africa*, pp. 671–672.

27. Ibid.

28. Dian Dincin Buchman, *Herbal Medicine : The Natural Way to Get Well and Stay Well* (New York: Wing Books, 1979), pp. 103–104, 121–122, 125,137–138, and 146–147.

29. Watt and Breyer-Brandwijk, *The Medical and Poisonous Plants of Southern and Eastern Africa*, pp. 671–674.

30. Ibid., p. 674.

31. Ibid., pp. 674–680.

32. Ibid.

33. Buchman, *Herbal Medicine*, p. 121.

34. Ibid.

35. Polunin and Robbins, *The Natural Pharmacy*, pp. 83–84.

36. Watt and Breyer-Brandwijk, *The Medical and Poisonous Plants of Southern and Eastern Africa*, p. 152.

37. Jan Huighen van Linschooten, *Discours of Voyages into Easte and Weste Indies,* in Lu Yü, *The Classic of Tea* (Boston: Little Brown, 1974), p. 36.

38. Ibid.

39. "Call Green Tea the Cure-All of Cure Alls," *Investor's Business Daily*, September 28, 1998, p. 1.

40. Yü, *The Classic of Tea*, p. 8.

41. That is, the rhizome aids in expelling gas from the stomach, and intestines, and increases the discharge of urine.

42. In seed catalogues, the madagascar periwinkle and its varieties are often grouped with true periwinkles (Vinca). Vinca (V. major or greater periwinkle; V. minor or lesser periwinkle) vining perennials and subshrubs with shiny green leaves that hail from Russia and Europe. Kristo Pienaar, *The Ultimate Southern African Gardening Book* (Halfway House, RSA: Southern Book Publishers,1994), pp. 82, 150, 467; see also Christopher Brickell, Elvin McDonald, Trevor Cole, eds., *American Horticultural Society Encyclopedia of Gardening.* (New York: Dorling Kindersey, 1993), pp. 431, 259, 175, 176, 173.

43. Watt and Breyer-Brandwijk, *The Medical and Poisonous Plants of Southern and Eastern Africa*, p. 1065.

# 13

# Bridging the Gaps for Industrialization in Africa

The structured world of information and ideas seems to be entering a complex age of an information deluge. In Japan it has been called *johoka*; in North America it is called an information explosion. In Africa it may mean mountains of information to sort through in order to identify information needed in a dynamic pro-industrial environment.[1]

In an age of an information explosion there appear to be chasms in many places in Africa between consumers and producers, government and business, and management and workers. An information explosion has not been adequately compensated with an increase in communication. These chasms in communication are fundamental problems that such places will surmount during industrialization.

In Africa and in many less developed nations around the world when one mentions the problems and barriers to communication, many persons immediately mention the dearth of modern communications devices. Unlike the industrialized world, there are relatively few radios, television sets, newspapers, and computers in Africa and the rest of the developing world. According to a UNESCO dictum, "for every 100 persons there should be at least 10 copies of newspapers, 5 radio sets, 2 cinema seats, and 2 television receivers."[2] Fundamentally, this paucity of communication media poses a serious hindrance to the creation of more modern attitudes toward education, using programmed instructional materials.

The major forms of communication are reading, writing, speaking and listening. Although constructive efforts have been made in this area, some nations have not yet been able to increase, adequately, domestic production for reading and writing materials. As a result scarce foreign exchange is expended on these imported items. Television and radio also have the capacity to circumvent the relatively high adult illiteracy rates still prevalent in some places in Africa. Television and radio take advantage of speaking and listening, thus breaking down barriers that may be posed by illiteracy or the unwillingness to read.[3]

The communications media, communications devices, and sound communication infrastructure are absolutely indispensable to industrialization. The mass media is very effective in disseminating knowledge, in enhancing skill set, and in influencing the attitudes of the population at large, including special groups.[4] Ironically, small minorities who have access to such media are often functionally literate and, therefore, tend to need them least for the type of basic knowledge, skills, and attitudes that are most needed in an industrializing environment. In Africa, the media will be harnessed to spread the critical mass of general technical and scientific knowledge required for industrialization, thus supplementing efforts deriving from the seats of higher learning, laboratories, and Africans who studied in industrialized nations.

An audit of the labor market on the eve of industrialization often depicts profound deficiencies in the stock of skilled labor—technicians, experts, scientists, manufacturers, designers, engineers, agronomists, diamond cutters and polishers, horticulturists, irrigation engineers, and the like—which tends to establish the essential precondition for rising productivity. Surmounting part of this deficit quickly using the mass media is possible. Israel is an example of a nation in which new labor skills were imparted within a very short period. Jews migrating to Israel were from all walks of life, with very skilled labor and sometimes unskilled labor. Those with no skills were quickly taught how to do mundane tasks like turning a lathe, tilling the ground, guarding property, and even sailing the seas.[5]

In an era of an information explosion, much of the basic information will be inculcated to children through entertainment programs that also have educational components. This information front load will supplement the formal schooling of children and youth, for example, in public television programming. On the other hand, the industrial system is highly dependent on commercial television. Television programs have the capacity to capture and hold the attention of consumers for considerable periods and in a comparatively effortless manner.[6] Corporations take advantage of this captive audience and advertise products during program intermissions.

Developing nations in general have relatively few of these devices that tend to break down the barriers of illiteracy. However, the volume of communication devices will increase as nations attain higher levels of industrialization.[7] This is because, as national productivity increases, incomes will increase, and more persons will be able to afford previously unaffordable communication devices and related equipment. The Conference on Pulp and Paper Development in Asia and the Far East held in Tokyo in 1960 concluded in its report that positive action should be taken to encourage the development of paper industries or else "there is a serious danger that current educational programmes will be jeopardized, the creation of an informed citizenry retarded, antiquated distribution systems retained, and industrial progress hampered."[8] This conclusion, drawn almost four decades ago, may still hold for much of Africa, on the eve of industrialization.

Newspapers and pamphlets were important communication devices, at the outset of the industrial revolution. Printed information was very potent, and laws were written to control or negate the influences of publications on the masses. Laws that were effective during the Industrial Revolution included libel, sedition, blasphemy, newspaper stamps, duties on paper and advertisement, and licensing. As a result, the initial costs of newspapers were generally high, and the number and circulations of newspapers were much smaller than the technical developments warranted.[9] There was a campaign against the many restrictions. Reforms were slow. By 1861 enough changes had been made in the laws to bring the prices of newspapers within the purchasing power of the masses.

Another significant impact of communications media on industrialization was in the twentieth century, with the invention of radio and television. Radio, originally, was envisioned as an advance on the telegraph as a medium of personal communication. Government control of radio in Europe, therefore, was a natural extension of European governmental monopolies of postal and telegraphic communication. There were many hours of air time slots to fill. Because of this void, European state broadcasters became major consumers and patrons of the arts. The *modus operandi* was to bring the "good life" to the average citizen, providing to the masses what the privileged classes had provided for themselves, on an individual basis. Cultural programs that were once seen as luxuries have increasingly devolved into necessities in which money is no object.

Radios and, especially, televisions are *the* major media of cultural dissemination. They have become the leaders in the culture industry, mainly because of the size of the audience, the variety of "products," and their influence on the rest of the audiovisual sector. They introduce thousands of products to consumers within the comfort of homes, through advertisements. They also raise the level of consciousness of consumers to the plethora of new products that generally flood the marketplace as a result of industrialization.[10] Radio and television are also important because they tend to respond to the needs and aspirations of the population for information, communication, education, and entertainment.[11]

The culture industry is generally labor-intensive and tends to employ a sizable cross-section of the human resources of an industrializing environment. For example, it still takes as many people to produce an opera today as it did in the eighteenth century. Film, music, theater, museums, libraries, sports, cinema, radio and TV, newspapers and so on, all employ numerous artists, managers, and other experts with skills that are often transferable to other sectors of an industrializing economy. The forerunners of contemporary arts programs in the United States of America were artists' programs of the New Deal, in which artists were just one more group of unemployed for whom work had to be created because of the Great Depression of the 1930s. The gainful employment of many artists was made possible by the revolution in the communications media in the twentieth century.[12] Many persons who had never entertained the thought of buying a ticket to an opera, or a ballet or other forms of art became converts after seeing such programs on television. They became patrons and will buy tickets for live performances. This propensity became real with mechanization. The average hours worked per week were shortened, and there was more free or leisure time. Similarly, retired persons suddenly found themselves with less money to spend but more time to kill. By initially patronizing the cultural industry, they also provided the energy to establish "cultural industries" as magnets for tourism and therefore restaurants, hotels, transportation, and other allied industries.

Unlike in a previous era when accomplished artists might have been beneficiaries of the virtues of princely or ecclesiastical commissions, the works of contemporary artists tend to reside in the aegis of mass consumption and the resources of mass communications media.[13] This does not in any way discount the significance of the contemporary role of government as impresario or the various systems of public and private support for cultural endeavors that have evolved in many countries. Whatever the case may be, modern communications, by themselves, do not guarantee effective communication in an industrializing environment. The most prevalent barriers to communication are not only physical. They are also psychological.

Communication, in this context, is the intercourse of messages by words, letters, symbols, and nonverbal behavior. It is the concrete that cements an organization. It is a tool to exert influence, understanding, planning, organization, and control. By contrast, information is purely formal. It is impersonal rather than interpersonal. When information is impersonal and, therefore, less charged with emotions, values, expectations, and perceptions, it tends to be validated as reliable. It, therefore, becomes more informative. The formidable challenge, therefore, resides in decoupling the intimate intercourse between information and communication content.

The vital component of communication has been demonstrated throughout history by methods such as speech, music, drama, sculpture, drawing, poetry, and prose. Medieval aesthetics maintained that a work of art communicates at multiple levels, at least three and possibly four: the literal; the allegorical; the moral, and the mystical. A paradigm of this artistic analogy was Dante's *Divina Commedia* (Divine Comedy). For generations, *Divina Commedia* has been projected as a work of supreme art and potent communication. The fable tends to be fuzzy. It is the element of ambiguity that lends itself to multiple gradations of comprehension and readership. It may be construed by some as a fairy tale, while others see it as a grand synthesis of metaphysics. In this instance of communication, perception, rather than information, has primacy. Opera is considered by some to be the highest form of art because it simultaneously conjoins many methods of communication including music, drama, poetry, design, and dance.

To enhance communication mankind devised various means of sending messages. In Africa, a common method of transmitting messages was by "talking drums." African communities, separated by sizable distances, played special drums in order to send messages. Within African communities, the town crier was typically used to relay messages. In ancient Greece, runners carried news from one city to another. The story of communication devices has been one marked by continual progress. Three important hallmarks in world history are observed by the invention of communication devices: the development of the alphabet; the invention of the printing press; and the application of electricity to communication with the invention of the telegraph in 1844. The telegraph was followed in quick succession by the invention of the telephone, motion picture, radio, television, satellite stations, and computers. These devices have virtually compressed the world into what seems to be a global village. Information stored at locations, thousands of miles away, may be retrieved in a matter of seconds or minutes.

Communication may be formal or informal. Formal communications follow the official channels of sending messages inside and outside the organization. These channels are often rigidly canalized by the organizational structure. Generally the predominant flows of communications tend to be from top to bottom. Communications are usually in the form of primary publications such as newsletters and newspapers; written memoranda; questionnaires; bulletin boards on walls; E-mail bulletins; computer bulletin boards; and manuals. Presentations and meetings (task forces, training committees, breakfasts, lunches, etc.) are other forms of formal communications.[14]

Although informal communication channels maybe notorious for rumors and gossip, they are needed in organizations. Informal channels are the unofficial networks that supplement the formal channels. An employee may use informal networks to consult other colleagues for expert opinions on issues. In an academic setting, headmasters or principals may use informal networks to talk with teachers, students, custodians, suppliers, and the general population to enhance the scope of understanding of the institutional environment. Such knowledge gathered may include "shared meanings," concerns, and priorities.[15] Managers have been known to employ informal communication channels to monitor employee reaction to controversial issues. Generally, such balloons are released to float over the *grapevine* on the eve of formal announcements. If employee reaction is very caustic and negative, then, plans may be ameliorated before announcement. Ignoring these channels may result in loss of important information. However, one must constantly be aware of the high incidence of unfounded rumors and tittle-tattle that tend to choke these informal channels. Encouraging the use of formal channels is, therefore, important.

Persons tend to interpret or understand messages according to their psychological needs and motives. We generally hear and perceive what we expect to see, hear, and perceive. Communication is also expectation; therefore the unexpected are ignored, mis seen, misheard, or misunderstood. If we understand this marginal propensity for perceptual distortion, alerting the human mind is possible, that what is perceived is contrary to expectation. Messages are susceptible to distortion, when transmitted from one person to the next. This is often because of barriers to communication that may be related to the *sender,* the *receiver,* or the *environment.*[16]

When an organization culture becomes hostile, people may become defensive, angry, suspicious, and distrustful of each other. People may be skeptical of messages, and the process of communication becomes ineffective. Other barriers may embrace poor communication skills (whether written or spoken) and perhaps insufficient nonverbal behavior. Communication barriers can easily be erected because of the profuse use of inappropriate language.[17] When talking, refining the language to the intended audience is important. Language used appropriately in one environment may be inappropriately employed elsewhere. Improper timing may also pose a barrier to communication. For example, a person who is stressed, fatigued, and already satiated with information may not be as receptive to as many messages as a person who demonstrates a good mood and seems unsaturated. Similarly, defensive communication may break down effective communication. In this case, people tend to send messages that overly protect their self-esteem. Often, a message that may arouse discomfort is suppressed through a process called *denial*.

Barriers to communication are not necessarily permanent physical and psychological fixtures. Most barriers to communication are surmountable. Because some barriers are apparent, while others are not immediately obvious. It is, therefore, imperative to analyze and to evaluate constantly, the status of communication in an organization. Once the barriers have been identified and uncovered, some of these solutions may apply:

• Foremost, listening to one's audience is important. It is necessary to find out what the audience is interested in, receptive to, and wants to know.

• It is also important to understand one's audience. This is because communication may be distorted when one does not understand the receiver.

• The use of appropriate language eases communication. Here the idea is to avoid profane and offensive language. Biased and caustic remarks or innuendoes are generally counterproductive in communication. They may be perceived as an affront to a person's integrity and dignity and may lead to an immediate breakdown of civilized forms of communication. Some persons or groups may resort to primal instincts that may be very destructive.

• If feasible, repeated messages, using multiple channels of communications, enhance the objectives of communication if there is no communication overload. When audiences are bombarded with a plethora of messages, the objectives of the communication may not be easily discernible.

Another method of breaking down barriers may be by empathy, that is, we try to visualize things as seen by other persons, or to figuratively put our feet in the shoes of others. By increasing the opportunities for informal interaction and casual conversations, the chances of being misunderstood are likely to be denuded, thus dislodging the roots of mutual distrust. By extension, people will tend to feel free in each other's company. The use of verbal feedback, or two-way communication, reduces the chances of misunderstanding. This is because conversations and dialogues offer many opportunities to pose questions when in doubt.

Businesses, especially if they are small or micro-businesses may take advantage of communication resources of government, to enhance effective communication in an industrializing environment. Such resources pertain to government agencies, chambers of commerce, public libraries, trade associations, industry associations, professional associations, cooperative associations, university research centers, syndicated business services, foundations, etc.

These organizations provide general business information and planning aids that may include labeling rules, legal abstracts, and accounting practice reports. More industry specific information may include general operating manuals for small stores, or even more specific operating manuals such as advertising, merchandising, sales promotion, sales training, and financing and record keeping. The channels of communication will be greatly improved for newly formed businesses if they are listed in business directories, have business telephones, use street addresses, are current/active members of their local chambers of commerce, have a summary of annually report of business transaction, hold membership in industry or trade associations, and the like.

When communication is effective, it bridges the gaping chasms between politicians and their constituents, managers and workers, consumers and producers, and business and government. Modern communication devices such as telephones, computers, radios, television, and newsprint have greatly enhanced the speed of communication within and without organizations. While poor communication distorts messages, successful communication is a fillip to understanding, planning, influence, organization, and control. Effective coordination, in a more sophisticated industrial environment in Africa, will require a sound organizational and physical communication infrastructure, entrenched across the continent, and interlaced with the global village.

## NOTES

1. The volume of information is easily expanded with computer networks. Networks bring a flood of useful and less useful information to desktops. The challenge is to consistently filter the sediment out of the less useful information. Networks tend to increase work efficiency, but network communication is not as cheap as it may seem. A connection requires computers (hardware and software), a modem, a telephone, monthly connection fees, and a network account. When institutions of learning, such as universities, provide subsidized connections students acquire accounts, which may be charged against tuition, fees, and overhead. Clifford Stoll, *Silicon Snake Oil: A Second Thought on the Information Highway* (New York: Anchor Books, 1995), pp. 96–98.

2. UNESCO, *Mass Media in Developing Countries*, Paris, 1961, p. 16., in Gunnar Myrdal, *Asian Drama: An Inquiry into the Poverty of Nations, Vol.3* (New York:Twentieth Century Fund, 1968), p. 1694.

3. Lyman K. Stell, "Communication Training: Listening," in William R. Tracey, ed., *Human Resources Management and Development Handbook* (New York: American Management Association, 1994), p. 914.

4. Myrdal, *Asian Drama*, p. 1651.

5. David Horowitz, "Israel," in Herbert V. Prochnow, *World Economic Problems and Policies* (New York: Harper & Row Publishers, 1965), pp. 223–253.

6. John Kenneth Galbraith, *The New Industrial State* (Boston: Houghton Mifflin Company,1971), pp. 208–209.

7. An analysis of national statistics consistently supports this statement in the following areas: number of daily newspapers, number of periodicals, number of television sets (per 1,000 inhabitants), number of radio sets (per 1,000 inhabitants), and the number of telephones (per 1,000 inhabitants).The number of radio receivers was less than 100 per 1,000 of population, in 40 countries in Africa, 17 in countries in Asia, and 15 countries in Latin America. An initial effect of the introduction of television was indicated by a negative impact on radio and newsprint: George Thomas Kurian, *The New Book of Rankings* (New York: Facts on File Publications, 1984), pp. 406–407, 393, 398–399.

8. United Nations, *Pulp and Paper Prospects in Asia and the Far East,* Vol. 1, in Myrdal, Asian Drama, *Vol.3,* p. 1696.

9. Pauline Gregg, *Social and Economic History of Britain*: 1760–1950 (London: Harrap & Co.,1950), pp. 267–275.

10. Kennard E. Goodman and William L. Moore, *Economics for Everyday Life* (Boston: Ginn and Company,1947), p. 9.

11. Milton C. Cummings, Jr., and Richard S. Katz, *The Patron State: Government and the Arts in Europe, North America and Japan* (New York: Oxford University Press, 1987), pp. 25–26.

12. The government also buys art to decorate public spaces and employs musicians to perform in public ceremonies. Examples include the U.S., New Deal make-work program and the Dutch program to buy paintings.

13. This new paradigm is unlike previously, when accomplished artists were beneficiaries of princely or ecclesiastical commissions for a painting, a court composer or *Kapellmeister,* or the building of a theater. Not all princelings supported the arts, and not every artist who received public patronage was a Beethoven, a Mozart, a Michelangelo, or a Racine. And obviously, not every great work of Renaissance art was the product of a public commission. In England, for example, there were concerts, plays, and operas that were purely commercial ventures, operating perhaps with royal license or patent, but without public financial support. Ibid., pp. 3–7.

14. Lin Kroeger, "Communication Within the Organization," in William R. Tracey, *Human Resources Management & Development Handbook* (New York: American Management Association, 1994), pp. 232–233.

15. Roald F. Campbell, John E. Corbally, and Raphael O. Nystrand, *Introduction to Educational Administration* (Newton, MA: Allyn and Bacon, 1983), p. 141.

16. Ibid., pp. 148–149. In this case, monitoring facilities tend to reduce the chances of message distortion, thus ensuring effective communication.

17. Ibid., p. 155.

# 14

# Transportation

For familiar and perhaps valid reasons, the African in the subcontinent neither developed nor participated proactively in the development of any elaborate forms of transportation, until the nineteenth century. Officially, the year 1885 marked the beginning of railway transportation in Africa. Then cars and airplanes had not been invented for transportation. Africa, therefore, had much transportation work ahead in the twentieth century. Unlike other nations that already had a head start in transportation networks, perhaps 2,000 years earlier in some cases, most of Africa had to catch up. Fortunately, the invention of the airplane meant practically every community could be reached, even without direct surface links. However, the challenges of transportation have significantly changed in the last hundred years, or so. Around the dawn of the twentieth century, the main challenge pertained to opening the hinterlands of Africa to the rest of the world. In the last several decades of the twentieth century it became, how to open the continent of Africa to itself. The challenge at the dawn of the twenty-first century in many places is how to use the available transportation resources, efficiently and effectively, in an industrializing environment. The focus, here, will be how some nations surmounted transportation challenges.

## ROAD TRANSPORTATION

Like others around the world, the nations of Africa invested tremendously in transportation infrastructure in the twentieth century. For example, roads were built in Africa just after 1960 at such paces that mileage statistics were sometimes obsolete before they were printed. Much progress has been made in this area, especially in places strategically weighted for nation building and in urban areas that are often commercial, manufacturing, and administrative centers. However, many problems still have to be solved in some places. This section focuses on some of these often familiar problems and a few practical solutions or advantages in good roads. In any case, with industrialization most problems associated with transportation, in a pre-industrial environment, are systematically eliminated. This explains why the types of problems subsequently discussed are generally not considered central problems in industrialized nations.

In Africa, the best roads were initially those linking the larger urban centers, reaching out to the immediate outskirts or support areas of urban centers and feeder roads to the new railway lines. In *Kenya* before the mid-1960s, the road system was comparatively extensive but uncoordinated and consisted mainly of gravel and earth roads. In 1963 about 4 percent or 1,800 kilometers of roads had asphalt surface, out of a total of 42,000 kilometers. The policies then had favored rail transport. Road transport development was discouraged through a highly restrictive operator-licensing program. As road development went on around the mid-1960s, operator restrictions were eased accordingly, particularly a national trunk-road system linking Nairobi and other major towns. By 1974, just about all major urban centers were linked by asphalt highways. In addition, the early development program also attached priority to the construction of feeder roads from certain agricultural areas. For example, roads in tea-growing regions and various settlement schemes were fed to the main roads. Similar road access was also provided to the sugarcane-growing region, and to various tourist centers. The Rural Access Road Program was initiated in 1974 and provided access to markets from the most promising farming areas. The goal was to create employment in rural areas through a labor-intensive undertaking. During this span, 14,000 kilometers of roads were to be newly constructed roads and rural tracks upgraded accordingly. A decade later, about 4,500 kilometers of roads had been built. This program was considered successful by international evaluations, and the methodology was recommended to other developing countries. By mid-1981, 100,000 kilometers of tracks and unclassified roads were estimated to exist in rural areas. In the same year, 12 percent, of the officially classified road network of 52,675 were paved. The classified road system was divided into five main categories, and three received special attention from the perspective of upgrading, improvement, and new construction. The international trunk roads that run to Ethiopia, Somalia, Tanzania, and Uganda were two-thirds paved in 1981, and work had been planned for a modern road to Sudan; the national trunk road was two-thirds paved; the primary road system, linking important provincial centers, was one-quarter paved; the remaining roads, secondary and minor, served rural needs and tied rural centers together and provided general access roads for rural areas. Here, less than 3 percent of the roads were paved.

In *Nigeria*, the government established a basic grid of two north–south trunk roads from Lagos and Port Harcourt to Kano, and several east–west roads: two north and two south of the natural division created by the Niger and the Benue rivers. In later decades, this system was expanded until most state capitals and large towns were accessible by paved road. In 1978, the express way was constructed, from Lagos to

Ibadan, and a branch from this route was later extended east to Benin City. Another expressway linked Port Harcourt with Enugu. In 1990, Nigeria had 108,000 kilometers of roads, of which 30,000 kilometers were paved, 25,000 kilometers were gravel, and the rest was unimproved earth. Here, roads convey 95 percent of the nation's goods and passengers and are the most significant element of the transportation network. Poor maintenance, in previous years, forced the government to shift emphasis in the 1980s from constructing new roads to repairing existing ones. Massive traffic jams were reported in large cities, coupled with long delays in the movement of goods.

Another example is in *Ghana*. Here, the Secondi-Takoradi-Kumasi-Accra triangle served to build up the revenues of the railways.[1] Ghana's transportation networks are centered in the southern regions, especially around the areas engaged in the production of gold, cocoa, and timber. A major road system connected the northern and central areas. Some areas, however, were said to remain relatively isolated. Difficulties in distributing economic inputs and food were partially attributed to the deterioration of the country's transportation network. As a result, it became a priority between 1983 and 1986.

Generally, the qualities of roads in Africa still vary greatly in some places from season to season. Rural roads, usually of unimproved earth, are especially susceptible to heavy traffic during long rainy seasons. In this case, laterite soil, favored in road construction, has a natural advantage since it is porous and rapidly dries up after rain.[2] In addition, its handling is easy. However, it also has detractors which may include its tendency to corrugate with heavy use, to be sprinkled with potholes during heavy rains, and to create dust in the dry season. As a result, maintenance costs may be high. Maintenance may even be poor if work crews are unskilled and inadequately supervised. It is not surprising therefore that in some places outside these large cities, motorable roads, in the dry season, are often punctuated by impassable, sometimes slithery tracks during the long rainy seasons. This is especially so, when roads (e.g., secondary and rural roads not built to handle heavy loads) are suddenly submitted to the stress of heavy freight traffic.

In places where the local earth is unsuitable, gravel or hardtop roads tend to be practical. Examples may be found in regions of unconsolidated sands and silted areas where the traffic is heavy or where freight is hauled by heavy trucks. Both gravel and hardtop roads, however, require more engineering, more materials, and more capital outlays. Although capital outlays may be initial detractors, once gravel and hardtop roads are built, they tend to be more easily maintained than dirt roads. Nevertheless, maintenance does not come very cheaply since, again, materials have to be hauled in from a distance, and there is heavy wear and tear on machinery. When the theoretical costs of tarred and gravel road construction is disciplined by building narrow single lanes, the shoulders tend to be aggravated by attrition, since motorists must use them as passing lanes and for parking. When the aforementioned scenario is considered, maintaining an asphalt road maybe expected, therefore, to be overall more costly than a gravel road.[3]

Without maintenance, thoroughfares can be easily swallowed up by the nearby bushes; parts of road networks can become roadless again. This was the case with Ethiopia between 1941 and 1951. This is especially so when road networks are not wide enough and are not used frequently by wheeled traffic. In addition, when roads are unkempt and narrow, they may look like paths beaten out of the bush by human feet, but they are still convenient for the motorcyclist. In practice, however, voluntary or pressed labor has been known to take charge of minor local road maintenance even in remote areas.

Other variable factors that can quickly escalate the cost of road construction include building bridges, erecting embankments, and creating drainage. Significant factors also include the nature of the bed rock, the proximity of labor crews, and the articulation of the terrain.

Previously, it was determined that most of the journeys the African undertook were to and from the local markets or from one market to the next. Such journeys were determined to be less than ten miles, or at most twenty-five miles in length. Here feeder roads were more serviceable than throughways. Noncommercial journeys (for reasons such as to visit friends, family relatives, and so on) were on the average not far. Interterritorial journeys were to places such as mines and factories. This explanation may be included in the catalog of reasons that the proportions of asphalt and gravel roads in some places have been increasing very slowly. At any rate, when such places decide to systematically engage in the production of important commodities, which must reach world markets, the analogy maybe weakened. The question becomes, therefore, how can an entrepreneur engage in the production of important commodities when the roads are unpredictable and seasonal? Since the answer is simple, it will not be discussed here.

In the 1960s and 1970s, as the demand for Ivory Coast's export increased, the government dramatically improved the road network. Paved roads linked Abidjan with all population centers in the country. These roads comprised only 7 percent of the total road network, and carried about 70 per cent of the total traffic. In addition, roads were the principal mode of domestic transportation, conveying 78 percent of interurban passenger traffic and 70 percent of freight traffic. From 1970 to 1980, traffic grew rapidly, expanding at a rate of about 10 percent per year for passenger traffic, and 7 percent annually for freight traffic. By 1986, approximately 14,000 vehicles entered and left Abidjan daily, a great contrast to an average of about 4,800 in 1969.

*Zimbabwe* has a fairly well developed road network that is made up of separate systems. Here, the high-standard road system connected the country's principal towns and commercial farming areas; served national development areas, such as the irrigated agricultural area around the Hippo Valley and the Triangle in Southern Lowveld; provided access to national parks and other tourist recreational areas; and linked the road system at border points with contiguous nations. The secondary roads system was composed of mainly gravel roads (about 23,400 kilometers) serving commercial farming places.[4]

Implications of poor roads will include accelerated depreciation of automobiles; the useful lives of intercity buses, cars, and other vehicles are generally very short. The costs of maintenance are high. When motor vehicles are used in poor road conditions, automobile parts may have to be replaced often. The downtime for commercial vehicles usually means forgone revenues. While this may nolonger be the case, it was not unusual to find one-third of intercity buses at any given time in repair shops. If there were no alternative forms of transportation, such as airlines, long-distance drives across vast regions, such as trans-Saharan journeys, can sometimes become an endurance test for motorists.

With industrialization, most of the familiar problems associated with poor roads tend to disappear. Settlements become economically more significant in an environment in which much more goods and services are produced. Income levels increase with growth in manufacturing and related services, and many persons can afford goods and services that were previously outside their reach. Some rural roads are upgraded because they become economically indispensable roads that link important agricultural or manufacturing districts: Big populations agglomerate around plantation estates and company towns. Residents here produce, process, assemble, or manufacture more goods, are engaged in the service sector, and command significant purchasing power.

If settlements must be connected, then it becomes necessary to do so efficiently. For some firms (e.g., firms engaged in seasonal products), transportation delays and other road inefficiencies may be the difference between staying in business and going out. Business earnings are important, and time is valued in terms of money. But timeliness is important and speed is not always the priority. Instead, in some cases where preventing a market glut enhances product value, delays can often increase market value. Logistically, therefore, storage that delays physical distribution also extends product availability in marketplaces, long after the actual production of goods ended.

Where speed is of essence, the business advantages of speed and convenience gained in one part of the country may be canceled by the costs and hazards of transportation associated with doing business in other parts of the country or economic region. An important consideration, here, is the rather lopsided freight movement during early industrialization, when economic growth poles may not be properly aligned. In this case, flatcars and trailers, used inbound, for example in transporting hardwood, may not always have cargo or adequate freight when needed during the outbound trip. When this predicament is resolved by low inbound and low outbound freight rates, it poses a problem for industrialization in that region because it encourages widespread use of raw materials, without value added in processing and manufacturing. Higher inbound freight rates for manufactured goods, on the other hand, are synonymous to tariffs. They add to regional retail prices, thus encouraging local manufacturing activities, while protecting novel and start-up business, from the forces of outside competition emanating from well-established competitors. Similarly, in an environment of high inbound rates, high outbound rates have the effect of depressing regional raw-material prices. The result is to encourage local manufacturing initiatives, which draw on such resources, and simultaneously to increase prices and the costs of manufacturing for outside competitors.

In Nigeria, linkage of urban markets to rural areas was most critical for fresh vegetable production. Previously, vegetable production had been limited, geographically, but became feasible and profitable in many areas, once efficient transport connections to urban areas were established. In an industrializing environment, even profits alone do not solve every problem, especially if the produce that leaves these areas is greater in bulk and less in value than the manufactured goods brought in. Ultimately, what is important is selling to markets that yield the largest return and not merely to markets with the lowest freight rates. Freight rates may be price determined or price determining. It should not be a bulwark to a producer or a manufacturer with an inventory of goods to sell. In *Ghana*, poor rural infrastructure was blamed for the problems in agriculture. At this time, it was determined that only one out of every three feeder roads could carry vehicular traffic. Transportation costs took up almost 70 percent of the difference between farm prices and retail prices. [5] It was said that freight rate made a substantial difference, but the paramount question in an industrializing environment or region, in additions to those previously mentioned should be: Should products be processed locally prior to shipment or should raw materials be shipped to or near their markets for processing or manufacturing? Freight rates make a great difference when substantial weight loss of final products is a factor.

In an industrializing environment, as the per capita income increases more persons can afford to travel and the number of personal, commercial, government, and other vehicles on the road increases. Generally with good roads it becomes easier for government to administer in a dynamic and industrializing environment. Roads become a source of business and government revenues, employ a significant proportion of the nation's workforces, add convenience and comfort to everyone and even beauty to the landscape. Roads, like transportation overall, facilitate interregional contacts and enhance the qualities of tastes, education, health, and way of life; political and cultural similarities are strengthened. The tendency is toward increased mutual understanding, and economic interdependence is magnified by large-scale production. Roads, airlines, railways, and waterways and other forms of transportation are all integral to industrialization at the very foundation.

### User taxes, roads, and hospitality

In a well-organized and industrializing environment, local government capital expenditures in transportation maybe effected from local sources of revenues. Gasoline taxes, manufacture and sale of license plates, special fees levied on trucks and buses, emission control decals, insurance taxes, toll bridges, and government securities obligations are all among the various ways local governments raise taxes to meet transportation obligations. This usually begins with defining transportation goals and objectives. Then, impact studies are analyzed and ramified. The government may proceed with arrangements on how to repay financial obligations to public and institutional lenders.

Worn-out roads and poor roads cost more in spare parts and tires than they do in taxes. To maintain these roads can be the responsibility of a local community or township. In the early days of automobile transportation in North America, farmers, were known to schedule a few days off to participate in road maintenance, instead of cash payments of their tax obligations. In other communities, road concerns began with a good roads colloquy, which eventually materialized in upgraded road construction or the fruition of the first experimental mile of country road.

Improved roads definitely were going to negate economic obstacles and social isolation of many farmers. In 1907 *Scientific American* reported that motorized traffic near Boston, "swept the [gravel] binder from the road and left it in windrows along the roadside." Although brick roads were considered the most satisfactory, the experts injected that the cost was prohibitive.[6] Those who favored paving included cyclists, bicycle manufacturers, automakers, and especially farmers, whose wagons constantly stuck in the mud. The prospects for concrete materials in road constructions were bright.

In North America, the Federal Aid Roads Act of 1916 made road-building funds available to states that would raise matching funds and set up state highway departments to administer them. Considering the muddy conditions during the wet seasons and the dusty environment during the drier seasons, the offer of the federal government to share the cost of road construction with the states was irresistible. To meet this obligation, in some places automobile license fees were increased, and taxes were collected at the pump, for example, a one-cent gasoline tax per gallon collected at the pump. The states had to submit an "orderly scheduling," so that the local roads they built were interconnected with other communities. This action preempted any remote possibilities of a thoroughfare suddenly terminating in cornfields at state lines. This network of roads was the genesis of the uniformly numbered U.S. highway routes that materialized after 1925. For example, U.S. 1 was the way to Maine from Florida. Highway 66 connected Chicago and Los Angeles. Good roads and personal automobiles increased the freedom of movement of many people. Many people for the first time saw other parts of the country, with appreciation and often without reservation.

Between 1945 and 1955, automobile registration doubled. Cars carried people to and from work. There were street congestion and increased traffic delays. A ten-year program was proposed for highway construction, at the cost of 101 billion in 1955 dollars. The reigning contention was that the existing highways were unsafe, inadequate, and prevalent traffic delays were a menace, with costly dimensions to individual operators, distribution, and consumers. Considering the cold war and the specter of the atomic bomb, commanding a better road network that lent itself to swift military movements and evacuations was necessary. In commerce and industry, better thoroughfares would be good for high-speed, long-haul traffic that bypassed downtown areas, with limited feeder highways linking networks with central business districts. At the time, this "grand plan" of pharaonic dimensions was considered among the largest public works project ever undertaken by man. It was dubbed the Interstate Highway and Defense System.[7]

To the public, the interstate highways were comfortable, efficient, and modern networks of roads that induced travel and vacation. In anticipatory delight, numerous people visited other states, visited national parks, and even went fishing for leisure. This trend in lifestyles was perceived and captured by enterprising individuals, who sought to supply motorists with their economic needs and wants.

Almost simultaneously a myriad of restaurants sprouted along roadsides, catering to the gastronomical delights of those motorists who had not patronized hotels. Another significant development was the motel. Typically, motels catered to tired families, who wanted to get off the highway for the night and have some rest before continuing their journey at daybreak. Motels were generally small family-run businesses. They were often owned and operated by retirement-age couples. The number of units often ranged from ten to fifteen units. Operating costs were kept low by the husband acting as room clerk, cashier, and repair person while the wife acted as house cleaner.

The 1950s were boom years for the motel business. Motel business became big business: the number of motels plummeted while the number of rooms escalated. Owners banded together in cooperative associations that specified standards for membership. They also offered joint services, such as for room reservations. Other motels emerged as chains, for example, Travelodge, Howard Johnson, and Holiday Inn. These big chains operated mostly as franchises, with a centralized authority that typically provided financing, coordinated management, architecture, and a host of other services. It was feasible to eat delectably and identically prepared culinary delights in any of the franchises, wash in identically sanitized bathrooms and sleep in identically laundered linens. One decade after the founding of Holiday Inn, in 1952, there were five hundred Holiday Inns. By 1974, the number had more than tripled; there were 1,679 Holiday Inns, with 264,117 rooms, along the nation's highways.[8]

Efficient and well-maintained highways, expressways, and byways are very important in industrial environments. They are important in the efficient distribution of industrial raw material and finished goods. This efficiency is enhanced by delivery vehicles, especially tractor trailers, light-duty commercial trucks, heavy-duty trucks, and vans that have the versatility of availing to the highways for fast and frequent dispatches. Their capacity for short-haul and small bulk transport, as well as the fact that they can go from door to door, gives them geographically localized advantages, vis-à-vis other forms of transportation.

In road transportation, it becomes necessary to have all the facts about transportation. For example, the maximum capacity of cars per lane per hour is two thousand; loop detectors can be used to avoid stalled traffic; ramp metering slows how fast cars get onto the highway; highways' electronic message signs improve traffic management. In the most advanced countries, highway radio stations are used to improve traffic management.

## AIR TRANSPORTATION

To enhance the efficiency of surface transport vehicles, challenges such as canyonlike valleys too wide to bridge and too steep to climb may have to be confronted. This is not so with air transport. Airplanes can fly almost anywhere away from airlanes, though air transport obviously has its own challenges. Storms that can wreck a train may quite easily overturn a plane with turbulence, all the more so at night, when such storms could not be easily seen or detected. Although planes can be as free as birds in the sky, in most cases they can only make scheduled stops at specific locations. Unscheduled stops may only be acceptable in cases of an emergency or impending disaster or in strategic free market competition, reminiscent of North America just after 1945. This discussion, therefore, will peer at some problems associated with ground facilities and operations within the context of an industrializing environment in Africa.

As in other parts of the world, air transport in Africa overcame some difficulties associated with surface transport. Mail and freight delivery was enhanced tremendously. Work productivity was enhanced since businesspeople and administrators could spend less time on the road and more time at work. In Africa, workers could fly in hours to destinations that previously took days and perhaps weeks. Airplanes brought distant businesses closer to their markets, and remote workers in places such as mines could sigh in contentment because they were perhaps only a few hours away from friends, relatives, medical care, supplies, and so on. In some places the plane could earn its keep as a long-distance hauler, transporting airmail, gold, diamonds, machine tools, replacement parts, medicine, periodicals, business samples, women's clothing, pedigree bulls, and even one-day-old chicks and perishables.[9]

Air transport has been very helpful in Africa, especially in places where the integrity of alternative forms of transportation was either undependable or unpredictable. This is even more so in an industrializing environment, where the quality of services offered is paramount. In any case, in recent decades, many airlines faced a series of trials and, if not errors, what were in the opinions of many errors also. Accordingly nations have been taking steps to confront the challenges meted out by a competitive market environment.

Schedule irregularities and passenger complaints were prevalent in Nigeria in 1990. As a result, government pressurized *Nigeria Airways* to improve the standard of service and to reduce financial losses. Despite problems, the number of passengers on domestic flights was increasing in the 1980s. In retrospect, this was mainly because of the unsatisfactory state of other modes of transportation during the same period. *Ghana Airways* has also had its own share of problems. Historically, these problems culminated in shortfalls in projected revenues. At worst this meant the airways could not purchase additional aircraft for strategic reorientation in the marketplace. Aircraft purchases to bolster Ghana's domestic and regional routes had to wait. In the 1990s, the government invested capital to improve the international airport facilities in the capital city, Accra. Here, the runway was resurfaced, the lighting system upgraded, and a new freight terminal was built. In Kumasi, the terminal building was given a facelift. Airport navigational apparatuses were upgraded, and improvements were also made in the freight landing infrastructure. Ghana has eleven airports. The most important are the Kotoka International Airport in Accra and the airports in Sekondi-Takoradi, Kumasi, and Tamale, which serve domestic air traffic.

Although airlines in some countries confronted challenges that were not easily surmountable, a few airlines operated in conducive environments. In the 1980s, the *Abidjan-Port Bouët International Airport*, on the outskirts of Abidjan was one of the busiest in Africa. Here, the number of passengers was around 1 million annually. The runway (3,000 meters in length) did handle all carriers, and so did the airports in Bouaké and Yamoussoukro. Thirty public airports are found in major towns, not including many more private airfields. *Ethiopian Airlines* was one of the profitable African airlines. Ethiopian Airlines provided training and maintenance services for over a dozen African and Middle Eastern airlines. In late 1986, this airlines corporation that began operations in 1946 responded to the need to support the nation's agricultural development and the agro-aircraft needs of other nations in Africa: the first agro-aircraft was assembled in late 1986. Air transport facilities added or expanded included: a gas production plant, base maintenance shops for ground equipment, and an expanded catering network. Ongoing was also a program to automate airline activities such as maintenance, engineering, ticket accounting, and crew and corporate data management. While the government, then, did not meddle in the airlines' operations, plans to expand into areas such as hotel construction and management, tourism, and catering were opposed. Instead, these areas were reserved for other state corporations, then operating at a loss. In mid-1989, Ethiopian Airlines, noted for an excellent reputation for safety, announced plans to spend US$1.2 billion on new aircraft. In 1991, financial arrangements were completed to purchase five new Boeing 757s and to refinance two Boeing 767s.[10] In Angola, the growth of air transport was largely attributable to difficulties with land transportation. Here, domestic service linked the capital, Luanda, with Benguela, Cabinda, Huambo, Lubango, Malanje, Negage, and Soyo. Angola Airlines sustained high profitability in an environment where prices for jet fuel were low, employee wages were low, fees were unrealistically low, demand for domestic flights was heavy, and the cargo loads on its flights were also high. By 1988, Angola Airlines (Linhas Aéreas de Angola-TAAG, formerly known as Transportes Aéreos de Angola) could afford to refurbish its fleet of Boeing 737s and 707s. Since then, this airline established an extensive international route network. Based at the major airport in Luanda, the airlines offered services from there to other countries in Africa (Zambia, Mozambique, Cape Verde, São Tomé and Principe, and Congo Republic and Democratic Republic of Congo) and internationally (Havana, Lisbon, Moscow, and Rome).

When commercial airlines are well managed, the operations become profit centers. Even then, the efficiency of operations must be consistently monitored for improvements. The following questions may or may not be helpful, in this regard:

- Are the seats at the terminal adequate for waiting passengers?
- Are the waiting areas comfortable?
- What is the safety record?

• Are the facilities well maintained or they are in melancholic disrepair?
• Are the newsstands and stores receptive and immaculate?
• Is ticket processing efficient (e.g., automated)?
• Are games /television receivers installed for entertainment?
• How are the hygiene standards?
• Are planes sometimes overloaded with cargo?
• What is the efficiency in handling peak traffic?
• Is the magnetometer operational?
• Are the emergency floor lights and exit door lights working?

## RAILWAYS

Factors used to determine the availability of transport in a nation include the following: the total length of railways in kilometers per 10,000 population; percentage of total rail and motor passenger traffic accounted for by rail; passenger kilometers per head; percent of rail, road, and inland waterway freight traffic accounted for by rail; ton-kilometers of road and rail freight per head; motor vehicles per 10,000 population.[11]

Africa, excepting a few countries, such as South Africa and Zimbabwe, is sparsely populated by rail lines. Although this may be a cause for concern, a historical overview of the state of rail lines in several countries in Africa recurrently indicated some challenges. Problems included lack of working locomotives, rolling stock, deteriorating rail beds, competition from other modes of transportation, slow passenger schedules, and declining revenues. In countries in Africa where railways have been successful, making expansions was quite easy based on projected demand.

In Nigeria, the rail lines seemed to reach out to most of the economically important regions of the country. The basic elements were two main lines from the coast, running inland. The start of the system was a line built between 1898 and 1901, linking Lagos and Ibadan. Between 1904 and 1912, the line was extended to Kano, through Ilorin and Zaria. With the opening of the tin mines at Jos, a line then linked it to Zaria. The line in the east, from Port Harcourt to a conjunction with the western line at Kaduna, opened in 1926. Major extensions were subsequently added. In 1929, the branch line connecting Zaria to Kuala Namoda (an important agricultural area in the northwest) was completed. In 1930, another branch line from Kano connected Nguru (in the cattle-raising region). The rail line also gave Enugu coalfield direct access to the deepwater harbor of Port Harcourt. Plans for renovations were shelved, and the system was said to be deteriorating because of poor maintenance, inadequate funding, and declining traffic.

In Ivory Coast, the rail became a long-distance hauler when rail transport was no longer important in the south and central regions. Here the railway contributed significantly to the development of agriculture and forestry, until the expansion and upgrading of the road network. The only places where rail services were still useful were found directly on the rail route. In the north, the railway was still vital to the economy and for new industries located similarly. Until the recession of the 1980s, which was complicated by misunderstandings, the railway was used by the inland nations of Burkina Faso and Mali for foreign trade that passed through the seaport of Abidjan.

In Algeria, unlike in Ivory Coast, the rail system was disabled by lack of long-distance traffic. Passenger traffic centered mostly in urban areas, and especially the capital city. Here iron ore and phosphate were the only commercially profitable freight. The rail carried 53 million passengers and 13 million tons of freight in 1989. The goal was to carry 40 percent of total freight, and plans included doubling the length and freight capacity of the existing rail network. The expansion program called for several new lines, freight centers, and stations, including a railroad tunnel. Several new lines were under construction in 1993.

In Zaire, less attention had been given to the rail system. As a result, it was in need of repairs by the 1980s. Transport was slow, cumbersome, and unreliable. Mineral shipment in one route could take two months and averaged forty-five days. Because the load on the route was limited, the country eventually resorted to South African rail lines for about 33 to 40 percent of its mineral export. Under a rehabilitation effort in the late 1980s, track beds had to be rebuilt and rail ties installed. The plan was to overhaul twenty diesel locomotives and thirty-eight electric locomotives, purchase new rolling stock, and materials to manufacture rail cars locally. The project was scheduled for completion at some time in the 1990s.

In Zimbabwe, the rail system also underwent renovations. Funds were applied in 1981 toward spare parts for locomotives, freight cars, machine tools, track equipment, and apparatus to maintain and improve the signaling system. Orders were placed for sixty-one new diesel electric locomotives. Here, domestic use took up 60 percent of the freight (about 12–13 million tons) hauled annually. Freights were mostly bulk goods, including coal, fertilizers, iron ore, and agricultural goods.[12] Export trade made up 33 percent, mainly maize, cotton, sugar, minerals, and steel. Import included general goods, fuels, and chemicals. Copper was carried in transit from Zaire and Zambia. In 1976, however, shipments on this line were interrupted because of trouble in Mozambique. When increases were projected in the volume of business activities, steps were taken accordingly. Locomotives were brought in, on loan from South Africa; overhauled locomotives for operational use also became handy. In 1981, the long-contemplated electrification of the railroad system began. Thirty locomotives were ordered in 1983.

Changes such as these in recent years are improving the overall transportation system in several countries. Although much work still needs to be done, it is also important to note that the supply of transport depends on expected demand. With appropriate planning and maintenance, the current transportation systems in Africa can, therefore, take advantage of unfolding opportunities deriving from a dynamic and industrializing environment.

# NOTES

1. George H.T. Kimble, *Tropical Africa: Land and Livelihood* (New York: Twentieth Century Fund, 1960), pp. 463–484.

2. This is reminiscent of McAdam's principle: John Loudon McAdam, a Scot who had made his fortune in America, proposed "that it is the native soil which really supports the weight of traffic; that while it is preserved in a dry state, it will carry any weight without sinking." He dispensed with the practice then (around 1836) of using stone foundation. He instead made optimum use of the soil already on the site. The idea was to keep the soil dry and this was achieved by constructing drains, to lower ground or by raising the soil above the water-level. The dryness of the road soil would be ensured by an impervious, compact, and indestructible cover or top layer capable of absorbing the weight of traffic. The camber will keep it free from puddles. These roads came to be known as 'metalled' or 'macadamized' roads. This improvement in road construction increased the speed of traffic and the average time of travel by coach was cut by more than half. The horse could haul three times more than on an unmetalled track. The burden of the laborer's walk to work was also reduced. By the close of the 19th century about 90 percent of principal European highways had been macadamized. While McAdam's faith in soil was marginalized in the late twentieth century, it had an inherent and enormous advantage of cheapness. Derry T.K. and Trevor I. Williams, *A Short History of Technology: From the Earliest Times to A.D. 1900* (New York: Oxford University Press, 1961), pp. 432–434.

3. Ibid., pp. 463–464. If history is still any guide, here, then Ghana's early experience in road construction may cast more light on this problem. Annual maintenance cost data pertaining to Ghana, then considered a fairly representative country, was estimated in 1954 to be more than £200 per mile for tarred roads and £167 per mile for gravel roads. In the then British East Africa, the average cost of building a mile of first-class roads was said to be between £8,000 and £10,000. In any given mile of first-class roads, the cost could range from between £200 and £20,000. In 1955 in then French Equatorial Africa, one mile of road with a high tonnage capacity was estimated to cost at most £184,000. It must be noted, however, that after World War II, practically all the financing of the infrastructure of the French speaking countries came from abroad. Ghana, Nigeria, and Uganda were able to finance nearly all of their needs from their own resources. In the post-1960 period, however, the plans showed that at least 50 percent of public capital investment was earmarked to be financed from abroad. In Tanzania (then Tanganyika), the plan showed that 90 percent of public investment was supposed to come from elsewhere; for Sudan it was 30 percent. This characteristic was unique to Africa, and no other region in the world was in a similar position. See: A.G. Thomson, "Cheap Roads for Africa," *New Commonwealth*, February 15, 1954, p. 178; "The Franco-African Transportation System . . . ," *African Affairs* (Ambassade de France), April 1955, p. 3; Melville J. Herskovits and Mitchell Harwitz, eds., *Economic Transition in Africa* (Evanston, IL: Northwestern University Press, 1964), p. 275.

4. Harold D. Nelson, ed., *Zimbabwe: A Country Study* (Washington, DC: GPO, 1983), p. 174.

5. Lavelle Berry, *Ghana: A Country Study* (Washington, DC: GPO, 1995), p. 181.

6. *Scientific American*, July 6, 1907; also March 29, 1909.

7. Joseph A. Loftus, "President offers a Roads Program ...," *New York Times*, February 23, 1955, p. 1.

8. *Highways and Economic and Social Changes* (Bureau of Public Roads, 1964), p. 12.

9. Airplanes are useful for passenger transport; cargo; business applications (like aerial photography, advertising, employee transport, etc.); agricultural applications (such as dusting,

spraying, seeding, weed control, checking unused land, counting cattle, studying soil erosion, surveying, hunting, and cloud seeding). The government also uses aircraft for training programs, research, testing airway radio ranges, forest patrol, fire fighting, fish and game management, exploration, chart making, and personnel transportation. The military, the police and the medical establishment use air transportation extensively. Among all these uses, commercial transportation has been the most captivating. This is because it is a profit center.

10. Thomas P. Ofcansky, and LaVerle Berry (eds.), *Ethiopia: A Country Study* (Washington, DC: GPO, 1993), pp. 198–199.

11. Gunnar Myrdal, *Asian Drama: An Inquiry into the Poverty of Nations* (New York: Twentieth Century Fund, 1968), pp. 540–541.Transportation is a component part of other factors used as indicators of the level of living, namely food (calories per head per day; proteins per head per day); clothing (annual textile consumption in kilograms per head); physicians (number per 100,000 population); literacy and education (literacy by sex of population aged 15 and over); newsprint, radios and television (each number per 10,000 population); telephones (number per 10,000 population); energy (annual consumption of coal equivalent, in kg per head); transportation.

12. Trains are structured to accommodate the spectrum of industrial activities, and freight cars are classified to serve the different sectors of industry. The following are some examples. *Box cars* are designed to carry merchandise such as grain, flour, dried and canned fruits, coffee, sugar, salt, and various packaged goods. *Platform cars* are widely used to transport lumber, logs, bridge girders, heavy machinery, military equipment, tractors, and so on. *Well cars* have very strong platforms designed to carry very heavy machines, engines, electric generators, and large wheels. *Gondola cars* are typically used for carrying coal, lumber, sand, sulfur, iron ore, cinders, and other bulky commodities. *Hopper cars* have an all-steel configuration, equipped with high harbor and a dumping mechanism. They are used for transporting sand, gravel, earth, slag, cinders, sulfur, phosphate, crushed stone and other commodities that can be dumped using a trip door. *Stock cars* are ventilated and are employed for shipment of cattle, horses, goats, sheep, pigs and so on. *Poultry cars* are used for transporting life poultry. *Tank cars* are used for shipment of crude oil, fuel oil, gasoline, naphtha, kerosene and the like. *Milk cars* are used for the shipment of fresh milk and cream. They are typically made of steel and aluminum. *Container cars* are gondola-style cars. They are typically fitted with four or five metals, waterproof and fireproof containers, some with special linings. They are generally used for the transportation of drugs, medicinal supplies, chemicals, e.t.c. They are easily transferred from, and to motor trucks. *Refrigerator cars* are insulated and are fitted with ventilators and airtight doors. They either have mechanical refrigerators or are fitted with bunkers for ice storage. They may also be fitted with heaters/heat pumps. Typically they are used to transport fresh meat, seafood, fresh fruits, vegetables, dairy products, cut flowers, and other commodities that are sensitive to adverse temperature conditions. *Interchangeable freight containers* are also used on railroads. Generally, containerization enhances the productivity of intermodal transportation, because giant box-like receptacles (containers) tend to be easily and quickly loaded and unloaded. Containers are locked against pilferage and sealed against adverse weather.

# 15

# Housing and Urbanization in an Industrializing African Environment

According to *Webster's New Universal Unabridged Dictionary*, housing refers to the act of sheltering. In much broader semantics, it means the problems related to providing adequate housing and the alternative solutions. This does not only mean striving to resolve the problem of housing in isolation. Instead, it means solving housing problems in the context of the immediate environment using tools such as policies, city planning, community services, standards, safety, security, and functions. Functions here refer to aspects such as work, plays, eat, sleep, and so on. Good housing, whether in an architectural jewel or public housing, should optimize health, happiness, comfort, convenience, aesthetics, and relationships with the physical and social environment.

Healthful housing, therefore, tends to respond to physical, physiological, and psychological needs.[1] Such housing tends to enhance the spirit of neighborhood and companionship. They tend to accommodate similar tastes and habits. They are generally in proximity to schools, hospitals, grocery stores, shopping centers, churches, parks, and playgrounds. They tend to make the neighborhood and community beautiful. This urban pattern of housing (or social organization) in an industrializing environment is in contrast with rural settlements that put premia on the social advantages of integrating village life and natural and artificial features. These *compact, nucleated,* or *loose-sprawl* arrangements of houses in rural settlements are generally along streams, spring lines, and roads.[2]

When housing is left not maintained for an extended period, the houses degenerate and become functionally inadequate. There is evidence that overcrowded and deteriorated housing may be associated with physical and mental illness.[3] In this case, these structurally retainable but functionally antiquated houses and other buildings tend to foster crime and breed disease that may affect the entire community. For example, it was observed that families who were removed from substandard housing into new public housing developments, had lower rates of illness and disability due to disease, than those families who were still living in such housing. This observation considered three major categories of children's health problems, namely, communicable diseases of childhood, digestive conditions, and accidents, and to a lesser extent respiratory infections.[4] A much earlier study, by the United Nations, determined that infectious, parasitic, and respiratory diseases, at high levels of mortality, had been drastically reduced. The reason was attributed to affordable modern medical techniques, widely available in urban settings in Africa.[5] However, the benefits of improved housing are not always guaranteed.

One reason is the *paradox of poverty and food*. An early example is when a government attempted to lift the most needy out of squalid environments by placing the residents in new, more hygienic government-issue flats. Surprisingly, the health status of those relocated declined instead. There was an increasing death rate among people in new housing, relative to the neighbors still living in substandard housing conditions. A study revealed that this disastrous outcome was because residents with very low income had to cut back expenses on their basic food requirements in order to meet their rent obligations.[6]

Nevertheless, there are several examples of ambitious and often successful housing efforts around the world. In Great Britain, about 1.5 million homes were built between 1918 and the mid-1950s. In Germany, about 2 million houses were built between 1919 and 1939 with Government aid. Austrian public housing, in Vienna, became the model for Europe. Public housing legislation in the Netherlands was adapted in 1901, supplying about 10 percent of the housing in the country. Some of the most successful public housing projects were built in Sweden, Denmark, Norway, and Finland. In the United States, the National Industrial Recovery Act (NIRA) of 1933 provided for the clearance of substandard dwellings.[7] The NIRA, under the auspices of the Public Works Administration (PWA), set up standards for site planning, design, community facilities, and construction methods. The PWA was set up to mitigate unemployment. Fifty-one projects were executed in thirty-six cities, canalized in zoning policies that extrapolated orderly growth and inculcated the utmost sanitary standards. Building codes also ensured safety and a healthful environment. Over 20,000 houses were constructed as a result of this effort.[8] In 1937, the National Housing Act was passed again with the major purpose of replacing functionally inadequate housing. This act encouraged the creation by local communities of independent agencies, chartered by the states and empowered to receive federal funds. These grants were to be applied toward building and managing housing. More than 260 communities benefited from these grants between 1939 and 1942, during which about 170,000 dwelling units were completed. During the war years, the federal government financed the building of 805,000 units of housing. Of this total, 195,000 units were of permanent construction.[9] Under the Lend-Lease Program, an arrangement was made to build thousands of prefabricated buildings for shipment to certain places in Europe, just after 1945.

There was public bias against government intervention, engineered by many landowners, and segments of the building industry. It seems some interests will exploit every opportunity to hamper changes that immediately threaten personal security and income, even when such changes are designed to benefit the community at large in the long term. Factions maintained that government intervention in housing was tantamount to unhealthy paternalism. The building industry remained, unlike other sectors of the economy, relatively underdeveloped in terms of management and technology and did not reap the benefits of economies of scale. The following statement may shed more light on this stagnation in housing that had acute and adverse ramifications for the lowest-income households in some places:

Localized, small-scale, speculative, and technologically [antiquated], it confronted a challenge of mass production for which it was structurally unequipped. . . . [B]uilding technology, such as the steel frame and elevator, had greater significance for commercial and office-building design than the wholesale construction of lowcost housing. [10]

It took crisis situations to drag the government in. And even at that juncture, the government viewed its role as purely ephemeral.

If governments were in the market for protracted periods, it was not deliberate. A conspiracy of socioeconomic trends determined that the elderly population had grown larger, marriage rates had increased, and there was widespread prosperity in the 1950s and into the 1960s. These were affluent years, and the bigger families found it feasible and comfortable to subdivide, thus increasing the demand for housing. This trend made the argument for government to invest in housing projects, coupled with the large number of migrant workers attracted by postwar expansion into the growing industrial centers of northern Europe and elsewhere.

## SUBSIDIZED HOUSING AND COMPETITION

A fundamental reason for government intervention in the housing market has been the poor and unhealthy state of housing. Frequently, the general solution is to replace unhealthy and inefficient shelters with simple, efficient, and functional structures.

Overall, by the 1930s, approximately 15 percent of the population of Western Europe occupied homes built with some form of government assistance.[11] In Britain, public housing comprised 90 percent of all new housing built in 1950, compared to 50 percent, in 1960. In 1959, 25 percent of all housing was publicly owned. Between 1945 and 1960 approximately 2 million public dwelling units were constructed.[12] In France, in 1984, public housing represented 1.1 percent of the market. In Germany, it represented 0.5 percent of the market in 1985; in Britain, it represented 15 percent (1985); in Japan, it was 7.1 percent (1984); and in the United States, it represented 2.3 percent (1970). Between 1945 and 1970, at least 75 percent of new residential construction in Western Europe received some form of government subsidies.[13]

In order to forestall any competition between subsidized housing and the private rental market, it may be necessary to consider demolishing substandard dwellings for every unit of public housing. Another possible stipulation maybe to keep public housing, as a percentage of the rental housing market, to a minimum. One more option may be to apply a relatively shallow subsidy to a broad spectrum of the housing market. This not only gives government an active voice in housing investments but also increases the ability to micromanage policy and planning (For example, location, volume, and timing).

Essentially, public housing is beneficial because it provides minimum standards without the high costs of private housing that are often associated with the handicraft and sometimes elegant technique of construction. It relieves the financial burden of the economically least-advantaged persons, thus increasing the purchasing power of the community. Better housing also alleviates disease, social tensions, crime, and juvenile delinquency. In the long run, the benefits tend to outweigh the initial cost of capital investment. However, such investments may be detested by ill-informed taxpayers who may send up an outcry often intended to drown any action signals. Urban housing renewal could be more effective, if it considers the short- and long-term tax ramifications in metropolitan areas.[14]

In Great Britain, public housing is not limited to low-income renters. It is made available to the entire public. The idea is well accepted and very popular. In fact, construction is done by the government.[15] In strategic policy formulation and implementation, government may subsidize either the producers or the consumers. Producer subsidies may be executed through government, for-profit corporations, and nonprofit corporations. When the government elects consumer subsidies, such subsidies may include cash outlay, cash allowances/housing allowances, and tax concessions to owner-occupiers.

Producer subsidies are generally encouraged when there is a dearth of houses and government wants to build more (seller's market). The snag intrinsic in this option is that it may not always reach the most qualified recipient. It becomes difficult to target and aid particular types of households. It generally tends to be inefficient. Some disadvantages may include restricted movement of people and regional unemployment that results when people cannot easily relocate to places where there are jobs, thus adversely impacting economic growth. For example, subsidized rents and the long waiting list for council houses, according to the British conservatives, is a reason workers cannot relocate to take advantage of new job opportunities.[16] Consumer subsidies may be administered in the form of housing allowances. This may have an advantage over producer subsidies because it tends to circumvent increased construction costs and marginal inflationary propensities. It targets population segments, especially those that would otherwise be unable to obtain decent dwelling. Such target segments include large families, pensioners, the disabled, and the elderly.

Sometimes *Housing allowances* encompass almost universal populations. Here, Sweden is a case in point. In France, the housing allowance was linked to the more general family allowance. The policy implication here was to encourage higher birth rates. In Germany, housing shortage was approached with government subsidies, encouraged by Article 7, Sections a–e, of the income tax law. The Housing Act of 1950 provided for publicly promoted social housing projects; housing projects aided by tax preference; and free, privately financed building projects. A dimension of the idea was for government to pick up the tab between the actual rent and the rent the family could reasonably afford, based on considerations such as family size and income.[17]

In the United States, public housing construction is by European standards negligible. However, the government provided insurance for Federal Housing Authority (FHA) mortgages and guaranteed Veterans Administration (VA) mortgages, within a secondary loan market. The government established a fixed interest ceiling on mortgages it insured, thus making the mortgage market very sensitive to interest rate changes.[18] As a result, an anti-cyclical variation component was built into the U.S. housing and construction. *Tax concessions,* also known as *tax credits* could be applied as a form of subsidies for the consumer. By this system, the government forgave taxable income that was applied toward interest on mortgage loans. This use of tax expenditure to subsidize housing was most prevalent in the U.S.A. Other forms of housing subsidies included deductible interest payment on property tax, and deferred capital gains tax on sale of property. Housing allowance could also take the form of a *voucher program,* payable to the landlord only. In the United States, this is called *Section Eight* (Housing and Development Act, 1974).

In a *privatized* housing environment, the tendency of the government is to allow the free forces of the market to determine demand and supply. Government, in this regard, may only intervene to correct factors that are not compatible with policy, for example, if small-scale artisans are disproportionately overpowered by the large realties in the housing industry.

By providing subsidies, to the housing industry, the government does not only perform its duties but also establishes leverage. In the housing industry, this leverage could be in determining the terms and conditions of interest-free /low-interest loans. Often, this is the occasion for government to inculcate or graft its policy into the momentum of industry.

In postwar France, the government did exactly this. In order to adequately execute the postwar program, it was essential to build capacity in the construction industry. Up to this juncture, most of the construction sectors comprised small, traditional-bound firms that generally offered resistance to the introduction of new building technologies and materials. In order to promote modern financial and management practices by house builders, the government determined the amalgamation of small firms. Thus, the French government used its leverage in the housing industry to encourage small mergers in the 1950s.[19]

Government housing policies may stimulate a housing boom, as was the case in some European countries. In Scandinavia, the Netherlands and England, sustained and deliberate efforts were made to eliminate dwellings determined beyond repairs and unsuitable. This ensured minimum standards of cleanliness and comfort. There were facilities for clearance and redevelopment, good neighborhood and city planning, and effective and well-enforced zoning. There were also financing and other aids to the house builder and owner and publicly supported research and architectural services for an industry that by its nature is equipped to do little on its own. There was a considerable amount of direct or assisted public construction for families in the lowest income brackets. In some cases, however, housing subsidies were disbursed indiscriminately, without due priority to slum clearance or urban planning. This was jeopardized by rent control, which resulted in very little spending on maintenance and repair.[20]

Ultimately, the quality of housing depends, not only on the industry, but also on what is invested in supplements and supports systems.[21] Thus, the value of a house is also a function of services accessible to its location. Generally, these would include hospitals, schools, sewerage, trash collection, water supply, electricity, macadamized/concrete roads, and telephones.

## BUILDING AND BUILDING INSPECTION

In an effort to affect standards in the building industry, the government employs *inspectors*. Their role is to make sure home builders, contractors, developers, and all concerned, abide by the *rules* and *regulations*. Building inspectors have to deal with a wide range of problems. These problems span from safety and security to potential environmental hazards.

Building inspectors look for home building-related problems such as drainage difficulties related to the yard, uneven walls, faulty plumbing, faulty wiring, foundation problems, quality of air-conditioning ducts, and potential health-hazards such as lead paint, ventilation, and the like. Other problems include the environmental impact of the landscaping, types of fences, and even the impact of the building on the rest of the community. Generally, after the initial building permit and the building inspector's stamp of approval, the structure qualifies for human habitation. The owner/contractor/developer is awarded a certificate of occupancy. The certificate of occupancy says that the building is habitable but does not confirm the absence of intrinsic violations that may not be immediately apparent to the naked eyes.

To overcome *code violations* emanating from structural deficiencies, technical complications and so on, government usually implements a *bond program for builders*. If code violations are uncovered within a legally acceptable period, typically one year after occupancy, the builder must repair the violations. If he or she fails to comply with the request, he or she runs a risk of forfeiting the bond.[22] In a well-structured building environment, building permits constitute an important *economic barometer*, for industrialization and the general health of the economy. The costs of the alternative forms of housing must not be discounted into the bargain.[23]

## HOUSING IN AFRICA

Despite the gigantic strides made in housing in the twentieth century, there is no nation that can confidently say that the problems of housing have been completely solved. In Africa, however, housing is still a very major problem or opportunity. Although by modern standards the stock of rural dwellings may leave much to be desired, the immediate problem of housing in Africa is foremost an urban problem. While the urban skyline of a few cities may impress the eyes, smaller cities and towns have been virtually given little attention. Where public housing exists, such housing privileges are typically for the lower- and middle-ranking civil servants. The least privileged, it seems, have been left to seek their own level. Incentives and institutional arrangements seem for the most part to have been left to the whims and caprices of the market forces.[24]

Increasing overpopulation in the rural areas, vis-à-vis relative life opportunities, has propelled rural–urban migration, especially among the young. With greater educational opportunities than their ancestors, many graduates will be trickling into the middle class, with great expectations of much better lifestyles. Unfortunately, the level of technology is not keeping pace with demand. There is still an acute shortage of healthful and decent housing for the masses, throughout urban Africa. This is aggravated by congestion, noise pollution, the absence of privacy, inconvenient layouts, lack of modern equipment, and difficult access to the outdoors. In the midst of these deficiencies, capital accumulation of real property investment tends to be less than optimal. In an industrializing environment these problems are resolved systematically.

In most states in *Nigeria,* 50 to 70 percent of all households occupied a single-room shelter during the early 1980s. This figure was worst in the city of Lagos. Indoor plumbing was unavailable to 30 percent of the households in Ilorin, and in Port Hacourt, it was as high as 75 percent. Flush toilets were virtually nonexistent in Kano, in 1980, and only 10 to 25 percent of housing had this convenience in other major cities.[25] The 1980s was almost a lost decade for Africa. It will, therefore, be surprising that any significant amelioration took place in the intervening period. There were some changes for the better, but they occurred at a snail's pace. In Lagos, for example, housing construction had boomed but rarely seemed to keep pace with demand. Noteworthy, is the ubiquitous government residential area (GRA), consisting of European-style housing, a hospital or nursing station, and educational, recreational, and religious facilities. In recent decades, these areas became upper-income suburbs, which sometimes spread outward into surrounding farmlands as well as inward to fill the space that formerly separated the GRA from the rest of the city. New institutions, such as university campuses, government office complexes, hospitals, and hotels, were often situated outside or at the peripheries of the city in the 1980s. The intervening space was later filled with further growth.[26] In many ways Nigeria is a virtual microcosm of the housing problems that span much of Africa.

Improvements have been made in rural and urban areas, but standards and strategies have not been dynamic enough to take advantage of contemporary housing technology. Providing running water in rural areas seems to have been a high priority across the continent. For example, in *Uganda* the government recognizing that many people had to walk several kilometers to carry water for household use, declared its intention to extend pipelines into rural areas. Projects in the late 1980s focused on drilling wells, protecting springs, replacing and repairing pumps, and training community workers to oversee water systems. In 1988, in several small towns work began on installing sewage systems. However, without discounting the value of such positive strides, much of Africa has yet to embrace basic technologies that will keep her in lockstep with a progressive world. In Mfilou, a suburban area on the outskirts of Brazzaville, after lots were acquired to build homes, it sometimes took as long as ten years to complete building construction. Utilities were similarly added at a snail's pace.[27] Similar areas were identified to the north of Dakar, the east of Libreville, and the south of Bamako.[28]

Municipal governments have city plans and have often guided land development, with propensities toward *laissez-faire* economy. However, the overall impact of this effort in many places is, justifiably and at best, image-oriented but without substantial economic grounding for sustainable industrialization. Urban housing strategies such as matching houses with stages of life have probably never been used in Africa. The idea is simple and straightforward: Newly married couples, families with children, and older persons in ill health all require different dwellings. Instead, housing in the nongovernment sector in many countries has an ineluctable association of certain districts with tribal and racial groupings. This tendency may have adverse effects in the real-estate market.

In Africa, decent housing for retirees is increasingly a problem because a substantial segment of the workforce, especially the management and leadership, live on government/company property. In *Zambia* this led to the virtual shortage of housing for retirees and their households. On the eve of their retirement, many in embarrassment, found themselves all packed up and almost 'nowhere' to go. In Zambia, the old system by which employers tied housing to benefits was discouraged. This has been replaced, however, by a vigorous market for owner-occupied housing.[29] Low-cost housing can be very effective in solving the problem of inadequate housing at the peripheries of urban settlements.[30] Nevertheless, if the implementation phases of lowcost housing construction projects are not carefully managed, even if the occupants are satisfied, the whole exercise may be a disaster for industrialization.

An approach used in Zambia, to resolve the housing problem, which has especially afflicted the low- and medium-income population, was dubbed Sites and Services. This allowed the procurement of serviced plots for supervised, loan-assisted, self-built, and owner-occupied housing. This housing development had to be 50/50 loan-assisted. Although the plan seemed ambitious on paper, it had inherent snags. For example, house completions were random and unsystematic. Some participants successfully completed their owner-occupied houses only to find that they had been transferred in their employment to other parts of the country. Houses of transferred owners were typically converted to rental property. Twenty percent of the houses were never completed. The sewerage system, which was in the original plan, was eventually eliminated. There was a shortage of procured building materials. The Zambian experience is not particularly unique. Variations of such projects are not uncommon across the continent.

Housing development in *Singapore* may be a handy example of successful housing in an integrated and industrializing environment. The Housing and Urban Development Board was established in 1960 to provide affordable and decent public housing in Singapore. The Land Acquisition Act of 1966, granted the board the power to purchase land (a scarce resource in Singapore) required for housing development. By 1979, the government controlled 67 percent of the land, up from 44 percent in 1960. The government subsidized rent for Housing and Development Board apartments. The selling prices for such apartments were below construction costs, excluding land acquisition costs. In the 1980s, the purchase prices for government-constructed apartments were, typically, 50 to 70 percent below similar privately owned apartments. The activities of the Housing and Development Board were largely successful because of access to large sums of government capital; [31] the spectrum of its authority in land acquisition; the ability to train its own workers and engineers; the freedom to act as a corporation in sourcing construction materials (in-house); the opportunity to enter partnerships and contracts with suppliers; and the ability to prevent corruption in contracting and allocating apartments to the public. In the 1960s and 1970s, before the growth of export-oriented industrialization, the housing construction industry was a major provider of employment and opportunities for workers to learn new skills. This program in Singapore put a lid on the pressure to raise wages. By controlling the tempo and scale of housing construction, the government was able better to regulate the economy and smooth out the cycles of economic activity. In Singapore, the government, in its efforts in rehousing a preponderance of the population, effectively was landlord or mortgage holder for most families. This, in turn brought them into close touch, thus promoting identification with the state. Unlike the preexisting settlement patterns, the outcome of the government housing and social engineering initiatives was a decomposition of ethnic enclaves. Multiculturalism became the dominant flavor of public-apartment residency.

## URBANIZATION AND INDUSTRIALIZATION

From the earliest times, urban communities were outcomes of particular functions each community had to discharge or fulfill. In some places or earlier periods a singular function was dominant while in other places or latter periods several functions were important. As a result, therefore, urbanization can be traced back or grouped into the following types of communities: crossroads community, primary agricultural community, commercial city, industrial city, transportation city, recreational city, educational city, mining community, retirement community, government centers, and combination (regional) city. Because of the nature and distinctive origins of early cities in preindustrial environments, the subsequent growth and expansion of such cities have not always fitted into the mold of industrial cities. In this case, it was not exactly practical to plan a city after it had been built, since planning implies a program before an act. While zoning canalizes the excrescences, it could hardly do more than freeze existing and inconsistent mixtures in land use. This is the reality and a problem of some early cities in Africa in an industrializing environment. Other pertinent problems pertaining to urbanization include rapid population growths, crime and delinquency, housing, and other hazards deriving from the physical, social, and economic environment.

In forest and savanna cities in *Nigeria,* for example, culture, landscape, and history generated different characters for most of the cities. Here, early Yoruba towns centered around the palace of the ruler or the *afin,* which was surrounded by a large open space and market. This arrangement was still evident in large older cities such as Ife. Many contemporary cities were founded during the Yoruba wars of the first part of the nineteenth century. They usually contained multiple centers of power, without a single central palace, thus reflecting their origins as war camps. Instead, the main market assumed the central position in the original town. Obeokuta, for example, had three leading families, of whom were headed by chiefs who had broken and become important rivals of Ibadan.[32] By 1990, this area (Yoruba southwest) was the most highly urbanized part of the country. In *Zambia,* several towns in the copper belt were associated with copper mining. Ndola, in Zambia, which was a trading center in an earlier period, had become and retained the character of a commercial, manufacturing, and administrative center. In *Ethiopia,* Bahir Dar was a newly planned city on Lake Tana and the site of several industries and a polytechnic institute. Here also, Akaki and Aseb were growing into important industrial towns, while Jijiga and Shashemene had become communications and service centers.

Cities that expect to grow with increasing opportunities in an industrializing environment would have to make allowances for increased demographic densities, sanitation, sewers, water distribution, and drainage. Heavy building cover negates natural drainage, but extensive paving enhances effective cleaning and utilization of storm sewers. When this is not so, the growing populations result in congestion in cities that was not present in earlier periods. Transportation traffic increases, narrow streets become crowded, and filth abounds, since provisions for the elimination of waste are inadequate.

While substantial populations still live in rural areas in Africa, people inevitably tend to desert communities without expected comparable economic opportunities, and gravitate to communities with such opportunities. In this case, it is hard to imagine educated persons such as an engineer, an accountant, or a nuclear scientist returning to their respective native villages when no immediate prospects for gainful employment are foreseeable. An example is Ghana, where most people still live in rural communities. Here, there was a high correlation between the economic well-being of the individual and his or her educational level and the tendency to migrate. A high proportion of migrants in urban areas came from the adjacent communities. Urban populations were characteristically multiethnic in orientation. Here, the degree of traditionalism or modernism was tempered by the lengths of stays in urban areas, educational levels, nature of work, religiosity, and living habits. Persons with the characteristics of an elite group membership, generally, did not see themselves as such. Most of them continued to participate in some aspects of traditional society and socialized with members of their own or other lineage groups. The family life of the affluent approximated those by international standards. Memberships in groups addressing societal, professional, and other concerns were also important. Examples here will include the Accra Turf Club, Ghana Red Cross Society, Ghana Bar Association, Ghana Medical Association, and Ghana National Association of Teachers.[33]

In *Ethiopia*, rapid rural-to-urban migration, between the period from 1967 to 1975, led eventually to decline in urban growth in the period spanning 1975 and 1987. Excepting Aseb, Arba, Minch, and Awasa, urban centers grew an average of 40 percent over a twelve-year period. Land reform programs provided opportunities and incentives for peasants and other potential migrants to stay in rural areas. Restrictions on travel, lack of employment, housing shortages, and social unrest in some towns (1975 and 1980) also contributed to the decline in rural-to-urban migrations. In *Kenya*, the ambitious program in educational expansion was not matched by an expansion of opportunities for graduates of the school system. As a consequence, by the mid-1970s, the rate of unemployment among secondary school graduates was reaching crisis proportions. This was exacerbated by high population growth in urban areas. In Nairobi, the rate of population growth was faster than the national average, between 1969 and 1979, during which population increased by 62 percent, reaching at least 800,000. Not surprisingly, and as in other parts of the world, crime rates varied directly with the size of the city. In sub-Saharan Africa, juvenile delinquency was a distinctly urban phenomenon. Unemployment among Kenya's youth was identified as an important underlying cause of the rising incidence of crime against property. Overall, crime was increasing in sophistication. While crime rates tend to increase with the size of cities, there are several practical ways to arrest and reverse the trend in an industrializing environment. Practical methods will include, massively increasing the police force, especially in patrolling; lighting streets; and other needed resources.

In *Nigeria*, rural-to-urban migration was speeded by the oil boom in the 1970s. Many energetic young men in rural areas abandoned farming opportunities, to seek their fortunes in cities such as Lagos, Port Harcourt, and Warri, which were directly affected by the oil economy. One would imagine several of these young men indeed attained their goals. Since then, migrations have waxed and waned with the state of the economy. Many young people were compelled to return to their villages by the late 1980s because of the sharp downturn of the economy and shortage of gainful employment opportunities in the cities. As a long-term phenomenon, however, migration from the rural areas, especially by young people, was expected to be an accelerating and largely irreversible process.[34]

Although the largest towns attract the greatest number of migrants, some migrations are to smaller towns, usually in response to economic opportunities. In *Zambia*, with a relatively high rate of urbanization in Africa, the towns of Kafue and Mazabuka are handy examples. Here, the former's growth was fueled by the textile and chemical fertilizer plants, and the latter attracted agricultural migrants responding to the establishment of a sugar estate and a refinery. In Nigeria, the effect of the departure of working-age men from rural areas was to generate a lively market for rural wage labor. As in most places in Africa, agricultural labor was traditionally specified by gender. As young men migrated from rural areas to seek their fortunes, a labor gap developed. This gap was met by others, usually wives or children or hired labor. By 1990, in many places, it was common practice to hire male and female laborers to do farm chores, which were once the responsibilities of household labor. With improvements in roads, the demand for hired labor was readily available, for such tasks as land preparation, weeding, and harvesting. The result was an increase in seasonal and longer-term *intra* rural labor migration. It became feasible for the Hausa and other northern workers to come south to work as hired labor in the cocoa belts and elsewhere and to return to their home villages in time to plant their own crops. The prospects for rural farming were brightened by better roads, which ensured supply of needed labor and transportation of farm produce to meet the vast increase in urban food demand. In this case, rural labor ensured the supply of food (and especially cassava, corn, and fresh vegetables) to the growing cities. The continued growth of urbanization and expansion of transportation capacity were likely to be major driving forces of agricultural production and modernization in the 1990s.

The Industrial Revolution was a dramatic watershed, in urban growth and public planning. It also ushered in an unprecedented period of urban overcrowding and substandard living conditions. In some places, municipal socialists arrested such conditions in the late nineteenth century, building public parks, upgrading the water and sewer systems, and taking over the control of private transportation companies. To get rid of substandard housing, construction projects were undertaken. Clearance of overcrowded and congested dwellings, unsatisfactory for renovation, is important in redevelopment that establishes adequate standards of low-rent housing for industrial workers. At the beginning of the twentieth century, healthier and more efficient communities and towns had gained roots among European planners. They were coined "garden cities" and satelite "garden towns."

Garden cities were intended to be self-contained and self-sustaining communities. Satelite garden towns, on the other hand, were situated close to large industrial cities to which the residents were attached for industrial employment or business. Both were similar in that they were residential areas of low density, with not more than twelve families per acre, and contained factory and shopping areas, parks, schools, other buildings, and protective buffers of permanent agricultural belts on the periphery.

These became the models for half a century, and they were not ignored by several European countries that wanted to build new towns. [35] The concept was successfully implemented in postwar London. At this time, its infrastructure was experiencing stress from demographic pressure. Policy makers therefore decided to slow population growth by establishing a permanent girdle, five miles wide around London. This ribbon of intervening land called the *Green Belt,* was imposed to put a check to urban sprawl. To absolve potential pressure in London, the government decided to build new towns within a radius of thirty-five miles from central London. This took place in the years just after 1945. To ascertain that such populations were not merely commuter populations, the communities were made relatively self-sufficient: municipal services were supplied, and the residents were able to shop and work in their own towns. In the 1960s, new locations were built, eighty miles farther away from central London. In a complex an industrializing environment, the provision of public services required by the residents can make the difference between success and failure. Important considerations, however, will also include the impact of transportation on residents of new-town projects or garden towns.

In Paris, the government embarked on a new-town project to stymie an imbalance in urban development that was straining the city's transportation network. Although people were living increasingly in the suburbs, they often had jobs in Paris proper. In the second half of the 1960s and the early1970s, the government built new towns adjacent to Paris. Additional nodes of development, were geared toward siphoning demographic densities away from the city center.[36]

In Sweden, between 1904 and the 1960s, the city of Stockholm purchased 20,000 acres of land surrounding the city. The land was incorporated and planned for garden suburbs. The varied methods employed in Sweden to maintain good housing ranged from municipal programs to rehouse households from dwellings considered unfit for renovation to housing for single women and for the aged.[37] Unlike London, Stockholm built suburban centers called satelite cities. The plan intentionally left the satelite cities dependent on the central city. However, these suburban centers had their own shopping, recreational, cultural facilities, and basic social services, like health care. Between 1952 and 1970, twenty-seven such plans were completed. Most experts acknowledge the general plan for Stockholm to be among the best-planned in the world.[38] In the Netherlands, a postwar concept for strategic urban development was the *Randstad* or *Ring City*. The randstad connected Rotterdam, The Hague, Amsterdam, Utrecht, and other smaller cities. The Dutch authorities foresaw an urban sprawl. The commissioning of the randstad checked the urban sprawl and the eventual conurbation.

*Shanghai* has a population in excess of 11 million, with more than 5.4 million people (inclusive) living in the fifty-eight-square-mile urban core. The city began as a fishing village before the tenth century. Around 1260 and 1378, it had become a minor cotton spinning and weaving center. By 1800 it was a flourishing port, with a population of approximately 50,000. Its strategic locality was recognized in foreign trade as a port of entry, to the great and wealthy Yangste Valley, where half China's millions lived. Until 1949, the area essentially evolved as a group of foreign enclaves or three cities within the city, thus complicating planning for the most populous city. Water, sewage, and road systems reflected the separation of authority and were not designed for intercommunity relationships or service. Coordination of the several communications and servicing systems were still considered critical problems in recent decades. However, ten industrial towns were constructed in the suburbs around Shanghai, about thirty to seventy kilometers (approximately eighteen to forty-three miles) away from the central city. These towns were based on principles in city planning and have industrial and residential areas, road networks, commercial centers, greenbelts, railway stations, and social service facilities such as schools, hospitals, and clinics. In *Beijing*, the proposed master plan called for the new development of satelites on the least productive agricultural land in the city periphery. The industrial plants proposed were located with reference to wind directions, in order to reduce pollution in both the local community and the city at large. Housing was separated by green belts and located close to industrial plants to encourage walking or bicycle riding to places of employment. Traffic arteries bypassed the city to reduce the amount of internal traffic and associated congestion.[39]

The government, in its constant effort to stay in control of the direction of urban development, participates in the business of buying and selling land. This hàs positive ramifications for controlling urban sprawls while actively retaining the voice of the government in the development of respective areas. Sometimes land purchased is not sold back in the private market. Instead, the land is leased long-term to developers. In this way, municipalities secure a steady flow of income, with an instrument useful in determining when and how landed property should be developed.

*Eminent domain,* the issue of expropriation though expedient, is often used as an instrument of last resort. It is politically a very sensitive instrument that tends to paralyze the free market forces of demand and supply. Land banking, however, is more acceptable and more practicable. The French adopted land banking policies in 1958 under the Gaullist minister of construction. This was a giant step away from the French traditional value that places premia on private property ownership. In parts of the industrialized world, government land ownership is generally in the wilderness. Government owns very limited land in urban settings. By implication, government does limited land banking to influence growth in cities. Typically, government expropriates land at the behest of a private developer. In Japan, government attitude toward land is similar to that of the United States. The authorities are reluctant to do land banking in order to control the direction of urban development. Instead, the Japanese government uses *Kukakuseiri* or *land Readjustment.* This is a technique similar to that used in Germany in 1899. The property owners band their holdings for a mutually beneficial venture. In return, they get an equitable share of the project. At the end of the project, they are entitled to their original landed property. While this technique is a money saver for the authorities, it is indifferent to urban sprawls. Urban sprawl poses a major planning problem in metropolitan Japan.

Besides land banking and eminent domain, governments have devised other control tools. In Europe, for example, a government may rely on a master plan for the city. The government also monitors developers, to make sure they abide by the blueprint. In the United States, where the authorities do not have the substantial benefits of land banking, *zoning ordinances* are used. They are statutes that group land-use according to functions. For example, the city may be zoned into residential, commercial, industrial, administrative, and military functions. The state in this case polices land use based on city functions.

*Land speculation* tends to be an endemic problem associated with urban development. The price of land tends to increase rapidly on the eve of a development project. In this process, land speculators may highly distort the profit potential of an otherwise viable business enterprise. Because of this seemingly irresistible proclivity by land speculators to inflate property value, through bids, the costs of land can contribute as much as 35 percent of the total cost of real estate development. This cost factor in the United States compared with only 15 percent to 20 percent during the same period in other advanced industrialized countries.[40] In Europe, this speculative value was dampened by a betterment tax. This tax was levied on "as is" land value and land value when applied to a superior investment.[41]

*Zoning* is very important for strategic industrial development. City planning, by definition, tends to be proactive planning that allows a city to grow into an ordered and attractive place to live. Therefore, modern cities have homes in one district and factories in another district. It is not a coincidence that they are marked off into city blocks by paved roads and sidewalks and underlaid by water, sewer, and cable lines. City planning strategically organizes priorities. For example, water pipes and sewer lines must be constructed before a road is built. When the converse is true, the constructed road is excavated leading perhaps to waste.

City planning puts elementary schools in residential districts, thus making it easily accessible by children. When elementary schools are juxtaposed with factories, markets, mechanic workshops, and pubs, they render the area dangerous for children. Such haphazard development increases the propensity for traffic congestion around schools and increases the risk of accidents as children constantly try to cross roads. City planning allocates industrial districts for factories and "town green" or parks. City functions (e.g., industrial parks in designated industrial zones and shopping malls in commercial districts) are moved or situated to invite the optimal number of people and businesses to use facilities. City planning commissions do the planning in most cities.

In city planning, desirable future developments are identified and allotted. The most common elements are streets, transit systems, railroads, waterways, airways, public utilities, parks and play grounds, public buildings, housing districts, business districts, and industrial districts. Once this plan is in place, it is then carefully controlled. An unplanned city tends to discourage industrialists and capitalists. Sometimes, tearing down factories can be expensive for moves to locations that were not anticipated. Location tends to be very important in investment decision making. A hotel magnate who locates a hotel within proximity of the airport because the hotel is used by airline pilots, flight crews, and administrators is likely to be aggravated when asked to relocate the business due to land use priorities.

Zoning tends to amalgamate buildings with similar functions. It divides the land into districts and regulates the use of land and buildings. It more specifically regulates the height of buildings, the size of buildings, and the balance between the size of each plot and the building on it. A zoning commission typically deals with height, use, and area. There is usually a zoning board of appeals, which on very rare occasions permit exceptions to the zoning laws. An example is a case where enforcement would mean hardship and injury to the public interest. In zoning, the laissez-faire spirit is put into check: buildings cannot be built very close to the sidewalk. Deed restrictions must not be violated. Deed restrictions forbidding commercial use of residential property must be respected. Residential property may not be turned into restaurants or electrical shops, nor living rooms into tailoring workshops and antique shops. Much zoning occurred in the 1920s in several places in the industrial north. Today it is as much a fixture of urban industrial life as the express way. When there is no zoning, property owners tend to make land development decisions based on their selfish interests, with little or no consideration given to the community at large. In this case, it is not impossible to have a tombstone cutter's shop with a yard full of granite urns and crosses across the street from a row of perfectly respectable middle-class homes.[42] Similarly, one may find a nightclub or pub next to residences. When zoning problems are not addressed in their infant stages, they only become worse with time. One of the reasons is that people tend to resist the urge to sell/give up their homes in areas designated for other land uses. In urban Africa, an overwhelming reason tends to be tribal. For example, a resource-constrained individual with property in a downtown district may refuse to sell the parcel of land with a dilapidated building on the grounds that it has been in the family for ages. So what happens is that one sometimes sees high-rises and other modern buildings juxtaposed with archaic habitats. Purchasing the property maybe possible, all the same, but often at unjustifiable and prohibitive benefit/cost structures.

## SOME CONTEMPORARY ASPECTS OF URBANIZATION

Urbanization is both a prerequisite and an outcome of industrialization. Yet it is also known that thousands of people may form demographic agglomerations without accruing the benefits of industrialization and without spawning it. Many cities in Africa grew very rapidly in the twentieth century, positioning themselves on the margins as *potential* urban engines that might be harnessed for industrial change. Most of the population increases were attributable to people leaving the countryside to seek economic opportunities in urban centers and mining districts.

For example, of the northern Nigerian migrants studied in Sokoto nearly all had an economic reason for migration. Fifty-two percent of them said they were seeking money; 16 percent said they were seeking food; and another 16 percent said they were going to trade.[43] Enugu, a regional urban center in eastern Nigeria, originated entirely out of the development of coalfields. Founded in 1909 as an empty site, this town had a population of 10,000 by 1921 and 62,000 by 1962. In 1990, the population was 272,000. Enugu endures as a major coal-mining and trading center, and manufacturing activities include steel, tiles, pottery, asbestos, cement, petroleum, pharmaceuticals, and machinery. It is also the administrative center of the railroad to Port Harcourt (since 1915) and the site of the Institute of Management and Technology since 1973. Port Harcourt, a leading port in Nigeria, was created as a terminus for the railway serving the Enugu coalfields. By 1953, the population was 72,000, and by 1990 the city had approximately 352,000 persons. In addition to its functions as a leading port, it is a road and railway hub as well as a major industrial center. Manufacturing activities have included saw milling, auto assembly, food canning, flour milling, tobacco processing, manufacture of rubber, glass, metal, paper products, cement, petroleum products, paint, enamelware, bicycles, furniture, and soap. It is the site of the University of Port Harcourt (since 1975) and the University of Science and Technology (since 1971). Export include palm oil, petroleum, coal, tin, columbite, palm products, cocoa, and peanuts. It serves the eastern region and parts of northern Nigeria.

Urbanism in North Africa dates back to pre-Roman times. With such a long and distinguished record it was only natural that individual towns and cities here, as in many similar places around the world, had to go through phases of changing fortunes. Despite such ups and downs, urban life somehow managed to retain its vitality. In Morocco, continuity is a striking feature of urbanism; the names of many cities reverberate deep into history. Of the earliest towns that had populations of at least 20,000, as early as the tenth century, three remain important centers, namely Meknes, Fez, and Salé. By the twelfth century, Marrakesh and Rabat had been added to the urban hierarchy. The city of Casablanca was a fishing village called Anfa that was selectively developed with the influence of the French.

In the last several decades, these urban centers, like those in many other parts of Africa, experienced population explosions. In Morocco, cities such as Casablanca, Kenitra, and Agadir absorbed migrants from many regions and social environments. The traditional city called the *medina* is composed of several quarters, or *derbs*. Residents of derbs were typically families that had lived there for several generations; they were naturally bound by feelings of solidarity and common identification. These families from every economic stratum lived in the same quarter, with the notables and wealthy assuming leadership positions. This traditional arrangement began to change, with increasing French influence. When the French arrived, unaccustomed to the ways of the indigenous population, they chose to live instead in the suburbs. The bounty of the Industrial Revolution in Europe was remarkable in Morocco, and European mass-produced goods came increasingly into general use. As it turned out, affluent Moroccans began trickling to the new suburbs, and eventually the traditional quarters were abandoned to the less affluent. The new divisions created by this movement to other parts of the city resulted in a new configuration of urban spaces, which were based on income, instead of the old residential divisions along ethnic lines. These new divisions were reinforced by the introduction of modern institutions that required education and technical expertise.

Social mobility was feasible under the new system, differing from the traditional system, which was static. Increasingly, education was recognized as a vehicle for social mobility, as French and other European technicians held important technical jobs for which qualified Moroccans could not be found. In a dynamic and industrially oriented environment, the educated elite garnered importance, since they were trained in understanding the new forces governing the environment. The traditional elite began losing influence and income as well. However, by the 1970s, there were more university graduates, especially in the liberal arts, than the job market could readily absorb in acceptable white-collar positions. Although the pure sciences also enjoyed great prestige, technical and engineering fields, especially those requiring manual labor, attracted few candidates, perhaps because of the traditional disdain for manual labor. By the mid-1980s, many young Moroccans were apprehensive that the status for which their education was to prepare them would prove illusory, coupled with the prospects for social mobility. Although industrial technology provided enviable opportunities for some, it did not offer them to all. Many skilled artisans who previously occupied respectable positions in the community found themselves being marginalized as mass-produced goods cut into the market share of handicrafts. Others managed to stay in business by changing their style or producing for the growing tourist trade. Although the government attempted to nourish the artisan tradition and find markets abroad, much of the work had become decorative rather than central to economic life.[44]

In Ivory Coast, *revolving national independence festivals* were held annually in different interior cities in order to motivate people to think nationally instead of in tribal terms. Typically the city's funding was approved a year in advance, to carry out major and minor development projects. These projects ranged from building a new hospital, high school, or electrification, to construction of a modern marketplace and paving of major city arteries. Whichever projects were chosen, the basic idea was to make the city a better place to live in. A major snag, however, was that the budget was very limited in terms of any significant impact on the city or region concerned. In addition, infrastructural facilities provided were poorly maintained, as was the case with paved roads and marketplaces, or undersupplied, as was the case with medical dispensaries. The projects were supposed to have long-term viability, for example, through adequate recurring revenues. In terms of human resources, the projects were beneficial because such decentralization in urbanizing programs gave regional officials an opportunity to improve their managerial and technical skills. A few of these projects were, however, massive in scale and had great potential in the areas and cities concerned. One of the projects was the Port of *San Pedro*: This port construction (1968–1971) was a response to the anemic development in the southwestern region, which was rich in forests and natural resources, including iron ore. The resources could not be exploited because of inadequate transportation facilities. A regional development authority was created and charged with coordinating the plan. The maximum benefits of the project to industrialization could not be realized, at least in the short term, because the industrial infrastructure was limited. Other projects included the *Dam of Kossou*, and the *Regional Development of the Savannah Zone*.[45]

The Tanzanians were not anxious in simply adopting an archetype from industrialized countries, or perhaps from Africa, that would precipitate positive industrial change. Instead, Tanzania moved gently toward an approach uniquely suited to the country's economic, political, cultural, and ideological requirements. In the city of Dar es Salaam (Tanzania) urbanization was influenced by *Ujamaa*; *Ujamaa* was predicated upon social organization, guided by the need to provide for both the common and the individual welfare. The idea was to reduce wide disparities in wealth, while enhancing at least a minimal economic and sustainable standard of living. Under *Ujamaa*, economic activities were oriented to increase the flow of goods and services to the countryside. An evaluation of this unique approach will determine the extent to which its engineering can be responsive and germane to the industrial market forces of the free enterprise system.[46]

Although urban areas and mining and industrial centers have provided a growing market for an increased number of African farmers, this outlet is still small relative to the value of agricultural exports. Urbanization represents an opportunity for farmers, since urban populations generally rely on purchased food. As incomes increase, the value of food consumed also increases; people tend to eat fewer starchy staples and more expensive foods that include meat, diary products, fruits, and vegetables. These foods make heavy demands on the agricultural resources and provide scope for improving the value of agricultural production. As a result, there is expansion in the manufacturing of processed foods, thus creating employment opportunities and demand for services in urban centers.

The existence of potential advantages in urbanization does not guarantee utilization. War, a political impasse, social discordance, lawlessness, lack of discipline, mismanagement, and a plethora of other factors can very easily detract earnest efforts in industrialization.

## LOCATION REQUIREMENTS AND INDUSTRIAL PARKS

Fundamentally, *location requirements* relate to health, safety, convenience, economy, and the general amenities of urban living. Such requirements involve health and safety hazards such as flood, fire, landslide, seismic activity, wind, volcanoes, extreme temperatures, and ecological ramifications; the nearness or remoteness of one use from another in time and distance; the compatibility or social implications of these uses to the people of the community; the economic feasibility of developing particular uses in particular locations; the practicalities from cost-revenue perspectives; and the livability and overall attractiveness as factors of location. Major functional areas in the urban complex are, therefore, for work (manufacturing, trade, services); living (residential communities, stores, playgrounds, local parks, elementary schools); and leisure time (educational, cultural, and recreational facilities).

As a rule of thumb, in urbanizing and industrializing environments, *work areas* should be in convenient proximity to living areas. They tend to be in interconnecting transit and thoroughfare routes and in convenient proximity to other work areas. Accessibility to heavy transportation facilities and large-capacity utility lines may be necessary. The best sites should be attractive economically and aesthetically, with a size that can probably accommodate contemplated industrial expansion over a period, of say twenty to twenty-five years. *Living areas* in urbanizing and industrializing environments, again as a rule of thumb, should be conveniently close to areas for work and leisure. Here again, convenient access by public and private transportation are important, and community facilities should be within walking distance. However, the location should be protected from traffic and incompatible uses, for example, cul-de-sac and loop streets that prevent through traffic. Open spaces are important. *Leisure-time areas* should be situated conveniently from living areas and should be accessible by public and private transportation. They should provide opportunity for a variety of recreational activities. Cultural and spectator sports are important, and parks and large open spaces should be situated to project the advantages of natural and unusual features of the landscape. The central business district is usually situated around peak flow of traffic and pedestrians. Institutions and businesses agglomerate here, such as government offices, banks, insurance companies, retail establishments, hotels, restaurants, and related financial, professional, and other service establishments. The central business district is usually easily accessible by public and private transportation and has adequate parking for employees, clients, and patrons. On the other hand *regional business centers* may be situated close to two major arterial tributary to trade areas; on intersections of radial and circumferential arteries; and on one or more major transit routes, with adequate parking and service areas. Such sites may have regional shopping centers or satellite CBD centers. Businesses here may include a complete line of shops, farmers' market, automobile sales and service centers, appliance centers, eating and entertainment facilities, and branch business and financial services. *Highway Service centers*, as the name implies, are on major highways, in outlying areas to urban areas. Here may be found motel accommodations and drive-in refreshments, produce stands, and automobile service facilities. On major trucking routes a few sites are open on twenty-four-hour schedules. Considerations here include highway safety, roadside beauty, and amenities for related uses. *Tourist service centers* may be along major tourist routes. Here facilities include modern motel accommodations, and the sites must be easily identified from the highway yet set back from noise and passing traffic.

*Industrial parks* are a convenient way of introducing the benefits of industrialization in an urbanizing environment without the associated health and safety hazards such as noise, odors, and so on. Electronics assembly plants, chemical plants, steel mills, food-processing plants, and research and development centers are among the choices available in an industrializing environment. Some modern industrial parks are noted for their excellent architecture, within landscape treatments of open areas, and overall high standards.

To decide locations for industrial parks, factors typically considered include topography, land size, direct accessibility of location by commercial transportation, public transit system, proximity of residential area of labor force and accessibility to transit service; major thoroughfare routes (major trucking routes, railway terminals, cargo airport facilities, deep water channels); availability of utilities at or near the site (water works, gas works, power plants and substation, communications facilities); sewage disposal and refuse disposal facilities; and fire protection station.

A manufacturing plant usually requires a large open site for modern one-story buildings and accessory storage. While site requirements of firms may vary on a case-by-case basis, structural densities require at least five acres and perhaps as much as a hundred acres, depending on the size of the urban area and the economic outlook of industrialization. In the industrialized world an assembly facility may occupy extensive areas, perhaps totaling around 825 acres.[47]

A planned industrial district is usually an enterprise under a singular management for marketing industrial sites on a sale or on a long-term lease arrangement. Developments are laid out in acreage lots of varying sizes, especially designed for modern industrial operations. Space is reserved for common facilities such as lunchrooms, exhibitions, recreation, and parks.[48]

Modern industrial parks can be beautiful, convenient, and comfortable places for work. They enhance organization in industrializing environments, completely integrating with the home areas of their employees, while maintaining, pollution-free operations and service roads designed not to conflict with the residential area of the community. Well contemplated and executed, they become important nodes in industrializing environments.

# NOTES

1. George Rosen, *A History of Public Health* (Baltimore, MD: Johns Hopkins University Press, 1993), p. 466.

2. Jan O.M. Broek and John W. Webb, *A Geography of Mankind* (New York: McGraw-Hill Book Company, 1989), p. 316. This is also in sharp contrast to the English enclosures and the commercial and isolated farmsteads more common in the United States and Canada. However, there are exceptions, such as the compact form of early New England settlements (possibly because of religion, security or plantations, that is, planting of immigrants) in closely knit communities. In the southern (United States), in neoplantations, the functional focus was the *tractor station* as opposed to clustering of housing units around the *plantation headquarters* of the Old South.

3. Ibid.

4. D.M. Wilner and R.P. Walkey, "Effects of Housing on Health and Performance," in *The Urban Condition*, Leonard J. Duhl, ed. (New York: Basic Books, 1963), pp. 215–228.

5. Melville J. Herskovits and Mitchell Harwitz, eds., *Economic Transition in Africa* (Evanston, IL: Northwestern University Press, 1964), pp. 248–249.

6. George Rosen, *A History of Public Health*, p. 389 in Robin Marantz Henig, *The People's Health: A Memoir of Public Health and Its Evolution at Harvard* (Washington, DC: Joseph Henry Press, 1997), p. 105.

7. Ibid., p. 466.

8. Ibid.

9. Ibid.

10. Melvin Kranzberg and Carroll W. Pursell, Jr., *Technology in Western Civilization, vol. 2* (New York: Oxford University Press, 1967), p. 470. Builders tended to erect one or a few buildings at a time. They did not appear to have the desire or opportunity to experiment with large building groups. These deficiencies were coupled with site plans that did not maximize light, ventilation, and space.

11. Ibid., p. 480.

12. Gustav Stolper, *The German Economy: 1870–Present* (New York: Harcourt, Brace & World, 1967), pp. 280–281: Housing shortage was a problem in Germany, in the twentieth century. Approximately, 8 million dwelling units were constructed between 1949 and 1964, initially at a rate of 215,000 units annually and after 1953 at a rate that surpassed 500,000 units per year. Per capita, more dwellings were built in Germany around this period than in any other Western nation.

13. Kranzberg and Pursell, *Technology in Western Civilization*, p. 481.

14. Ibid., p. 478.

15. In 1948 alone, 190,000 units of public housing were completed. In the 1950s and the 1960s at least 100,000 units were completed annually. In Britain, one in four persons is an occupant of a public housing unit.

16. Robert D. Hershey, "Britain . . . Awaken from a Long Economic Slumber," *New York Times*. June 8, 1980, pp. 1, 18.

17. Stolper, *The German Economy: 1870-Present*, pp. 103, 280–284. Housing was scarce in Germany during the Weimar period. This huge demand prompted government regulation to keep all rents down in old buildings and new building constructions, thus preventing rents in the two groups from drifting apart. Subsidies were also used. Financial institutions granted first mortgages (savings banks, insurance companies, mortgage companies), up to 50 percent of construction costs, and the government granted second mortgages, coupled with mortgage

revaluations. Reich funding derived from a *Hauszinssteuer* or house-rent tax (inflationary). As a result, many modern residential buildings were erected in German cities and towns.

18. Angus Maddison, *Economic Growth in the West* (New York: Twentieth Century Fund, 1964), p. 111.

19. J. Pearsal, "France" in M.Wynn, ed., *Housing in Europe* (London : Croom-Helm,1984).

20. Maddison, *Economic Growth in the West*, p. 111.

21. John K.Galbraith, *The Affluent Society* (Boston: Houghton Mifflin, 1969), p. 259.

22. *Atlanta Journal/Constitution*, May 22, 1993, pp. Al, A16.

23. "Consumer Prices: Examining Housing Rental Components," *Economic Review, Federal Reserve Bank Of Atlanta*, vol. 78, no. 3 (May/June 1993), pp. 32–46.

24. T. Barnett, A.J. Groth, and C. Ungson, "East-West Housing Policies: Some Contrasts and Implication," in Alexander Groth and Larry L. Wade, *Public Policy across Nations: Social Welfare in Industrial Settings* (Greenwich: JAI Press, 1985), p. 131.

25. *Nigeria, A Survey of U.S. Export Opportunities* (Washington, DC: U.S. Department of Commerce, International Trade Administration, 1981), pp. 43–45.

26. Helen Chapin Metz , ed., *Nigeria: A Country Study* (Washington DC: GPO, 1992), p. 133.

27. Alain Auger and Pierre Vennetier, "La croissance péripherique des villes: Naissance et développement d'une banlieue brazzavilloise," in "La croissance urbaine dans les pays tropicaux," *Travaux et documents de géographie tropicale, no. 26* (Talence, France: Domaine Université de Bordeaux, 1976), pp. 44–48, in Christopher Winters, "Urban Morphogenesis in Fancophone Black Africa," *Geographic Review*, April 1982, p. 150.

28. Roger Barnnet, "The Libertarian Suburb: Deliberate Disorder," *Landscape*, 22, no. 3, 1978, pp. 223–286 in Christopher Winters, "Urban Morphogenesis in Fancophone Black Africa,"*The Geographic Review*, April 1982, p.150.

29. *The Courier*, Jan–Feb. 1992, pp. 76–77.

30. Claude Robinson, *Understanding Profits* (New Jersey: D. Van Nostrand Company, 1961), pp. 112–120. By carefully managing sales, costs, earnings, cash receivables, liabilities, long-term debt, book value of shares, and so on, engaging profitably in prefabricated housing is possible. Here, prefabricated housing for low-income families may be an attractive alternative to custom-built homes. Prefabricated houses tend to use a wide range of materials, ranging from wood to gypsum board, plastics, and metals. One approach is the "you-finish-it-homes." This approach is especially attractive to families who have home-building skills and are willing to spend their leisure time on home construction. Before investing, families must be certain that such homes will be approved by the local home inspector. Typically, precut materials are brought from the factory to the building site, ready for final assembly. Huge multiple saws may do about ten operations in one. Nailing machines do in one minute what scores of carpenters may accomplish in one hour. The complex flow of pieces is controlled by computers, so that the right pieces, in the right number, arrive at the right shipping dock simultaneously. The package is then loaded on tractor trailers and hauled to the building site. The exterior walls arrive with already installed windows. Plumbing comes precut. Within twenty-four hours, on location, the shell is erected. By week three, utilities are installed and the new owner moves in. This is usually feasible, assuming the site experts had previously laid out the ground and engineered the roads and sewer.

31. Capital funds derived from the Central Providence Fund, a compulsory tax-exempt savings plan into which Singapore workers contributed 25 percent of their monthly earnings, and from low-interest long-term loans deriving from international financial institutions. The Central Provident Fund benefited the citizens by providing them with secure savings for their old age, and the satiety of their own account. This account could be drawn on to meet expenses

such as medical bills and tuition for colleges or to finance a pilgrimage to Mecca. Additionally, this savings margin was adjustable, thus enhancing government latitude in controlling not only wages, but other functions and the economy at large. In 1988, the fund absorbed 36 percent of all wages below the limit of $6,000. Here, 24 percent of the contribution derived from the worker, while the remaining 12 percent was made by the employer. Homeowners were encouraged to use their Central Provident Fund savings to pay for their apartments. Factors determining the selling prices of apartments included location, construction cost, ability of the applicant to pay, and the practical limits of government subsidies. Between 1960 and 1985, this government-owned board completed more than 500,000 high-rise and high-density public housing apartments and related facilities, known as housing estates. This was in sharp contrast to the period between 1927 and 1959, when Singapore Trust completed only 23,000 apartments. Generally, apartments enhanced community living, enhanced demographic integration, and encouraged upward social mobility (a built-in mechanism for upgraded homes), while preserving the Asian family structure. The function of the Housing and Urban Development Board after 1982 was redefined, and oriented to focus on building and marketing apartments for the middle income segments of the population, a function that really began earlier in 1974.

32. Metz, *Nigeria*, pp. 130–139.

33. LaVerle Berry, ed., *Ghana: A Country Study* (Washington, DC: GPO, 1995), pp. 96–99.

34. Metz, *Nigeria: A Country Study*, p. 138.

35. Pauline Gregg, *A Social and Economic History of Britain: 1760–1950* (London: George Harrap and Co., 1952), pp. 484–485.

36. Arnold J. Heidenheimer, Hugh Heclo, and Carolyn Adams, *Comparative Public Policy* (New York: St. Martin, 1989), p. 273.

37. Arthur B. Gallion and Simon Eisner, *The Urban Pattern: City Planning and Design* (New York: Van Nostrand Reinhold, 1986), pp. 110–112.

38. Heidenheimer et al., *Comparative Public Policy*, p. 273.

39. Gallion and Eisner, *The Urban Pattern*, pp. 116–120.

40. Organization for Economic Cooperation and Development, *Urban Policies in Japan* (Paris: OECD, 1986), p. 50.

41. *Betterment tax* revenue, siphoned from the pockets of land speculative enthusiasts, is deposited in the public coffers. Another instrument of intervention is the imaginative approach by which the government designates an area for development and during a period, for example fourteen years, the government reserves the right to buy the land once it is put up for sale. The price of the land is fixed at the value of the land one year before future development announcement. Urban growth can also be guided by discouraging traffic congestion in the cities. Fundamentally, this can be accomplished by the strategic location of facilities that invite mass traffic. For example, shopping centers, convention centers, hospitals, and sports stadiums, when located at the peripheries, tend to limit the traffic in the inner city. Taxes on gasoline, auto accessories, auto insurance companies, auto companies, and mechanics alike will be shifted to the automobile owner. This will place an unusual burden on persons for owning and running a car. Other methods include paid parking, no parking, no stopping/standing, parking from 9am-6pm, 30 minutes maximum parking, and so on. Another option is to provide affordable, safe, reliable, immaculate, comfortable mass transit. Also, important are areas designated: pedestrians only, automobiles prohibited; and token thoroughfares, coupled with control stickers, and well-equipped traffic police.

42. *Insight*, August 14, 1989, p. 16.

43. Kenneth Little, *West African Urbanization* (Cambridge: Cambridge University Press, 1965), p. 8.

44. Harold D. Nelson, *Morocco: A Country Study* (Washington DC: GPO, 1985), pp. 126–130.

45. Garland Christopher, "Urbanization, Rural to Urban Migration, and Development Policies in the Ivory Coast," in R.A. Obudho and Salah El-Shakhs, eds., *Development of Urban Systems in Africa* (New York: Praeger, 1979), pp. 157–176.

46. Edwin S. Segal, "Urban Development Planning in Dar es Salaam," in Obudho and Shakhs, *Development of Urban Systems in Africa*, pp. 258–269.

47. Gallion and Eisner, *The Urban Pattern*, pp. 340–342.

48. Theodore K. Pasma, *Organized Industrial Districts* (Washington, DC: GPO, 1954); Urban Land Institute, *Industrial Districts: Principles and Practice*, Technical Bulletin No. 44, *Industrial Districts Restudied*, Technical Bulletin No. 41; and *Planned Industrial Districts*, Technical Bulletin No.19 (Washington, DC: Urban Land Institute, December 1962; April, 1961; October, 1952, respectively), in F. Stuart Chapin, Jr., *Urban Land Use Planning* (Urbana: University of Illinois Press, 1965), p. 392–395.

# 16

# Covering the Downside during Industrialization

Many developing economies were rightly organized to operate in what in retrospect were fewer complex business environments than during industrialization. An industrialized business environment by definition has by far many more complex environments than an agriculturally oriented business environment. Because such economies were for the most part dominated by primary industries such as mining, forestry, and cash crops, the systems were not structured to handle the contemporary nuances and complexities of commerce and industrial mass production in increasingly highly technological environments. In an industrializing environment, economic growth and expansion will be enhanced and more organized when expansion in private sector manufacturing is coupled with coeval directions and regulations.

When this is not the case, disorganization and inefficiency may manifest themselves in the form of noncompetitive goods and services in the marketplace. In this case, therefore, a business boom will be accompanied by derangements such as long queues of people waiting at airports, banks hospitals, and so on; gridlocks in documentation handled in government offices; admixtures in residential, commercial, and office districts in urban settings; deficiencies in minimum standards in the housing and construction industry; filthy or no public restrooms, and so forth. Developmental impediments that are relatively nonexistent in rural settings and low-tech societies suddenly impose themselves as gigantic bulwarks against business opportunities.

When nations are posturing for industrial development, the ministerial functions of government may quickly become deficient in handling the new load of information and activities emanating from a highly technological and proindustrial environment. To canalize these overwhelming business activities, the government generally opts for new federal regulatory agencies in core areas of activities. Government agencies, thus, are empowered to microregulate private sector transactions. Government agencies, once formed, tend to have more impact on economic activities than regulations stemming from common law and the courts.[1] Some examples will include an occupational safety and health administration; a consumer product safety commission; and an environmental protection agency.[2]

Virtually every economic activity is subject to regulation at one stage or another, in the process of manufacturing, wholesaling, distribution, retailing, and so on. The regulatory spectrum inculcates novel initiatives that may span from transportation, communications, utilities, consumer products, energy, health and safety to innovation, patents/copyrights, and trademarks.

An industrializing environment does not only heavily regulate entrepreneurial activities; It also regulates consumers' interfacing with expansions in manufacturing. A remote rural African visitor who deplanes for the first time in the United States, France, Canada, Germany, Japan, or Great Britain, is likely to be accosted by a plethora of directions, street signs, rules and regulations, that may or may not be familiar. Some of the more common signs are: No Smoking; No Stopping or Standing; No U-turns; No Jaywalking; One Way Only; No Smoking in Government Buildings; Pedestrians Only; Minimum Speed 35 m.p.h.; Maximum Speed 70 m.p.h.; Refrigerate contents after opening; Chill before serving; Shake well before using; Do not purchase if safety button moves when pressed; Place a postage stamp here; Do not use content after the expiration date; Warning:This salt does not contain iodide, a necessary nutrient; Government Warning: According to the Surgeon General women should not drink alcoholic beverages during pregnancy because of the risk of birth defects; Consumption of alcoholic beverages impairs your ability to drive a car or operate machinery and may cause health problems; Warning: The federal law provides severe civil penalties for the unauthorized reproduction, distribution, or exhibition of copyright motion pictures, video tapes or video discs. Criminal copyright infringement is investigated by the Federal Bureau of Investigation and may constitute felony with a minimum penalty of five years in prison and/or a $250,000 fine; Warning: The Surgeon General has determined that cigarette smoking causes lung cancer, heart disease, emphysema, and may complicate pregnancy; Warning: Do not litter highway. Fine $25.00; Warning: Do not Enter! Violators will be prosecuted.

This is just a sampling of the directions, signs, rules, bylaws, and regulations, people in an industrializing environment will expect to deal with. As contradictory as it may sound, this is the essence of freedom. In a free and industrializing environment, there are infinitely more rules and regulations than in a simple or rural settlement. It is this body of rules and regulations that give structure and discipline to industrial development. Where originally individualism was freedom *from* society, it becomes freedom *within* an industrializing society. Self-reliance is transformed into other-directed sensitivity; independence becomes teamplay; and autonomy becomes initiative within organizational bounds.[3]

This does not in any way relegate traditional mores, customs, laws, and religious commandments, to a lesser place.[4] Instead, it tends to project the essence of these values onto the complex space and time of industrialization. These rules and regulations attempt to adorn the individual with maximum freedom without encroaching upon the freedoms of others, and/or the freedom of society at large. The absence or deficiency in this structure and discipline is often breeding ground for anarchy and authoritarianism with a highly centralized power nexus.[5] In an industrializing environment, therefore, there can be no freedom without laws; without justice there can be no law.

The subsequent discussions in the rest of this chapter are simplified for a gist of the flavor and substance of the ethical environment of business. Illustrations, for the most part, have been drawn from the business (and evolution of business) in North America. However, there may be some variations in other similar places and in industrializing countries. The issues therefore discussed are intended for the sake of familiarity and may not be construed or quickly generalized as finite in their applications, in dynamic and geographically diverse business environments.

Agencies combine the duties and the responsibilities of the judiciary, the legislative, and the executive branches of U.S. government. Agencies promulgate rules and are endowed with policing powers to ensure compliance. These bureaucratic extensions of government render judgment and impose penalties or remedies as prescribed by law. There is room for appeal to the courts in case a party is not satisfied with an administrative decision. However, it is important to inject that such decisions are seldom reversed because of the technical nature of subject matter. Agencies tend to consider evidence that is generally not accepted in the court of law. On very rare occasions, the courts may reverse decisions construed to be capricious, arbitrary, and blatantly inconsistent with legal precedent.

Over the years, as society has assumed a more complex configuration, administrative agencies have been endowed with discretionary powers that authorize administrators to formulate goal-oriented rules and guidelines.

Administrative agencies also have investigatory powers. They reserve the right to investigate the records, practices, or premises of businesses once a warrant is procured. Such investigations may be prompted when it is believed the health and safety of employees are in jeopardy. In the U.S., OSHA may exercise such investigatory powers by physical entry of employment premises deemed questionable by law. The following are examples of other investigatory powers: inspection of records; completion of questionnaires, often triggered by complaint or adjudicative action; subpoenas of witnesses; and examination under oath. In some cases rule making may preempt state law.

Administrative agencies are generally given the power to settle disputes, where the respective parties are unable to reach an informal agreement. This generally begins when entities or businesses violate agency rules or standards. Concerned parties are then involved in a hearing, presided over by an administrative law judge, who in this case is an employee of the agency, not a member of the federal judiciary. The setting of a trial resembles that of a typical courtroom trial, except that they tend to be informal.

In the mass consumption oriented society of the twentieth century, consumer protection became preeminent. The twentieth century, relative to the nineteenth century, has indeed been a giant step for mankind.[6] Comparatively much more food, shelter, and clothing have been available to the average person. In the twentieth century, production became more and more impersonal as labor specialized and the assembly line engaged mass production for an increasingly urban population. People enjoyed many household conveniences that were virtually unheard of a century earlier.

Household conveniences included the vacuum cleaner, the transistor radio, the television, washing machines, clothes dryers, air cleaners, toasters, VCRs, camcorders, and personal computers. These inventions and technological strides were sometimes not without consumers' grievances. As the volume of goods and services multiplied rapidly, the number of real or potential conflicts between consumers and merchants also escalated.[7]

Because many inventions were very lucrative, the tendency was for profit-seeking businesses to venture these domains. Often, money was made but sometimes consumers were dealt a bitter experience: consumers bought goods that did not stand the test of performance. With time, consumer complaints mounted with ever-increasing dissatisfaction. It became clear that there were increasingly dishonest people inhabiting the business world. The government had to do something to stamp out what might be tantamount to a social evil![8]

Consumers had to be protected against any deficits in the qualities and plethora of goods and services that emerged daily in the marketplace: the price and terms of credit; repossession practices; warranties; after-sale-service of consumer goods, and so on. Consumer protection became the clarion call, resonating across the halls of Congress/Parliament and the judiciary. In the ears of the appropriate authorities, this call came across as a plea to reverse the unconscionable exposure of the consumer in everyday business transactions.

In the United States, consumers are protected under the Federal Trade Commission Act of 1914 as amended in 1938. Essentially, the law seeks to protect the consumers against unfair and deceptive practices that may influence, inhibit, or restrict consumers unfairly in their purchasing decisions. Violators of guidelines/rules and regulations stand to be prosecuted. Consumers may use the court system to obtain remedies for their grievances. To further empower consumers, the prohibitive costs of private lawsuits were diminished by offering consumers *free legal services*, small claims court, and recovery of attorneys' fees in class actions.

Although the general climate of business transactions was ethical there were a few pockets of, or potential for, unfair practices that led to consumer protection. In many countries, areas of consumer protection ranged from labeling and packaging; door-to-door sales; mail order transactions; food quality and food inspection; real estate settlement procedures to consumer credit protection; truth-in-lending; and fair debt collection practices.

In the twentieth-century mass production/mass consumption environment, individual manufacturers were obliged to meet certain minimum standards in order to produce and sell their products in the global marketplace. Manufacturers that overlook obvious minimum standards while engaging in these complex production processes are likely to be marginalized sooner or later by the market forces or to run aground consumer protection legislations. By the same token, firms cannot always vouch to protect consumers from the independent and sometimes careless choices made in the marketplace.[9] Although firms typically demonstrate sensitivity to the rational consumers' rights to be *informed*, to *safety*, and to *choose*, firms rarely volunteer all information about the shortcomings of their products or services, in a competitive marketplace. This void is therefore filled by public-interest organizations, individuals, and businesses—serving as "professional consumers"—constantly patrolling the marketplace, performing laboratory tests, evaluating and comparatively rating products. The findings, including product recalls, are disclosed in publications to interested consumers.[10]

Standardization and disclosure, even where such disclosure may impede the competitive advantage of a manufacturer, may therefore occur. Let us put the case of sausages. Although many people like to eat sausages, not everybody may like exactly the same condiments in them. For example, some people may have an aversion for salt, while others stay away from pepper and some may be allergic to monosodium glutamate or MSG, which is used in manufacturing many food products. For such reasons, it became expedient and essential to *label* and package products in a manner that disclosed as much information as possible about the products being purchased. One major reason for labeling is that it facilitates comparison among similar products in the marketplace. Pertinent information such as net quantities must be conspicuously displayed in a uniform location, on packages of similar or competing products in the marketplace. In the case of potentially poisonous substances, poison prevention packaging is the rule. Manufacturers are obliged to provide childproof devices on all household products that may be harmful to children, due to mishandling and/or accidental ingestion. The idea is, therefore, to assure the best possible conditions for consumers as they evaluate and choose goods and services.

In the United States, the Fair Packaging Act requires that consumer goods have labels that identify the product; the manufacturer; the packer or distributor and the place of business; the net quantity of contents; the net quantity of each serving if the number of servings is stipulated; ingredients that were used in the manufacture of food and nonfood products; standards for partial filling of packages and other mundane instructions such as how to treat unused portions in packages, for example Discard remaining contents, Refrigerate any unused portion of content, Keep at room temperature, Keep out of reach of children.

*Door-to-door sales* are increasingly common in the urban settings of Africa and many developing countries. In West Africa, many young people, with exceptional effort, foresight, resourcefulness, thrift, and the ability to perceive economic opportunity, gainfully find subsistent employment in this domain. Their skill is not only in selling. To many, trading is the essence of social life, from childhood upwards. Not only are there bargains to be made, but an opportunity for gossip, banter, and perhaps the chance assignation. The per unit profits are usually razor-thin, and everything hangs on quick turnover, an eye for fashion, a knowledge of market prices, and the extras to be made by breaking bulk and selling in small quantities down to a single cigarette. No one could fail to admire the energy and vitality of these traders, the range of their contacts and interests, their sharp eye for the slightest chance of trade, and their hard work for disproportionately small nominal returns.[11]

Although this kind of selling is not common in industrialized nations, it is nonetheless given ample treatment by the law. The door-to-door seller typically has a captive audience of individuals immobilized at home. The impact of sales generally begins to trigger if the sales person gains entrance. Sometimes there may be signs, like No Trespassing, No Soliciting!, Wild Dogs!,—all designed to keep unwelcome visitors at bay. Compared to shops, the door-to-door vendor has very little incentive to establish goodwill. Relatively, repeat purchases are random and less likely than in shops that command large inventories and variety. In the United States, the door-to-door vendor is regulated by the Federal Trade Commission (FTC) and is required to give consumers a three-day grace period to rescind sales. This, coupled with other state statutes, has protected consumers.

The consumer's health is protected by laws governing the processing and distribution of diverse products, such as meat, poultry, hazardous substances, drugs, cosmetics, and so on. The rules and regulations may be either implicit or explicit.

The law holds manufacturers responsible for a consistent aseptic quality of food. Guidelines and rules are established that are averse to toxicity and pathogenic microbes. Early food laws were generally geared against misbranding and adulteration of food and drug products. With technological breakthroughs, more and more substances appeared on the market as preservatives and additives. Some of these substances used in accordance with manufacturers' instructions or guidelines were consumer friendly. Others, as it turned out, were health hazards to subpopulations and even carcinogenic in laboratory tests.

In 1906, the U.S. Congress passed its first act regulating drugs. The Food and Drug Administration was endowed with rights in 1958, to define food additives and to set safe levels. Food additives determined to be carcinogenic were outright forbidden. Shipment of perishables such as meat and poultry were regulated for wholesomeness and accuracy in labeling. The Food, Drug and Cosmetic Act of 1938 and later amended in 1962 required that all drugs be proven effective and safe before they can be marketed. The FDA monitors and reserves the authority to enforce the laws.

Some of the responsibilities of the Food and Drug Administration included the following: developing regulations for food and food standards, with regard to the use of additives and the use of color; developing safety standards for over the counter drugs; approving of requests of drugs for experimental use; disseminating information pertaining to the toxicity of household products and medicines; developing safe, effective open policies regarding labeling of all drugs for human consumption; researching and developing standards on food composition, food quality, nutrition, food safety, food additives, colors, and cosmetics; inspecting manufacturing outfits for compliance with stipulated standards.

## CARE AND VIGILANCE IN BUSINESS

When care and vigilance are not exercised in output production in an industrializing environment, manufacturers of consumer goods sooner or later become familiar with the complaints of dissatisfied consumers and the barrage of litigations that may emanate from *product liability*. Liability exposure, based on negligence, breach of contracts as stated or implied by warranty, or strict liability have prompted managers to take counteractive proactive measures. Here, consumer products manufactured tend to be user friendly and safe. Liability prevention programs are written, if necessary, for the entire corporations. Constructive efforts are also made to educate consumers about products.[12]

A classic product liability case is the 1916 case of *MacPherson v. Buick Motor Company*. It deals with an outdated product (wooden wheels for cars). It is generally considered a useful backdrop for later developments in product liability in the United States.

Macpherson bought a car from a dealer. However, MacPherson brought a lawsuit against the manufacturer, Buick Motor Company for injuries sustained when he was suddenly ejected and thrown out of the car because one of the wheels had embarrassingly and abruptly collapsed. The analogy of the court was that if the manufacturer of a finished product, places the product in the market when danger is foreseeable, whether or not it is a tool of destruction, such as a poison or an explosive, the manufacturer is liable. The idea here is that the manufacturer is duty bound to exercise care and vigilance.

Originally, a plaintiff was able to bring action if there had been a direct relationship between plaintiff and seller, that is, if the purchaser bought the product directly from the manufacturer. This requirement, however, became more and more difficult to meet in the mass market environment, with complex formal and informal networks with sometimes enormous geographical spans. *MacPherson v. Buick Motor Company* was a landmark case eliminating this direct relationship requirement in a tort action.[13]

Sometimes product liability cases may be derived from warranties. There are two kinds of warranties: implied and express warranties. An *express warranty* is created when a seller represents a product to a buyer and the buyer relies on such representation when purchasing the product. An express warranty may be a statement of fact about a product, whether it is made in writing, orally, on a label or in any form of promotion. In other words, it is an assurance of quality or a promise of performance made by a buyer to a seller.[14] An *implied warranty* is imposed by law. Essentially, an implied warranty requires that sellers provide certain minimum standards of quality and performance, even if no explicit promises are made contemporaneously with and as part of a contract of sale.[15] An implied warranty is twofolds: An implied warranty of merchantability, or fitness for a particular purpose. An implied warranty of merchantability is a promise arising by operation of law that the product being sold is guaranteed fit for ordinary uses and the product is safe and reliable when used as originally envisioned by the manufacturer or as would ordinarily be expected.

An example is if a person steps on a coffee table and uses it for a ladder. In a product liability case, it is a jury that determines if a product's use or misuse could have been foreseen by the manufacturer and whether the product is safe enough for a specific use. An implied warranty of fitness for a particular purpose is invoked when a retailer, distributor, or manufacturer has reason to know any particular purpose for which the consumer goods are required and further that the buyer has relied on the skill and judgement of the seller to select and furnish suitable goods.[16] An implied warranty of merchantability or an implied warranty that goods are merchantable means that the goods pass without objections, in the trade under the contract description; fit the ordinary purposes for which such goods are used; are adequately containerized, packaged, and labeled; conform to the promises or affirmation of fact stipulated on the container or label.[17] Other dimensions of warranties include *extended warranty, full warranty, limited warranty, presentment warranty, warranty of title, and written warranty.*

When product liability arises from tort, it may be broken down into *misrepresentation, negligence* and *strict liability.* In *misrepresentation,* the product in question does not have to be defective, but an injury must have been sustained when the product was used. The burden of proof rests on the plaintiff-buyer. The plaintiff-buyer must prove that the product was falsely represented and that he relied on this misrepresentation, from which injury was sustained. Importantly, the representation must be a "material fact" and not simply a seller's opinion or "puffing" statements. The definition of "reasonable reliance" and "material fact" are left to the the courts to determine. Legal action, in the case of misrepresentation, is not limited to the manufacturer.

In the case of *negligence*, the product must have been defective. Damage must have occurred from the *defective product*, and the damage must have been caused by the product made by the defendant. Negligence is generally invoked when the plaintiff charges a defendant of failing to exercise "ordinary" care or such care as a reasonable person would use under similar circumstances.[18] Negligence may be said to exist when a product design is unsafe or when a manufacturer fails to warn users adequately, of the inherent dangers of using the products or failure to test and inspect product for safety during the expected useful life of product. In a negligence case, the burden of proof rests on the plaintiff, and the jury determines whether a manufacturer acted reasonably and whether a reasonable person would have acted in similar fashion, given similar circumstances.

*Strict Liability* means liability regardless of a fault. Under tort law, strict liability is imposed on a manufacturer who introduces or markets any product that is unreasonably dangerous when in a defective condition. According to the 1963 decision of the California Supreme Court (U.S.A.), *Greenman v. Yuba Power Products Inc.*, strict liability obtains when . . . a manufacturer places an article on the market, knowing that it will be used without inspection and the article is proven to have a defect that causes injury to a human being. The plaintiff is expected to prove that a defect existed and that defect caused injury. The burden of proof rests squarely on the shoulders of the manufacturer, who must show that the product was not defective when it left the factory. A manufacturer who fails to give appropriate warnings or instructions, on how to use respective products, increases the company's exposure to strict liability lawsuits in an industrializing environment. Generally, strict liability offenses tend to be concerned with the public welfare or regulatory offenses that evolved in England and the United States with industrialization.[19] The trend toward strict criminal liability was captured in the well-known opinion of Justice Robert Jackson:

> The industrial revolution multiplied the number of workmen exposed to injury from increasingly powerful . . . mechanisms . . . Traffic . . . came to subject the wayfarer to intolerable casualty risks if owners and drivers were not to observe new cares and uniformities of conduct. Congestions of cities . . . called for health and welfare regulations undreamed of in simpler times. Wide distribution of goods became an instrument of wide distribution of harm . . . Such dangers have engendered . . . detailed regulations which heighten the duties of those in control of particular industries, trades, properties, or activities that affect public health, safety, or welfare.[20]

## INDUSTRIAL GAINS AND LIABILITIES

Although many manufacturers in the twentieth century had to go through a difficult learning curve of a litigious industrial environment, overall manufacturers are largely responsible for contriving the unusually high standard of living enjoyed by many.

The discovery of antibiotics (also known as miracle drugs) has not only improved the quality of life for many, but is a life-saving drug *per se*. We live in a sea of countless microbes, some of them (pathogens) very infectious and debilitating to health. Antibiotics are said to be the doctors' best friends because they slow the growth of pathogenic bacteria. Thus, they are effective against pneumonia, tuberculosis, syphilis, typhoid fever, dysentery, bone infections, and many other diseases.[21] Not long ago, bacterial pneumonia was among the chief killers of human beings. With the discovery of antibiotics, the number of casualties was drastically reduced. Similarly deaths from *streptococcic* and *staphylococcic* bacterial infections as well as blood poisoning and osteomyelitis (bone infections) have been reduced. *Tularaemia*, which was almost always fatal can now be easily cured, and typhoid fever and dysentery are no longer considered dangerous diseases. Cures in these areas were realizable with antibiotics—the outcome of the efforts of researchers and manufacturers.

Vitamins are essential to health and growth. Vitamins were discovered in 1911 by a Polish biochemist called Casimir Funk at Lister Institute in London. For many years the cause of a disease called *beriberi* had puzzled scientists. Funk isolated, from the material discarded in steam-powered mills for polishing rice, a certain substance that would cure artificial beriberi in pigeons. He later proved that the same substance would cure beriberi. The deduction he made from this association was that a diet rich in polished rice would likely cause beriberi. He suggested that these accessory food factors, whose absence caused these diseases, should be called "vitamines" (*Vita* implying that they were necessary for life, and *amine* their supposed chemical composition).[22]

Vitamins are essentials and are noninterchangeable. A shortage of any vitamin may affect a person's health. Although the best kinds of vitamins are those that occur naturally in food, the manufacture of vitamins has been one of the great scientific breakthroughs of the twentieth century. Consumers have been very satisfied with their vitamins. However, there were a few bulwarks outside successes such as vitamins and antibiotics.

In 1947, diethylstilbestrol (DES) came onto the market as an experimental drug to prevent miscarriages. Unfortunately, the downside of administering the drug turned out to be devastating even to unborn children, as was found out three decades later. Before approval, DES had been used as an animal supplement. Studies later showed it was ineffective in preventing miscarriages. It was determined that women exposed to DES before birth may develop cancerous vaginal and cervical growths. *Adenocarcinoma* manifests itself after at least ten to twelve years. It is pervasive and deadly and requires radical surgery.[23]

Litigation was brought against the industry, alleging product liability, negligence, strict liability, and violations of express and implied warranty. This case held manufacturers jointly and individually liable, despite the plaintiff's inability to identify the specific manufacturer.

The plaintiff, who was then an unborn child, sued the companies that manufactured DES between 1941 and 1971. Although a class action suit was filed against six companies, almost 200 different manufacturers had marketed DES, so that it was not possible to pinpoint the manufacturer that had produced the specific batch that had caused the plaintiff's injury. In litigations of DES cases filed later manufacturers were not specifically identified. It was alleged that manufacturers were jointly liable: they relied on each other's tests and lack of warning and abided by industry-wide standards. This suggested that the manufacturers had jointly controlled the risks, and were jointly responsible for the harm. Besides, the manufacturers had jointly collaborated in the marketing and promotion efforts. The court, using market share liability, a doctrine of causation and product liability, held each of the drug companies potentially liable, in proportion to its share of the DES market.

The market share liability rule is a step away from *caveat emptor* (let the buyer beware) and a step toward *caveat venditor* (let the seller beware). It implies that for manufacturers to reduce their exposure to the potential, futuristic, litigious populace, accurate and detailed records spanning ages may have to be kept. Although through the years some companies ceased to exist, those that survived and thrived were the very ones held responsible for a common sin. By keeping all records of business transactions, it is possible for a company to extricate itself from the fangs of liability litigation under the market share liability rule.

## REGULATING IN AN INDUSTRIALIZING ENVIRONMENT

In an industrializing economy, a highly regulated business environment is imperative. Rules and regulations that address minimum standards should be able to protect manufacturers, distributors, retailers, consumers, and the environment at large.

When the rate of literacy is very low, the nuances of technology must be highly regulated to prevent individual and general catastrophes. For example, chemicals must be highly regulated. A needy hard-working, illiterate and ignorant manual laborer who happens to work with obscure and hazardous/carcinogenic compounds may not be immediately aware of the deadly effects of the chemicals he or she may be breathing. As long as he or she does not have familiar experiences, like that from a gunshot, a snakebite, or a "physical" industrial accident in which, say, an arm or a leg is injured, he or she is inclined to nurse a false sense of security. Injuries deriving from chemicals are not always easily or immediately identifiable. In a pre-industrial environment, the level of knowledge about chemicals is often very low. Sometimes, a country's best and brightest may live a vigorous but shortened life because the ignorance of the masses was not properly addressed. On December 2 and 3, 1984, an industrial chemical accident in Bhopal, India, took the lives of 2,500 people, and 200,000 persons were injured. There was an explosion, followed by the leak of fumes. A highly regulated industrial environment tends to negate and possibly diminish the regressive ramifications of the less informed. A permissive environment only hurts the community itself, possibly stalling industrialization efforts.

Around 1990, a visitor to Nigeria might have remarked that the Nigerian currency, the naira, was relatively devalued. Products made in Nigeria might have been comparatively inexpensive in the eyes of an alien visitor, before taxes, duties, and other charges. Many entrepreneurs from neighboring countries sought profitable opportunities to import from Nigeria. Among these were also smugglers, who bought cheap petrol (gasoline) from Nigeria to sell in the contiguous countries that at the time possessed relatively stronger currencies. The lucrative nature of this underworld trade in gasoline lured many high school graduates who were either unemployed or marginally employed at the time. Because these creative entrepreneurs were thinly capitalized, the tendency was to use nonstandardized containers to transport and distribute petrol. This resulted in the mishandling of a hazardous chemical compound.

Motorists who succumbed to the temptation of buying this street brand, sometimes sadly found out that the gasoline had been watered down. Adulterated fuel eventually led to increased frequency in auto repairs. Many motorists used leaded gasoline because it was cheaper than unleaded petrol. Lead had been the most economical additive to boost the octane rating of gasoline and, thus, automobile performance. More user-friendly but expensive substitutes for lead in gasoline are ethanol and methanol. Meddling with illicit petrol trade may have adverse effects on human health. An environmental protection agency, determined that lead in gasoline is a leading cause of high blood pressure. It is also related to heart attacks, strokes, and other heart and blood-vessel diseases. Research studies have also shown that high levels of lead in the bloodstream cause mental retardation in children and permanent damage to the nervous system.[24]

Social balance in an industrializing environment is not only restricted to the production of goods and services by the public and private sectors, but it is extended to individuals, corporations, and other entities and social institutions. A sound legal framework balances the rights and responsibilities of consumers against that of producers. It ensures fairness and protects consumers, businesses, the public, and the environment at large.

## NOTES

1. Kenneth W. Clarkson et al., *West's Business Law* (Saint Paul, MN: West), p. 808.

2. It must be remarked, however, that consumer protection in some countries has been approached by some scholars in terms of models. The following are some examples of such models: free market model; consumer cooperative model; independent consumer association model; corporatist model; quasi public agency model; and political/bureaucratic elite model.

3. James W. Kuhn, "Unions in the Nineties: Implications for Business Ethics," in Clarence C. Walton, ed., *Enriching Business Ethics* (New York:Plenum Press, 1990), p. 149.

4. Ibid."One should understand, however, that the traditional understanding of individualism rested upon a moral foundation that the new one does not. That foundation [in the U.S.A.] was rooted in the Puritan tradition that gave religious sanction to both individualism and 'work' as a 'calling.' Prudence, sobriety, propriety, and dignity in work easily attached themselves to the worker imbued with the old values of individualism. Whether they accompany the new individualism is a question to consider carefully. Do those who sit at or near the apex of many layered hierarchies have a careful regard for the values generally held by those beneath them?"

5. Sven Kuhn Von Burgsdorff, *The Courier* (Brussels), July-Aug. 1992, p. 61.

6. Lawrence E. Rose, "Consumer Protection in Scandinavia," in Alexander J. Groth & Larry L. Wade, *Public Policy Across Nations: Social Welfare in Industrial Settings* (Greenwich, CT: JAI Press, 1985), pp. 151–152. In Norway and Sweden, for example, one can find laws dating from the seventeenth and eighteenth centuries or earlier, which served to govern the conduct of business and certain trades or professional groups as well. These laws set quality standards for specific goods (e.g., precious metals) and the operation of public services (e.g., pharmacies and postal services). Such laws became more common in the 19th Century, as new services (e.g., railroad, telegraph and telephone) and new products or forms of services (e.g., guns, margarine, tobacco, fish and meat processing, and hotel services) were subject to official control. To the extent that consumers benefit from these efforts to standardize commercial practice, these laws could be deemed to constitute a form of consumer protection. In general, however, the primary intent of these laws was to protect the commercial interests of those engaged in specific forms of production, trade, or service provision rather than consumers of these goods and services.

7. Ibid., p. 170.

8. The law does not only seek to protect consumers but protects businesses from other business. An example is the *principle of constructive effort*. The idea here is that, competing businesses will succeed by their own positive efforts rather than by undermining their competitors. They see their competitors, not as obstacles to be eliminated, but as fellow seekers after a common prize. It is, therefore, ethical that businesses compete by focusing on their strengths rather than seeking to identify and capitalize on the weaknesses of their opponents—even if they are genuine and relevant. There is no room, therefore, for commercial disparagement—the making of false statements about the quality of a business's products or services with intent to cause financial harm to the business. From a macro perspective, permitting the less successful to defame and sabotage the more successful would frequently result in a net loss to the economy and especially an industrializing economy. See, Lynn Sharp

Paine, "Ideals of Competition and Today's Marketplace," in Walton, ed., *Enriching Business Ethics*, pp. 100–102.

9. Tom L. Beauchamp & Norman E. Bowie, eds., *Ethical Theory and Business Practice* (Engelwood Cliffs: Prentice-Hall,1979), p.451. "But given the dependence effect — given that the consumer wants are created by the process by which they are satisfied—the consumer makes no such choice. He is subject to the forces of advertising and emulation by which production creates its own demand." Advertising operates exclusively, and emulation mainly, on behalf of privately produced goods and services. The pressure exerted on communities to emulate other communities in the production of public goods (e.g., a new school and a new highway) while realistic, the intercommunity effect is obviously small. See, John Kenneth Galbraith, *The Affluent Society*, (Boston: Houghton Mifflin Company, 1969), pp. 147–154.

10. Consumer Union of the U.S., Inc., is the largest of such an organization, and is the publisher of *Consumer Reports.*

11. Guy Hunter, *The New Societies of Tropical Africa: A Selective Study* (London: Oxford University Press, 1962), pp. 129–158.

12. Pablo A. Iannone, *Contemporary Moral Controversies in Business* (New York: OUP, 1989), p. 244.

13. A tort action is a private civil wrong or injury other than a breach of contract. A tort action requires three components: a legal duty must bond the parties; that duty must have been breached; and damage must have been sustained from the breach. There are three tort theories: negligence, strict liability and misrepresentation.

14. *A Guide to American Law: Everyone's Legal Encyclopedia,* vol. 10 (Saint Paul, MN: West Publishing Co., 1984), p. 301.

15. Ibid.

16. Henry Campbell, *Black's Law Dictionary* (Saint Paul, MN: West Publishing Co., 1990), p. 1587.

17. Ibid.

18. Iannone, *Contemporary Moral Controversies in Business*, pp. 365–375.

19. Sanford H. Kadish, ed., *Encyclopedia of Crime & Justice* (New York: Free Press, 1983), pp. 1512–1518.

20. *Morissette v. United States*, 342 U.S. 246, 253–256 (1952).

21. Wayne Biddle, *A Field Guide to Germs* (New York: Henry Holt and Co., 1995), pp. 9–10, 57, 63–65, 97, 110, 126, 140–152.

22. Charles Singer and Ashworth Underwood, *A Short History of Medicine* (New York: Oxford University Press, 1962), p. 612. It was later shown that they were not amines, but the name gradually became accepted, with the final e being dropped to avoid the unjustified chemical assumption.

23. Iannone, *Moral Controversies in Business*, pp. 365–375.

24. *Reader's Digest,1986, Almanac/Yearbook*, p. 191.

17

# Agriculture: *Sine qua non* for Industrialization in Africa

A *sine qua non* for an irreversible industrial takeoff is a sound agricultural foundation. The industrial revolution, therefore, is a corollary of an agricultural revolution. This was the case with all industrialized nations, with a few unique exceptions. Although the traditional system of agriculture in Africa underwent substantial modifications in the twentieth century, overall one may say it has been successful in some ways, relative to the beginning of the century. Nevertheless, this achievement is not good enough in an industrializing environment.

Several modifications started ranged from the introduction of cash crops, to farms that supply seeds to local communities, and research activities in areas such as hybridization and breeding. Plowing with animal draft power was started in some places coupled with irrigation projects and even mechanization schemes, for example, in Zimbabwe, then Southern Rhodesia.

The African subsistent farmer was quick to adapt to new opportunities, even when that meant spontaneous and substantial changes in traditional agriculture. Here an example was when the responsibilities of cash crop farming were added to the chores of subsistent farming. When cocoa was introduced in the Gold Coast (Ghana) at the end of the nineteenth century, it was widely accepted, and Ghana became a leading exporter of cocoa in the world market. When cotton was introduced as an export crop in Uganda at the beginning of the twentieth century, it also gained acceptance. Kenya is renowned for its coffee, and this credit may also be shared by traditional African farmers. The mechanization of rice production started in the Bonthe-Pujehun District of Sierra Leone was also deemed successful.[1]

These efforts were largely successful because African males saw cash crops as a "man's crop." The traditional division of labor by sex relegated light but routine and recurrent duties, such as agricultural and household tasks to females and children. By contrast, men did the heavier tasks, for example breaking up fields for new cultivation, felling trees, fishing, and the more risky hunting.

Heavy work functions also left men with substantial leisure time, and when cash crops were introduced, men not seeing any serious conflict in the scheduling of work readily accepted the offer to participate in export production.[2] This consideration of conflict was important to foreclose the scourge of famine or the pinch of preharvest hunger. Fears had been expressed concerning food shortages that would emerge as a result of neglect of food crops owing to preoccupation with export production. This concern was valid, but the reasons were different. There was considerable anxiety in West Africa in 1948–1949 and in 1950–1951 because of sharp increases in the prices of staples prompted by a sharp rise in cocoa prices that led to an abrupt increase in consumer purchasing power in the midst of a substantial reduction in maize supplies due to an outbreak of maize rust, introduced in West Africa in 1949. In some places, the introduction of cash crops led to liberal adjustments in dietary intakes and, therefore, changes in local food crop cultivation. A case in point was in the Ubangi-Shari area of Central African Republic. Here, the introduction of the cotton crop conflicted with the seasonal peaks in the labor requirements for the traditional millet and sorghum crops. Adjustments were made by traditional farmers, and the more convenient manioc production was expanded at the expense of cereal crops. This technically valid adjustment, however, represented a deterioration in the nutritional quality of the diet and from an economic point of view.[3] Where there were setbacks, these were often not deliberate, but were perhaps due to the traditional farmer's lack of acquaintance with the technicalities of the circumstances. By constantly making less risky and realistic marginal changes, the families of traditional African farmers therefore became responsible for growing staples for domestic consumption as well as cash crops for export.

Unfortunately, the changes grafted in the twentieth century on traditional farming are not good enough in an industrializing environment. Traditional shifting cultivation, a common practice in growing staples, is not suited for a commercially oriented economy. Shifting cultivation takes place in scattered plots in bush clearings or in plots in the forest. The logistics for bulking produce from such random locations are difficult to rationalize. Such plots held in temporary usufruct provide only minimal incentives to invest resources for land improvement, including transportation, public utilities, and communications. The types of long-term planning and rational management that accrue to well-defined farm holdings are divorced in the case of farms under shifting cultivation. The effectiveness of agricultural extension programs becomes impaired and overall poses problems to technical innovations.[4] The system of shifting cultivation may be at the very root of problems in Africa pertaining to increasing output and productivity.

In an industrializing environment the incomes and savings of farmers increase with increased crop yields. Farmers have a very high purchasing power in the marketplace and command necessities such as enough food, clothing, adequate transportation, and modern farm equipment. The peaceful rural scene is rehabilitated into modern villages with electricity, communication infrastructure, clean water supply, warehouses, mills, and beautiful permanent residential buildings with alleys adorned with flowers. This was accomplished in South Korea in just ten years.[5] In this regard, given the right stimulation, the abilities of the traditional African farmers to adjust to changing conditions and adapt to better practices that will improve their lives must not be underestimated. This is especially so when one factors in the delight in hard work and ambition to succeed. Nevertheless, for all these to come to fruition, reevaluating the synergy of agriculture and urban industries will be necessary.[6]

Economic progress is retarded in the very early stages of industrial expansion when people decide to quickly engage in the consumption of luxury goods and services instead of investing in capital equipment. In this case, comfort and well-being are given priority over production increases. This may result in a tragic economic impasse that borders on famine and greatly slows down economic progress.[7] In order to surmount this grim dilemma in Africa, there will have to be systematic and sustainable increases in agricultural productivity. To ensure rapid and sustainable growth in food production, initial steps, taken to revolutionize agriculture, tend to include some combination or all of the following: intensive agriculture; small plot size increase where feasible; abandonment of the fallow system; crop rotation; large-scale farming; mechanized farming; selective-breeding of farm animals;[8] improved or developed seed banks; food storage/preservation; stabling; educating farmers; agricultural research /information gathering, storing, and analysis for strategy and policy applications; accommodation of transportation needs of farmers; disseminating pertinent information to farmers and industry in a timely manner; and using underutilized labor.

The possibilities of farming in the twentieth century are almost without natural limitations. Where land is limited, *intensive farming* is practiced, and where land is plentiful and fertile, *extensive farming* may be preferred. Unlike extensive cultivation, farming a small tract of land requires great diligence and skill in order to produce a maximum yield. This is usually the case in countries with high population densities. Fruit growers, vegetable growers, and farmers in general, adjacent to large urban centers, may use intensive methods such as green houses and hydroponics. This, therefore, means that people do not necessarily have to wait for rains in order to harvest a crop, and vegetables can be grown without soil.[9] High-quality tomatoes can be harvested from plants grown in *nutrient* solutions, warmed by electricity. These plants may reach heights of fifteen feet or more, with annual outputs per acre of at least 200 tons. Potatoes have been grown at a rate of 2,500 bushels per acre. Similarly, remarkable yields have been obtained from beets, turnips, carrots, and celery.[10]

Besides lands that are naturally arable, marginal lands, including those in arid and semiarid regions, can be brought under cultivation. There are hundreds of millions of acres in Africa that can be put into productive agricultural use. Radically reducing or eliminating the endemic problem of *postharvest food losses* will sharply increase agricultural output. Cassava, very familiar in much of Africa, is a valuable food crop that is tolerant to poor soils and harsh climatic conditions. Once established, the plants can withstand at least six months of drought, and the cyanide content tends to deter rodent pests. Because of such demonstrated stamina, it is also called a food security and famine reserve crop. Cassava, therefore, is important to farmers living on marginal soils, since it is easily propagated (by woody stem pieces) and yields are generally in excess of ten tons per hectare.[11] In Democratic Republic of Congo (formerly Zaire) most of the total vegetable consumption (70 percent, by weight) comprises cassava leaves.[12] In an industrializing environment, cassava can be useful in manufacturing a variety of food products, which may include the familiar gari, farinha, tapioca or sago, chips, wafers, glucose, vermicelli, spaghetti, and cattle feed. In an industrializing environment, cassava will not only be used as food and animal feed. It will also be useful in manufacturing soap and detergent; paper; cosmetics (toilet paper, shampoo); pharmaceuticals (making pills, insecticides, disinfectants); fireproofing preparations; explosives (construction industry); drilling muds; optical whiteners; leather treatment; plastics (filler in PVC plastics, and in rigid urethane foam); and even as a replacement for carbon black. In Australia, as an example, ninety miles of desert were brought under cultivation by adding a few soil nutrients and other available technologies. In fact, given the current level of technological progress, the world is capable of feeding at least 38-40 billion people.[13]

Although much food can be produced in Africa in the short term, much of this food will also have to be processed for efficient distribution and consumption. Without foresight, food production, a fundamental requirement, may unnecessarily become overly dependent on the import sector— in this case, fertilizers, pesticides, milling, packaging and distribution, hardware and materials. In fact, this was the case with some countries in Africa, where agricultural development efforts have been stagnating or retrogressing.

The worst thing that can happen to a humanbeings and their dignity is that they cannot fathom where the next meal will come from. They cannot feed themselves, let alone their families. Life at this point, it seems, has no meaning and death stands at the door steps staring and beckoning to the bag of bones. Although many Africans may not be aware of this tragedy, this is the quiet reality of millions of Africans, starving in obscure locations in the last quarter of the twentieth century or so. The problems of agriculture in Africa are unnecessarily elusive. Low-tech and simple solutions to agriculture can adequately feed whole communities in just a few growing seasons. Widely known scientific solutions can permanently guarantee self-sufficiency. In fact, the problem should never be food. Instead, the problem should be how efficiently to provide employment to those displaced from farms. In an industrializing nation, the problems of the destitute and hungry may vitiate whole communities. Again, a *sine qua non* for an irreversible industrial take off is a sound agricultural foundation. The industrial revolution, therefore, is a corollary of an agricultural revolution.

## ENVIRONMENTAL PROTECTION

It is quite easy to lay emphasis on alleviating poverty while neglecting the long-term effects of industrialization on the environment. It is not always possible to control the forces of nature, such as volcanoes, earthquakes, landslides, floods, tornadoes, hurricanes, cyclones, extreme temperatures, and lightnings that result in fires. It is possible, however, to protect against land degradation and environmental deterioration resulting from human activities.

Much topsoil is lost annually through soil erosion caused by wind and water, but this problem is worsened overall by deforestation and specifically by inadequate standards in activities such as in mining, construction, agriculture, and tree harvesting. While some bodies of water may be naturally polluted and unfit for direct human use, unregulated human activities may also result in contamination of streams, lakes, and wells used for drinking water. Human activities that cause pollution, in this case, are like adding insults to injury. It is therefore imperative to have environmental impact assessments, for major development and construction projects. *Rules and regulations*, or *guidelines* aimed at environmental conservation are, therefore, likely to ensure the benefits of industrialization, without the concomitant environmental hazards. What may be difficult to control are the violent forces of nature that can wreak havoc on natural ecosystems in just hours, or perhaps minutes.

## NOTES

1. Bruce F. Johnson, "Changes in Agricultural Productivity," in Melville J. Herskovits and Mitcell Harwitz, eds., *Economic Transition in Africa* (Evanston, IL: Northwestern University Press, 1961), p. 174. Here the land was level grassland with rich and fertile soil replenished by annual flooding. The flooding was deep, but the land was dry enough during the dry season to support crawler tractors. Owing to the heavy grass cover and short dry season, rice cultivation was virtually unfeasible without tractors for clearing and preparing seedbeds. Mechanical cultivation was done on a contract basis, with payment in kind at harvest time.

2. The heaviest labor requirements for cocoa and coffee occurred precisely during the slack periods of staple cropping, from August to December. Activities such as hunting and fishing could be scheduled around cocoa harvest. Tree crops could be planted with food crops on the same plot. In this way, the food crops provided the needed shade that was required by the cash crop during the first three to four years.

3. R. Guillemim, "Evolution de l'agriculture dans les savannes de l'Oubangi," *Agronomie Tropical*, 2 (1956), pp. 281–299.

4. Bruce F. Johnson, "Changes in Agricultural Productivity," in Herskovits and Harwitz (eds.), *Economic Transition in Africa* p. 176.

5. Park Chung Hee, *Korea Reborn* (Englewood Cliffs,NJ : Prentice Hall, 1979), pp. 68–69, 91. South Korea is unendowed with natural resources and is bound by long traditions. Historically, Korean major export items were tungsten ore, squid, laver or silk. With industrialization its major export items also included synthetic yarns, plywood, cars, ships, machinery, electronic devices and construction materials. South Korea's economic performance was aptly called Miracle on the Han River.

6. Cyril E. Black, Marius B. Janson, Herbert S. Levine, Marion J. Levy, Jr., Henry Rosovsky, Gilbert Rozman, Henry D. Smith II, S. Frederick Starr, *The Modernization of Japan and Russia* (New York: Free Press, 1975), p. 167. When reforms are not accompanied by proper stimulation, the whole exercise may be futile. The period between the 1860s and 1880s in Russia (as in Japan) was more significant for its institutional reforms than for its economic growth. The abolition of serfdom, for example, did not produce the immediate desired results because of the way in which it was administered. Labor mobility continued to be restricted,

agricultural technology was not stimulated, and the development of an internal market was not enhanced. Industrial output increased, but only at a sluggish rate of 2 percent per year.

7. Gunner Myrdal, *Asian Drama: An Inquiry into the Poverty of Nations* (New York: Twentieth Century Fund, 1968), pp. 1241–1384.

8. Wayne D. Rasmussen, *Taking the University to the People* (Ames: Iowa State University Press, 1989), p. 128. In the 1950s, the average dairy cow produced 5,314 pounds of milk; in 1984, production had increased to 12,495 pounds.

9. Similarly the technique of artificial insemination in cows increases livestock output: Myrdal, *Asian Drama*, pp. 1253.

10. Kennard E. Goodmam and William Moore, *Economics in Everyday Life* (Boston: Ginn & Company, 1947), p. 123–133.

11. On an annual basis, cassava can yield as much as 50 tons of tubers per hectare, when grown in high fertility soils coupled with good agronomic practices. Well-suited soils tend to be well-drained, loamy, or sandy-loamy with sufficient organic matter. Optimal tuber formation occurs in soils that are loose and friable. On heavy clay and rocky soils the yield tends to be less because of restricted tuber development. Soil may be loosened, however, by tractor plowing or spade digging to enhance crop rooting. Cultivation using soil mounds tends to be best for soils that are high in clay content and have restricted drainage, whereas the ridge method is used on slopes to prevent soil erosion; the flat method is used in well-drained land. With irrigation, cassava may be planted any time of the year. Traditionally it has been inter-planted with other crops such as maize, cowpea, millet, and sorghum. More recently, it is being cultivated on an industrial scale. Countries such as Nigeria, Thailand, Indonesia, and Colombia, introduced new and improved varieties, in terms of yield, adaptation to environmental and biotic stress, and root quality. C. Balagopalan, G. Padjama, S.K. Nanda and S.N. Moorthy, *Cassava in Food, Feed, and Industry* (Boca Raton, FL: CRC Press, 1988); O.O. Onyekwere, I.A. Akminrele, O.A. Koleojo, and G. Heys, "Industrialization of Gari Fermentation," in *Industrialization of Indigenous Fermented Foods* (New York: Marcel Dekker, 1989), pp. 363–408; J. Muchnik, and D. Vinck, *La Transformation du Manioc: Technologies Autochtones* (Paris: Presses Universitaires de France, 1984); J.H. Cock, "Cassava Plant and Its Importance," in *Cassava, New Potential for a Neglected Crop* (Boulder, CO: Westview Press, 1985).

12. Although cassava is a high-energy food that can be grown with little effort, it may also impart toxicity and several nutritional deficiencies when poorly prepared and when consumed indiscriminately and without adequate protein supplements. The toxicity is usually the result of cyanide consumption. In addition, thiocyanate interferes with iodine uptake by the thyroid gland, leading to goiter, and in extreme cases cretinism. Although cassava is considered a good hedge against famine, epidemic spastic paraparesis has been reported on several occasions in Africa since 1981, affecting between 5,000 and 10,000 persons with paralysis. Each outbreak was obviously associated with famine-induced consumption of poorly processed cassava and lack of protein in the diet. H. Rosling, *Cassava Toxicity and Food Security: A Report for UNICEF African Household Food Security Programme* (Uppsala : International Child Health Unit, University Hospital, 1988).

13. Orville Freeman, "The Family Farm: A Success Story with Global Implications," in Howard F. Didsbury, Jr., *The Global Economy: Today, Tomorrow, and the Transition* (Bethesda, MD: World Future Society, 1985), p. 139.

# Tempering the Economic Tenor and Rhythm for Sound Fiscal and Monetary Policies in Africa, during Industrialization

Historically, the rate of inflation in *South Africa* was closely intertwined with those of its major trading partners. Annual inflation rates in the 1960s averaged around 3 percent. In harmony with global trends, interest rates rose above 10 percent in 1974 and gyrated between 11 and 14 percent during the early 1980s. However, in the late 1980s it trended away from those of its Western partners, who were then experiencing declining interest rates. Inflation peaked at 18.6 percent in 1986, prompting the depreciation of the rand, and continued in double digits in the subsequent period. The erratic price of oil, deriving from circumstances unique to South Africa, was a source of consistent inflationary pressure. Inflation persisted into the early 1990s and continued to erode economic vigor. The erratic price of gold in the 1980s led to other budget problems, fueling the cycle of reduced industrial revenues, currency devaluation, and high inflation. The government tried to increase its revenues through lenient tax policies, but average incomes sustained at low levels to bring in the needed government revenues. By 1994, interest rates had declined to 9.1 percent, but trended upward in early 1995 under the pressure of new social spending, taking a respite at 8.7 percent, by the end of the same year. This lower rate was attributed to declining prices for food, lowering import tariffs, and the relative stability of the currency (the rand). However, with increased credit purchases and strong labor demand, inflationary pressures persisted.

Manufacturing in South Africa is among the most evolved on the continent. However, this sector suffered serious effects from chronic high inflation that eroded other sectors of the economy. The high inflation of the late 1980s coupled with general economic downturn and debt crises, took a toll on manufacturing, especially capital intensive manufacturing. The annual increase in manufacturing in 1981 was 3 percent. In 1991, the decline was 2.5 percent, with the biggest decreases registered in textiles, footwear, industrial chemicals, and nonferrous metal-base industries. The lackadaisical performance of these industries mirrored falling inventories, and weakness in local demand due to higher interest rates. In agriculture, input costs such as fertilizers and machinery escalated 10 to 20 percent in some years. By 1992, farm debt had reached R17 billion, or at least four times the amount owed in 1980. This was jeopardized by severe drought in the early 1990s, thus compelling the government to spend vital foreign exchange on food imports.

In *Nigeria*, the average annual rate of inflation was 20 percent, between 1973 and 1980 and at least 20 percent between 1980 and 1984, based on the consumer price index. In 1985 the rate of inflation plummeted to 5.5 percent, and with a record good harvest in 1986 the rate eased at 5.4 per cent. The good harvest of 1986 was followed by a year of poor harvest. In 1987, therefore, inflation rose to 10.5 percent. Food prices in 1987 had a domino effect on 1988 prices, speeding inflation to 38.3 percent. In late 1989, inflation stood at 47.5 percent, where it abated as food supplies grew. Inflationary pressures in the late 1980s coupled with wage controls and drastically eroded the incomes of salaried workers. This propelled public sector workers to moonlight in the private sector in areas such as farming, trade, consultancy, and business. Some skilled workers, including doctors, lawyers, and professors, analyzing the possibilities of better opportunities abroad sought to emigrate. Businesses, particularly traders, were less affected. In rural areas, salaried workers resorted to farming to supplement incomes and maintain real wages. By the late 1980, the average income of all rural households in Nigeria exceeded the average income for urban households. For the first time, since 1960, more Nigerians were migrating to the country than to urban areas.

From the early 1960s to the early 1970s, the rate of inflation in *Kenya* was very moderate. In 1973, inflation rose sharply to 15 percent; in 1974 it was 16.1 percent, and in 1975 it reached 20.3 percent. Inflationary pressures during this period were attributed to high prices for imported oil, a liberal credit policy, the effects of adverse weather on food production, and official price increases for the main staples.[1] Inflation in *Uganda* had staggered to 300 percent in 1986. However, the government succeeded in pulling down the rate to 72 percent in 1988. This downward inflationary trend proved transient, spiraling upward to more than 100 percent in 1989, as money supply increased to purchase coffee and other farm produce and to meet increased related costs. The situation was aggravated by food shortages due to low rainfall levels in the south. During this period, prices rose for bananas, corn, and other foodstuffs, coupled with shortages of consumer goods and bottlenecks in transportation, distribution, marketing, and production. The cost of import, from Japan and Europe increased with the depreciation of the dollar. The Ugandan government resorted to tightening controls on credit and to increase disbursements of import-support funds. These measures checked inflation, bringing down the rate to 30 percent by mid-1990. However, in late 1990 an upward trend had resumed.

In *Ghana,* inflation averaged more than 50 percent a year, between 1976 and 1981, the year it peaked at 116.5 per cent. Real-minimum wages dropped, from an index of 75 in 1975, to 15.4 in 1981. In 1973, tax revenue was 17 percent of GDP, and in 1983 it was only 5 percent of GDP. The volume of actual import, in 1982, was 43 percent of the average levels in 1975 and 1976. Overall, productivity, the standard of living, and government resources had ebbed dramatically. The nation's problems were initially attributed to festering corruption. However, it was not long when in 1981 it was realized that Ghana's problems were far more dynamic and intricate than festering corruption. The problems were aggravated in 1982 and 1983 by severe drought, bush fires that destroyed crops, and the very low cocoa prices, which were perhaps enough to compel Ghana to resort to external debt obligation. Economic recovery, thereafter, focused on political, social, and economic reorientation, aimed to repay foreign debt obligations. Fiscal stringency was enforced to eradicate budget deficits, and foreign trade was emphasized. Here, the export-producing industries received the most direct support. They also received the most indirect support through the improvement of their proximate infrastructure. By promoting export, the government sought to obtain foreign exchange essential to repay debt and to restrict import. This effort, however, was negated by smuggling activities. In 1982, it was estimated that parallel, or black, market activities comprised 32.4 percent of all domestic trade. Smuggling had cut down the amount of foreign exchange required for official transactions, leading to a reduction in official import. Those most affected were manufacturers dependent on external sources for raw materials and equipment. Consequently many consumer goods were no longer available in Ghana, and this in turn reinforced smuggling activities across borders where the goods could be obtained. This problem, however, was officially resolved. While this economic recovery program faithfully gained the support of the international financial community, it did not enhance the levels of living for most Ghanaians: better living standards were delayed but not forgotten.

During the 1980s, Ghana's economy registered strong growth averaging about 5 percent per year, reflecting the pace of economic recovery. Inflation was reduced, and export earnings increased. Most production came from the export sector and by 1992 and 1993 cocoa production exceeded 300,000 tons, placing Ghana third in the world. In 1990, mineral export fetched 23 percent more earnings than the previous year. To stimulate production in various sectors, products such as machinery, fertilizer, and petroleum were imported. The debt service ratio for 1992 was 27 percent, an improvement over the late 1980s when the average was as high as 62.5 percent. To cover deficits deriving from increased import and external debt obligations, the government came to rely on rising levels of foreign aid.

Although agriculture (i.e., including forestry and fishing) continued to be the bedrock of Ghana's economy, contributing 48 percent of gross domestic product (1991), the long-term importance of agriculture in Ghana was declining in favor of industry and services. For example, from 1988 to 1991, industry's contribution to GDP doubled, comprising 16 percent of GDP while services contributed 35.3 percent in 1991.

Throughout the history of capitalism, perturbing events have deranged the tenor and rhythm of economic life. Wars, augmentations in political regimes, resource changes, new technologies, shifts in demand, and other factors all disturb the equilibrium of the marketplace, as pebbles cast ripples in a pond.

Inflation is one of those ancient and lingering problems that has disaffected the tenor and rhythm of economic life. Efforts by Diocletian (285–305 A.D.) to curb the Roman inflation proved abortive. Between 1150 and 1325, the cost of living in Europe rose fourfold. Between 1520 and 1620, prices doubled and then quadrupled largely because of the massive and sustained importation of gold, which the Spaniards had systematically filibustered from the Americas. The Spanish gold inflation is the only chronicle in which increase in physical gold in circulation was sufficient to depreciate significantly the exchange value of gold already in circulation.

It must be remarked that inflationary episodes that occurred in earlier epochs, for example in 1790s France, took place in an economic, technological, and social environment very different from today's. This may also be said of the ferocious inflation that ran concurrently with the civil war of the American revolutionary period. Probably, a more illustrative example is the German experience of the early 1920s.

On the eve of the German crisis, politicians, like pundits, made strident claims that the economy was in high gear. The combined aggregates of notes in circulation and bank deposits had risen from 12 billion marks prior to World War I to 63 billion marks during the war. The general price level was lagging and only rose at about 150 percent during the same period. This spell indeed appeared to the relatively uninformed public as if there was national prosperity. But this economic tenor seemed to reverse itself between 1921 and the beginning of 1923: when the money supply doubled, prices quintupled. Throughout 1922 and 1923, the gait of price increases was bigger and faster than that of the money supply. By August of 1922, the money supply had reached 252 billion marks, and in January 1923 it stood at 2 trillions. In September 1923, it had reached 28 quadrillions. In November 1923 it was 497 quintillions, or 497 with eighteen naughts affixed after it. The Germans were paying a billion marks for a loaf of bread by mid-1923. People went shopping with baskets full of money and returned home with purchases in their pockets. Needless to say frustration, violence, and chaos erupted in the streets of major cities, almost consuming the last vestiges of law and order. Much later paradigms of pressures emanating from fiscal deficits include some nations in Latin America in the 1980s and the former eastern bloc nations immediately after the end of the cold war.

Early inflations were often triggered by war. The reasons were obvious: wars greatly increased public expenditure. However, governments in wartime do not curb private investments by an equal amount, through taxation. Instead, wars tend to be financed invariably and extensively by borrowing, and the total amount of spending, public and private, rises rapidly. Meanwhile, the quantity of goods available to households is cut back to make room for wartime production. As a result, an environment is sculptured where very much money chases very few goods—the classic phenomenon called inflation.

The causes of inflation are manifold and sometimes not immediately obvious. They may range from high interest rates (that may choke the economy and produce recession) to concentrated economic power (e.g., frequent demands by labor unions for management to shore up wages). They may include the high cost of government regulations (e.g., antipollution), high cost of raw materials (oil in the 1970s), drooping productivity, and even the state of mind that may be diluted by insatiable appetites and the desire to have more than one can afford.

Indexing makes inflation contagious. One reason is that the cost-of-living allowance is kept on an even keel with the cost of living. Unlike the maxim that what goes up must come down, indexing ensures that what goes up stays upwards.

Theoretically, a rise in interest rates could encourage consumer savings from current income and by the same token reduce spending from current income. In reality, this is not always practical as a tool in monetary policy. The money supply tends to increase or decrease with corresponding increases or decreases in commercial bank lending. An increase in money supply affects prices through increased spending of borrowers from borrowed funds, as well as through the multiplier by those from whom they buy. When the supply of funds available for lending is reduced and interest rates are raised to discourage borrowing, the effects are not always as expected. For example, increases in interest rates do not appear to reduce consumer borrowing and spending. One reason is that consumer credit is often repaid in installments, and mathematically very large increases in interest rates bring about very minute increases in monthly payments.[2] Although some critics maintain that high interest rates may serve as a catalyst for inflation, others say that high interest rates would mitigate the rate of inflation. One reason advanced is that it becomes harder to finance investment spending. The pangs of tighter purse strings are sharp and immediate but the effects slowly infiltrate the economic infrastructure. In a well-developed industrial infrastructure, high interest rates cut into home building and there is a slowdown in investments, thus causing unemployment to rise.

Unlike industrializing economies, an economy may be less inflation prone after industrializion. This is because industrialization deploys resources and transforms the infrastructure into a goods-oriented economy. Postindustrial economies tend to be service-oriented economies. Productivity tends to rise faster in factories and manufacturing plants than in the service sector. Productivity increases the stock of goods, thus negating the classic phenomenon of too much money chasing too few goods.

Inflation may be negated by exporting domestic inflation. In a well-developed industrial economy, foreign central banks may decide in concert to shore up a specific currency (e.g., U.S. dollars). During the inflationary period of the 1970s, there was growing demand abroad for dollars. Foreign purchases of dollars reduced the domestic supply, thus slowing inflation. Foreign central banks also purchased U.S. treasury securities. Had they bought U.S. domestic investments instead, and/or deposited their money into U.S. banks, this would have boosted the domestic money supply, thus propping up inflation.

In Western capitalism, a floor of economic stability is provided by the large public sectors that are typically responsible for 30 to 50 percent of all expenditures.[3] While this economic cushion does not immunize the economy from the vagaries of inflations and recessions, it negates the gravity of movements from recession to depression. The downward spiral of production and employment are checked by "safety nets" on government floors. Such safety nets include social security and unemployment insurance. During inflationary periods, pay revision for public servants tends to be delayed because of the fear of setting a poor example for private employers. Because private wages in an industrial environment tend to rise faster than public wages, opportunities to move from a public to a private sector tend to be favorable. Nevertheless, it must be also recalled that there is relatively more unemployment in the private sector than in the public sector. This relative insecurity may be counterbalanced by social security benefits.

Inflation might be checked by several measures, used in some combination or another. An example is a budget discipline. A goal of a balanced budget may be achieved by freezing expenditure while imposing higher taxes as a downward shocker. Alternatively, government spending may be slashed; the problem often confronted is not that of cutting the budget, but the crux is where to trim the fat without disaffecting sectors of the economy that may result in idle capacity and increased unemployment. When the fat is trimmed, social assistance programs may be abandoned: health care expenditure may be reduced if preventive measures are proving effective; research and development expenditure may be slashed if productivity, efficiency, and the quality of products are higher than the forecast targets; and educational budgets may be trimmed if there appear to be diminishing returns.

Some countries that employ cheap migrant labor in industrial plants have stopped inflation by rounding up foreign workers and simply sending them back to their native lands. Switzerland and the former West Germany have been known to resort to such remedies—sometimes at the expense of adverse social and political ramifications. In Africa, the converse occurred: migrant labor was encouraged and recruited to work in the mines. Increasingly, industrial nations have resorted to employing seasonal labor in agriculture and temporary workers in industry and commerce. While temporary and seasonal jobs may increase the credit-risk exposure of such workers, the workers cannot rationally commit to long-term financing of major purchases, such as homes and automobiles.

Inflation may affect persons in low-income brackets rather than persons in high-income brackets. This is because the prices of necessities (e.g., food) tend to rise faster than those of luxury items. Low-income-bracket persons spend more income than the counterparts do on necessities. A 50 percent increase in the prices of food items dramatically increases the percentage of income expended on food, by a low-income-bracket person. To the rich, changes in the prices of food may even go unnoticed, because cumulatively food disbursements are minutiae of the household budget.

Borrowing money at normal interest rates during inflationary episodes is obviously advantageous. This is especially so because such debts will be repaid with cheaper and more plentiful money. Similarly businesses seek to borrow, but banks are disinclined to lend for the same reasons. If rates increase to the extent that they are more than counterbalanced by the fall in value of the currency, then banks will find it profitable to lend. Such loans, when and if they are extended, are usually short-term in nature at high interest rates.

Inflation may restrain an economy from reaching potential growth because of the affinity of full employment to jeopardize inflation. Government therefore opts to tolerate or encourage a certain level of unemployment in order to prevent inflation from getting worse. Inflation tends to be widespread and more urgent than unemployment, which typically afflicts economic pockets or minority enclaves. The real costs and dangers of taming inflation must be carefully examined under a microscope, and the imaginary consequences separated from the real consequences. Inflation is ultimately a zero-sum game in which some win, what others lose, or vice versa. Higher prices always mean higher incomes for someone, if not at home, then abroad.

Commodity money was the earliest and easiest medium of transaction. Because the commodity by itself had value in other uses, the masses of the population had a demand for it. Different commodities have been utilized as money at different times and various places. For example, rice was used as money in China; nails and tobacco were used as money in the United States; salt was used as money in Africa; in the Roman times, the soldiers were sometimes paid in salt. This explains why salt is the root word for salary. The latin word *Salarium* originally meant salt money, money given to buy salt, as part of the pay of Roman soldiers. However, precious metals such as gold and silver were the preferred forms of payment.

Inflations of ancient monetary systems proceeded in more or less the following sequence: It typically began with the decreed replacement of the private goldsmiths' weight and fineness certification on coins with the official seal as certification. Next, names were affixed on the face of the official coins in place of weight and the fineness certification. Invariably, the ruler sooner or later decreed monopoly of issue. The ruling authority maintained monopoly power in minting legal tender. This inherent authority implied the power to officiate in calling in all circulating coins for reminting and reissue. This was often the case during coinage debasement or inflationary financing. It was not uncommon for coinage debasement to be repeated until the coin became almost devoid of its intrinsic value. Some economies (for example, Rome) circulated fiat coinage composed of base metals. When coins depreciated to the extent that they became almost valueless for all intents and purposes, no one would accept them in business transactions. What often followed was a period of trade by barter and economic stagnation (and not infrequently) rebellion. The crown was forced to reissue genuine precious metal coins, in order to resurrect trade and industry (and to ease the ability to collect taxes).

*Coinage* eliminated the need to weigh bullion in every transaction in order to determine the value. The marginal costs of making coins from bullion were minimal. Unlike other commodities (such as rice, nails, tobacco, salt, and bullion), coins had desirable attributes such as durability, divisibility, portability, homogeneity, difficulty of counterfeiting, and a stable demand for and supply of legal tender.

In spite of the aforementioned glowing attributes of coinage, *paper currency* evolved as a substitute for money. In this case, paper currency coexisted with coinage and did not seek to relegate coinage into oblivion. The first veritable paper currency was introduced in China, during the Sung dynasty, in the tenth century. The paper money was a substitute for the iron coinage then used as the medium of transactions: typically, people deposited these heavy and bulky coins in banklike institutions and held in exchange more portable and more convenient receipts for the deposits. The receipts functioned as *"representative money "* or currency. Initially, the government offered a group of families the privilege of organizing and issuing paper claims that bore the nomenclature *chiao-tzu* (or exchange medium).[4] However, in due course, the provincial government withdrew these privileges and took on the role of issuing money.

China experienced inflation amid wartime expenditures. The initial money system collapsed sometime after 1127, with the invasion of the Tatars. In 1161, a new currency, the *hui-tzu* (or check medium) was circulated. The hui-tzu was adequately backed by coinage reserves. This was tantamount to a pledge by the authorities to convert the paper currency to coinage on demand. It must also be remarked, however, that the conversion rate was not at 100 percent. In order to win the trust and credibility of the public, the government carefully regulated the amount of currency outstanding. For two decades the market-determined rates of exchange between paper currency and copper coins were kept stable. The net result was that the credibility of the government was enhanced, and the use of paper money spread like wildfire, across to many places. Under this commodity-money standard of the Chinese, the government maintained an iron hand. The currency that was outstanding was carefully controlled, and the currency supply could increase without inflation because it increased with the volume of economic transactions. In other words, currency supply increased because of corresponding elevations in demand, rather than excess currency supply generated by monetary authority.

Acute fiscal pressures, possibly caused by military expeditions, forced the Chinese government to relax its iron hand over monetary policies: the government resorted to paper money creation to raise revenue. This was jeopardized by the absence of a viable market for sovereign debt. The backing of money reduced, thus resulting in a depreciation of the currency's value. Between 1160 and 1240, the annual rate of inflation averaged between 4 and 5 percent or a fortyfold cumulative increases, over an eighty-year span. The Chinese experience is another example showing that inflationary financing and seigniorage may result in persistent inflation, currency depreciation, and the loss of purchasing power.

Chronicles of the evolution of paper money in China and in the Western world are not disparate. In medieval times, it was customary for *goldsmiths* to serve as depositories for the safekeeping of gold bullion owned by wealthy customers. Business transactions often required the payer party to carry, physically, bullion to the payee or accompany the customer to the goldsmith's shop to witness the transfer of ownership. As the use of paper gained popularity and acceptance, the goldsmith would simply issue a receipt to the *depositor*. The depositor could later present the receipt for *withdrawal* of his gold or exercise the option of endorsing the receipt to a third party, to whom he was making payment. In this fashion, the *receipt* itself became a money substitute and a medium of transaction. The recipient enjoyed the same option: he could either turn in the receipt for the gold, or *endorse* it to yet another recipient. At this juncture, it was not long before the goldsmiths began to issue *bearer receipts*, which required no endorsement. The bearer receipts proved to be a great convenience, and they were accepted in circulation. These were the first *banknotes* in the Western world.

The goldsmiths (bankers), in issuing "bearer" receipts, including smaller denominations, were clearly transgressing the domain of the royal coinage monopoly. Ironically, royalty, instead of demonstrating outrage, was apparently fascinated to observe that the public appeared to prefer the goldsmith's paper to the king's often underweight and impure metal coins. It cannot be stipulated with absolute certainty that the crown did not decipher the duplicity of the goldsmith in issuing more receipts than he had gold in deposit.[5] In any event, it was through such collaborations between the monarch and the banker that *fractional reserve* banking became legalized. The king offered immunity from fraud prosecution (regarding unbacked bearer receipts or banknotes) and the protection from anyone who objected, in exchange for the banker's financial backing. The king was entitled to unsecured loans. Such loans would be extended whenever the king demanded them.

When the banker was immoderate, the depreciating effect on the value of receipts outstanding became noticeable by the public. Depositors became wary of his *solvency* and demanded their gold. When this transpired, the banker became bankrupt because he was able to pay out only a fraction of the reserve of the full amount owing. When the banker could anticipate this impending catastrophe, he would call upon the king to issue a decree to *close* the bank. This forestalled the depositors who could not immediately redeem their gold reserves. By closing the bank, the suspect "bearer" receipts remained in circulation, often at deep discounts, relative to their face value. This respite was often a window of opportunity for the banker himself, or (on some occasions) the king, to arrange a bridge loan to meet the gold obligations. When the bank reopened its doors to meet its obligations, some depositors, seeing that the redemptions were being made, would disregard presenting their notes for redemption. Other disgruntled depositors sooner or later returned their gold to the same previously troubled bank.

With the passage of time, the public confidence in the notes was gradually restored. This was often observed when the notes circulated at a relatively small discount from their face value in gold. At this juncture the banker and/or the king would become encouraged to inflate further the notes in circulation. Each successive cycle was pregnant with the proclivity to discount the notes marginally.

## WAGE-PRICE CONTROLS

Wage-price controls cannot replace responsible fiscal and monetary policies. But sometimes responsible fiscal and monetary policies may require the firm hand of government in holding down the wage-price spiral. Although inflation can be checked with manifold solutions, controls have the inherent advantage of choking down inflation dead in its tracks. It is usually among the solutions of last resort.

Controls maintained for protracted periods have the disadvantage of blocking the normal operation of the economy. This market distortion tends to result in shortages in some areas and surpluses in others. They may also lead to the development of a black market. When wage-price guidelines, designed to hold down inflation, are accompanied by an expansion of money supply, the results are almost invariably cataclysmic. In Germany in 1923, wage-price controls could not have been effective because of the expansion of the money supply. When inflation is demand-pull, protracted controls might not be very effective because people would sooner or later resort to the black market to make their purchases. When this environment prevails, the sooner the government abolishes controls, the better.

During the second world war and the Korean war, wage-price spiral in the United States was successfully contained. Between 1941 and 1942, the industrial production wholesale prices index rose slightly more than seven points. In the subsequent three years the index increased by only 2.4 points. During this period, the controls were in effect although there were greatly increased demand and virtual full employment. Between 1950 and 1951, after the outbreak of the Korean War, the wholesale index of capital goods showed prices rose by seven points while prices for consumer durables rose by only five points. The following year, after wage-price controls went into effect, each index rose by only about one point.

When wage-price controls are mandatory, such controls may have to be backed by heavy taxes and a huge bureaucracy. For example, 18,000 wage-price control inspectors were needed in the United States during the Korean War to make the system work. Although computers can replace some inspectors, in industrializing highly technological environments, it is not possible to replace all inspectors. In cases where wage-price controls are voluntary, major industries may have to abide by government guidelines for acceptable wage and price increases that exceed productivity. Because of the voluntary nature of these measures, they seem to work best when they are sugar coated—they are made profitable as well as patriotic—for example, tax incentives. Common ground and incentives have to be sought because of the economic power wielded by big businesses, governments, and professional people, among others. Because of these pockets of power strewn across the economic landscape, prices do not always respond to the natural market forces of demand and supply. Instead, prices tend to respond to the whims and caprices of a plethora of power centers.

When wage and price controls are imposed at the front end of industrialization, the cost of production is also kept in check. When the economy is overwhelmingly dependent on imported industrial raw materials, and prices are escalating disproportionately, industrial and agricultural producers will become risk averse. In the case of a latent increase in the cost of production, businesses will be less willing to risk the additional capital to produce the bare essentials.

By the beginning of the 1870s the trading partners of the United States were demonstrating a growing unease about the large and persistent negative balance of payments. It seemed they were nursing a cause for concern about the overvalued dollar. By mid-July 1971, the president and his economic advisers knew that the dollar could not continue to be pegged to gold at the fixed rate and would have to be devalued. Gold price had been fixed at $35 per ounce since 1934. The Swiss franc had been fixed at $0.2320 since 1940, and the U.S. government had been fixing the price of silver in one way or the other since 1878.

Although devaluation appeared to be a positive response for healthy trading relationships, it was known to have daunting ramifications. Devaluation per se was probably going to ignite adverse political reaction if it were not cloaked with other major decisions. On August 15, 1971, the "new economic policy" was born. It was an embodiment of price control and precipitated economic growth—the "gold window" would be closed and a surcharge imposed on all imports. The basic idea was to ensure an attractive position for American products in the world market. It is important to reiterate that, given the intricate pattern of the U.S. economy, wages and prices could not be kept frozen for an extended period without causing acute market distortions. It was therefore imperative at the outset to stipulate unequivocally and irrevocably that the freeze was a ninety-day ephemera. For the freeze to be effective, it had to be sold to the public. It had to garner an acceptance and popular accolade. It had to be fair, comprehensible, and workable, inculcating procedural considerations. For the rules and regulations to amass popular consent and for the people to abide by them by their own volition, there had to be an initial publication of draft regulations with opportunity to vent comment and justified criticism. The administering boards had to be organized so that vocal parties would feel that the board was receptive and attentive to hear their arguments and concerns. Finally, the process would be deemed successful if the public retained the confidence and the integrity of the program. At the end of the ninety-day ephemera, wages and prices would be decontrolled, often simultaneously. Disengagement of the controls could be as an edict of some kind—the private sector would defy it and the whole program would explode into vestigial fragments.

Alternatively, self-administration may be adapted, at the end of the ninety-day period. In this case, companies and unions would be relieved of bureaucratic entanglements that derived from wage-price controls. Once the rules are published, the burden of responsibility would be shifted to invested parties for proper self-administration. The tactic of delaying wage and price increases would drop out of the system. The parties would reserve the right to decide for themselves if and when to raise wages and prices. They can then cross-check to ensure that the increments do not violate the rules and regulations.

Wage-price controls may be disengaged by using the sector-by-sector approach. However, the nervous system of the economy often renders this technique a little delicate. In this case, those sectors itching to be decontrolled would be asked to pledge guarantees. They may be asked to maintain about average price behaviors over a stipulated time frame, in the immediate future. They may be asked to limit the export of critical materials, make investment commitments, plans, and so on. This sector-by-sector approach tends to relieve the pressure very slowly, leading to slight increases in prices. However, the goal is to disengage as rapidly as possible without causing havoc.

When controls go awry, they pose a dangerous dilemma for businesses, in domestic and international matters. For example, if the controlled price of a domestically produced good is below the world market price, export will surely rise. By the same token, export may result in domestic scarcity, thus allowing the price of the good (e.g., rice) to escalate to world market price levels. When export controls result in shortages in the world market (e.g., the brief experiment with soybeans by the

United States in the 1970s) the obvious tendency is to undermine the confidence of the importing countries that rely on this particular nation as a secure source of supply. This may even result in importing nations sourcing alternative suppliers. Another example is anchovies, food fish also used in fish meal. European farmers normally used fish meal as cattle feed—a source of protein. Oddly enough, these herring-like saltwater schooling fishes used in fish meal disappeared without leaving behind any clues. They had swum away from their preferred habitat around the coast of Peru. The fish that preyed on anchovies followed them, thus leaving the fishermen without bounty.[6] European farmers were compelled to switch to feed grains. In the case of the broiler (chicken) industry, this was tantamount to disaster. Price increases of certain commodities may be negated by selling out of government stockpiles no longer considered strategic. The immediate effect was sharp increases in grain prices, thus increasing the tide of inflation, which was jeopardized by the OPEC oil crisis (1970s).

Autonomous groups may be formed under the auspices of the executive branch of government. Generally, such groups tend to command a sizable staff with experts who can develop independent information and analysis, which form the basis for affronting departmental perspectives. Because their singular mission is to contain the tide of inflation, they therefore work toward expanding rather than contracting the stock of supply of goods and services available. Control programs may have administrative integrity, to command staying power. They may reconcile themselves with being denounced and repudiated for their innovative views. Administrators in this domain may frequently remind themselves not to take vilifications and imprecations too seriously or very personally, because they are fighting a battle against inflation.

## DEVALUATION

To diversify and expand the economy in the 1960s, *Ghana* used cocoa revenues. These revenues were applied as the basis for loans to establish import substitute manufacturing and export processing plants. Unfortunately, this plan was impeded by the collapse of the price of cocoa in the mid-1960s. Ghana therefore obtained less foreign exchange to repay loan obligations, which had increased almost tenfold between 1960 and 1966. The nation's currency was overvalued, and devaluation had to be seriously considered.

Nations prefer, however, to maintain the integrity of their respective currencies, since significant gyrations in the currency *status quo*, may erode confidence in the currency. Rapid price increases may compel advance purchases, delays in selling, and increases in speculation and hoarding. Significant devaluation may be an added incentive for smuggling activities and perhaps capital flight. Under the pressure of speculative behavior, prices might as well spiral upward, ultimately compelling the government to further currency devaluation. Nevertheless, the likelihood of such adversities unfolding could be reduced.

Devaluation may be feasible if the decision to devaluate was carried out, in an orderly manner and at a time when prices were stable, thus maintaining a tight rein on domestic prices, foreign exchange transactions, and capital transfers. Devaluing

Ghana's currency would have made its cocoa price more attractive in the world market, but *devaluation* would have also made loan obligations, which had to be repaid in United States dollars, more difficult. Import costs for nascent industries and consumers would have also increased. Given this predicament and the tension that it might have created in the political climate, devaluation was therefore postponed. With overall low cocoa prices, therefore, production was discouraged and smuggling of cocoa to neighboring countries became an enticing option, since prices offered there were more attractive. Cocoa production dropped to 50 percent from the mid 1960s to late 1970, and Ghana's share of the world market shrank, from 33 percent in the early 1970s to around 12.5 percent in 1982–1983. Additionally, mineral production fell by 32 percent; gold production dropped by 47 percent, diamonds by 67 percent, manganese by 43 percent, and bauxite by 46 percent. Official export dropped, drastically curtailing foreign exchange earnings and compelling Ghana to incur more external debt obligations.

In every economic climate, opportunities usually exist for some people to prosper. However, throughout the 1960s, the Ghanaian gross domestic product, *per capita*, was not impressive and declined by 3.2 percent per year between 1970 and 1981.[7] Excepting a momentous attempt in 1971, Ghana postponed currency devaluation until 1981, when it was coupled with an economic recovery program. Currency devaluation, coupled with raising producer prices for export and the introduction of an interbank–foreign exchange market, negated the advantage of smuggling such goods across borders. In addition, many import duties and trade taxes were revised and reduced, thus easing importation of essential capital and consumer goods. In the early 1990s, cocoa regained its dominance in export earnings. In 1993, gold fetched the most export earnings, although timber, electricity, and bauxite were also significant.[8]

In *Uganda*, the 1981 budget attempted to reestablish financial control by reducing government borrowing and by floating the shilling in relation to world currencies. The official exchange rate before 1981, was USh9.7 per SDR or USh7.3 per US$1. When the Ugandan shilling was floated in mid-1981, it dropped to only 4 percent of its previous value, before settling at USh78 per US$1. In the 1980s, the currency was repeatedly devalued. A two-tier exchange rate was introduced in August 1982 and lasted until June 1984, when the two rates became one. Foreign exchange shortages aided the continued decline of the value of the currency in 1985 and 1986. In May 1987, the government introduced a new shilling, worth a hundred old shillings, and coupled it with an effective devaluation of 76 percent. According to consumer complaints in the marketplace, the new currency's value was quickly eroded by rising prices. Consequently, the revised rate was soon out of line with the parallel rate. The money supply was expansionary following the May 1987 devaluation. The currency was subsequently devalued by 60 percent, in July 1988, followed by other currency devaluations in December 1988, March 1989, and October 1989. By late 1990, the official exchange rate was USh510 per US$1, and in the black market it was USh700 per US$1.[9] The government's efforts to curb inflation were helpful when disbursements were increased for import-support funds and in tightening controls on credit. These measures helped to reduce inflation to 30 percent by mid-1990.[10]

In 1964, *Kenya* exported to more than seventy countries around the world including in Africa, where a substantial portion of foreign trade went to Tangayika and Uganda. About 29 percent of trade went to Britain and the European Economic Community (EEC), while Tangayika and Uganda received at least 30 percent. Britain absorbed 21 percent of export destined for areas outside East Africa, while the former West Germany accounted for about 23 to 24 percent. Export to EEC (Common Market) was composed of mostly coffee, tea, sisal fibers, pyrethrum extract, meat, and meat products. About half the export to Uganda and Tangayika comprised a variety of consumer manufactures, and the remainder was composed of mostly foodstuffs, beverages, and tobacco. Other significant destinations of export from Kenya during this period were the United States, Canada, India, Japan, and South Africa. In 1977 to 1979, the coffee and cocoa boom years, export to EEC was raised to an average of around 45 percent of the total. In Africa, by 1977, Uganda was the largest single importer of Kenyan export. By the early 1980s, Zambia, Zaire, Burundi, Rwanda, and Sudan were more important purchasers. Here, trade was largely to neighboring countries, where export goods were transported mostly by road, rail, and inland lakes.

Initially, *Kenya* applied government revenue surpluses toward development of the economic infrastructure. Many new additions in the manufacturing sector were privately financed, including significant foreign investments. Existing and newly created statutory bodies actively supported industrial efforts. However, the government later faced budgetary problems affecting economic revitalization and balance of payments. In any case, visible progress was being made toward industrialization, and devaluation was not a pressing problem. The Kenya shilling (KSh) replaced the East African shilling, the common currency of Kenya, Tangayika, and Uganda from 1920 to mid-1966. Until June 1973, the exchange rate was maintained at KSh7.14 per US$1, or Ksh1 to US$0.14. Later in 1973, it was revaluated, and KSh6.90 equaled US$1; the earlier rate was restored in January 1974. In October 1975 the currency was pegged to IMF's special drawing right, at KSh8.16 to US$1. After two devaluations of the shilling in 1981, the rate at the end of the same year dropped to KSh10.29 to US$1. In December 1982 it dropped again to KSh12.73 per US$1. On March 31, 1983, it stood at KSh13.06 per US$1.[11]

More than 60 percent of Kenya's import in 1964 came from the industrialized West, Japan, and India. During this period Tanzania and Kenya supplied 11 percent. In 1964, Britain supplied 27 percent, of Kenya's total import. This share, however, declined in subsequent years. In 1975 it was 20 percent and in the early 1980s it was around 17 percent. A preponderance of the total import derived from the industrial West and mostly comprised industrial materials and supplies, machinery, capital equipment, and transport-related items. Import from Tanzania and Uganda comprised mostly foodstuffs, basic supplies such as vegetable oil and electric power, and some manufactured goods. Kenya experienced a favorable balance of trade with trading partners in Africa. Trade with the rest of the world was not as favorable as in Africa, and the overall deficit grew substantially after 1974. The coffee and cocoa export boom years aided to reduce the deficit. However globally, high oil prices added to import costs between 1974 and 1979. This was coupled with an expansionary domestic policy that relied on credit and government overspending, leading to a slower rate of growth in export than in import. Here, the regular deficit in the trade and invisible transactions (i.e., current account of balance of payments) resulted, when net invisible receipts on freight, insurance, and tourism could not absorb all of the merchandise trade deficits. About 50 percent of the time in the 1970s, current account deficits were covered by capital inflows. Between 1972 and 1977, long-term capital inflows from external sources were just about equal to net private long-term capital inflows. Until 1978, external loans and grants (capital inflows) to the public sector were applied toward development projects. As the foreign exchange reserve declined below the desirable minimum (equivalent of four months' cost of import coverage), external lending sources were employed to cover balance of payments shortfalls. Between 1977 and 1981, external debt repayable in foreign exchange increased quickly. Funds were borrowed from the Eurodollar market, but at high interest rates.[12]

The trade balance experienced a parallel growing deficit: in 1981, export earnings could only cover 46 percent of import costs, a much lower proportion than in 1975, when it was 76 percent. Debt service cost, which was 11.5 percent of merchandise export receipts in 1975, rose to 19 percent in by 1982.[13]

Devaluation tends to depress foreign prices and makes export goods more affordable. In case of a sustained balance of trade deficits, devaluation tends to reduce the demand for foreign exchange. This increases the propensity for an increase in the supply of foreign exchange that unequivocally mitigates against the deficit. The supply of foreign exchange may fall, however, if the demands by the rest of the world for imports are inelastic. In a case where lower prices of commodities in the world market are directly related to a surplus of primary products, or substandard quality, devaluation will not significantly increase the supply of foreign exchange, for the exporting country.[14] Devaluation or depreciation may therefore result in a reduction in a nation's real income, because of an overall deterioration in the terms of trade.

Devaluation may or may not be a fillip to industrialization. One reason is that growth in real income does not proportionately translate into an increase in demand for primary products in industrialized countries. This therefore exposes primary products as poor opportunities for expansion, a crucial consideration in economies that engage the majority of the labor force in agriculture and other primary industries. An alternative tendency will be to step up industrialization on the home front. Industrialization requires an injection of technology. It is worth noting, however, that even when technological improvements are applied in the primary export markets the benefits (i.e., the cheapening of production) are often transferred to the importing countries.[15] In the industrial sector, there would be a stronger incentive for private entrepreneurs to produce for export markets. In an environment of import controls the aforementioned effect would be minor, and the tendency would, therefore, be to produce for the home market, thus making it a lucrative field for enterprise, at least in the near term.

Domestically, devaluation may postpone substantial improvements in the levels of living in order to permit capital accumulation and higher productivity. But in parts of Africa and many developing countries, an improved level of living is a precondition for higher labor input and efficiency. When levels of living are very low, worker health, vigor, and attitudes toward work are impaired. In this case, consumption is really an "investment" that tends to ameliorate productivity, possibly boost foreign exchange, and stimulate growth. Depending on the policy ramifications, export may be subsidized at this stage, and workers may be offered higher wages. The idea here is to attract and keep labor in sectors that are the powerhouses of industrialization.

Devaluation may be an impetus for wealthy Africans who previously invested their savings abroad. Such funds may be repatriated, at windfall rates, to unmistakably take advantage of industrial opportunities on the home front. Unfortunately, the wealthy classes in Africa in the past demonstrated relative disinclination to risk funds in productive long-term investments. Instead, a pension for quick profits in investments and conspicuous consumption were demonstrated. Many Africans as investors tend to be unusually afraid to commit to projects that at first sight may be risky. Instead, there is much enthusiasm for quick turnover of near-term investments, often at the expense of bigger profits that tend to accrue in the remote and hazy future. Perhaps wealthy African investors may want to consider more closely alternative investment vehicles such as equity markets.

Devaluation does not necessarily guarantee a positive outcome, nor does it necessarily have a negative connotation. The twain dollar devaluation of 1971 and 1973 was recanted by major trading partners who commanded substantial dollar-denominated balances. This was also demonstrated by their purchase of dollars in the foreign exchange markets in order to maintain exchange rates favorable to their export industries, thus resulting in a great increase in their foreign exchange reserves. This increase in world money supply was a major contributor to the worldwide inflation spanning the period 1972 to 1975.

The net result of devaluation depends on well-coordinated strategic policy decisions and calibrations. When policy decisions are not constructively coordinated and effected, devaluation may have to contend with other market forces such as protectionist policies, substitute products, recycled products, and inflationary pressure that tends to prevail when a currency chases a relatively smaller basket of goods.[16]

Some countries have addressed the problem of trade deficits by imposing export taxes. The idea is to create scarcity in the world market and eventually raise revenue. This prescription has been used mostly by developing countries. It is extremely rare in industrialized nations. Brazil taxed coffee. Ghana taxed cocoa. Thailand and Burma taxed rice. An option to devaluation may be an export quota. In years of poor harvest, export quotas may be instituted to keep prices relatively low on the home front. Export duties tend to be anti-inflationary. If the foreign demand for import does not change significantly, with changes in the volume of certain commodities available in the world market (e.g., coffee), then an export tax may improve the balance of payments (and not a subsidy). In case of a subsidy, it makes no difference whether the higher prices were fueled by subsidy or depreciation. In any case, national income changes through the foreign exchange multiplier.

## CAPACITY UTILIZATION

Although investments in new plants and equipment are generally large relative to the existing stock of capital and total new investments, such investments are often necessary. This is because economic development is directed at industrialization, and it is therefore important that capital investments factor in expected growth in demand. Industrialization normally results in an increase in the proportion of the nation's capital, procured in indivisible manufacturing units. Much of the necessary social overhead capital and the basic structure of industry consists of large indivisible capital, such as in power, steel, transport, housing, and government buildings. For a given level of investment, therefore, the amount of extra output can vary over a wide range. Small additions, in the form of extensions of existing plants, sometimes yield a large amount of extra output per unit capital. On the other hand, the extra output per unit of capital of large additions involving the construction of new plants may yield less. If long-run costs are declining, even if demand is expected to remain constant and no indivisibilities exist, it pays to build a larger plant than that which is optimally adapted to the desired output and to underutilize. This is because the unit cost of production of the optimum plant will be higher than the unit cost of the same output produced by the larger plant. If demand is expected to increase, initial construction of excess capacity may be desirable even if it results in greater production costs of initial output.

Here, future costs of expanding and rebuilding equipment and the interruptions of production while expansion is underway may be averted. Again, this is feasible, if an initial outlay is geared to future larger demand instead of being adapted to current demand. Overall, much fuller utilization will depend on the project's own capacity, coupled with capacities deriving from other already-existing enterprises and the readiness to seize consequential investment opportunities for output generation. For example certain projects, such as improvements in farming methods may by themselves require little capital but may require complementary investments in transport, power, storage, and related facilities. It will, therefore, be misleading to focus solely on initial investments and its direct effects.

The aforementioned does not in any way discount the significance of micro enterprises, or small industry. Instead it creates opportunities for small-scale businesses, since obviously large outfits are not self-sufficient islands. Here, maintaining and upgrading workshop, handicraft and cottage industry is important. Typically such outfits derive from an earlier stage in development and are not creations of small industry. Once native small industry has been disrupted, revitalizing it may be difficult. In fact it is an opportunity for gradual technological improvement and learning from experience. It is also an opportunity for the distribution of technology consistent with local factor endowments and culture. Obviously this notion is not new to many countries in Africa, which have extension, credit, and industrial estate programs to encourage small-scale manufacturing establishments. For example, Nigeria since 1960 or so supported the establishment of small-scale industry through subsidies, tariff drawbacks, training, and extension services. Outside Africa, a handy example is Japan, where small industry was retained and encouraged by government to take cooperative action even in textiles, then in the leading manufacturing industry.

Here, large-scale enterprise created external economies in the supply of raw materials, working capital, and markets. Additionally, these enterprises could not manufacture every item needed, and found it cheaper to buy parts and components from independently-run small workshops. The large firms provided technical advice, scarce inputs, credit, and, where needed, access to large international trading companies, *sogo shosha*, which could avoid deficiencies in language skills of both Japanese and foreign businesses. From 1884 to 1930, small industry, defined here as establishments with fewer than fifty workers, increased its real output (though not output share) and absorbed 65 to 75 percent of Japan's employment. Small industry also contributed 45 to 50 percent of Japan's gross manufacturing output in 1934. However, small firms were not independent, being dominated by major banks, industrial companies, and trading corporations.[17] Much earlier, in the *Meiji* period, technical and management assistance coupled with credit facilities were availed to increase the scale of small workshops, handicraft producers, and cottage industry left from before 1868. This therefore meant less social disruption, since small industry's environment was not alien. The 1884 plan laid emphasis on improving traditional technology through applied science and favored postponing massive foreign large-scale factory transplantation until traditional enterprises could use new techniques.[18]

In capacity utilization, therefore, the output effects of one investment depend on other investment projects embarked upon simultaneously or in sequence as a coordinated program. Output varies sharply, based on the availability of complementary supplies such as appropriate construction elsewhere and other pieces of equipment and the existence of appropriate demand. Capital, therefore, is not treated as a homogeneous entity. Instead, it is treated as heterogenous, like a collection of specific bits and pieces that have to be fitted together in a jigsaw puzzle. What matters is the juxtaposition of the pieces in functional relation to each other, not the display of singular pieces nor the misplaced aggregation or the counting of the total number of pieces thrown together at random. Much investment, particularly public investments, such as in highways, power, stations, ports, railways, and housing, provides opportunities and possibly incentives for consequential output generating investment. Nevertheless, many forms of private investments are of this nature. The opportunity to raise production by a selective encouragement of expenditure is likely to bear fruits in parts of Africa, where much underutilization of resources still prevails. If, therefore, a series of investment projects is interrelated, either by sectoral or temporal arrangements, each depending on the others for its success, the notion of *a capital/output ratio* for any one of them in isolation becomes meaningless.

Therefore, if changes in attitudes and institutions are taken into consideration when appraising capital projects, some projects are seen as more productive than others. This is not just because of their physical effectiveness. It is also because of their impact on attitudes toward work and venture, on the formation or destruction of habits on traditions, on customs, on the aspirations of workers and entrepreneurs, on entrepreneurial action, on decision making, and on incentives. Improved techniques are in many ways related to investment and improving levels of living, especially levels of nutrition, health, and education, will raise output. The success and effectiveness of capital, in contributing to the growth of output and industrialization depends on its locus and the momentum of present and future policies with which it is packaged. Here, it is within the constellation of dynamic forces in an industrializing environment.

## NOTES

1. Harold D. Nelson, ed., *Kenya: A Country Study* (Washington, D.C.: GPO, 1984), pp. 175–176.

2. John K. Galbraith, *The Affluent Society* (Boston:Houghton Mifflin,1958), pp. 226–238.

3. Robert Heilbroner and Lester Thurow, *Five Economic Challenges* (Englewood Cliffs, NJ: Prentice-Hall, 1981), p. 7.

4. Francis T. Lui, "Cagan's Hypothesis and the First Nationwide Inflation of Paper Money in World History," *Journal of Political Economy*, Dec. 1983, pp. 1064–1074.

5. Like you, the goldsmith (banker) had an idea of how large his money balance should be. His objective was to have an adequate nominal reserve to cover any likely withdrawal requests, to have money available to pay his bills, and to make loans to good customers on short notice.

6. Some species of anchovies are filleted, salted, and sold as a delicacy. These tiny fishes are also used in animal meal, oil, and fertilizer. The disappearance came as a great surprise, as they were one of the world's most important commercial fishes.

7. LaVerle Berry, ed., *Ghana: A Country Study,* (Washington, DC: GPO, 1995), pp. 135–145.

8. Ibid., p. 141.

9. Rita M. Byrnes, ed., *Uganda: A Country Study* (Washington, DC: GPO, 1992), p. 136.

10. Ibid., p. 137.

11. Harold D. Nelson, ed., *Kenya: A Country Study* (Washington, DC: GPO, 1984), p. 322.

12. Ibid., pp. 173–179.

13. Ibid.

14. Poor export quality tends to tarnish the reputation of whole industries. For example, a few farmers with poor rice quality, when left unchecked, may dent the image of a nation's rice output in international trade. This applies to other products such as watches, radios, and so on.

15. This may explain why some economies reasoned against devaluation where demand and supply are roughly at equilibrium and in favor of "overvalued" currencies in some combination with import controls. Devaluation is not an alternative to import controls. The idea here is to promote industrialization by holding down the cost of development goods (capital equipment). In the case of Pakistan, the rupee was not devalued when the sterling and a number of other currencies were devalued in September 1949 (United Nations, ECAFE, *Economic Bulletin for Asia and the Far East*, November, 1956, p. 57). As in Africa, here also the supplies of traditional export goods are relatively price inelastic. Here technological innovations improved yields (e.g., rubber and tea in the former Malaya and Ceylon), principally by using export revenues. Mainly export taxes were applied to subsidize replanting. Gunnar Myrdal, *Asian Drama: An Inquiry into the Poverty of Nations* (New York: Twentieth Century Fund, 1968), pp. 2079–2082.

16. In the case of Ghana, the depreciation of the currency, the *cedi*, resulted in higher prices in local currency terms, for local producers. This had the seeds of inflation.

17. Howard Stein (ed.), *Asian Industrialization and Africa: Studies in Policy Alternatives to Structural Adjustment* (New York: St Martin's Press, 1995), p. 78–78.

18. Inukai, Ichirou, "The Kogyo Ikem: Japan's Ten Year Plan, 1884," *Kyoto Sangyo University Economic and Business Review*, May 1979, p. 5 in Stein, ed., *Asian Industrialization and Africa*, p. 78.

# Appendix: Glimpses of Africa

# ALGERIA[1]

| Area: 919,595 sq. mi. (2,381,741 sq. km.) | Monetary Unit: dinar<br><br>Official Language: Arabic (83%)<br><br>Other Languages: Berber; French | Agriculture (wheat, barley, potatoes, tomatoes, melons, grapes, dates, olives, tobacco, livestock); fishing (sardines, anchovies, sprats, tuna, shellfish) | Major Export<br>—natural gas, petroleum, iron ore, vegetables, tobacco, phosphates, fruits, cork, hides | Places of Interest: Sahara Desert; Atlas mountains; Court of the Great Mosque (Algiers); Perregaux Bridge (in Constantine) | Number of physicians: 23,550 (1990); Number of public libraries: n.a.; Volumes (000): n.a.; Literacy rate: 49.6 % (1987); Daily newspapers: 5 (1992); Daily newspaper circulation (1/000 pop.): 38 (1992); Number of nondailies: 37 (1990); Number of TV sets per 1000 pop.: 79 (1993); Number of radios per 1000 pop.: 236 (1993); Museums: n.a.; Annual attendance ('000): n.a.; R&D expenditure: n.a. |
| Population: 29.8 million (1997 est.) | Main Ethnic Groups: Arabic-Berber (98%) | Manufacturing (carpets, textiles, chemicals, oil refining, plastics, construction material, olive oil, wine, processed tobacco, iron and steel, paper, electrical items) | Major Import<br>—machinery, textiles, sugar, cereal, iron and steel | Temperature: Extreme High, 107°F; Extreme Low, 32°F; Total annual rainfall, 30 inches | |
| Capital: Algiers (Alger) | | Mining (petroleum, gas, phosphates, iron ore, coal, lead, zinc, mercury) | | | |

1. Algeria has a beautiful Mediterranean climate around the coastal region. Inland, the *Sahré* (Arabic word for desert) is predominant. Although, only 3 percent of the landmass is arable, there are sizable quantities of oil and gas deposits in the Sahré. Algeria has been considered one of the wealthiest nations in Africa. Much of the wealth is tied to mineral wealth. However, in recent years, this wealth was adversely affected by sagging world prices for primary products.

# ANGOLA

| Area: 481, 354 sq. mi. (1,246,700 sq. km.) | Monetary Unit: New Kwanza (Kz); 100 Lwei per Kwanza<br><br>Official Language: Portuguese | Agriculture [1] (coffee, cassava, sugarcane, bananas, corn, vegetables, cotton, palm products, sisal, and livestock); fishing | Major Export<br>—petroleum, coffee, diamonds, sisal, fish, palm oil, salt, natural gas | Places of Interest: Government buildings in Luanda; Matala Dam on the Cunene River | Other Information: Number of physicians: n.a.; Number of public libraries: n.a.; Volumes (000): n.a.; Literacy rate: 41% (1986); Daily newspapers: 4 (1992); Daily newspaper circulation (1/000 pop.): 12 (1992); Number of nondailies: (1992); Number of TV sets per 1000 pop.: 7 (1993); Number of radios per 1000 pop.: 29 (1993); Museums: n.a.; Annual attendance ('000): n.a.; R&D expenditure: n.a. |
| Population: 10.6 million (1997 est.) | Main Languages: Umbundu, Kimbundi, and Kikongo<br>Main Ethnic Groups: Orimbunda; Mbanda; | Manufacturing (beverage, processed foods, refined sugar, fish meal, flour, beer, others: textiles, cement, glass, chemicals, and petroleum refining) | Major Import<br>—textiles, foodstuff, heavy machinery, iron and steel | Temperature: Extreme High, 98°F; Extreme Low, 58°F; Total annual rainfall, 12.7 inches | |
| Capital: Luanda | Bakongo or Kongo; Lunda-chokwe; Nganguela | Minerals (petroleum, diamonds, iron ore, copper, uranium, phosphates, and salt) | | | |

1. In Angola, about 2.8 percent of the land is arable of which less than one-sixth is under permanent cultivation. Near the town of Benguela, irrigation transformed dusty plains into green blankets of rice fields. Agricultural potential was acutely disaffected by protracted domestic skirmishes.

# BENIN

| Area: 43,484 sq. mi. (112,622 sq. km.) | Monetary Unit: CFA franc<br><br>Official language: French<br><br>Main Ethnic Groups: Fons or Dahomeans/ Adja (59%); Somba and Bariba (15%); Yoruba (9%) | Agriculture (Food crops: corn, cassava, sorghum, yams, millet, beans. Cash crops: cotton, palm kernels, peanuts, cacao. Livestock: sheep, cattle, goats); fishing;[1] forestry[2]<br><br>Manufacturing (Mostly processing of primary products that include palm oil, textiles, cement, sugar refining, wire and steel manufacturing) | Major Export —crude petroleum, cotton, palm products, cacao<br><br>Major Import —textiles, clothing, machinery | Places of Interest: Pendjari Game Reserve; national park of the "W"; Cotonou floating fishing village, Port Novo Ethnographic Museum; Temple of the serpents in Ouidah; Abomey Historical Museum<br><br>Temperature: Extreme High, 83°F; Extreme Low, 73°F; Total annual rainfall is 14.4 inches | Other Information: Number of physicians: n.a.; Number of public libraries: n.a.; Volumes (000): n.a.; Literacy rate: 29.3 % (1992); Daily newspapers: 1 (1992); Daily newspaper circulation (1/000 pop.): 2 (1992); Number of nondailies: 3 (1992); Number of TV sets per 1000 pop.: 6 (1993); Number of radios per 1000 pop.: 91 (1993); Museums: n.a.; Annual attendance (000): n.a.; R&D expenditure: n.a. |
| **Population:** 5.9 million (1997 est.)<br><br>**Capital:** Porto Novo | | | | | |

1. There are some commercial fishing activities (mainly shrimp). Most of the fish caught are from inland waters, and are for domestic consumption (41,000 metric tons). 2. Most wood harvested annually (about 5.2 million cu meters or 184 million cu feet) is for fuel.

# BOTSWANA

| Area: 231,805 sq. mi. (600,372 sq. km.) | Monetary Unit: Pula<br><br>Official Language: English<br><br>Other Languages: Setswana is predominant<br><br>Main Ethnic Groups: [1] Tswana (98 %) | Mining (diamonds, [2] copper, nickel, coal, cobalt, manganese, soda ash, asbestos, salt, gold)<br><br>Agriculture (cattle, sheep, goats, corn, sorghum); food processing; tourism | Major Export —meat, hides, diamonds, copper, nickel, manganese, coal<br><br>Major Import —grains, fuel, motor vehicles, textiles, clothing | Places of Interest: Kalahari Desert; Okavango swamps; Makarikari salt pans; game and bird sanctuaries; Gaborone gambling casino; Stone Age rock paintings on cliffs of Tsodilo Hills<br><br>Temperature: Extreme High, 90°F; Extreme Low, 41°F; Maximum average monthly rainfall, 4.2 inches | Other Information: Number of persons per physician: n.a.; Number of public libraries: n.a.; Volumes (000): n.a.; Literacy rate: 69.8% (1995); Daily newspapers: 1 (1992); Daily newspaper circulation (1/000 pop.): 29 (1992); Number of nondailies: 4 (1992); Number of TV sets per 1000 pop.: 17 (1993); Number of radios per 1000 pop.:119 (1993); Museums: n.a.; Annual attendance (000): n.a; R&D expenditure: n.a. |
| **Population:** 1.5 million (1997 est.)<br><br>**Capital:** Gaborone | | | | | |

1. The name Botswana is derived from the main ethnic group, Tswana, comprising eight tribes. 2. Botswana was noted as the world's largest supplier of gem-quality diamonds.

# BURKINA FASO

| Former Country Name: Upper Volta

Area: 105,869 sq. mi. (274,200 sq. km.)

Population: 10.9 million (1997 est.)

Capital: Ouagadougou | Monetary Unit: CFA franc

Official Language: French

Main Ethnic Groups: Voltaic (includes Mossi) and Mande; Others: Fulani, Lobi, Bobo, Sénoufo, Gourounsi, Bissa, Gourmantche | Agriculture (Cash crops: cotton; Food crops: sorghum, corn, pulses, rice, peanuts); fishing; forestry and lumbering

Manufacturing (processing agricultural products such as cotton, oils and fats, sugar, soap, footwear, motorcycles, motorscooters)

Mining [1] (manganese, gold, copper, iron ore, cassiterite or tin ore, phosphates) | Major Export —raw cotton, gold, livestock products

Major Import —foods, petroleum products, textiles, clothing, iron, steel, metal products, vehicles, electrical equipment, machinery | Places of Interest: Spiked mosque at Bobo Dioulasso; Ouagadougou

Temperature: Extreme High, 118°F; Extreme Low, 45°F; Total annual rainfall, 35.2 inches | Other Information: Number of physicians: n.a.; Number of public libraries: n.a.; Volumes (000): n.a.; Literacy rate: 19.2% (1995); Daily newspapers: 1 (1992); Daily newspaper circulation (1/000 pop.): 0.3 (1992); Number of nondailies: 10 (1990); Number of TV sets per 1000 pop.: 6 (1993); Number of radios per 1000 pop.: 27 (1993); Museums: n.a.; Annual attendance ('000): n.a.; R&D expenditure: n.a. |

1. Mining contributed less than 1 percent of GNP and about 20 percent of export earnings. Principal export items include manganese, phosphates, and gold. About 10 percent of the land is arable, and 37 percent is pasture. Most of the farmland is in the south, where the land is less susceptible to aridity and erosion. Principal wealth, deriving from agricultural activities, includes cattle, sheep, pigs, horses, and poultry.

# BURUNDI

| Area: 10,747 sq. mi. (27,834 sq. km.)

Population: 6.1 million (1997 est.)

Capital: Bujumbura [1] | Monetary Unit: Burundi franc (BurFr)

Official Languages: Kirundi and French

Other Languages: Swahili is predominant

Main Ethnic Groups: Hutu (85%); Tutsi (14%); Twa (1 %) | Mining (small amounts of gold and peat and reserves of uranium and nickel)

Agriculture (Food crops: sweet potatoes, cassava, bananas, beans, maize. Cash crops: coffee, cotton, tea. Livestock: 440,000 cattle, 932,000 goats, 370,000 sheep.); fishing

Manufacturing (textile, cement, insecticides) | Major Export —coffee, cotton, tea, hides

Major Import —clothing, textiles, motor vehicles, flour, petroleum products | Places of Interest: Lake Tangayika; Ruvuvu River, the source of the Nile; Bujumbura

Temperature: Extreme High, 88°F; Extreme Low, 64°F; Maximum average monthly rainfall is 4.9 inches | Other Information: Number of physicians: n.a.; Number of public libraries: n.a.; Volumes (000): n.a.; Literacy rate: 35.3 % (1995); Daily newspapers: 1 (1992); Daily newspaper circulation (1/000 pop.): 3 (1992); Number of nondailies: 3 (1992); Number of TV sets per 1000 pop.: 2 (1993); Number of radios per 1000 pop.: 62 (1993); Museums: n.a. Annual attendance ('000): n.a.; R&D expenditure: n.a. |

1. Commodities traded internationally, such as coffee, are transported by ferry service on Lake Tangayika, at Bujumbura, to Kigoma-Ujiji in Tanzania, where they continue by rail to Dar es Salaam (Tanzania) for export. There is a dense road network, but no railroads. Goods traded internationally are shipped via Congo (Zaire), Tanzania, and Zambia.The manufacturing industry is focused on processing agricultural and consumer goods, intended to decrease national reliance on imports. Retained cattle herd (as symbol) tends to be economically underutilized. The consequences of overgrazing and attendant soil erosion may not be overlooked.

# CAMEROON

| Area: 183,569 sq. mi. (475,442 sq. km.) | Monetary Unit: CFA franc<br><br>Official Languages: French and English | Mining (petroleum, limestone, tin ore. Other mineral resources: uranium, diamonds, thorium, manganese, copper, bauxite, iron ore)<br><br>Agriculture (Commercial crops: cocoa, coffee, tobacco, cotton, bananas, pineapples. Others: rubber, palm products, sugarcane. Subsistence crops: plantains, sweet potatoes, cassava, corn, millet); forestry: mahogany, teak, ebony; fishing[1]<br><br>Manufacturing (processing agricultural products, aluminum smelting, aluminum products, fertilizers, cement, textiles); food processing | Major Export —petroleum, coffee, cocoa, cotton, timber, prawns, aluminum<br><br>Major Import —machinery, textiles, transport equipment, consumer goods, alumina, chemicals | Places of Interest: Waza wildlife reserve; Bamiléké plateau; Bamoum country; beaches<br><br>Temperatures: Extreme High, 86°F; Extreme Low, 71°F; Maximum average monthly rainfall, 29.2 inches | Other Information: Number of persons per physician: 12,540 (1986); Number of nonspecialized libraries: 14 (1989); Volumes (000):50 (1989); Literacy rate: 63.4% (1995); Daily newspapers: 1 (1992); Daily newspaper circulation (/1,000 pop.): 4 (1992); Number of nondailies: 25 (1988); Number of TV sets per 1000 pop.: 25 (1993); Number of radios per 1000 pop.: 146 (1993); Museums annual attendance (millions): 4.641(pre-1986); Museum annual attendance (/1,000): 560; Performing arts annual attendance (/1,000 pop.: 5 (pre-1986); R&D expenditure: n.a. |
| Population: 14.7 million (1997 est.) | | | | | |
| Capital: Yaoundé | | | | | |

1. Fishing in Cameroon is dominated by freshwater subsistence activities. Deep-sea fishing has been increasing in recent years.

---

# CAPE VERDE

| Area: 1,750 sq. mi. (4,352 sq. km.) | Monetary Unit: Cape Verde Escudo<br><br>Official Language: Portuguese<br><br>Main Ethnic Groups: Creoles or Mestiços (71%); Blacks (28%) | Agriculture[1] (Cash crops: bananas, sugarcane; Staples: beans, corn; Others: sweet potatoes, coconuts, cassava, dates, vegetables); fishing; food processing; tourism | Major Export —tuna, lobsters, bananas, coffee, salt, peanuts<br><br>Major Import —petroleum, consumer goods, corn, rice, sugar | Places of Interest: White-sand beaches; chã das caleiras; black sand lake on Fogo; ruins at São Tiago<br><br>Temperature: Max. High, 85°F; Extreme Low, 67°F; Max. average monthly rainfall is 4.5 inches | Other Information: Number of physicians: n.a.; Number of public libraries: n.a.; Volumes (000): n.a.; Literacy rate: 71.6 % (1995); Daily newspapers: n.a.; Daily newspaper circulation (1/000 pop.): n.a.; Number of nondailies: 3 (1992); Number of TV sets per 1000 pop.: 3 (1993); Number of radios per 1000 pop.: 176 (1993); Museums: n.a.; Annual attendance (000): n.a.; Performing arts annual attendance (/1000 pop.: n.a.; R&D expenditure: n.a. |
| Population: 393,943 (1997 estimate) | | | | | |
| Capital: Praia | | | | | |

1. The fishing industry in Cape Verde was slated for modernization. Agriculture is limited by scarce arable land. Land suitable for agriculture is estimated around 9 percent. Sugarcane is used to manufacture rum.

# CENTRAL AFRICAN REPUBLIC

| Area: 240,535 sq. mi. (622,984 sq. km.) | Monetary Unit: CFA franc | Mining (diamonds; Deposits: uranium, iron ore, gold, lime, zinc, copper, tin) | Major Export [1] | Places of Interest: | Other Information: |
|---|---|---|---|---|---|
| | | | —diamonds, coffee, tobacco, timber, cotton, timber | Game reserves in the north; Bangui | Number of physicians: 113 (1990); Number of public libraries: n.a.; Volumes (000): n.a.; Literacy rate: 60% (1995); Daily newspapers: 1 (1992); Daily newspaper circulation (1/000 pop.): 1 (1992); Number of nondailies: 2 (1988); Number of TV sets per 1000 pop.: 5 (1993); Number of radios per 1000 pop.: 7 (1993); Museums: 7 (1987); Annual attendance (000): 8 (1987); Number of telephones (/1000 pop.): n.a.; R&D expenditure: n.a. |
| Population: 3.4 million (1997 est.) | Official Language: French  Other Languages: Sango (Sangho)  Main Ethnic Groups: Banda, Baya, Sara, Mboum, M'Baka, Mandjia | Agriculture (Cash crops: coffee, cotton; Basic foods: cassava, plantains, corn, peanuts, sweet potatoes, millet)  Manufacturing (cotton seed, peanuts, sesame oils, textiles, leather goods, tobacco products, soap, flour, bricks, paint); lumbering | Major Import —machinery, textiles, leather | Temperature: Extreme High, 101°F; Extreme Low, 57°F; Total annual rainfall, 60.8 inches | |
| Capital: Bangui | | | | | |

1. Export is hindered by difficulty of transporting goods to a seaport. There are no railroads. Ubangi river and the Chari and Logone river systems are important transportation arteries. There are about 23,738 kilometers of roads, of which 2 percent were paved. Some trade is done with Cameroon, Congo, and Gabon, all member nations of Customs and Economic Union of Central Africa. The chief trading partners are France and Belgium. Gem diamonds comprised 63 percent of export earnings. There are petroleum and uranium reserves, and other minerals include tungsten, tin, bauxite, gold, iron ore, and titanium.

---

# CHAD

| Area: 495,755 sq. mi. (1,284,000 sq. km.) | Monetary Unit: CFA franc | Mining (natron or sodium carbonate) | Major Export | Places of Interest: Lake Chad, Sahara Desert | Other Information: |
|---|---|---|---|---|---|
| | | | —cotton, livestock | | Number of physicians: n.a.; Number of public libraries: n.a.; Volumes (000): n.a.; Literacy rate: 48.1% (1995 est.); Daily newspapers: 1 (1992); Daily newspaper circulation (1/000 pop.): 0.4 (1992); Number of nondailies: 1 (1988); Number of TV sets per 1000 pop.: 1 (1993); Number of radios per 1000 pop.: 245 (1993); Museums: n.a.; Number of telephones (/1000 pop.): n.a.; R&D expenditure: n.a. |
| Population: 7.2 million (1997 est.) | Official Language: French  Other Languages: Arabic; Sara  Main Ethnic Groups: Arabs, Black Africans | Agriculture (cotton, rice, millet, potatoes, squash, beans, peanuts, and other vegetables) livestock  Manufacturing (textiles, processing of cotton, cottonseed oil, peanut oil, meatpacking, fresh, dried, and smoked fish) | Major Import —petroleum products, machinery, motor vehicles | Temperature: Extreme High, 114°F; Extreme Low, 47°F; Total annual rainfall, 29.3 inches | |
| Capital: N'Djaména | | | | | |

# COMOROS

| Area: 694 sq. mi. (1,797 sq. km.) | Monetary Unit: Comorian franc | Agriculture [1] (maize, cassava, rice, bananas, and vegetables; scent-bearing flowers and spices include ylang-ylang, vanilla, cloves, copra, a valuable oil derived from coconut); fishing; poultry | Major Export —vanilla, cocoa, coffee | Places of Interest: Karthala volcano (7,746 ft.) on Grande Comore | Other Information: Number of physicians: 57 (1990); Number of public libraries: n.a.; Volumes (000): n.a.; Literacy rate: 57.3 % (1990); Newspapers: 2; Daily newspaper circulation (1/000 pop.): n.a.; Number of nondailies: n.a.; Number of TV sets: 200 (1991); Number of radios per 1000 pop.: 129 (1991); Number of telephones: 3,000; R&D expenditure: n.a. |
|---|---|---|---|---|---|
| Population: 589,737 (1997est.) | Official Languages: French and Arabic | | Major Import —food, consumer goods | Temperature: Extreme High, 80°F; Extreme Low, 70°F; Total annual rainfall is 200 inches, on the slopes on Karthala | |
| Capital: Moroni, on Grande Comore | Main Ethnic Groups: mixed Arab-Malay-African ancestry | Manufacturing (artisan workshops engage in gold-smithing, boat building, clothing manufacture, scent processing) | | | |

1. Cash crops take up a significant portion of the best land. Food comprised 40 percent of import.

---

# REPUBLIC OF CONGO

| Proper Name: République du Congo (Republic of Congo) | Monetary Unit: CFA franc | Mineral resources (petroleum, gold, lead, zinc, copper, natural gas, iron ore) | Major Export [1] —Petroleum, forest products | Places of Interest: Mayombé mountains, Bateke Plateau, rain forest, Brazzaville | Other Information: Number of physicians: n.a.; Number of public libraries: n.a.; Volumes (000): n.a.; Literacy rate: 74.9 % (1995); Daily newspapers: 6 (1992); Daily newspaper circulation (1/000 pop.): 8 (1992); Number of nondailies: 3 (1992); Number of TV sets per 1000 pop.: 7 (1993); Number of radios per 1000 pop.: 115 (1993); Number of telephones: n.a.; R&D expenditure: n.a. |
|---|---|---|---|---|---|
| Area: 132,047 sq. mi. (342,000 sq. km.) | Official Language: French Other Languages: Lingala; Kikongo | Agriculture (Cassava, pineapples, plantains, bananas, maize, avocadoes; cash crops: sugar cane, palm kernels, cacao, coffee) | Major Import —machinery, vehicles | Temperature: Extreme High, 98° F; Extreme Low, 54° F; Total annual rainfall, 58 inches | |
| Population: 2.6 million (1997 est.) Capital: Brazzaville | Main Ethnic Groups: Bakongo (50%); Teke; MBoshi; Pygmies (12,000) | Manufacturing (textiles, cement, footwear, soap, petroleum refining, consumer goods, processing agricultural products including tobacco) | | | |

1. About 75 percent of export earnings derived from petroleum. Congo engages in substantial trade with members of Economic Union of Central Africa (Cameroon, Central African Republic, and Gabon). Congo also provides key port activities for Central African Republic, Chad, and Gabon. The Congo–Ocean railroad passes through swamps, twelve tunnels, and 172 bridges, and links Brazzaville to Pointe Noire (317 mi.) and a spur links to Gabon. Five percent of the road (about 7,500 mi.) is tarred. The Zaire river system is considered a major transportation network for Central Africa.

# DEMOCRATIC REPUBLIC OF CONGO

| Proper Name: | Monetary | Agriculture | Major | Places of | Other Information: |
|---|---|---|---|---|---|
| République Démocratique du Congo (Democratic Republic of The Congo)[1] | Unit: New Congo (issued 1997) | (coffee, palm kernels, cottonseeds and lint, rubber, plantains, cassava, maize, groundnuts, bananas, rice, yams, cattle, goats, sheep, chickens); forestry; fishing | Export —copper, coffee, diamonds, cobalt, crude petroleum | Interest: Boyoma falls, Point Kalina, Cristal mountains, Botanical and zoological gardens (in Kinshasa), Museum of native life | Number of persons per physician: 23,192 (1985); Number of public libraries: 11 (pre-1986); Volumes (000): 177 (pre-1986); Literacy rate: 77.3% (1995); Daily newspapers: 9 (1992); Daily newspaper circulation (1/000 pop.): 3 (1992); Number of nondailies: 77 (1990); Number of TV sets per 1000 pop.: 2 (1993); Number of radios per 1000 pop.: 97 (1993); Museums: n.a.; Number of telephones ('000): 38.8 (1985); R&D expenditure: n.a. |
| | Official Language: French (also used in business and social settings) | | | | |
| Aeaa: 905,568 sq. mi. (2,345,409 sq. km.) | | | Major Import —consumer goods, foodstuffs, mining and other machinery, transport equipment, fuels | Temperature: Extreme High, 97° F; Extreme Low, 58° F; Total annual rainfall, 53.3 inches | |
| | Other Languages: Swahili (eastern); Kikongo (around Kinshasa and coastal); Tshiluba (southern); Lingala (riverine) | Manufacturing (petroleum products, cement, sulfuric acid, refined metals, petroleum products, cement, tires, shoes, textiles, processed foods, beer, cigarettes) | | | |
| Population: 47.5 million (1997 est.) | | | | | |
| Capital: Kinshasa (Since 1960) | | Mining (copper, industrial diamonds, gem diamonds, uranium, tin, gold, silver, zinc, manganese, offshore crude oil) | | | |
| | Main Ethnic Groups: Bantu (80%) | | | | |

1. The hydroelectric potential is about 13 percent of the world total. Congo Kinshasa also has 6 percent of the world's total woodlands. Copper has been the leading source of export revenues (more than 50 percent). Zaire (informally called Congo Kinshasa and properly DROC) was determined as the largest producer of cobalt and industrial diamonds in the world. Cattle raising is mainly around regions with high elevations not susceptible to tsetse flies.

# DJIBOUTI

| Area: 8,958 sq. mi. (23,200 sq. km.) | Monetary | Leading | FOREIGN | Places of | Other Information: |
|---|---|---|---|---|---|
| | Unit: Djibouti franc | Industries: n.a. | TRADE (excluding transit shipment to and from Ethiopia) | Interest: Free-port shops in Djibouti, beach resorts, Lake Asal (512 ft. below sea level) | Number of physicians: 92 (1988); Number of public libraries: n.a.; Volumes (000): n.a.; Literacy rate: 46.2 % (1995 est.); Daily newspapers: n.a.; Daily newspaper circulation (1/000 pop.): Number of nondailies: 2 (1988); Number of TV sets per 1000 pop.: 45 (1993); Number of radios per 1000 pop.: 81 (1993); Number of telephones ('000 ): 14; R&D expenditure: n.a. |
| | Official Language: Arabic | | | | |
| Population: 434,116 (1997 est.) | | | Major Export —Coffee (from Ethiopia), hides, cattle | | |
| | Other Languages: Somali, Afar, French | | | Temperatures: Extreme High, 110°F; Extreme Low, 90°F; Annual average rainfall is 5–15 inches | |
| | | | Major Import —food, textiles, consumer goods | | |
| Capital: Djibouti | Main Ethnic Groups: Issa (Somali, 45%); Afar (45%) | | | | |

# EGYPT

| Area: 386,900 sq. mi. (1,002,066 sq. km.) | Monetary Unit: Pound (E£) Official Language: Arabic Other Language: English | Agriculture[1] (cotton, rice, tomatoes, wheat, maize, sugarcane, potatoes, oranges; livestock: cattle, buffalo, sheep, goats, poultry); fishing | Major Export —Petroleum, textile yarn, fabrics, vegetables and fruits, clothing, accessories | Places of Interest: Pyramids and Sphinx at Giza; Nile River; Abu Simbel temples; Aswan | Temperatures: Extreme High, 117°F; Extreme Low, 34°F; Total annual rainfall, 1.1 inches (8 inches along the Mediterranean coast) |
|---|---|---|---|---|---|
| Population: 64.8 million (1997est.) | Main Ethnic Groups: Egyptian, Copt, Bedouin, Nubian | Manufacturing (refined petroleum, textiles, chemicals, cotton yarn and fabrics, wool yarn, raw sugar, sulfuric acid, fertilizers, paper, cement, motor vehicle assembly, oil refining in several locations; Small-scale significant industry: tanning, brewing, pottery, perfumes, handicraft, cottonseed oil, flour, food processing, asphalt) | Major Import —machinery, transportation equipment, basic manufactures, especially iron and steel, paper, food products, chemicals | Dam; Alexandria; Luxor and Karnak temples; Valley of the Kings; Queen Hatshepsut Temple; Memmon Colossi at Luxor. In Cairo: Citadel; Mohammad Ali Mosque; Coptic churches | Other Information: Number of persons per physician: 576 (early 1990s); Number of nonspecialized libraries: 105 (1991); Volumes (000): 832; Literacy rate: 51.4% (1995 est.); Daily newspapers:16 (1992); Daily newspaper circulation (1/000 pop.): 41 (1992); Number of nondailies: 35 (1991) Number of TV sets per 1000 pop.: 113 (1993); Number of radios per 1000 pop.: 307 (1993); Museums: 54; Annual attendance ('000): 6,659 (1980); R&D expenditure: n.a. |
| Capital: Cairo | | Mining (iron ore, petroleum, uranium, phosphate rock, manganese, natural gas) | | | |

1. Less than one-tenth of the land is settled or cultivated. Egyptian farm yields (three crop yields per year) rank among the highest in the world. Egyptian yields in metric tons are approximately as follows: cotton (324,000), rice (3.9 million), tomatoes (4.7 million), wheat (4.6 million), maize (5.2 million), sugarcane (11.6 million), potatoes (1.8 million), oranges (1.7 million); livestock: cattle (3 million), buffalo (3 million), sheep (4.4 million), goats (4.8 million), poultry (44 million); fishing (298,000). Egypt is a leader in the production of long-staple (long-fiber) cotton lint. Most industrial activities are around Cairo and Alexandria. Petroleum is the main export earner.

# EQUATORIAL GUINEA

| Area: 10,831 sq. mi (28, 051 sq. km.) | Monetary Unit: CFA franc (CFA was adopted in January 1985) Official Language: Spanish Other Languages: Ethnic tongues | Agriculture (Main foodcropss: cassava, sweet potatoes, commercial crops: cocoa, coffee); Forestry and lumbering; food processing | Major Export —cocoa, coffee, tropical hardwood timber | Places of Interest: Beaches; tropical islets; art exhibits at the Cultural center in Malabo; art Museum in Bata | Other Information: Number of physicians: 99 (1990); Number of nonspecialized libraries: 1 (1993); Volumes (000): n.a.; Literacy rate: 78.5% (1995); Daily news papers:1 (1992); Daily Newspaper circulation (1/000 pop.):3 (1992); Number of nondailies: n.a.; Number of TV sets per 1000 pop.:10 (1993); Number of radios per 1000 pop.: 422 (1993); Number of telephones (/1000 pop.): n.a.; R&D expenditure: n.a. |
|---|---|---|---|---|---|
| Population: 442,516 (1997est.) | | | Major Import —Food, tobacco, textiles | | |
| Capital: Malabo (formerly called Santa Isabel) | Main Ethnic Groups: Fang (80 %); Bubis (15%) | Manufacturing: soap, cocoa, yucca, coffee, seafood Mineral Resources: petroleum | Temperature: Extreme High, 89°F; Extreme Low, 67°F; Total annual rainfall, 80 inches | | |

261

# ERITREA

| Area: 46, 482 sq mi. (121,320 sq km.) | Monetary Unit: birr (Br) | Agriculture | Major Export | Temperature: | Other Information: |
|---|---|---|---|---|---|
| Area: 46, 482 sq mi. (121,320 sq km.)<br><br>Population: 3.6 million (1997 est.)<br><br>Capital: Asmara (formerly Asmera) | Monetary Unit: birr (Br)<br><br>Languages: Afar, Amharic, Arabic, Italian, Tigre, and Kunama<br><br>Main Ethnic Groups: Tigrinya (50%); Tigre & Kunama (40%); Afar (4%); Saho of the Red Sea coast (3%); others (3%) | Agriculture (sorghum, lentils, vegetables, maize, cotton, tobacco, coffee, sisal (for rope making), livestock, fish)<br><br>Resources (gold, potash, zinc, copper, salt, and perhaps oil)<br><br>Manufacturing (food processing, beverages, clothing ) | Major Export —Livestock, hides, sorhu, textiles, gum arabic<br><br>Major Import —Processed goods, machinery, petroleum products | Temperature: Extreme High: n.a.°F; Extreme Low: n.a.°F; Total annual rainfall is up to 61 cm. | Other Information: Number of persons per physician: n.a.; Number of public libraries: n.a.; Volumes (000): n.a.; Literacy rate: n.a.; Daily newspapers: n.a; Daily newspaper circulation (1/000 pop.): n.a.; Number of nondailies: n.a.; Number of TV sets per 1000 pop.: n.a.; Number of radios per 1000 pop.: n.a.; Number of telephones (/1000 pop.): 40; R&D expenditure: n.a. |

# ETHIOPIA

| Area: 436,300 sq. mi. (1,130,000 sq. km.) | Monetary Unit: Birr | Agriculture | Major Export[2] | Places of Interest: | Other Information: |
|---|---|---|---|---|---|
| Area: 436,300 sq. mi. (1,130,000 sq. km.)<br><br>Population: 58.7 million (1997est.)<br><br>Capital: Addis Ababa | Monetary Unit: Birr<br><br>Official Languages: Amharic<br><br>Other Languages: Gallinya, Tigrinya, Arabic<br><br>Main Ethnic Groups: Galla (40%); Amhara (25%); Tigre (12%); Sidama (9%); Somali (2%) | Agriculture (coffee, cotton, sugarcane, cattle, pulses, oilseeds, cereal grains, fruits, vegetables); livestock<br><br>Manufacturing (textiles, cement, food processing)<br><br>Mining[1] (gold, platinum, iron, copper, petroleum, salt, potash) | Major Export[2] —coffee, cereal, oilseeds, hides and skins, gold<br><br>Major Import —vehicles, machinery, steel, textiles | Places of Interest: Lalibela churches carved out of solid rock; ruins at Axum (Āksum); Asmara; Harar; Addis Ababa<br><br>Temperature: Extreme High, 94° F; Extreme Low, 32° F; Total annual rainfall, 48.7 inches | Other Information: Number of physicians:1,466 (1988); Number of public libraries: n.a.; Volumes (000): n.a.; Literacy rate: 35.5% (1995 est.); Daily news papers: 4 (1992); Daily newspaper circulation (1/000 pop.): 1 (1992); Number of nondailies:4 (1988); Number of TV sets per 1000 pop.: 3 (1993); Number of radios per 1000 pop.: 197 (1993); Number of telephones ('000) 154.5 (1992); R&D expenditure: n.a. |

1. Since ancient times, inhabitants have mined outcroppings of iron, copper, zinc, and lead. Gold and platinum are mined in small quantities. 2. Coffee fetches about 62 percent of export earnings and engages about 25 percent of the labor force. The origin of C. Arabica has been traced to Ethiopia. From here it was introduced into Persia, Egypt, and Arab lands. Initially, and for a long time, the manipulation (that is roasting, grinding, brewing) and consumption of the berries of this shrublike trees were the province of priests and medicine men. By the fifteenth century, there were several coffee houses in Mecca. As coffee consumption spread to other parts of the world, the Arabs remained the sole source of supply, since most of the beans moved through the port of Mocha. As a beverage, coffee stimulates cerebral activity; the central nervous system is affected, blood flow is increased, the heart beats faster, the muscles are more responsive, and the kidneys work a little harder. Besides its capacity to sharpen alertness and readiness to face daily activities, consumption of this popular beverage may prevent kidney stones. However, after an intake of about five or six cups, this mild stimulant may render one restless and perhaps irritable. Decaffeinated coffee allows for the enjoyment of this drink without the effects of caffeine. Extracted caffeine is useful in the pharmaceutical industry, where it can be incorporated into pain remedies. The stimulating effects hasten substances such as aspirin and phenacetin into the bodily system. As a cardiac and respiratory stimulant, it is useful in fighting overdoses of depressants as alcohol.

# GABON

| Area: 103,347 sq. mi. (267,667 sq. km.) | Monetary Unit: CFA franc<br><br>Official Language: French<br><br>Main Ethnic Groups: Fang (32%); Eshira (19%); Adouma (12%); Okande (5%) | Agriculture (food crops: cassava, plantains, sugarcane, yams, and taro; cash crops: coffee, cocoa, palm oil, peanuts, pepper);[1] forestry;[2] fishing<br><br>Mineral Resources: (petroleum, high grade manganese ore, uranium, iron ore, lead and silver ores, zinc, copper, diamonds, gold) | Major Export —petroleum,[3] wood, manganese, uranium<br><br>Major Import —petroleum products, iron and steel, trucks, agricultural machinery, clothing | Places of Interest: Dense hardwood forest, Crystal Mountains, Mt. Iboundji, national parks, Libreville<br><br>Temperature: Extreme High, 89°F; Extreme Low, 68°F; Total annual rainfall, 50–80 inches. Total annual precipitation reaches 120 inches near the coast | Other Information: Number of physicians: 448 (1989); Number of public libraries: n.a.; Volumes (000): n.a.; Literacy rate: 63.2 % (1995 est.); Daily newspapers: 1; Daily newspaper circulation (1/000 pop.): 16 (1992); Number of nondailies:1 (1988); Number of TV sets per 1000 pop.: 38 (1993); Number of radios per 1000 pop.: 147 (1993); Number of telephones (/1000 pop.): n.a.; R&D expenditure: n.a. |
|---|---|---|---|---|---|
| Population: 1.2 million (1997est.)<br><br>Capital: Libreville | | | | | |

1. Pepper is mostly grown for export. 2. Gabon is the world's largest producer of *Okoume*, a softwood used for plywood. 3. The level of economic activities may be sensitive to vibrations in world petroleum prices.

# GAMBIA

| Area: 4,361 sq. mi. (11,295 sq. km.) | Monetary Unit: Dalasi<br><br>Official Language: English<br><br>Main Ethnic Groups: Mandingo (42%); Fulani (18%); Wolof (16%); Serahuli (7%); Jola (10%) | Agriculture [1] (peanuts, rice, millet, cattle, sheep, goats, bees, vegetables, fruits); tourism; fishing<br><br>Manufacturing (peanut processing, beverage, clothing, footwear, handicraft) | Major Export [2] —peanuts, hides, fish, beeswax<br><br>Major Import —textiles, food, machinery, hardware, consumer goods | Places of Interest: Flora and fauna along Gambia river; Banjul; beaches<br><br>Temperature: Extreme High, 110°F; Extreme Low, 60°F; Total annual rainfall, 30–55 inches | Other Information: Number of persons per physician: n.a.; Number of public libraries: 2 (1992); Volumes (000): 94; Literacy rate: 39.6 % (1995); Daily newspapers: 2 (1992); Daily newspaper circulation (1/000 pop.): 2 (1992); Number of nondailies: 6 (1990); Number of TV sets per 1000 pop.: n.a.; Number of radios per 1000 pop.:162 (1993); Number of telephones (/1000 pop.): n.a.; R&D expenditure: n.a. |
|---|---|---|---|---|---|
| Population: 1.3 million (1997est.)<br><br>Capital: Banjul (formerly Bathurst) | | | | | |

1. The economy depends on peanuts, cultivated mainly for export. In an effort to diversify agriculture, the government introduced cotton, sisal, and citrus fruits. 2. In the early 1990s, export (including reexport) were in the vicinity of $174 million, while import were around $133 million.

# GHANA

| Area: 92,100 sq. mi. (238,537 sq. km.) Population: 17.5 million (1995 est.) Capital: Accra | Monetary unit: Cedi Official Languages: English Others:[1] Ethnic languages and French Main Ethnic Groups: Fanti, Ashanti, Nzima, Ahanta, Ga, Moshi-Dagomba, Gonja. | Agriculture (main crops: cacao, coffee, palm kernels, shea nuts, palm oil, corn, plantain, peanuts, yams; others: oil nuts, cotton, tobacco, rice, dura, millet, cow peas, citrus fruits); livestock; forestry; fishing  Manufacturing (large-scale: beer, cigarettes, soft drinks, edible oils, nails, oxygen, acetylene, sheet aluminum; others: textiles, footwear, iron and steel, sugar, flour, glass); forestry and lumbering; fishing  Mining (gold, diamond, manganese, bauxite) | Major Export —gold, cocoa, aluminum, petroleum, tuna, wood, diamonds, manganese  Major Import —auto parts, food, medicines, machinery, automobiles | Temperature: Extreme High, 100°F; Extreme Low, 59°F; Total annual rainfall, 28.5 inches | Other Information: Number of physicians: 700 (1990 estimate); Number of public libraries: n.a.; Volumes (000): n.a.; Literacy rate: 64.5 % (1995 est.); Daily newspapers: 4 (1992); Daily newspaper circulation (1/000 pop.): 18 (1992); Number of nondailies: 87 (1992); Number of TV sets per 1000 pop.: 16 (1993); Number of radios per 1000 pop.: 269 (1993); Museums: n. a.; Number of telephones ('000): 81.3 (1992); R&D expenditure: n.a. |

1. According to *Jeune Afrique Plus* (May 13, 1997, p. 38) gold had superseded cacao (an important export crop) and fetching as much as 35 percent of total export earnings. Ashanti Goldfields operates eleven mines. The labor force is 10,000, including 900 expatriates. Sixty percent of the labor is employed directly in mining activities, 15 percent in security and processing, and the rest in administrative functions. In the early 1990s, there were approximately 1.4 million cattle, 2.6 million goats, 2.5 million sheep, and 12 million chickens. Offshore waters provide a useful fish resource. Manufacturing in Accra includes vehicle and appliance assembly, petroleum refining, manufacturing foodstuff, textiles, plastics, pharmaceuticals, and wood products. The principal industry in Kumasi (a commercial and transportation center and rich cacao producing area) is food processing. It is the site of the University of Science and Technology (founded 1951), and the Research Institute for Ghana Academy of Sciences. There are two teacher-training colleges in Tamale (a road hub and trading center) and a technical institute.

# GUINEA

| Area: 94,926 sq. mi. (245,857 sq. km.) Population: 7.4 million (1997est.) Capital: Conakry | Monetary Unit: Guinean franc Official Language: French Other Languages: Fulani, Malinké, Susu, Kissi, Basari, Loma, Koniagi, Kpelle Main Ethnic Groups: Fulani, Malinké, Susu | Agriculture and Manufacturing (rice, coffee, cotton, cassava, maize, groundnuts, millet, sorghum, yams, pineapples, sweet potatoes, plantains, palm oil, cattle, fish, sheep/goats)  Mining[1] (Bauxite, alumina, diamonds, gold, platinum, uranium) | Major Export —alumina, pineapples, bananas, palm kernels  Major Import —Machinery, metals, food, transport equipment | Places of Interest: Mount Nimba National Reserve; national museum  Temperature: Extreme High, 96°F; Extreme Low, 63°F; Total annual rainfall, 169 inches | Other Information: Number of physicians: 773 (1981); Number of Higher Education libraries: 6 (1988); Volumes (000): n.a.; Literacy rate: 34.9 (1995); Daily newspapers: n.a.; Daily newspaper circulation (1/000 pop.): n.a.; Number of nondailies: 1 (1990); Number of TV sets per 1000 pop.: 8 (1993); Number of radios per 1000 pop.: 43 (1993); Number of telephones ('000): 18.7 (1991); R&D expenditure: n.a. |

1. Has a significant proportion of the world's bauxite mines and known reserves of high-grade bauxite ore.

# GUINEA-BISSAU

| | | | | | |
|---|---|---|---|---|---|
| **Area**[1]: 13,948 sq. mi. (36,125 sq. km.)<br><br>**Population:** 1.2 million (1997est.)<br><br>**Capital:** Bissau | **Monetary Unit:** peso<br><br>**Official Language:** Portuguese<br><br>**Other language:** Crioulo<br><br>**Main Ethnic Groups:** Fulani, Malink, Pepel, Balante, Mandyako, Cape Verdians | **Agriculture** (food crops: rice, plantain, cassava, maize; commercial crops: cashew nuts, palm products, cotton, peanuts, cattle); fishing; forestry | **Major Export** —cashew nuts, cotton, peanuts, palm products, fish, wood<br><br>**Major Import** —Petroleum products, food, consumer goods | **Places of Interest:** Bissau, islands of the Bijagos archipelago; Boloma, capital until 1948<br><br>**Temperatures:** Extreme High, 109° F; Extreme Low, 73° F; Total annual rainfall, hovers between 80 and 120 inches | **Other Information:** Number of physicians: 112 (1988); Number of public libraries: n.a.; Volumes (000): n.a.; Literacy rate: 54.9% (1995); Daily newspapers: 1 (1992); Daily newspaper circulation (1/000 pop.): 6 (1992); Number of nondailies: 1 (1988); Number of TV sets per 1000 pop.: n.a.; Number of radios per 1000 pop.: 40 (1993); Number of telephones ('000): 11.9 (1992); R&D expenditure: n.a. |

1. Area includes about sixty offshore islands. Cashew nuts fetch as much as 50 percent of export income.

---

# IVORY COAST

| | | | | | |
|---|---|---|---|---|---|
| **Area:** 124, 504 sq. mi. (322,463 sq. km.)<br><br>**Population:** 15 million (1997 est.)<br><br>**Capital**[1] Yamoussoukro | **Monetary Unitt:** CFA franc<br><br>**Official Language:** French<br><br>**Other Languages:** African languages<br><br>**Main Ethnic Groups:** Akan-speaking people, Kru, Malinke, Mande; a significant Lebanese community | **Agriculture** (cash crops: coffee, cocoa, cotton, pineapples; crops for domestic consumption: yams, cassava, plantains, rice, maize); forestry<br><br>**Manufacturing** (automobile and bicycles plants, textiles, shoes, plywood, cement, steel containers, aluminum-sheet products, consumer products)<br><br>**Mining** (petroleum, gold, diamonds, iron ore) | **Major Export** —cocoa, coffee, petroleum, timber, palm oil, cotton, pineapples, sugar<br><br>**Major Import** —cotton fabrics, automobiles, tractors | **Places of Interest:** Abidjan plateau; Ebrié lagoon; Banco National Park; Grand Bassam; Dabou; Bingerville; Beach resorts<br><br>**Temperatures:** Extreme High, 104°F; Extreme Low, 72°F; Total annual rainfall ranges from 80 to 120 inches | **Other Information:** Number of physicians: 1,020 (1990); Number of public libraries: n.a.; Volumes (000): n.a.; Literacy rate: 64% (1995); Daily Newspapers:1 (1992); Daily newspaper circulation (1/000 pop.): 7 (1992); Number of nondailies: 1 (1992); Number of TV sets per 1000 pop.: 60 (1993); Number of radios per 1000 pop.:143 (1993); Number of telephones ('000): 206.6 (1992); R&D expenditure: n.a. |

1. *Abidjan* (pop: 2.7 million) is defacto capital, largest city, and center for cultural and commercial life. A village in 1904, it has grown into a fairly modern city with parks, broad boulevards, and elegant residential areas such as Cocody, east of the CBD. The urban area has several converging peninsulas and islands are connected by bridges. Industrial activities include vehicle and radio assembly, textiles, metal products, clothing, foodstuff, plastic, rubber, and petroleum products. There are several technical colleges and libraries. It is the terminus of a regional railroad and is linked to the Atlantic Ocean by a lagoon and a canal. Much of West Africa's import/export trade is processed here. Tourism is important. *Bouaké* is a road-hub city. Gold and manganese deposits are in the vicinity. There are sisal-cordage and cotton mills. There is also a school of forestry, government livestock, veterinary, meteorological stations, and a cotton textile research institute. *Yamoussoukro* (the nation's Capital) is the site of the Higher Institute of Technical Training. It is also the site of Our Lady of Peace of Yamoussoukro Basilica, the largest Christian church in the world dedicated in 1990, by Pope John Paul II.

# KENYA

| Area: 224,961 sq. mi. (582,646 sq. km.) | Monetary Unit: Kenyan shilling (Ksh)  Official Language: Swahili Others widely spoken: Kikuyu, Luo and English  Main Ethnic Groups: Kikuyu; Luhya; Kamba, Luo. There is a small, but significant, group of Europeans, Asians, and Arabs | Agriculture[1] (coffee, tea, cattle, sugarcane, dairy products, poultry, pyrethrum (flower used for insecticide), sisal, corn, fruits, vegetables)  Manufacturing (processing farm products, oil refining, cement, small-scale consumer goods)  Mining (copper, soda ash, salt, fluorspar, gold, garnets, and limestone); tourism | Major Export —coffee, tea, sugar, sisal, petroleum products, canned pineapples, hides and skins, soda ash, pyrethrum  Major Import —crude petroleum, industrial machinery, iron and steel, agricultural implements, vehicles, fertilizers, pharmaceuticals | Places of Interest: Rift Valley; Treetops Hotel; national museum in Nairobi; Nairobi; Tsavo National Park; Marsabit National Reserve  Temperature: Extreme High, 87°F; Extreme Low, 41°F; Total annual rainfall, 41.8 inches | Other Information: Number of physicians: 1,063 (1990); Number of public libraries: n.a.; Volumes (000): n.a ; Literacy rate: 78.1% (1995); Daily newspapers: 5 (1992); Daily newspaper circulation (1/000 pop.): 14 (1992); Number of nondailies: 8 (1988); Number of TV sets per 1000 pop.: 11 (1993); Number of radios per 1000 pop.: 87 (1993); Museums: n.a.; Number of telephones ('000): 420.6 (1992); R&D expenditure: n.a. |
|---|---|---|---|---|---|
| Population: 28.8 million (1997est.)  Capital: Nairobi | | | | | |

1. Agricultural system is highly diversified, although about 4 percent of the land is arable. Almost every basic food crop is produced. Manufacturing is more significant here than in several other African nations. The city of *Mombasa*, founded in the eighth century, is the site of Mombasa Polytechnic. There are extensive docks, and shipyards. There are also sugar and petroleum refineries. Textiles and processed foods are important in *Nakuru*, where development was facilitated when it was linked by railroad to the coast at Mombasa. The seaport at Mombasa serves Uganda and northeastern Tanzania. The role of mining is minuscule. There are few developed mineral resources. Large deposits of lead and silver have been discovered.

# LESOTHO

| Area: 11,720 sq. mi (30,355 sq. km); Area is surrounded by Rep. of South Africa | Monetary Unit: loti  Official Languages: English and Sesotho  Main Ethnic Group: Basotho | Agriculture[1] (corn, wheat, sorghum, fruits and vegetables); Livestock: cattle, sheep, goats  Manufacturing (carpets, candles, fertilizer, pottery, jewelry)  Mining (diamonds) | Major Export —wool, mohair, wheat, peas, beans, hides, baskets  Major Import —Building materials, clothing, food, medicine, petroleum, machinery, vehicles, consumer goods | Places of Interest: Drakensberg Mts.; Bushmen cave and cliff paintings in Cave Sandstone area; National Park  Temperature: Extreme High, 70°F; Extreme Low, 45°F; Total annual rainfall, 3.6 inches | Other Information: Number of physicians: 74 (1990); Number of public libraries: n.a.; Volumes (000): n.a.; Literacy rate: 71.3% (1995); Daily newspapers:2 (1992); Daily newspaper circulation (1/000 pop.): 7 (1992); Number of nondailies:3 (1988); Number of TV sets per 1000 pop.: 7 (1993); Number of radios per 1000 pop.: 32 (1993); Number of telephones ('000): 22.4 (1992); R&D expenditure: n.a. |
|---|---|---|---|---|---|
| Population: 2 million (1997estimate)  Capital: Maseru | | | | | |

1. Ten percent of the land area is arable. Four out of every ten adult males (Basothos) worked in South Africa. There are several small airports. Most of the trade is with South Africa.

# LIBERIA

| Area: 43,000 sq. mi. (111,369 sq. km.)<br><br>Population: 2.6 million (1997est.)<br><br>Capital: Monrovia | Monetary Unit: Dollar (L$)<br><br>Official Languages: English<br><br>Other Languages: Include ethnic tongues of Mande, West Atlantic or Kwa<br><br>Main Ethnic Groups: Kpelle, Bassa, Gio, Kru; American-Liberians comprise five percent | Agriculture[1] (foods consumed locally: rice, cassava; others: fruits, vegetables, sweet potatoes; Cash crops: coffee, cocoa, rubber, palm kernels); fishing; forestry<br><br>Mining (iron, ore, diamonds, gold); shipping; forestry & lumbering; tourism<br><br>Manufacturing (plastics, paint, soap, paper products, textiles, building materials, fertilizer, tobacco products) | Major Export —Iron ore, rubber, diamonds, timber, coffee, cocoa, palm kernels<br><br>Major Import —mineral fuels, machinery, metals, foodstuffs, textiles | Places of Interest: Atlantic coast beaches and resorts; Lake Piso; Bong mine; LAMCO mining site; Providence Island; Monrovia<br><br>Temperature: Extreme High, 97°F; Extreme Low, 62°F; Total annual rainfall, 174.9 inches | Other Information: Number of physicians: n.a.; Number of public libraries: n.a.; Volumes (000): n.a.; Literacy rate: 38.3% (1995); Daily newspapers: 8 (1992); Daily newspaper circulation (1/000 pop.): 13 (1992); Number of nondailies: 8 (1988); Number of TV sets per 1000 pop.: 19 (1993); Number of radios per 1000 pop.: 227 (1993); Number of telephones ('000 ): 15 (1991); R&D Expenditure: n.a. |

1. Civil strife disrupted agriculture. Expansion efforts in deepwater fishing resulted in catches such as sole, lobster, crayfish, shrimp, and crabs. Liberia engages about 70 percent of the population in agriculture and forestry, although 50 percent of the population lives in towns and cities. Educational resources were scarce and tended to jeopardize educational access for many children. Monrovia is the site of College of Technology (founded in 1978), Cuttington University (founded in 1889), and University of Liberia (founded in 1862). Significant industrial activities have included food, refined petroleum, chemicals, pharmaceuticals, and building materials. Rubber fetched 25% of export income. Significant portions of import were earmarked for transshipment to neighboring countries. Although Liberia has a local currency, the U.S. currency has been utilized since 1943.

# LIBYAN ARAB JAMAHIRIYA

| Area: 679, 362 sq. mi. (1,759,540 sq. km.)<br><br>Population: 5.6 million (1997est.)<br><br>Capital: Tripoli | Monetary Unit: Libyan dinar (LD)<br><br>Official Language: Arabic<br><br>Other Languages: Berber<br><br>Main Ethnic Groups: Arab, Berber | Agriculture (cattle, sheep, goats, peanuts, olives, grapes, dates, barley, wheat, potatoes, tomatoes)<br><br>Manufacturing (petroleum products, textiles, tobacco products)<br><br>Mining (Petroleum) | Major Export —petroleum, refined petroleum products, natural gas<br><br>Major Import —machinery, transport equipment, food, manufactured goods | Places of Interest: Marble arch of Marcus Aurelius in Tripoli; 2d Century amphitheater at Sabratha; ancient city of Leptis; Cyrene archaeological site<br><br>Temperature: Extreme High, 114°F; Extreme Low, 33°F; Total annual rainfall, 15.1 inches | Other Information: Number of physicians: 4,749 (1991); Number of public libraries: n.a.; Volumes (000): n.a.; Literacy rate: 76.2%; Daily newspapers: 4 (1992); Daily newspaper circulation (1/000 pop.):15; Number of non-dailies: n.a.; Number of TV sets per 1000 pop.: 100 (1993); Number of radios(/1000 pop.): 226 (1993); Number of telephones ('000): 800 (1985); R&D expenditure: n.a. |

# MADAGASCAR

| Area: 226,658 sq. mi. (587,041 sq. km.) | Monetary Unit: Malagasy franc (Malfranc)

Official Languages: Merina and French

Other Languages: Ethnic tongues

Main Ethnic Groups: Merina (Hova), 27%; Betsimisaraka, 15%; Betsileo, 12%; Tsimihety (7%); Sakalave (6%); Antaisaka (5%) | Agriculture [1] (coffee, cotton, cloves, vanilla, tobacco, rice, sugar, sisal, cattle, corn, beans, potatoes, cassava); livestock; fishing

Mining (chromite, graphite, mica, unrefined salt)

Manufacturing (Food processing: meatpacking, brewing, sugar refining; Others: petroleum refining; motor vehicle assembly, textiles, electrical equipment, glass, printed material, tobacco) | Major Export (by value) —vanilla (19%); shrimps and lobsters (15%); coffee (12%), clove and clove oil (4%); others: cotton, fabrics, refined petroleum, chromium

Major Import —crude petroleum, chemical products, machinery, electrical equipment, rice, textiles, vehicles and vehicle parts | Places of Interest: Antananarivo market places

Temperature: Extreme High, 95°F; Extreme Low, 34°F; Total annual rainfall, 53.4 inches | Other Information: Number of physicians: 1,392 (1990); Number of public libraries: n.a.; Volumes (000): n.a.; Literacy rate: 80% (est. early 1990s); Daily newspapers: 7 (1992); Daily newspaper circulation (1/000 pop.): 4 (1992); Number of nondailies: 37 (1992); Number of TV sets per 1000 pop.: 20 (1993); Number of radios per 1000 pop.: 192 (1993); Number of telephones ('000): 67.7 (1992); R&D expenditure: n.a. |
|---|---|---|---|---|
| Population: 14.1 million (1997est.) | | | | |
| Capital: Antananarivo (formerly Tananarive) | | | | |

1. In Madagascar, the mountainous landscape disallowed extensive use of land for farming. About 5 percent of the land area is cultivated. Rice, the chief staple, takes up about 50 percent of cropland. Fishing (shrimps and lobsters) increasingly constitutes an important source of export revenues. Countries may fish in the exclusive maritime area in exchange for compensation. There are mineral resources that have yet to be exploited. Chromite is the most valuable mineral. *Antsiranana* (pop. about 55,000) has one of the finest harbors in the world. Here, industry includes shipbuilding, meat processing, tuna fishing, salt extraction, and oxygen manufacturing. *Toliara* (pop. about 61,000) is the site of a large agricultural experimental station and a technical school.

---

# MALAWI

| Area: 45,747 sq. mi. (118,484 sq. km.) | Monetary Unit: Kwacha; 100 tambala = one Malawian kwacha

Official Languages: Chichewa and English

Main Ethnic Groups: Chewa, Nyanja, Tumbuko, Ngoni, Yao | Agriculture (cotton, peanuts, coffee, tea, tobacco, maize, cattle, sorghum, sugar, millet); fishing

Manufacturing (processed food, chemical products, textiles, beverages)

Mining (marble, limestone) | Major Export —tobacco, tea, sugar, peanuts, coffee, peanuts, wood products

Major Import —food, petroleum products, semimanufact-ures, consumer goods, transportation equipment | Places of Interest: Lake Malawi, Great Rift Valley, public gardens at Lilongwe, Blantyre-Limbe tea estates

Temperature: Extreme High, 86°F; Extreme Low, 45°F; Total annual rainfall, 35–50 inches | Other Information: Number physicians:186 (1989); Number of public libraries:[1] 1 (1992); Volumes (000): 237; Literacy rate: 56.4% (1995); Daily newspapers: 1 (1992); Daily newspaper circulation (1/000 pop.): 2 (1992); Number of nondailies: 4 (1992); Number of TV sets per 1000 pop.: n.a.; Number of radios (/ 1000) pop.: 226 (1993); Number of telephones (/1000 pop.): 56.8 (1992); R&D expenditure: 0.2% GNP; Country rank: 46 (1980) |
|---|---|---|---|---|
| Population: 9.6 million (1997est.) | | | | |
| Capital: Lilongwe | | | | |

1. The public library has seven service points, according to UNESCO, *1996 Statistical Yearbook*.

# MALI

| Area:464, 874 sq. mi. (1,204,02 sq. km.) | Monetary Unit:[1] CFA franc (reintroduced in 1984 to replace Mali franc)<br><br>Official Languages: French<br><br>Other Language: Bambara<br><br>Main Ethnic Groups: Mande (50%); Peul (17%); Voltaic (12%); Songai (6%); Tuareg and Moors (5%) | Agriculture[2] (cattle, cotton, rice, peanuts, sorghum, millet, goats, sheep)<br><br>Manufacturing (textiles, cigarettes, matches, baskets, food processing)<br><br>Mining (phosphate rock, salt, uranium, gold, diamonds) | Major Export —cotton, processed foodstuff, mangoes, peanuts, fish, livestock<br><br>Major Import —textiles, food, machinery, motor vehicles, petroleum products | Places of Interest: Cliff-dwelling Dogon tribes near Sangha; Bamako; Timbuktu; Lake Débo<br><br>Temperature: Extreme High, 117°F; Extreme Low, 47°F; Total annual rainfall, 44.1 inches | Other Information: Number of physicians: 435 (1988); Number of public libraries: n.a.; Volumes (000): n.a.; Literacy rate: 18.8% (1988); Daily newspapers: 2 (1992); Daily newspaper circulation (1/000 pop.): 4 (1992); Number of nondailies: 7; Number of TV sets per 1000 pop.: 1 (1993); Number of radios per 1000 pop.: 44 (1993); Number of telephones ('000): 14.6 (1990); R&D expenditure: n.a. |
|---|---|---|---|---|---|
| Population: 10 million (1997est.)<br><br>Capital: Bamako | | | | | |

1. CFA franc means Communauté Financière Africaine Franc (also CFAF). 2. The River Niger is a lifeline and provides surplus fish that is exported. The riverine soil is very rich. Agriculture was adversely affected by drought in the mid-1980s. Livestock are very significant. In the early 1980s, there were 5.4 million cattle, 6.7 million sheep, 6.7 million goats, and 22 million poultry birds. *Bamako*, the administrative capital, is also the center of commerce, finance, manufacturing, and transportation. Here, industrial activities have included the production of motor vehicles, processed foods, printed material, farm machinery, metal goods, batteries, and building materials. Colleges include administration, engineering, medicine, dentistry, teachers training, and many research institutes. There are mineral reserves.

# MAURITANIA

| Area: [1] 397,955 sq. mi. (1,030,700 sq. km.) | Monetary Unit: Ouguiya<br><br>Official Languages: Hasaniya Arabic & Wolof<br><br>Other Languages: Pular, Soninke, French<br><br>Main Ethnic Groups: Arab-Berber; Black Africans, in the Senegal Valley | Agriculture (cattle, sheep, goats, horses, millet, dates, rice, pulses, yams, maize); fishing<br><br>Manufacturing (fish processing, foodstuffs)<br><br>Mineral Resources (iron ore, chrome, gold, lead, lithium, phosphate, tin, uranium, zinc) | Major Export —iron ore, fish and fish products<br><br>Major Import —food products, consumer goods, petroleum products, capital goods | Temperature: Extreme High, 115°F; Extreme Low, 44°F; Total annual rainfall, 6.2 inches | Other Information: Number of physicians: 127 (1990); Number of public libraries: n.a.; Volumes (000): n.a.; Literacy rate: 37.7 (1995 est.); Daily newspapers: 1; Daily newspaper circulation (1/000 pop.): 0.5; Number of nondailies: 25 (1992); Number of TV sets per 1000 pop.: 23 (1993); Number of radios per 1000 pop.: 147 (1993); Number of telephones ('000): 7.8 (1992); R&D expenditure: n.a. |
|---|---|---|---|---|---|
| Population: 2.4 million (1997est.)<br><br>Capital: Nouakchott | | | | | |

1. Some of the richest fishing grounds in the world are found within Mauritania's exclusive economic zone. Fishing tends to rival iron ore in foreign exchange earnings contribution. Mining contributed about 80 percent of export earnings. However, weak global demand, high production costs, and decreasing productivity, have in the past devitalized some gains.

# MAURITIUS

| Area: 790 sq. mi. (2,045 sq. km.) | Monetary Unit: Mauritian rupee (MauRs)<br><br>Official Language: English<br><br>Main Ethnic Groups: Indian Asian descent (67%); Creole (28%); Chinese descent (3%) | Agriculture[1] (sugarcane, rice, tea, tobacco, aloe, potatoes, onions, vegetables, livestock, poultry)<br><br>Manufacturing (refined sugar, sugar by-products; fertilizers; beverages; electronic components; leather goods; textiles); food processing; fishing | Major Export —textiles, sugar, molasses, light manufactures<br><br>Major Import —rice, wheat, cotton, fabrics, petroleum products, fertilizers, machinery, consumer goods | Places of Interest: Pamplemousses Garden; Nicolière Reservoire; Plaine Champagne; Black River gorges; Grand Bassin Lake; Morne Brabant; Mahebourg Naval Museum; Blue Bay Beach; Belle Mare<br><br>Temperature: Extreme High, 95°F; Extreme Low, 50°F; Total annual rainfall, 50.6 inches | Other Information: Number of physicians: 850 (1990 estimate); Number of public libraries: n.a.; Volumes (000): n.a.; Literacy rate: 79.9% (1990); Daily newspapers: 6 (1992); Daily newspaper circulation (1/000 pop.): 74 (1992); Number of nondailies: 25 (1992); Number of TV sets per 1000 pop.: 23 (1993); Number of radios per 1000 pop.: 147 (1993); Museums: 5; Museums attendance (000): 600 (1990); Number of telephones ('000): 100.2 (1992); R&D expenditure: n.a. |
| Population: 1.2 million (1997est.)<br><br>Capital: Port-Louis | | | | | |

1. Over half the land has been useful in cultivating sugarcane. Textiles flourished in the 1980s.

---

# MOROCCO

| Area: 275,117 sq. mi. (712,550 sq. km.) | Monetary Unit: Dirham<br><br>Official languages: Arabic<br><br>Other Languages: Berber tongues, French, Spanish<br><br>Main Ethnic Groups: Arab, Berber, Black (There are about 100,000 Europeans, mostly French, and some 12,000 Jews) | Agriculture[1] (Poultry, sheep, goats, cattle, tomatoes, melons, dates, olives, raisins, barley, wheat, corn, potatoes, grapes, vegetables, mandarin oranges, tangerines, oranges, figs); Lumbering; Fishing (pilchard, tuna, mackerel, anchovies, shellfish, etc.)<br><br>Mining (phosphate rock, coal, manganese ore, silver, iron ore, lead, zinc, tin, petroleum)<br><br>Manufacturing (food processing, wine, paint, cement, construction materials, chemicals, textiles, footwear); Artisans produce fabrics, leather goods, rugs, carpets, and woodwork | Major Export —phosphates and phosphoric acid, fruits, tomatoes, preserved fish, manganese<br><br>Major Import —industrial equipment, fuels, food products, manufactured goods | Places of Interest: Tombs of the Merinides princes and 1,000-year-old university at Fez; Bahia Palace and tombs of the Saadians in Marrakech; the Casbah in Tangier; Mohammad V Mausoleum in Rabat; Casablanca<br><br>Temperature: Extreme High, 118°F; Extreme Low, 32°F; Total annual rainfall, 19.8 inches | Other Information: Number of physicians: 4,924 (1992 estimate); Literacy rate: 30.3 % (1982); Daily newspapers: 14 (1992); Daily newspaper circulation (1/000 pop.): 13 (1992); Number of nondailies: 5 (1988) Number of TV sets per 1000 pop.: 79 (1993); Number of radios per 1000 pop.: 219 (1993); Number of telephones (/1000 pop.): 714.2 (1992) R&D expenditure: n.a. |
| Population: 30.4 million (est.1995)<br><br>Capital: Rabat | | | | | |

1. In the early 1990s, in Morocco, there were approximately 17 million sheep, 5.5 million goats, and 3.3 million heads of cattle.

# MOZAMBIQUE

| Area: 308,641sq. mi. (799,380 sq. km.) | Monetary Unit: Metical | Agriculture[1] (Cash crops: cashew nuts, cotton, sugarcane, copra, tea; Basic foods: | Major Export —Shrimp, cashew, cotton, sugar, copra | Places of Interest: Maputo; Cabora Bassa dam on Zambezi River | Other Information: Number of physicians: 388 (1990 estimate); |
|---|---|---|---|---|---|
| | Official Language: Portuguese | cassava, corn, wheat, potatoes, peanuts, and beans); fishing (lobsters, shrimps) | | | Number of public libraries: n.a.; Volumes (000): n.a.; |
| | Other Languages: Swahili and ethnic tongues | | Major Import —machinery, electrical equipment, vehicles, iron and steel | Temperature: Extreme High, 114°F; Extreme Low, 45°F; | Literacy rate: 40.1% (1995 est.); Daily newspapers: 2 (1992); Daily |
| Population: 30.4 million (1997est.) | Main Ethnic Group(s): Makua-Lomwe, from the north (about 47%); Tsonga, from the south (about 23%); Malawi; Shona; Yao | Manufacturing (machinery; electrical equipment, motor vehicles, iron and steel; processing agricultural products, cotton ginning, clothing, and textiles)  Mining (mineral resources include coal, salt, diamonds, asbestos, bauxite, and small amounts of copper, gold, manganese, titanium, and natural gas, in the early 1990s) | | Total annual rainfall, 29.9 inches | newspaper circulation (1/000 pop.): 5 (1992); Number of nondailies: 5 (1992); Number of TV sets per 1000 pop.: 4 (1993); Number of radios per 1000 pop.: 48 (1993); Number of telephones ('000): 74.6 (1992); R&D expenditure: n.a. |
| Capital: Maputo | | | | | |

1. About 80 percent of the labor force is employed in agriculture, and 4 percent of the land is cultivated. Agriculture was adversely affected by civil war that kept farmers off the land, scarcity of labor, wartime disruptions of transportation systems, and drought. Coal is a significant. Coal, gold, asbestos, and uranium are mined at the city of Tete (pop. 112,200 est.). Here the cathedral dates from 1563. Shrimp and lobster fetched 50 percent of export revenues, in the early 1990s.

# NAMIBIA

| Area: 318, 252 sq. mi. (824, 268 sq. km.) | Monetary Unit:(new) Namibian dollar (N$); old currency: S. Af. rand | Agriculture (corn, millet, sorghum, livestock); fishing: (mackerel, pilchard; hakes, anchovies)[1] | Major Export —diamonds, copper, lead, zinc, vanadium, fish, cattle, karakul fur pelts | Temperature: Extreme High, 74°F; Extreme Low, 57°F; | Other Information: Number of physicians: 321 (1991); Number of public libraries: n.a.; |
|---|---|---|---|---|---|
| | Official Language: Afrikaans, English, German | Manufacturing (processed foods, textiles, clothing); ore smelting | Major Import —Construction materials, fertilizers, grain, food products, consumer products | Total annual rainfall, 22 inches inland (2 inches around the coast) | Volumes (000): n.a. Literacy rate: n.a.; Daily newspapers: 4 (1992); Daily newspaper circulation (1/000 pop.): 147 (1992); Number of |
| Population: 1.7 million (1997est.) | Other Languages: Ethnic tongues  Main Ethnic Groups: | Mining (diamonds, copper, lead, silver, zinc, vanadium, uranium, tungsten, and salt) | | | nondailies: 18 (1992); Number of TV sets per 1000 pop.: 23 (1993); Number of radios per 1000 pop.: 140 (1993); Number of |
| Capital: Windhoek | Blacks (85%); Whites (6.6%); Mixed (7.4%) | | | | telephones ('000 ): 93 (1992); R&D expenditure: n.a. |

1. Overfishing in the 1970s adversely affected the rich marine life that thrives in the cold Benguela currents on the coast. Namibia has some of the richest diamond fields in the world and supplies about one-third of the total output. Almost all diamonds recovered are of gem quality. Mining contributed 32 percent of GDP of about $2.2 billion, in the early 1990s.

271

# NIGER

| Area: 489,191 sq. mi. (1,267,000 sq. km.) Population: 9.4 million (1997est.) Capital: Niamey | Monetary Unit: CFA franc Official Language:[1] French Other Languages: Ethnic tongues Main Ethnic Groups: Hausa (50%); Djerma (23%); Fulani (15%); Tuareg (10%) | Agriculture (cowpeas, millet, sorghum, manioc, rice, pulses, cotton, cattle, sorghum); Fishing (Lake Chad and Niger River) Manufacturing (food processing, construction) Mining (uranium, tin, coal, iron ore, copper, and phosphates) | Major Export —Uranium, cowpeas, cotton, meat, hides Major Import —petroleum, machinery, food, consumer good | Places of Interest: Lake Chad; Native villages Temperatures: Extreme High, 108°F; Extreme Low, 58°F; Total annual rainfall, 21.8 inches | Other Information: Number of physicians: 142 (1990); Number of public libraries: n.a.; Volumes (000): n.a.; Literacy rate: 13.6% (1995); Daily newspapers: 1 (1992); Daily newspaper circulation (1/000 pop.): 1 (1992); Number of nondailies: 1 (1988); Number of TV sets per 1000 pop.: 5 (1993); Number of radios per 1000 pop.: 61 (1993); Number of telephones ('000 ): 14 (1992); R&D expenditure: n.a. |
|---|---|---|---|---|---|

1. Ninety percent of Nigeriens live near the southern border. The Niger River begins in Guinea and flows through Mali, Niger, and Nigeria. Most of the river's length is navigable, making it potentially a useful option in transportation of freight and passengers in an industrializing environment. The combined population in these countries is about 130 million.

# NIGERIA

| Area:[1] 356,669 sq. mi. (923,768 sq. km.) Population: 107.2 million (1997est.) Capital: Abuja | Monetary Unit: Naira Official Language: English Other Languages: Hausa, Yoruba, Ibo, Fulani, Kanuri, Tiv, and other ethnic tongues Main Ethnic Groups: Hausa (21%); Yoruba (20%); Ibo (17%); Fulani (8%) | Agriculture (yams, cassava, sorghum, rice, millet, maize, sugarcane, taro, plantains, peanuts, palm oil, peppers, tomatoes, cotton, cocoa beans, rubber; livestock); fishing; forestry Manufacturing (processed foods, brewed beverages, refined petroleum, iron and steel, textiles, cigarettes, footwear, vehicles assembly, pharmaceuticals, paper, cement, traditional crafts) Mining (petroleum, natural gas, tin and columbite in the Jos Plateau, black coal (Onitsha region), iron ore, limestone, lead, and zinc) | Major Export —crude petroleum, cocoa beans, rubber, palm oil, urea and ammonia, fish, shrimp, textiles, cotton Major Import —machinery, transportation equipment, manufactured goods (mostly iron and steel, textiles, paper products), chemicals, food products | Places of Interest: The museum of Nigerian antiquities in Lagos; Muslim City of Kano; City of Ibadan; Benin City Temperature: Extreme High, 104°F; Extreme Low, 60°F; Total annual rainfall, 72.3 inches | Other Information: Number of physicians: 17,960 (1990 estimate); Number of public libraries: 12 with 76 service points (1992); Volumes (000): 611 (1992) Literacy rate: 57.1% (1995 estimate); Daily newspapers: 26 (1992); Daily newspaper circulation (1/000 pop.): 18 (1992); Number of nondailies: 11 (1990 estimate) Number of persons per TV set: 38 (1993); Number of persons per radio: 196 (1993); Number of telephones ('000): 457.6 (1992); R&D expenditure: n.a. |
|---|---|---|---|---|---|

1. Nigeria is a mosaic of more than 250 ethnic groups. Others include Edo, Ijaw, Ibibio, Nupe, Tiv, and Kanuri. Livestock included approximately the following: cattle, 15.7 million; goats, 24 million; sheep, 13.5 million; pigs, 5.3 million; poultry, 135 million. In the early 1990s, petroleum contributed 98 percent of export earnings and comprised 80 percent of government revenues.

# RWANDA

| Area: 10,169 sq. mi. (26,338 sq. km.)

Population: 7.7 million (1997 est.)

Capital: Kigali | Monetary Unit: Rwanda franc (Rwfr)

Official Languages: French and Kinyarwanda

Main Ethnic Groups: Hutu (90%); Tutsi (9%); Twa (1%) | Agriculture (coffee, cattle, pyrethrum, tea, beans, corn, sorghum, potatoes, cassava, dry peas)

Manufacturing (light consumer goods)

Mining (tin ore (cassiterite), tungsten ore (wolframite) | Major Export —Arabica coffee, tin, tea

Major Import —Motor vehicles, fuels, textiles, machinery | Temperature: Extreme High, 81°F; Extreme Low, 54°F; Total annual rainfall, 46.5 inches | Other Information: Number of physicians: 275 (1990 estimate); Number of public libraries: n.a.; Volumes (000): n.a.; Literacy rate: 60.5% (1995 estimate); Daily newspapers: 1 (1992); Daily newspaper circulation (1/000 pop.): 0.1 (1992); Number of nondailies: 15 (1990); Number of TV sets per 1000 pop.: n.a.; Number of radios per 1000 pop.: 66 (1993); Number of telephones ('000): 21.2 (1992); R&D expenditure: n.a. |
|---|---|---|---|---|---|

# SENEGAL

| Area: 75,750 sq. mi. (196,192 sq. km.)

Population: 9.4 million (1997 est.)

Capital: Dakar | Monetary Unit: CFA franc

Official Languages: French

Other Languages: English and ethnic tongues

Main Ethnic Groups: Wolof (44%); Fulani and Toucouleur (24%); Serer (15%); Diola (5%); Malinke (4%) | Agriculture[1] (sugarcane, millet, sorghum, peanuts, rice, maize, livestock, vegetables, and fruits); forestry; fishing; tourism

Manufacturing (peanut oil, refined sugar, canned tuna, flour, cement, fertilizers, textiles, chemicals, tobacco)

Mining[2] (phosphates) | Major Export —basic manufactures, peanuts, petroleum products, phosphates, fish;

Major Import —crude petroleum, consumer goods, grain, machinery, transport equipment | Places of Interest: Fine beaches; national parks; wild game reserve; Gorée Island

Temperature: Extreme High, 109°F; Extreme Low, 53°F; Total annual rainfall, 21.3 inches | Other Information: Number of physicians: 407 (1990); Number of public libraries: n.a.; Volumes (000): n.a.; Literacy rate: 33.1% (1995 est.); Daily newspapers: 1 (1992); Daily newspaper circulation (1/000 pop.): 6 (1992); Number of nondailies: 10 (1988); Number of TV sets per 1000 pop.: 37 (1993); Number of radios per 1000 pop.: 116 (1993); Number of telephones ('000): 55 (1987); R&D expenditure: n.a. |
|---|---|---|---|---|---|

1. Senegal is among the world's leading producers of peanuts. However, in recent years this contribution declined from 29 percent of export earnings in the 1980s to 12 percent in the 1990s. Efforts were made (such as increasing output of rice and tomatoes) to diversify agriculture in order to attain self-sufficiency.
2. Although Senegal has a good road network, reserves of iron ore were yet to be exploited mainly because of remote locations.

# SIERRA LEONE

| Area [1]: 27, 699 sq. mi. (71,740 sq. km) | Monetary Unit: Leone<br><br>Official Language: English<br><br>Other Languages: Pidgin English (Krio); Ethnic tongues<br><br>Main Ethnic Groups: Mende (30%) in the south; Temne (30%) in the north; Others (40%) | Agriculture (cassava, millet, sorghum, peanuts, ginger, palm oil, palm kernel, coffee, cocoa, kola nuts, piassava or palm fibers); livestock<br><br>Manufacturing (processing palm kernels, rice, light industries that include furniture, textiles, cigarettes, cement)<br><br>Mining (rutile, diamonds, iron ore, bauxite, small quantities of gold and platinum) | Major Export —rutile, diamonds, iron ore, palm kernels<br><br>Major Import —Mineral fuels, machinery, vehicles, foodstuff | Temperature: Extreme High, 87°F; Extreme Low, 73°F; Total annual rainfall, 160–180 inches | Other Information: Number of physicians: 300 (1990 estimate); Number of public libraries: n.a.; Literacy rate: 31.4% (1995); Daily News papers: 1 (1992); Daily newspaper circulation (1/000 pop.): 2 (1992); Number of nondailies: 6 (1990 estimate); Number of TV sets per 1000 pop.: 11 (1993); Number of radios per 1000 pop.: 233 (1993); Number of telephones ('000 ): 56.2.; R&D expenditure: n.a. |
|---|---|---|---|---|---|
| Population: 4.8 million (1997est.) | | | | | |
| Capital: Free Town | | | | | |

1. A preponderance of the population is dispersed in 29,000 rural settlements. Minerals are the principal export, fetching 70 percent of export revenue, while agricultural commodities (coffee, cocoa, etc.) provide 30 percent of export income. Sierra Leone has been known to be one of the world's leading producers of diamonds. In recent years annual output of diamonds plummeted, however, from about 2 million carats per annum in the 1970s to around 312, 000 carats in the early 1990s. This decline in production has been attributed to exhausted supplies from some fields, relentless smuggling activities, and pockets of civil strife. Diamonds have been replaced by rutile (a titanium ore) as leading export.

# SOMALIA

| Area: 246,201 sq. mi. (637,657 sq. km.) | Monetary Unit: Shilling (SoSh)<br><br>Official Languages: Somali and Arabic<br><br>Other Languages: English and Italian<br><br>Main Ethnic Groups: Somali (Arab, Persian, and Cushitic descent) | Agriculture [1] (cattle, sheep, goats, camels, sugarcane, bananas, sorghum, corn, beans, peanuts, cassava, watermelons, mangoes); fishing<br><br>Manufacturing (food processing, leather products, textiles, low-tech assembly, furniture assembly, chemicals, metal products, beverages)<br><br>Mining (tin) | Major Export —livestock, bananas, hides and skins<br><br>Major Import —food, rice, cotton, fabrics, petroleum products, machinery, transport equipment, paper products, beverages, tea | Places of Interest: Lac Badana National Park; Indian Ocean resorts; Bajuni Islands; wildlife reserves<br><br>Temperature: Extreme High, 97°F; Extreme Low, 59°F; Total annual rainfall, 16.9 inches | Other Information: Number of doctors: 450 (1990 estimate); Number of public libraries: n.a.; Literacy rate: n.a.; Daily newspapers: 1 (1992); Daily newspaper circulation (1/000 pop.): 1 (1992); Number of nondailies: 4 (1990 estimate); Number of TV sets (/000 pop.): 13 (1993); Number of radios (/000 pop.): 41 (1993); R&D expenditure: n.a. |
|---|---|---|---|---|---|
| Population: 6.5 million (1997est.) | | | | | |
| Capital: Mogadishu | | | | | |

1. Most people are employed in the livestock industry. Agriculture in general has been in a recovery phase in recent years. Somalia has mineral resources that have yet to be exploited. Frankincense and myrrh are among the major export items.

# SOUTH AFRICA

| Area: 471,445 sq. mi. (1,221,037 sq. km.) | Monetary Unit: rand (R) | Agriculture (Sugarcane, grapes, maize, wheat, apples, oranges, sheep, cattle, goats, pigs, chicken); fishing | Major Export —gold, metal products, food, diamond, wool | Places of Interest: Kruger National Park; Kalahari Gemsbok National Park; Oudtshoorn caves; | Other Information: Number of physicians: 25,967 (1993); Number of public libraries: 671 (1990 estimate); |
|---|---|---|---|---|---|
| | Official Languages:[1] Afrikaans, English, isi Ndebele, Sesotho sa Leboa, isi Sesotho, isi Swati, Xitsonga, Setswana, Tshivenda, isi Xhosa, isi Zulu | Manufacturing (chemical products, petroleum and coal products, processed foods and beverages, transportation equipment, iron and steel, metal products, machinery, paper, and textiles) | Major Import —automobiles, petroleum, machinery, manufactured goods | Johannesburg gold mines; Kimberly diamond mines; Zululand game reserves; Sudwala caves and adjoining Dinosaur Park | Volumes (000): 15,863 (1990 estimate); Literacy rate: 89.8 (1995); Daily newspapers: 20 (1992); Daily newspaper circulation (1/000 pop.): 32 (1992); Number of nondailies: 10 |
| Population: 42.3 million (1997 est.) | | | | | |
| | Main Ethnic Groups: Black Africans (76.1%); Whites (12.8%); Coloreds (8.5%); Indians (2.6%) | Mining (Chief contributors: gold, diamonds and coal; Others: copper, nickel, platinum, asbestos, chromium, fluorite, phosphates, vanadium, tin, titanium, antimony, manganese and iron ores, uranium) | | Temperatures: Extreme high, 103°F; Extreme low, 28°F; Total annual rainfall, 20 inches | (1991); Number of TV sets per 1000 pop.: 101 (1993); Number of radios per 1000 pop.: 314 (1993); Number of telephones('000): 5,222.1 (1992) |
| Capital: Pretoria (administrative) | | | | | |

1. Afrikaans is the first language of all Afrikaners and many coloreds. It is a variant of the Dutch language. English is the primary language of many Whites. It is also spoken by Blacks and Asians. South Africa is endowed with almost every essential commodity pertaining to industry. In the fishing industry, a preponderance of the catch is processed into fish meal.

# SUDAN

| Area: 967,500 sq. mi. (2,505 sq. km) | Monetary Unit: pound (Sud£) | Agriculture (livestock, cotton, sorghum, wheat, sesame, peanuts, castor beans, fruits, vegetables) | Major Exports —cotton, sesame, peanuts | Places of Interest: Archaeological ruins along the Nile; Nubian Desert; machinery, petroleum, chemicals | Other Information: Number physicians: 2,095 (1992); Number of public libraries: n.a.; Literacy rate: 46.1% (1995 est.); |
|---|---|---|---|---|---|
| | Official Language: Arabic | Manufacturing (textiles, handicraft) | Major Imports —fertilizers, sugar, wheat, flour, machinery, petroleum, chemicals | | Daily News papers: 5 (1992); Daily newspaper circulation (1/000 pop.): 24 (1992); Number of nondailies: 10 (1990 estimate); Number of TV sets per 1000 pop.: 80 (1993); Number of radios per 1000 pop.: 257 (1993); Number of telephones ('000 ): 91.9 (1992) R&D expenditure: n.a. |
| Population: 32.6 million (1997 est.) | Main Ethnic Groups: Arabs (70%); Blacks (23%) | Mining n. a. | | Temperature: Extreme High, 118° F; Extreme Low, 41° F; Total annual rainfall, 6.2 inches | |
| Capital: Khartoum | | | | | |

# TANZANIA

| Area:[1] 364,900 sq. mi. (945,087 sq. km.) | Monetary Unit: Shilling (Tshs)<br><br>Official Language: Swahili<br><br>Other Languages: English widely spoken<br><br>Main Ethnic Groups: Blacks | Agriculture (sisal and cloves, cotton, coffee, tobacco, tea, cashews, peppers, livestock); fishing; forestry (camphor, podo, African mahogany)<br><br>Manufacturing (processing raw materials, including coffee, grain, sisal, kapok, and jute; auto assembling, cement, and tannery)<br><br>Mining (Diamonds, gold, coal, tin, salt, lead, iron ore, tungsten, pyrochlore, kaolin, phosphates) | Major Export —cotton, coffee, tobacco, cloves, tea, sisal, diamonds<br><br>Major Import —petroleum, machinery, transportation equipment, iron and steel | Places of Interest: Mount Kilimanjaro; Ngorongoro crater; nine national parks; five game reserves; Olduvai Gorge; Amboni caves; Pemba and Mafia islands<br><br>Temperature: Extreme High, 96°F; Extreme Low, 59°F; Total annual rainfall, 41.9 inches | Other Information: Number of physicians: 1,200 (1990 estimate); Number of public libraries: n.a.; Volumes (000): n.a.; Literacy rate: 67.8 % (1995 est.); Daily newspapers: 3 (1992); Daily newspaper circulation (1/000 pop.): 8 (1992); Number of nondailies: 9 (1988); Number of TV sets per 1000 pop.: 2 (1993); Number of radios per 1000 pop.: 26 (1993); Number of Telephones ('000): 150.7 (1992); R&D expenditure: n.a. |
| Population: 29.5 million (1997est.) | | | | | |
| Capital: Dodoma (official); Dar es Salaam (actual) | | | | | |

1. Tanzania is the world's largest producer of sisal and cloves (mostly from Zanzibar and Pemba islands). Diamonds are very important.

# TOGO

| Area: 21,295 sq. mi. (56,785 sq. km.) | Monetary Unit: CFA franc<br><br>Official Language: French<br><br>Other Languages: tribal tongues<br><br>Main Ethnic Groups: Ewe; Kabre (kabye); Gurma | Agriculture[1] (coffee, cotton, cocoa, palm kernels, corn, millet, manioc (yams), cassava, corn, millet, sorghum)<br><br>Manufacturing (cement, flour, palm oil, cotton, textiles, beverages, soap)<br><br>Mining (phosphates, limestone and marble) | Major Export —phosphates, cotton, cocoa, coffee, cement, karite nuts, palm kernels<br><br>Major Import — food and food products, textiles, machinery, electrical equipment, construction materials, transportation equipment | Places of Interest: Togo Mountains; Native villages; Lomé<br><br>Temperature: Extreme High, 94°F; Extreme Low, 58°F; Total annual rainfall, 31 inches | Other Information: Number of persons per physician: 319 (1991); Number of public libraries: 1 (1989); Volumes (000): 63 (1989); Literacy rate: 51.7% (1995); Daily newspapers: 2 (1992); Daily newspaper circulation (1/000 pop.): 3 (1992); Number of nondailies: 1 (1988); Number of TV sets per 1000 pop.: 7 (1993); Number of radios per 1000 pop.: 211 (1993); Number of telephones ('000): 30.7 (1992); R&D expenditure: n.a. |
| Population: 4.7 million (1997est.) | | | | | |
| Capital: Lomé | | | | | |

1. Togo is self-sufficient in basic foods. A preponderance of the population (about 78 percent) is engaged in agriculture. The land under cultivation is about 26 percent. Among the Ewe people, property is held in common. Inheritance of landed property is usually through maternal uncles. Movable property goes to a paternal uncle. Descent is patrilinear. Hunting is monopolized by a caste. The Ewe people, also found in Ghana and Benin, tend to be organized in judicial matters. Togo is a leading world producer of phosphates. Mineral income is the main source of foreign exchange (about 50 percent).

# TUNISIA

| Area: 63,170 sq. mi. (163,610 sq. km.)<br><br>Population: 9.2 million (1997est.)<br><br>Capital: Tunis | Monetary Unit: dinar<br><br>Official Language: Arabic<br><br>Other Languages: French<br><br>Main Ethnic Groups: Arab-Berber (98%) | Agriculture (wheat, barleys, tomatoes, vegetables, melons, grapes, oranges, olives, dates, sheep, goats, cattle, camels, poultry); fishing (sardines, pilchards, tuna, whitefish)<br><br>Manufacturing (petroleum refining, sugar refining, phosphate processing, cement, sulfuric acid, textiles, forest products, food processing)<br><br>Mining (petroleum, natural gas, phosphate rock, iron ore, lead, zinc) | Major Export — petroleum, clothing, fertilizer, olive oil, phosphoric acid, wine, citrus fruits, iron and steel, lead<br><br>Major Import —machinery, petroleum products, iron and steel, electrical machinery, food | Places of Interest: fine beaches; archaeolo-gical sites; ancient city of Carthage<br><br>Temperature: Extreme High, 118°F; Extreme Low, 30°F; Total annual rainfall, 16.5 inches | Other Information: Number of physicians: 4,482 (1991); Number of public libraries: 250 (1992); Volumes (000): 2,493; Literacy rate: 66.7% (1995); Daily newspapers: 9 (1992); Daily newspaper circulation (1/000 pop.): 49 (1992); Number of nondailies: 9 (1988); Number of TV sets per 1000 pop.: 81 (1993); Number of radios per 1000 pop.: 198 (1993); Number of Telephones ('000): 464.8 (1992); R&D expenditure: n.a. |

# UGANDA

| Area: 93,104 sq. mi. (241, 139 sq. km.)<br><br>Population: 20.6 million (1997 est.)<br><br>Capital: Kampala | Monetary Unit: Ugandan shilling (USh)<br><br>Official Language: English<br><br>Other Languages: Luganda and Swahili (widely used)<br><br>Main Ethnic Groups: Baganda (17%); Karamojong (12%); Basogo (8%); Iteso (8%); Langi (6%); Rwanda (6%); Bagisu (5%); Acholi (4%); Lugbara (4%); Bunyoro(3%); Batobo (3%); European, Asian, and Arab descent (1%); others (23%) | Agriculture (cotton, coffee, tea, bananas, plantains, sweet potatoes, sugarcane, maize, millet, beans, sorghum); livestock (cattle, sheep, goats, poultry)<br><br>Mineral and Other Resources (gold, copper, tin, tungsten, phosphate rock, limestone, other minerals (reserves), and ample water for hydroelectricity)<br><br>Manufacturing (food, beer, soft drinks, matches, shirts, footwear, construction materials) | Major Export —coffee (97%), cotton, tea<br><br>Import —Petroleum products, machinery, cotton piece goods, metals, transportation equipment, food[1] | Temperature: Extreme High, 97°F; Extreme Low, 53°F; Total annual rainfall, 46.2 inches | Other Information: Number of physicians: 710 (1990 estimate); Number of public libraries: 1; Volumes (000): 82; Literacy rate: 61.8% (1995); Daily newspapers: 6 (1992); Daily newspaper circulation (1/000 pop.): 4 (1992); Number of nondailies: 5 (1990); Number of persons per TV receiver: 44 (1989); Number of radios per 1000 pop.: 107 (1993); Number of telephones ('000): 55.3 (1992); R&D expenditure: n.a. |

1. Principal trading partners: Kenya (25 percent), United Kingdom (14 percent), Italy (13 percent).

# ZAMBIA

| Area: 290,586 sq. mi. (752,614 sq. km.) | Monetary Unit: Kwacha | Agriculture (corn, sugarcane, cassava, sunflower seeds, peanuts, sweet potatoes, tobacco, beef and dairy cattle) | Major Export[2] —copper, cobalt, zinc | Places of Interest: Victoria Falls; Lake Tanganyika; Zambezi River; national parks; Livingstone Museum | Other Information: Number of physicians: 713 (1990); Number of public libraries: n.a.; Volumes (000): n.a.; Literacy rate: 78.2 % (1995); Daily newspapers: 2 (1992); Daily newspaper circulation (1/000 pop.): 8 (1992); Number of nondailies: 1 (1988); Number of TV sets per 1000 pop.: 27 (1993); Number of radios per 1000 pop.: 82 (1993); Number of telephones ('000): 112.6 (1992); R&D expenditure: n.a. |
|---|---|---|---|---|---|
| | Official Language: English | | Major Import —Machinery, transport equipment, mineral fuels and lubricants, chemicals, food and basic manufactured goods | Temperature: Extreme High, 100°F; Extreme Low, 39°F; Total annual rainfall, 32.9 inches | |
| Population: 9.3 million (1997est.) | Other Languages: Bemba, Lozi, Luvale, Tonga, Nyanja | Manufacturing[1] (copper smelting and refining, metals, vehicle assembly, petroleum refining, food processing, fertilizers, explosives, textiles) | | | |
| Capital: Lusaka | Main Ethnic Groups: Bemba, Nyanja, Tonga | Mining (copper, zinc, cobalt, lead, diamond) | | | |

1. Manufacturing employed 16.7 percent of the workforce and contributed 33.3 percent of the GDP in the early 1990s. 2. The economy is coupled to export earnings deriving from copper (93 percent in the early 1990s). This relationship with commodity prices while practical and useful in a synergy, may, in the converse, express a downside economic overexposure.

# ZIMBABWE

| Area : 150,873 sq. mi. (390,759 sq. km.) | Monetary Unit: Zimbabwe dollar (Z$) | Agriculture (tobacco; cotton, maize, sugarcane, coffee, cassava, wheat, sorghum, millet, peanuts, potatoes, beans, oranges, cattle, goats, sheep, hogs, poultry; dairying); forestry; fishing | Major Export —tobacco, ferrochrome, gold, nickel, cotton, steel, and textiles | Places of Interest: Victoria Falls; Wankie National Park; Inyanga and Vumba mountains; Mana Pools; Harare; Bulawayo; Zimbabwe ruins | Other Information: Number of physicians: 1,320 (1990); Number of public libraries: 76 (1989); Volumes (000): 1,038 (1989); Literacy rate: 85.1 % (1995); Daily newspapers: 2 (1992); Daily newspaper circulation (1/000 pop.): 19 (1992); Number of nondailies: 16 (1990); Number of TV sets per 1000 pop.: 27 (1993); Number of radios per 1000 pop.: 86 (1993); Museums: 11 (1990) Annual attendance ('000): 100; Number of telephones ('000): 306.2 (1992); R&D expenditure: n.a. |
|---|---|---|---|---|---|
| | Official Language: English | | Major Import —machinery, transport equipment, basic manufactures, chemicals, fuels | Temperature: Extreme High, 95°F; Extreme Low, 32°F; Total annual rainfall, 32.6 inches | |
| Population: 11.5 million (1997est.) | Other Languages: Shona, Ndebele | | | | |
| | Main Ethnic Groups: Bantu: Shona (80%); Ndebele (19%); European/Asian Descent (1%) | Manufacturing (food products, ferrochrome, steel, nickel, chemicals, textiles) | | | |
| Capital: Harare (formerly Salisbury) | | Mining (Leading minerals:[1] Chromium, copper, asbestos, nickel, gold, silver, and iron, coal, platinum, kyanite, zinc, lead; cobalt, tin, emeralds, diamonds) | | | |

1. Zimbabwe has been ranked as the world's fifth largest supplier of chromium ore, and is one of the leaders in the production of gold, nickel, and asbestos. Tobacco accounted for approximately 25% of export earnings.

# Selected Bibliography

Adjibolosoo, Senyo B.-S. K., ed. *Human Factor Engineering and the Political Economy of African Development*. Westport, CT: Greenwood, 1996.

Agonefer, Mulugeta, ed. *Africa in Contemporary International Disorder: Crisis and Possibilities*. Lanham, MD: University Press of America, 1996.

Ake, Claude. *Democracy and Development in Africa*. Washington, DC: Brookings Institution, 1996.

American Horticultural Society. *Encyclopedia of Gardening: The Definitive Practical Guide to Gardening Techniques, Planning, and Maintenance*. London: Dorling Kindersley, 1994.

Askew, R.R. *Parasitic Insects*. New York: American Elsevier Publishing Company, 1971.

Auty, R. M. "The Macro Impact of Korea's Heavy Industry Drive Re-evaluated." *Journal of Development Studies*, 29, no. 1 (October 1992), pp. 24–48.

Bain, David. *The Productivity Prescription: The Manager's Guide to Improving Productivity and Profits*. New York: McGraw-Hill, 1982.

Bates, Robert L. *Industrial Minerals*. Hillside, NJ: Enslow Publishers, 1988.

Bartomé Fernando. *Articulate Executive: Orchestrating Effective Communication*. Boston: Harvard Business School Press, 1993.

Bauer, Max. *Precious Stones*. Vol.1. New York: Dover Publications, 1968.

Bebbington, Anthony, and John Farrington. "Governments, NGOs, and Agricultural Development: Perspectives and Changing Inter-Organizational Relationships." *Journal of Development Studies*, 29, no. 2 (January 1993), pp. 199–219.

Berle, Adolf A., Jr. *Power without Property*. New York: Harcourt, 1959.

Biggs, Tyler. *Africa Can Compete! Export Opportunities and Challenges for Garments and Home Products in the European Market*. Washington, DC: World Bank, 1996.

Boring, John Kadel et al. *Natural Gardening: A Nature Company Guide*. Sydney, Australia: Time-Life Books, 1995.

Brookfield, Harold. *Transformation with Industrialization in Peninsular Malaysia.* New York: Oxford University Press 1994.

Brown, George W. *The Economic History of Liberia.* Washington, DC: Associated Publishers, 1941.

Cairncross, Alec, Sir. *Home and Foreign Investment, 1870–1913: Studies in Capital Accumulation.* Cambridge: Cambridge University Press, 1953.

Cameron, Rondo E. *France and the Economic Development of Europe, 1800–1914.* New York: Octagon Books, 1975.

Clapham, John Harold, Sir. *The Economic Development of France and Germany, 1815–1914.* Cambridge: Cambridge University Press, 1928.

Clough, Shepard Bancroft. *European Economic History: The Economic Development of Western Civilization.* New York: McGraw-Hill, 1975.

Clower, Robert W., et al. *Growth Without Development.* Evanston, IL: Northwestern University Press, 1966.

Craft, Betsy Harvey. *Oil and Natural Gas.* New York: Franklin Watts, 1982.

Cummings, Milton C., Jr., and Richard S. Katz. *The Patron State: Government and the Arts in Europe, North America and Japan.* New York: Oxford University Press, 1987.

Curran, Donald J. *Metropolitan Financing: The Milwaukee Experience, 1920–1970.* Madison: The University of Wisconsin Press, 1973.

Denison, Edward F., and William K. Chung. *How Japan's Economy Grew So Fast.* Washington, DC: Brookings Institution, 1976.

Desautels, Paul E. *The Gem Kingdom.* New York: Random House, 1976.

Didsbury, Howard F., Jr., ed. *The Global Economy: Today, Tomorrow, and the Transition.* Bethesda, MD: World Future Society, 1985.

Dietrich, William S. *In the Shadow of the Rising Sun.* University Parks: Pennsylvania State University Press, 1991.

Drucker, Peter F. *Management: Tasks, Responsibilities, Practices.* New York: Harper & Row, 1974.

—————. *Managing the Future: The 1990s and Beyond.* New York: Truman Talley Books/Plume, 1993.

Einzig, Paul. *Primitive Money in Its Enological, Historical, and Economic Aspects.* New York: Pergamon Press, 1966.

Fass, Simon M. *Political Economy in Haiti: The Drama of Survival.* New Brunswick, NJ: Transaction Publishers, 1993.

Flinn, Michael W. *The Origins of the Industrial Revolution.* New York: Barnes & Noble, 1966.

Forbes, Munro J. *Africa and the International Economy, 1800–1960.* London: J. M. Dent & Sons, 1976.

Fox, Michael W. *Agricide: The Hidden Crisis That Affects Us All.* New York: Schockton Books, 1986.

Galbraith, John Kenneth. *The Affluent Society.* Boston: Houghton Mifflin, 1969.

—————. *The New Industrial State.* Boston: Houghton Mifflin Company, 1971.

Gelfand, Michael. *Lakeside Pioneers.* Oxford: Basil Blackwell, 1964.

Gregg, Pauline. *A Social and Economic History of Britain, 1760–1950.* London: George G. Harrap & Co., 1952.

Groth, Alexander, and Larry L. Wade. *Public Policy across Nations: Social Welfare in Industrial Settings.* Greenwich, CT: JAI Press, 1985.

Habakkuk, Hrothgar J. *American and British Technology in the Nineteenth Century.* New York: Cambridge University Press, 1962.

Haggard, Stephan, Chung H. Lee, and Sylvia Maxfield, eds. *The Politics of Financing Developing Countries*. Ithaca, NY: Cornell University Press, 1993.

Hahn, Emily. *Love of Gold*. New York: Lippincott & Crowell, 1980.

Hamada, Robert S. "Financial Theory and Taxation in an Inflationary World: Some Public Policy Issues." *Journal of Finance*. Papers and Proceedings, Thirty-seventh Annual Meeting, American Finance Association, Chicago, Illinois, August 29–31, 1978.

Hammer, Michael, and James Champy. *Reengineering the Corporation: A Manifesto for Business Revolution*. New York: Harper Business, 1993.

Hance, William A. *African Economic Development*. New York: Frederick A. Praeger Publishers, 1967.

Hausmann, Ricardo, and Reisen Helmut, eds. *Securing Stability and Growth in Latin America: Policy Issues and Prospects for Shock-prone Economies*. Paris: Organization for Co-operation and Economic Development, 1996.

Hee, Park Chung. *Korea Reborn*. Englewood Cliffs, NJ: Prentice Hall, 1979.

Heilbroner, Robert, and Lester Thurow. *Five Economic Challenges*. Englewood Cliffs, NJ: Prentice-Hall, 1981.

Henig, Robin Marantz. *The People's Health: A Memoir of Public Health and Its Evolution at Harvard*. Washington, DC: Joseph Henry Press, 1997.

Hermes, Niels, and Robert Lensink, eds. *Financial Development and Economic Growth: Theory and Experiences from Developing Countries*. New York: Routledge, 1996.

Hobsbawm, E. J. *Industry and Empire: The Making of Modern English Society*. New York: Pantheon, 1968.

—————. *Labouring Men: Studies in the History of Labour*. New York: Basic Books, 1964.

Hughes, Jonathan R. T. *The Vital Few: The Entrepreneur and American Economic Progress*. New York: Oxford University Press, 1986.

Hugon, Philippe, Guy Pucet, and Suzanne Quiers-Valette, eds. *L'Afrique des Incertitudes (Africa with Uncertainties)*. Paris: Presses Universitaires des France, 1995.

Hunter, Guy. *The New Societies of Tropical Africa: A Selective Study*. London: Oxford University Press, 1962.

Hunter, Louis C. *Water Power: A History of Industrial Power in the United States, 1780–1930*. Charlottesville: University Press of Virginia, 1979.

Hutchins, Ross E. *Insects*. Englewood Cliffs, NJ: Prentice-Hall, 1966.

Jeffreis, Ian. *A guide to Economies in Transition*. New York: Routledge, 1996.

July, Robert W. *A History of the African People*. New York: Charles Scribner's Sons, 1970.

Kemp, Tom. *Industrialization of Nineteenth-century Europe*. London: Longman, 1985.

Landes, David S. *Revolution in Time: Clocks and the Making of the Modern World*. Cambridge, MA: Belknap Press of Harvard University Press, 1983.

Lane, Peter. *The Industrial Revolution: The Birthplace of the Modern Age*. New York: Barnes & Noble Books, 1978.

Lanham, Url. *The Insects*. New York: Columbia University Press, 1964.

Licht, Walter. *Industrializing America: The Nineteenth Century*. Baltimore, MD: Johns Hopkins University Press, 1995.

McLindon, Mihael P. *Privatization and Capital Market Development: Strategies to Promote Economic Growth*. Westport, CT: Praeger 1996.

Maddison, Angus. *Economic Growth in the West*. New York: Twentieth Century Fund, 1964.

Medhi, Krongkaew, ed., *Thailand's Industrialization and Its Consequences*. New York: St. Martin's Press, 1995.

Muscat, Robert J. *The Fifth Tiger: A Study of Thai Development Policy.* Helsinki: United Nations University Press/World Institute for Development Economics Research (UN/WIDER), 1994.

Pienaar, Kristo. *The Ultimate Southern African Gardening Book.* Halfway House, RSA: Southern Book Publishers, 1994.

Rasmussen, Wayne D. *Taking the University to the People.* Ames: Iowa State University Press, 1989.

Robinson, J. C. *Bananas and Plantains.* Wallingford, U.K.: CAB International, 1996.

Rogers, Bruce A. *Nature of Metals.* Cleveland, OH: American Society of Metals, 1966.

Rosen, George. *A History of Public Health.* Baltimore, MD: Johns Hopkins University Press, 1993.

Sarton, George. *A History of Science: Ancient Science through the Golden Age of Greece.* Cambridge, MA: Harvard University Press, 1960.

Seligman, Edwin R. A. *Essays in Taxation.* New York: Augustus M. Kelley Publisher, 1969.

Selya, Roger Mark. *The Industrialization of Taiwan.* Jerusalem: Jerusalem Academic Press.

Singer, Charles, and E. Ashworth Underwood. *A Short History of Medicine.* New York: Oxford University Press, 1962.

Smith, Adam. *The Wealth of Nations.* New York: Modern Library, 1994.

Solberg, Carl. *Oil Power.* New York: American Library, 1976.

Speedy, A. (ed.). *Developing World Agriculture.* Hong Kong: Grosvenor Press International, 1991.

Spufford, Peter. *Money and Its Use in Medieval Europe.* New York: Cambridge University Press, 1989.

Stolper, Gustav. *The German Economy: 1870–Present.* New York: Harcourt, Brace & World, 1967.

Strauss, John, and Thomas Duncan. "Health, Nutrition, and Economic Development." *Journal of Economic Literature,* June 1998, 766–817.

Summers, Gene F., Sharon D. Evans, Frank Clemente, E. M. Beck, Jon Minkoff. *Industrial Invasion of Nonmetropolitan America.* New York: Praeger Publishers, 1976.

Toynbee, Arnold. *The Industrial Revolution.* Boston: Beacon Press, 1956.

Tugendhat, Christopher. *Oil: The Biggest Business.* New York: G.P. Putnam, 1968.

Veblen, Thorstein. *Imperial Germany and the Industrial Revolution.* Ann Arbor: University of Michigan Press, 1966.

Vicker, Ray. *The Realms of Gold.* New York: Charles Scribner's Sons, 1975.

Vogel, Ezra F. *The Four Little Dragons.* Cambridge, MA: Harvard University Press, 1992.

Walker, Laurence C. *Forests: A Naturalist's Guide to Trees & Forest Ecology.* New York: John Wiley, 1976.

Walton, Clarence C., ed. *Enriching Business Ethics.* New York: Plenum Press, 1990.

Watt, John Mitchell, and Maria Gerdina Breyer-Brandwijk. *The Medicinal and Poisonous Plants of Southern and Eastern Africa.* Edinburgh: E. & S. Livingston, 1962.

Wionczek, Miguel S., ed. *Latin American Economic Integration: Experiences and Prospects.* New York: Praeger, 1966.

# Index

**About the Author**

THOMAS A. TAKU is an export/import manager and investment consultant with Camafric International Company and a grants/contracts specialist at Lincoln University.

ISBN 0-275-96498-1

HARDCOVER BAR CODE